# HOUSECRAFT AND STATECRAFT

# HOUSECRAFT AND STATECRAFT

Domestic Service
in Renaissance Venice,
1400–1600

Dennis Romano

The Johns Hopkins University Press

Baltimore and London

This book has been brought to publication with the generous
assistance of the Gladys Krieble Delmas Foundation.

The Johns Hopkins University Press
2715 North Charles Street, Baltimore, Maryland 21218-4319
The Johns Hopkins Press Ltd., London

*Frontispiece:* Paolo Veronese, *Giustiniana Barbaro and Her Maidservant,*
Villa Barbaro, Maser. Photograph from Alinari / Art Resource, New York.

Library of Congress Cataloging-in-Publication Data
will be found at the end of this book.

A catalog record for this book is available
from the British Library.

ISBN 0-8018-5288-9

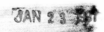

*For My Parents*
*Dante A. and Mary G. Romano*

It is evident that the art of Housecraft is older than that of Statecraft, since the Household, which it creates, is older; being a component part of the Nation created by Statecraft.

Pseudo-Aristotle, *Oeconomica*, 1.1

# Contents

List of Plates and Tables ........................................ *xi*

Acknowledgments ............................................. *xiii*

Introduction ................................................. *xv*

**Part I Norms**

One

**Treatises on Household Management and Service** ............... 3

Paolino the Minorite, Francesco Barbaro, and the Venetian
    Tradition of Treatises on Household Management .............. 5

Giovanni Caldiera and the Apogee of the Political Metaphor ....... 13

Giacomo Lanteri and the Social Utility of Servants .............. 16

Agostino Valier and "Christian" Economy ...................... 21

An Encyclopedia, a Book of Fashion, an Oration, and a
    Treatise on Death ........................................ 23

Two

**The Venetian Government and the Regulation of Domestic Service** . . 43

The *capi di sestieri* and the Registration of Servants .............. 44

The *capi di sestieri* and the Capitulary of 1503 ................... 49

The Transfer of Authority to the *censori* and the Capitulary of 1541 . . . 54

Later-Sixteenth-Century Legislation Concerning Servants ......... 59

The Censors as Judges ....................................... 63

**Part II Structures**

Three

**Servants in the Venetian Household** ........................... 77

The Ducal Household ........................................ 77

The Patrician Household ..................................... 85

The *cittadino* Household ..................................... 95

The Artisan Household ....................................... 99

Toward a Quantitative Analysis of Servant Keeping: Census Data  . . 106
*Status animarum* Records . . . . . . . . . . . . . . . . . . . . . . . . . . . . . . . . . 110

**Four.**
**Recruitment, Contracts, and Wages: The Mechanics of Labor**  . . . . 118
Finding Work  . . . . . . . . . . . . . . . . . . . . . . . . . . . . . . . . . . . . . . . . . 119
Recruitment of Servants  . . . . . . . . . . . . . . . . . . . . . . . . . . . . . . . . 122
Contracts  . . . . . . . . . . . . . . . . . . . . . . . . . . . . . . . . . . . . . . . . . . . 129
The Length of Contracts  . . . . . . . . . . . . . . . . . . . . . . . . . . . . . . . . 135
Wages . . . . . . . . . . . . . . . . . . . . . . . . . . . . . . . . . . . . . . . . . . . . . . 138
Payment Schedules . . . . . . . . . . . . . . . . . . . . . . . . . . . . . . . . . . . . 145

**Five**
**The Lives of Servants**  . . . . . . . . . . . . . . . . . . . . . . . . . . . . . . . . . . . 151
Childhood . . . . . . . . . . . . . . . . . . . . . . . . . . . . . . . . . . . . . . . . . . . 152
Marriage  . . . . . . . . . . . . . . . . . . . . . . . . . . . . . . . . . . . . . . . . . . . 155
Work and Associative Life . . . . . . . . . . . . . . . . . . . . . . . . . . . . . . . 167
Old Age . . . . . . . . . . . . . . . . . . . . . . . . . . . . . . . . . . . . . . . . . . . . 178
Death and Burial  . . . . . . . . . . . . . . . . . . . . . . . . . . . . . . . . . . . . . 182

**Part III  Practice**

**Six**
**The Dynamics of Master-Servant Relations**  . . . . . . . . . . . . . . . . . . . 191
Loyalty and Obedience  . . . . . . . . . . . . . . . . . . . . . . . . . . . . . . . . . 193
Disloyalty and Disobedience  . . . . . . . . . . . . . . . . . . . . . . . . . . . . . 207
Punishment and Submission  . . . . . . . . . . . . . . . . . . . . . . . . . . . . . 222

**Seven**
**The Significance of Service** . . . . . . . . . . . . . . . . . . . . . . . . . . . . . . . . 227
Domestic Service in Renaissance Venice . . . . . . . . . . . . . . . . . . . . . 228
Service, Honor, and Class Relations in Early Modern Venice  . . . . 235

Appendix A. The *capi di sestieri*'s Capitulary of 1503  . . . . . . . . . . . . . . . 241
Appendix B. The Censors' Capitulary of 1541 . . . . . . . . . . . . . . . . . . . . . 245
Notes  . . . . . . . . . . . . . . . . . . . . . . . . . . . . . . . . . . . . . . . . . . . . . . . . . 249
Bibliography . . . . . . . . . . . . . . . . . . . . . . . . . . . . . . . . . . . . . . . . . . . . . 305
Index . . . . . . . . . . . . . . . . . . . . . . . . . . . . . . . . . . . . . . . . . . . . . . . . . . 321

# Plates and Tables

## Plates

Cesare Vecellio, *Barcaruoli* . . . . . . . . . . . . . . . . . . . . . . . . . . . . . . . . . . . . . . . . 29

Cesare Vecellio, *Fantesche* . . . . . . . . . . . . . . . . . . . . . . . . . . . . . . . . . . . . . . . . . 30

Titian, *Portrait of Fabricius Salvaresius with a Black Page* . . . . . . . . . . . . . . . . . 33

Vittore Carpaccio, Detail of Gondoliers from *The Healing
     of the Possessed Man* . . . . . . . . . . . . . . . . . . . . . . . . . . . . . . . . . . . . . . . . . 34

Cesare Vecellio, *Cavalier del doge* . . . . . . . . . . . . . . . . . . . . . . . . . . . . . . . . . . . 82

Cesare Vecellio, *Scudieri del doge* . . . . . . . . . . . . . . . . . . . . . . . . . . . . . . . . . . . 83

The Tabernacle of the *traghetto* of the Ponte della Paglia . . . . . . . . . . . . . . . . 169

Lorenzo Lotto, *Pala di Sant'Antonino* . . . . . . . . . . . . . . . . . . . . . . . . . . . . . . . 174

Palma il Giovane, *Pasquale Cicogna Assists at the Mass* . . . . . . . . . . . . . . . . . 181

## Tables

2.1. Accusations in Censors' Trials, 1569–1600 . . . . . . . . . . . . . . . . . . . . . . . . 65

2.2. Accusations, by Gender of Defendant, 1569–1600 . . . . . . . . . . . . . . . . . . 67

2.3. Average Penalties Expressed in Years, 1569–1600 . . . . . . . . . . . . . . . . . . . 69

3.1. Venetian Census Figures, 1509–1642 . . . . . . . . . . . . . . . . . . . . . . . . . . . . 106

3.2. Population of Venice, 1563 . . . . . . . . . . . . . . . . . . . . . . . . . . . . . . . . . . . . 107

3.3. Servant Population of Venice, 1563–1642 . . . . . . . . . . . . . . . . . . . . . . . . . 109

3.4. Gender Distribution of Servants, 1563–1642 . . . . . . . . . . . . . . . . . . . . . . 110

3.5. Parish Populations and Servant Populations, 1590s . . . . . . . . . . . . . . . . . 111

3.6. Total Households and Servant-Keeping Households, 1590s . . . . . . . . . 112

3.7. Distribution of Households by Size, 1590s . . . . . . . . . . . . . . . . . . . . . . . . 114

3.8. Servants in Noble Households, 1590s . . . . . . . . . . . . . . . . . . . . . . . . . . . . 115

3.9. Non-Noble Titled Households, 1590s . . . . . . . . . . . . . . . . . . . . . . . . . . . . 115

3.10. Distribution of Servants by Household Type, 1590s ............... 116

3.11. Gender Distribution of Servants, 1590s .......................... 116

4.1.  Origins of Barbarigo Family Servants, 1460–1582 ................. 124

4.2.  Geographic Origins of Barbarigo Family Servants,
      by Time Period and Account Books, 1460–1582 ................ 125

4.3.  Geographic Recruitment of Barbarigo Servants,
      by Gender, 1460–1582 ..................................... 126

4.4.  Geographic Origins of Servants Based on Testaments,
      15th and 16th Centuries ................................... 127

4.5.  Geographic Origins of Servants Based on
      Censors' Trials, 1569–1579 ................................. 128

4.6.  Average Length of Indentured Service Contracts,
      by Gender, 15th and 16th Centuries ......................... 136

4.7.  Contracted and Actual Length of Indentured Service,
      by Gender, 15th and 16th Centuries ......................... 137

4.8.  Servants' Wages in Ducats per Year, 15th and 16th Centuries ....... 139

4.9.  Wet Nurses' Wages in Ducats, 1438–1598 ....................... 141

4.10. Wage Comparisons in Ducats per Year, 1407–1580s ............... 143

5.1.  Professions and Trades of Servants' Fathers, 1569–1600 ............ 154

5.2.  Dowries of Servants, Boatmen, and Others, 1400–1599 ............ 158

5.3.  Professional Endogamy and Exogamy of
      Female Servants, 1416–1589 ................................ 163

6.1.  Executors Selected by Servant Testators, 15th and 16th Centuries .... 199

6.2.  Accusations, by Plaintiff's Status, 1569–1600 ..................... 215

# Acknowledgments

THE RESEARCH FOR this project has been generously assisted by numerous organizations, whose support I gratefully wish to acknowledge. Major support was provided by the Gladys Krieble Delmas Foundation. Additional assistance was supplied by a National Endowment for the Humanities Travel-to-Collections Grant, a Syracuse University Senate Research Grant, and a grant from the Appleby-Mosher Research Fund of the Maxwell School of Citizenship and Public Affairs at Syracuse University.

This study also would not have been possible without the capable guidance and assistance I received from the staffs of the Biblioteca Nazionale Marciana, the Museo Civico Correr, the Biblioteca Querini-Stampalia, the Archivio Curia Patriarcale, and the Archivio degli Istituzioni di Ricovero e di Educazione (IRE). I especially wish to acknowledge the assistance of the late Monsignor Fulvio Parisotto at the Archivio Curia Patriarcale and the generosity of Dr. Giuseppe Ellero at the Archivio IRE. My largest debt, however, is to the entire staff of the Archivio di Stato di Venezia, whose professionalism and patience make research in Venice a particular pleasure. Additionally, I wish to thank the very capable staff in the Interlibrary Loan Department of the E. S. Bird Library at Syracuse University.

Over the course of many years I have accumulated innumerable debts to fellow *studiosi,* colleagues, friends, and students—more than I can ever repay or even name. A few, however, must be singled out. First, I wish to thank Alessandra Sambo for the generous help she has provided on innumerable occasions in the Archivio di Stato. Marion Leathers Kuntz provided special assistance with particularly intractable problems in Latin. Former students Dennis Frey, Michelle Langin, and Arthur Siegel assisted with computer issues, analysis of the parish registers, and a search for images of servants in Venetian art. James Grubb's thoughtful and careful reading of the manuscript for the Johns Hopkins University Press is much appreciated.

A very special debt is owed to John Martin and Edward Muir, both of whom took the time to read and comment extensively on an earlier version of this study. Their broad vision, intellectual acuity, and generosity of spirit represent what is best in the community of Venetian scholars. Finally, I wish to recognize Michela dal Borgo not only for her assistance in the Archivio di Stato but especially for her friendship over many years.

I dedicate this book to my parents, Dante A. and Mary G. Romano. It is but a small repayment for their support and love.

# Introduction

*AUCTORITAS* HAD REPLACED *CARITAS.*" With these words I concluded my study *Patricians and Popolani: The Social Foundations of the Venetian Renaissance State,* an examination of Venetian social relations in the fourteenth century.[1] In that work I attempted to map the networks and ties that united and divided Venetians of various social classes and to understand how those associations shaped and affected Venetian politics in the century following the Serrata, or closing of the Great Council, in 1297. I identified as well an underlying ideological shift in which the communitarian values of the early fourteenth century gradually gave way in the last quarter of the fourteenth century and the early fifteenth century to a new emphasis on rank and hierarchy.

In this book, I continue my examination of Venetian society by delineating the increasing sense of social stratification that characterized the city in the fifteenth and sixteenth centuries. But rather than doing so by charting the networks that linked unskilled workers, artisans, citizens, and nobles as I did earlier, I do so by examining one particular social tie that bound together Venetians of varied station—the relationship between master and servant. Venetian humanist writers emphasized repeatedly that the household was the analogue of the polity; they firmly believed that there was some essential connection between social organization at the domestic level and the larger political order. And so from the perspective of the household, from within the confines of the domestic sphere, through the lens of intimate relations between masters and servants, I hope to outline shifts in Venetian social organization and ideology during a period when republican Venice stood increasingly alone in an absolutist world.

The decision to use domestic service as the key was not a difficult one since the master-servant tie was one of the fundamental relationships that characterized European society before the era of the French Revolution. Like the bonds between lords and vassals, masters and apprentices, even fathers and sons, ties between masters and servants linked tens of thousands of Europeans in relationships imbued with economic, social, and political significance. No relationship, with the exception of that between husbands and wives, better expressed the patriarchal and hierarchical ideals of early modern society—ideals institutionalized in the three estates—than the master-servant bond. And there is no greater testimony to the symbolic power of this relationship than the fact that the supreme pontiff, who claimed universal dominion over emperors and kings, simultaneously styled himself the *servus servorum Dei,* "the servant of the servants of God." One cannot understand late medieval and early modern society without understanding the role of service.

Despite its importance both as a social reality and as an ideological construct, the bond between master and servant has received only sporadic attention from historians of Venice and elsewhere. One authority on domestic service in nineteenth-century France and England attributes the neglect to several factors. First, since servants did not constitute a distinct social class, they have not elicited much interest from labor or social historians interested in class struggle. Second, since the majority of servants were female, the study of domestic service has fallen victim to the neglect until recently of women and women's work in historical research. Finally, since few servants left written accounts of their lives, scholars have avoided a topic studded with archival and methodological pitfalls.[2] Only with the burgeoning interest in social history, especially family and women's history, have a significant number of historians taken up the study of domestic service.

What studies do exist have looked at the issue from a variety of particular perspectives. Several examinations of slavery in the late Middle Ages have indirectly considered the question of domestic service, since in Western Europe the vast majority of slaves were used as household servants or artisan laborers rather than as agricultural field hands. These analyses approach service from the vantage point of labor and economic history. Notable is Charles Verlinden's two-volume *L'esclavage dans l'Europe médiévale.*[3] Verlinden concentrates on uncovering the extent and nature of the slave trade, the ethnic composition of the slave force, and the legal status of the enslaved. Domenico Gioffrè's detailed and valuable study of slavery in fifteenth-century Genoa focuses on many of the same concerns.[4] In both works, the authors' consideration of the master-servant relationship and characteristics of domestic service is peripheral to their interest in the economics of the slave trade and slavery as an institution.

Susan Mosher Stuard's article "Urban Domestic Slavery in Medieval Ragusa" is a narrowly focused but sophisticated analysis of the impact of domestic slavery on one urban economy.[5] Stuard argues that the availability of a cheap supply of slave labor contributed to Ragusa's commercial success in the late Middle Ages. The low cost of slave labor allowed Ragusa's merchants to accumulate the capital necessary for mercantile expansion. Stuard extends her analysis to the social sphere by suggesting that deferential ties forged in households between masters and servants created a peculiarly stable and secure urban environment that further facilitated Ragusa's growth.

Far removed in time and place from these studies is Theresa McBride's examination of domestic service in England and France, which also details the economic impact of service. Entitled *The Domestic Revolution: The Modernisation of Household Service in France and England, 1820–1920,* her work argues that "domestic service is an occupation central to the transition from a purely familial economy to an industrial mass-production economy."[6] According to McBride, domestic service, which in the nineteenth century was controlled by the bourgeoisie and overwhelmingly employed women, helped effect the shift from the rural to the urban world as tens of thousands of young girls made the transition from peasants into French- or Englishwomen. Avowedly materialist in her focus (and either unaware or unconcerned with developments prior to the nineteenth century), McBride claims that "the history of domestic service has more to do with stages of economic development than with particular cultural styles."[7]

Two works that emphasize cultural or social style rather than economics as central to understanding domestic service are Cissie Fairchilds's and Sarah Maza's studies of domestic service in Old Regime France.[8] According to both authors, the keeping of servants, particularly male servants, was crucial to the aristocratic style of life. Servants, who were expected to exhibit loyalty and obedience, were in their livery and demeanor quite literally personifications of the deferential and paternalistic ideals of Old Regime society. Both authors believe, however, that the years leading up to the French Revolution witnessed fundamental changes in domestic service. Increasingly the bourgeoisie gained power and defined a new cultural style, including a new form of servant keeping based primarily on economic ties. For Maza, this transformation was brought about by the feminization of service and by Enlightenment ideas that labeled male domestic service a source of economic stagnation and the vestige of an outmoded system of production.[9] Fairchilds agrees that there was a feminization of service but emphasizes the emergence of the affectionate family as the primary factor leading to a redefinition of master-servant ties. Servants were no longer viewed as members of the family but rather as workers, and strangers at that.[10] Neither author believes that the Revolution itself played much of a role in transforming the bond between masters and servants.

While Fairchilds and Maza have emphasized the interaction between masters and servants, other practitioners of social history have concentrated on understanding the place of servants and servanthood within the structures of society. Iris Origo's 1955 article "The Domestic Enemy: The Eastern Slaves in Tuscany in the Fourteenth and Fifteenth Centuries" has been especially influential. Origo called attention to this little-known stratum of Renaissance Italian society at a time when historians were devoting their attention almost exclusively to the elites. Although much of her essay is devoted to an examination of the mechanisms of the slave trade and the legal status of slaves, she also draws attention to the dynamics within households, especially to the property crimes of slaves and the jealousies attractive slave girls aroused in their mistresses.[11] Origo's characterization of master-slave ties as essentially antagonistic, best exemplified by her title, which is itself a borrowing from Petrarch, who referred to slaves as *domestici hostes,* has had an important impact on subsequent interpretations of master-servant relations.[12]

Two recent works that also concentrate on late medieval and Renaissance Italy largely duplicate Origo's pioneering study. Piero Guarducci and Valeria Ottanelli's *I servitori domestici della casa borghese toscana nel basso medioevo* relies heavily on *ricordanze,* or family diaries, and on literary sources such as Boccaccio's *novelle.* It provides a useful overview of not only slave but free domestic labor in Tuscany from the thirteenth through the fifteenth century.[13] Jacques Heers's *Esclaves et domestiques au Moyen Age dans le monde méditerranéen* is more ambitious.[14] Drawn from a wide range of secondary sources and archival materials from Genoa (and to a lesser degree from Venice), Heers finds that domestic service was dominated by women, that freed slaves assimilated rapidly with the rest of the populace, and that domestic slavery was only a temporary condition for the individual slave.[15] Heers concludes that slaves did not form a distinct class or even a distinct "social category" in late medieval society. His interpretation differs from that of Bronislaw Geremek, who places servants on the margins of society in late medieval Paris.[16]

The chief impetus for research on masters and servants in recent years has come from the growing interest in family history and especially women's history.[17] Indeed, some of the works discussed above owe their origin, if not their focus, to these concerns. The most notable recent contributions to the study of servants in Renaissance Italy are those of Christiane Klapisch-Zuber. Her study of the Florentine *catasto* of 1427, which she coauthored with David Herlihy, contains a wealth of information on household structure and kinship relations, including some information on servants.[18] In a series of articles in which she combined demographic data with a reading of ricordanze, she has explored service as an aspect of women's work.[19] She finds that poor women went into service at an early age in order to accumulate a dowry that would allow them to marry and leave service. But in the late fifteenth century the conditions of female domestic service declined as more and more men entered service. Ironically, one consequence of the new interest in domestic service as an aspect of women's work has been the almost total neglect of male domestic servants.

Finally, other scholars have examined servants as cultural types or the master-servant bond as a trope. One such work is Michael Goodich's essay "*Ancilla Dei:* The Servant as Saint in the Late Middle Ages." In his essay Goodich examines the lives of female servant-saints whose cults were especially popular in Italy. He argues that the stories of women such as Zita of Lucca, Margaret of Città di Castello, and Sibillina Biscossi of Pavia, who performed acts of charity and showed strength in adversity, provided solace for the poor and dispossessed women who made up the servant population. At the same time, official veneration of these women may have helped secure the loyalty of the lower classes, who were increasingly attracted to heretical movements, to the church.[20]

In a different vein, Frances Dolan explores the master-servant bond in relation to the development of early modern notions of political and social order. In *Dangerous Familiars: Representations of Domestic Crime in England, 1550–1700,* Dolan dissects narratives of petty treason. In English law, a wife's killing of her husband or a servant's murder of his master was defined as petty treason. Drawing upon both accounts of infamous crimes and fictional narratives, including Shakespeare's *The Tempest,* Dolan argues that both disobedient servants and negligent masters undid the social order. She notes that "in these various representations of petty treason, any pressure from either above or below so destabilizes social structure and dramatic form that they collapse." At the end of each story, however, the "social and aesthetic order" is restored when subordinates are put in their proper social and narrative place.[21]

Taken together, these studies, which range in time from the twelfth to the twentieth century and geographically from the Mediterranean to the North Sea, suggest several elements that domestic service in preindustrial and industrializing societies shared in common. First, service constituted an important sphere of women's work. Time in service was part of the curriculum vitae for many poor women who wished to marry. While their male counterparts spent time learning a trade, young women were "apprenticed" into household service. At the same time, domestic service was generally a temporary occupation. Men and women might spend some part of their life in service, but it was seldom a permanent job. With regard to the relationship between masters and servants, in all of the societies studied, masters viewed servants in paternalistic terms. Servants were likened to children for whom the master as "father" was responsible. Finally, the master-servant relationship was characterized by sexual tension. The coming together of rich and poor in personal relationships within the confines of the household appears to have elicited surprisingly similar responses in very dissimilar societies.

Yet there are also telling differences from one society to another and from one time period to another, and these suggest a tentative chronology for the history of domestic service. In northern Europe the servants of the aristocratic household were to some degree part of the nobleman's affinity, the network of associates that formed his base of power.[22] Many posts in the royal governments of England and France evolved from positions in the king's household. And through the sixteenth century, part of the education of a young gentleman included a period of service in the household of a nobleman. Given these origins, for a long time most servants in large aristocratic households were men. They even performed the cooking and cleaning, tasks that later would be associated with women.[23] Furthermore, these aristocratic households were often large and ambulatory. In 1420 the earl of Warwick's household numbered 125; in 1526 the duke of Norfolk's domestic staff included 144 persons.[24]

The pattern of domestic service in southern Europe, especially Italy, was different in this period. The regions bordering the Mediterranean Sea were the first to see a revival of trade in the Middle Ages and the development of commercial capitalism. In the cities of northern and central Italy especially, a mercantile class of bankers, notaries, and traders controlled politics and created the dominant cultural style, including humanism. Unlike the aristocratic households of northern Europe, these bourgeois households were quite small, often with no more than two or three servants, the vast majority of whom (including slaves) were women.[25]

In the seventeenth and eighteenth centuries, the number of servants in the aristocratic households of northern Europe remained high, if not as high as in the fifteenth and sixteenth centuries. One seventeenth-century French domestic manual, for example, recommended a staff of fifty-three for a great noble household; and although few nobles could support that many domestics, it was not unusual for a Parisian noble to have between twenty and thirty servants.[26] But the aristocratic domination of servant keeping declined in the late eighteenth century and was accompanied by the feminization of service. The middle-class householders of the nineteenth century preferred small staffs of predominantly female servants, whom they treated as employees rather than as family members.

This rough chronology reflects changing patterns of servant keeping and illustrates the extent to which the maintenance of servants was tied to the elites' sense of self. As the composition of the elite and their self-identity changed, so too did the characteristics of servant keeping. For Italy, the preliminary evidence provided by Klapisch-Zuber suggests that a crucial period of transition occurred during the later fifteenth and early sixteenth centuries, when the bourgeois style of servant keeping (the maintenance of a small number of female servants) was replaced by the aristocratic style more typical of northern Europe (larger household staffs with proportionally more males).[27] This seems to have coincided with the political subjugation of Italy by northern European powers and with the accompanying trend toward aristocratization characteristic of Italy in this period. Until now, however, there has been no systematic exploration of servants in a Renaissance city over this period. Furthermore, most studies have examined service either as an economic and social relationship or as a cultural metaphor but have not fully integrated the perspectives.

These are the goals of this book. A study of domestic service in Venice from the beginning of the fifteenth to the end of the sixteenth century, it examines the economic and social realities of service, that is, the sociology of service, and the symbolic use of the master-servant relationship as a construct for understanding and shaping politics and society, that is, the ideology of service. The central concern of this study is the often uneasy fit between the analogic uses of the master-servant relationship in the creation of the dominant ideology and the economic and social realities of service. Simply stated, the servant-keeping elite invested what was essentially a contractual labor relationship with broad political and social significance. They made the master-servant tie a metaphor for the relationship between rulers and subjects and, at the same time, transformed servants into symbols of their own exalted and morally superior station. The first was part of the development of a patriarchal theory of authority; the second, of a hierarchical vision of society based upon notions of inborn virtue and honor. But in so doing, masters created a situation fraught with danger for themselves, for by challenging their masters, even by doing things as simple as breaking contracts, servants could call into question and subvert their masters' position. By examining the interaction between masters and servants and the interplay of ideology, structure, and practice, this study explores social relations in a crucial period that saw the rise of commercial capitalism and the development of absolutism.

While on one level, then, this study should be read as an examination of the connection between social relations and political ideology in early modern Europe, it should also be considered as an analysis of transformations in one particular polity, namely, republican Venice. In 1400, when this study begins, Venice stood as one of several vibrant republics on the Italian peninsula. Ruled by an elite heavily involved in banking and trade with the eastern Mediterranean, the city was only beginning to embark on a policy of expansion onto the Italian mainland. The elite themselves were still debating the criteria for inclusion within the ruling class and wrestling with the problem of how to reinvigorate demographically their own ranks. The prevailing ethos still favored a measured frugality and modesty in social display. However, by 1600, when this study ends, republican Venice stood nearly alone in an Italy now dominated by foreign powers, native princes, and absolutist ideals. Rulers of an extensive *terraferma* dominion that required significant expenditures of money and manpower, the ruling elite themselves were increasingly divided into rich and poor and had moved from risky business ventures to safer investments in land, government bonds, and offices. At the same time, some members of the elite now favored an aristocratic style of life that included magnificent urban palaces and rural villas, costly entertainments, and extravagant acts of patronage. Through an examination of domestic service, it is possible to chart these changes and evaluate the transformation of republican Venice.

In order to accomplish these goals, I have divided this work into three sections. The first explores the ideological and normative role of domestic service in Venetian political thought and legislation. It begins, in chapter 1, with an examination of humanist treatises on household management and wifely duties and compositions in other genres in which members of the servant-keeping elite expressed through the metaphor of the master-servant tie their vision of the political and social order. Chapter 2 looks at the ways the Venetian government sought to institutionalize and enforce these norms through administrative procedures and by legislative and judicial action.

In part 2 the concern shifts from ideologies to structures and, to a lesser degree, from masters to servants as it explores the economic and social realities of service. Chapter 3 is devoted to an examination of the composition of Venetian households and a demographic analysis of the service-performing population. Chapter 4 considers the mechanisms, conditions, and movement of the service labor market. Servants' lives are the subject of chapter 5. Just as the focus shifts in this section from norms to structures, so too does the evidentiary base. Treatises and statutes yield to account books and notarial instruments, especially dowry receipts and testaments.

The third and final part examines master-servant relations in practice and the broader significance of service. Chapter 6 considers master-servant interaction and the factors that contributed to harmonious or dysfunctional relations between masters and servants. It also explores the strategies servants used to resist domination and the ways masters sought to put bad relations aright. Chapter 7 tries to make sense of service by asking what domestic service tells us about Venice and about the broader issue of the relationship between "superiors and inferiors" in early modern Europe.

Before proceeding to that examination, however, I need to say something about several issues that inevitably arise in conjunction with any consideration of domestic service in Renaissance Venice. The first has to do with the vexing problem of terminology, particularly that referring to the family and to servants. Renaissance commentators on the family and subsequent historians have employed the term *famiglia* in a variety of competing and often contrasting ways.[28] In the best-known Renaissance treatise on family life, *I libri della famiglia*, Florentine Leon Battista Alberti at times used the term to indicate a small domestic group, comprising the husband, wife, children, *and* servants. When Giannozzo Alberti, one of the interlocutors in the dialogue, was asked what he meant by the family, he responded, "E' figliuoli, la moglie, e gli altri domestici, famigli, servi."[29] At other points in the discussion, however, Alberti used *famiglia* to refer to the larger lineage or group of men sharing a common surname. Clearly there was some overlap between these definitions, but they were not synonymous, since servants were not part of the lineage.

Modern anthropological attempts to create a terminology are not necessarily applicable to Renaissance Italian society. For example, in an effort to distinguish the household from the family, anthropologist Donald Bender argues that "the referent of the family is kinship, while the referent of the household is propinquity or residence."[30] Such a distinction directly contradicts Alberti's first definition of the family as a small domestic unit including servants. In the Renaissance, the term *family* encompassed persons who were not related to one another by blood or marriage ties.

The terms *domestici* and *familiari*, which were frequently employed in the Renaissance, offer some guidance. The term *domesticus* (It., *domestico*) comes from the Latin root *domus* (house), and indicates a close relationship to the house, home, or household. *Familiaris* (It., *familiare*), on the other hand, derives from the Latin *familia* and could mean one who belongs to a household, one who is closely related or akin, or one with whom one is intimate. Generally speaking, it indicated a close relationship to persons. Implicit in the terms *domestici* and *familiari* is an element of distinction or hierarchy. Those who enjoyed the status and title of familiars usually enjoyed more rank and prestige than domestics. Indeed, the term *familiar* could be applied to persons at the very highest levels of society in Renaissance Italy. Courtiers were considered familiars of the prince they served. And in papal Rome, it was possible, even necessary, to obtain patents of familiarity from cardinals or the pope.[31]

In this book, I have attempted to maintain a distinction in my use of the terms *family* and *household.* When *family* is employed, it implies a relationship between persons who may or may not be related by kinship ties. *Household,* by contrast, indicates a relationship to the house or home. And in part 3 the term *family* takes on the additional sense Klapisch-Zuber applied to it, of a "cluster of values."[32]

As Alberti's multiple meanings for *famiglia* indicate, words are often employed in promiscuous ways; and in Venice at least, the distinction between familiars and domestics was not always so clear-cut. Venetians had a rich terminology in Latin and the vernacular referring to servants. Male servants were known by a variety of terms. The most frequently employed terms were *servitor* (It., *servitore*) and *famulus* (It., *fameglio*), which can be translated as "servant" and "manservant." Often these terms were further qualified; for example, a male servant might be referred to as a *famulus in domo* (manservant in the house) or a *servitor in cymba* (servant in the gondola). Since many male servants served as gondoliers for their masters, they were often referred to as *barcaruoli* (boatmen), again with further distinctions, such as *popier* (the gondolier who served in the rear, or poop, of the gondola) and *de mezo* (the gondolier who rowed at the front of the craft). But other terms were also employed, although much less frequently. Among these were *fante* (boy servant), *familiaris* (familiar), *cameriere* (chamberlain), *remer* (oarsman), *nauta* (sailor), and *gastaldus* (steward).

A rich terminology was used to describe female servants as well. By far the most common were *ancilla* (handmaid), *fantesca* (serving girl), and *massara* (housekeeper). *Famula* (woman servant) was also used, as were *domicula* (housegirl), *pedisqua* (footmaid), *cameriera* (chambermaid), and *donzella* (lady-in-waiting). The terms *balia*, *nena*, and *nutrix* were used to refer to wet nurses and governesses.

It is tempting to see distinctions between the terminology for male servants and that for female servants and to relate those to the differences between familiars and domestics. For example, while women were commonly referred to as *massare*, which is closely related to *masserizia* (household goods), men were generally referred to as *famuli*, again indicating a relationship to persons. In other words, some of the terminology suggests relations to persons, while other terms suggest a relationship to the household. And indeed, as we shall see, female servants were closely associated with the house and its care, whereas the primary responsibility of male servants was to row and escort their masters and mistresses. However, not too much should be made of this difference, since it is unclear what role notaries and secretaries (who probably had little or no acquaintance with the practices of the particular households to which they were referring) played in assigning titles to particular servants. What we can say is that terminology tended to become more precise as staffs grew larger and more specialized, especially in the latter part of the sixteenth century, when the impulses toward hierarchy were strongest. Only then did the term *familiar* begin to take on in Venice the more exalted sense that it connoted elsewhere. Indeed, as will become clear in chapter 7, the absence of familiars, that is, of a corps of distinguished personal retainers, was one of the characteristics that set the Venetian elite off from their contemporaries in other societies and that points to the republican distinctiveness of Venice, even at the opening of the seventeenth century.

*Servi,* the third term in Alberti's trilogy of words referring to servants, is similarly ambiguous. In Italian, *servo (serva)* usually indicates free servants, but when employed in Latin as *servus* (It., *schiavo*) it refers to slaves. This raises another issue, namely, the presence of domestic slaves in Venice. I have chosen to include, where appropriate, material about slaves in this book, although this is not a study of slavery per se. I have made this choice for two reasons. First, as many of the works cited above indicate, in practice, if not in legal terms, slaves were virtually indistinguishable from other servants.[33] They performed the same tasks as other domestics, and when manumitted, they blended imperceptibly into the larger populace. Second, since many households included both free and slave laborers, as well as indentured servants, whose status lay somewhere in between, there is no way to isolate one from another in a study of domestic service. Throughout this study, slaves are clearly identified as such so that readers may draw their own conclusions about the conditions of free, indentured, and slave labor, as well as the relationship between them.

A final point has to do with efforts to recover servants' mentality and attitudes toward their situation. It goes almost without saying that virtually all of the extant documentation, with the possible exception of servants' testaments, was written from the point of view of masters. But while it is true that masters generally set the terms of relationships, it does not necessarily follow that servants either passively accepted or necessarily agreed with their masters' will. This study demonstrates that servants shared with masters the same complex vision of master-servant ties, that they too saw the bond as an economic arrangement invested with larger meanings, but that they also manipulated and appropriated these ties to create their own patterns and understandings, that they could at times turn patriarchy on its head. Indeed, servants and their masters were engaged in a struggle to control the meaning of the relationship.

From the perspectives of the family and the household, then, this book seeks to cast light on a number of issues of interest to historians of late medieval and early modern Venice, Italy, and, more generally, Europe, including the growth of hierarchy, shifting concepts of honor among urban elites, modes of resistance by the lower classes, appropriation and contestation of cultural symbols, and the development of the ideology of patriarchy. If it does nothing else, I hope this work illustrates that an analysis of domestic service leads from questions of family and household life to larger issues about shifting relations between social classes and changing conceptions of society and politics in the Renaissance.

# Part I
# Norms

# Chapter One

# Treatises on Household Management and Service

During the late medieval and early modern periods many writers composed treatises and books of advice on proper household management. In fourteenth-century Paris a bourgeois of substance known as the ménagier de Paris wrote an extensive handbook for his young bride in which he advised her on everything from tending a garden to planning banquets.[1] In Elizabethan England John Dod and Robert Cleaver composed a treatise entitled *A Godly Form of Household Government, for the Ordering of Private Families,* in which they developed their vision of the proper household.[2] The most famous Italian example of the genre is Alberti's *I libri della famiglia.* Responding in part to a perceived crisis in the family life of the Florentine upper class and perhaps to his own illegitimacy as well, Alberti composed an encomium to family values and prudent household management. Book 3 in particular is filled with advice to women about garnering and preserving supplies, regimenting servants, and providing for family and guests.[3]

The genre enjoyed widespread popularity for several reasons. First, treatises on household management had a classical pedigree. In the Renaissance a work entitled *Oeconomica* was widely believed to be part of the Aristotelian corpus. The three books of the tract deal with various subjects, including management of slaves, public finance, and relations between husbands and wives.[4] Another ancient text, Xenophon's *Oeconomicus,* likewise enjoyed wide readership and inspired imitators. Written in the form of a Socratic dialogue, the work concerns the art of managing the household and treats a variety of issues, such as the duties of husbands and wives, training of stewards, and farming.[5] By composing treatises on household management, Renaissance writers were able to imitate ancient authors. Interest in the genre was one aspect of the Renaissance classical revival in which works dealing with this-worldly concerns took their place alongside works of theology and moral philosophy as subjects of learned discourse.[6]

A second explanation for the widespread popularity of treatises on house-hold management was their versatility. Through them authors could expound upon a variety of issues and concerns. As Daniela Frigo has noted in her masterful study of such works in sixteenth-century Italy, the genre was extraordinarily flexible and able to encompass within its form the shifting preoccupations of society.[7] In her view, during the thirteenth and fourteenth centuries, treatises on the household were part of the larger debate about politics and political forms. They represented one strain of the "mirror for princes" genre. By the sixteenth century, however, they were composed as part of the debate over nobility, that is, over what constituted "the civilized life" [il vivere civile].[8]

Such treatises were also read because they contained some practical information. Although the authors who wrote these works did not intend them as step-by-step manuals to be followed painstakingly, the advice they offered had a commonsensical quality. Admonitions to use older provisions before newer ones, to assign duties and responsibilities to various members of the household, and to assess carefully the character of potential servants were universally valid precepts worth repeating generation after generation. The popularity even today of columns of practical household advice (although now often relegated to the pages of "women's magazines") attests to the continuing desire or need to impart information of this sort to a new generation of "homemakers." Although these treatises were composed by and for men, the advice found in them could make its way to women, children, and servants via sermons, plays, and verbal orders.[9]

Finally, and most importantly, treatises on household management were composed and read because they reinforced the prevailing social and political ideologies of late medieval and early modern Europe. Aristotle's central notion that households were the building blocks of the larger collectivity—the polity—meant that treatises on household management had wide significance. Writers on economics did not relegate their subject matter to the realm of private concerns. Indeed, contemporaries did not see public and private spheres as contrasting or contending realms. As Giorgio Politi argues, the antipode of the *bene pubblico* was not the "private" but rather the "particular," because "the public or general good was not conceived as anything other than the sum or, better, the mediation of a plurality of distinct interests."[10] Through their discussion of ruling servants, admonishing wives, rearing children, and managing household provisions, then, writers on economics were able to express their concerns and ideals for the wider world. These ideals in turn influenced the ways masters and servants interacted.[11]

## Paolino the Minorite, Francesco Barbaro, and the Venetian Tradition of Treatises on Household Management

A number of writers from Venice and the Veneto composed works in the Aristotelian/Xenophonic tradition. From the early fourteenth century through the sixteenth century and beyond, authors composed tracts on the organization of the household, wifely duties, and related subjects. The earliest surviving tract is Fra Paolino the Minorite's treatise *De regimine rectoris,* composed at the beginning of the fourteenth century. The work raises many of the issues and themes common to the genre and so warrants detailed examination.[12]

The author, a Franciscan friar, was probably born in Venice sometime during the late thirteenth century. Little is known about him except that he had a fairly distinguished career in service to both the Venetian republic and the papacy. He served on a diplomatic mission from Venice to Robert of Naples and assisted the church in its investigation of heretics. For his service to the church he was rewarded in 1324 with the bishopric of Pozzuoli. He died around 1344. Two of Paolino's works have come down to us: a Latin chronicle and the treatise *De regimine rectoris.* The treatise is dedicated to Venetian nobleman Marino Badoer, duke of Crete. Badoer held that post from July 1313 to September 1315, and these dates provide a *terminus ad quem* for the composition of the treatise.[13]

The tract itself consists of a brief dedicatory prologue in Latin followed by eighty-four chapters in Venetian dialect. Paolino modeled his work closely on Giles of Rome's *De regimine principum,* a work with which his own shares a tripartite division. The first book, or section (chs. 2–45), concerns governing oneself, or morals. Here the author discusses the virtues a "retor" [ruler or governor] should cultivate and the vices he should avoid. The second book (chs. 46–64) deals with the family, or economics. The third and final book (chs. 65–85) treats governance of public things, or politics. In this way the work covers the three divisions of practical philosophy, following the example of Aristotle.[14]

In the second book, concerning governance of the family, Paolino discusses a wide variety of issues or topics. He begins by noting that it is natural for humans to live together and that this takes three forms: the household, the neighborhood, and the city or other large district, such as a kingdom. Within proper households there will be four types of persons—husbands, wives, children, and servants—and three kinds of "rule" [reçimento] by husbands—over wives, children, and servants.[15]

Wives require particular attention, since women have little reason and are likewise defective in spirit. Nevertheless, when seeking a wife, a man should search for one who has a nobility similar to his own and who is well mannered. Since the primary purpose of marriage is procreation, a man should seek a woman who is the proper age and size for childbearing and well formed. While wealth is helpful, it is not essential. A man who seeks in a wife that which he seeks in prostitutes [putane] will be punished with disobedient children. For her part, a wife has five duties or obligations: to honor her in-laws, love her husband, raise her family, maintain her home, and be above reproach in both words and deeds. A husband should gently instruct his wife in these skills using "kind words" [bone parole], and he should strike her only after great deliberation, since "in many ways she is his equal" [en molte cose si è engual de lu] (68–74).

Turning to the regimen of children, it is a father's duty to instruct and correct them so that they will not go to ruin. A father should instruct his children first in faith, then in good manners, and finally in knowledge (80–81). They must be taught to avoid vices, including gluttony and drunkenness. At age seven sons should be sent to school to learn grammar, dialectic, and rhetoric. They should also exercise in order to avoid falling into vices. At age fourteen boys enter a dangerous period when they are especially susceptible to carnal concupiscence; hence they need to be instructed in temperance and other virtues. They must obey their elders in order to provide an example to those who serve. Finally, boys should be instructed in horsemanship and arms so that at age eighteen they can begin to defend the fatherland (81–89).

Girls need particular attention, since as members of the female sex they have "little reason" [pocha raxon]. They should be instructed in "some skill" [alguna cosa] so that their minds will not wander to evil things. They should not be allowed to travel about freely and must be taught to speak with few words since, as Aristotle said, "silence is the ornament of woman" [silencio è ornamento de la femna]. Above all, Paolino warns fathers "to keep daughters under tight control" [tengnir le fiole molto strecte] (89–91).

Having dealt with the first two forms of household rule, Paolino turns to the governance of servants in the final two chapters of book 2 (91–94). First, he advises the father to decide how many servants he needs to run his household. When one servant will suffice, he should not employ more. But if the father decides that he needs more than one servant, then he should select one to take charge; otherwise there will be confusion. To back up this principle, Paolino cites the example of the Queen of Sheba, who was overwhelmed by the order and efficiency of Solomon's court, especially by the "discipline of the well-dressed squires, who served without fault." In selecting the chief servant, the ruler must be sure that he is equal to the task. If this principle is followed, the servants will better carry out their tasks.[16]

Continuing with this theme, Paolino advises the rector to determine which servants serve out of fear or pressure—"per presio"—and which out of love—"per amor"—for those who serve out of love will be more loyal. Likewise he must discern which are more intelligent and provident. Having found a servant who is loving, loyal, and discreet, he should assign him the most important office in the household. To this same servant he can reveal more of his private affairs and allow him to discipline and rule the other servants. If the father or rector follows these precepts, he will find peace in the right ordering of his household. For their part the servants will be rewarded according to their merits (92).

Next Paolino turns to the difficult question of rewarding and punishing servants. The first reward one can offer is food—here he advises the father to provide his servants with food that is suitable for them, but not with delicacies, since these will make them lazy and corrupt. As for clothing, servants should be dressed according to the customs of the land. They should not be clothed to satisfy the ruler's vainglory, but to honor the post he holds. Servants occupying different positions should be dressed in different ways. To back up this principle, Paolino cites the "example of God" [exemplo da Dio], who has dressed his "house," namely, the earth and sky, with different ornaments of plants, animals, and stars. In addition, the father should grant servants rest and even recreation as long as it entails "licit games" [zogi liciti]. To support this precept, Paolino cites Ecclesiasticus 33:31: "If you have a servant, treat him as a brother, for as your own soul you will need him."[17]

But if a servant is not good, then one should follow another precept of Ecclesiasticus (33:24), namely: "Fodder and a stick and burdens for an ass; bread and discipline and work for a servant."[18] One must correct both men and animals who are "without reason." Nevertheless, this must be done without anger. If a servant shows that he does not wish to be corrected, then the master should dismiss him. And if a servant wishes to leave the master's service, then it would be disgraceful for the master to try to keep him by force. Paolino cites as evidence the example of the philosopher Diogenes, whose servant Mathan escaped. When he was shown a way to retake Mathan, Diogenes replied, "How would it appear if Mathan could live without me, yet I could not live without Mathan."[19]

Paolino concludes his discussion of servants and book 2 by noting that women should also play a part in ruling the household. Citing Saint Jerome, he notes that women should nourish the servants—"la fameja"—like mothers and advises that, like fathers, women should strive to be more loved than feared. This applies only to servants who are good; those who are bad, especially maidservants, should be dismissed. Paolino notes that according to Jerome, a mistress is judged by the behavior of her maidservants (94).

Having concluded his discussion of governance of the self and governance of the household, Paolino turns in the final book of his treatise to governance of the city. After a brief discussion of Aristotle's six forms of government, he concludes that rule by one man is the best form of government. He makes an analogy to the body, in which different parts are subordinate to the heart (97–98). The exposition continues with a consideration of the qualities of a good ruler, his counselors, and laws. Above all, laws should be suitable for the city. In his only explicit reference to Venice, Paolino notes that many laws that are good for Venice would be of no use on the terraferma (107). A city is not likely to find peace when it is controlled by men who are unequal in wealth, for the rich despise the poor and the poor are jealous of the rich (113–14). Paolino concludes his treatise by noting that he does not wish to discuss what will occur if a city is not at peace. If the rector follows his precepts in governance of self, household, and city, things should come to an good end; if not, God will be "his master and defender" [so maistro e so defendedor] (115–16).

Throughout book 2, Paolino presents the household as a natural, orderly unit in which each member has assigned roles and responsibilities. As Daniela Frigo has observed, the underlying premise of this and other treatises on economics is that the inequalities and hierarchies found in the household (and by analogy in the city) are the product of nature, not human invention.[20] Husbands rule their wives and keep watch over their daughters because women are naturally lacking in reason. Sons must be supervised until they acquire adult reason. And masters rule servants, who, like children, naturally follow their baser instincts.

The notion that servants are naturally inferior to their masters is subtly reinforced through analogies to the animal kingdom. Servants are explicitly compared to asses, animals known for their stubborn nature. And the livery of servants are likened to the flora and fauna with which God ornaments the earth. Such arguments from nature are taken up again in book 3 when the polity is compared to the human body. By arguing that inequalities within the household and the city are based on inherited traits, Paolino justifies and legitimizes a hierarchical ordering of household and society that awards power and position to some and denies it to others. Such an ordering is not a human convention but a divinely ordained and natural phenomenon.

Above all else, it is the job of the father or rector to discern the natural hierarchy of his household. And having done so, the master must work to maintain it through a complicated system of rewards and punishments. In this he is assisted by his wife who also enjoys a role—albeit an inferior one—in ruling the household. For the master, maintenance of order is a delicate balancing act, and the well-run household is always in a state of precarious equilibrium. The slightest misstep can have disastrous consequences. Throughout it is clear that nature predisposes servants to vices and their masters to virtue. Through rewards and punishments, masters have an obligation to help the higher instincts prevail.[21]

In the treatise, Paolino also uses three exempla to indicate that the governance of servants reflects the reputation of the master. First, he notes that the Queen of Sheba was amazed by the "ordene" of Solomon's household. In a fuller example, Paolino uses the words of Diogenes to indicate that it would be disgraceful if the natural order were inverted and Diogenes became dependent on his servant Mathan. The third exemplum is accompanied by an explicit statement of principle. The author notes that a woman's reputation will be judged by the behavior of her maids. Servants' vices and virtues reflect those of their masters and mistresses; masters and servants are inseparably linked by reputation. This theme will be taken up more forcefully by writers in the sixteenth century.

Finally, although Paolino never explicitly compares the household to the polity, it is clear from the organization of the treatise and from frequent references to various kinds of rule that such an analogy exists. Right rule of the polity depends upon a prince who knows how to rule himself and who has a well-ordered household. He must be wise like Solomon. By extension, the rule of servants is preparation for the rule of men.

Paolino's *De regimine rectoris* was the product of the city-state environment of late-thirteenth- and early-fourteenth-century Italy. Dedicated to a Venetian nobleman, the work offers advice to the *signori* (princes) who ruled most of the cities of northern and central Italy. The work also had special significance for republican Venice. Despite the obligatory bow to the principle of enlightened monarchy, Paolino believed that a tranquil state was one in which most men were relatively equal in wealth. Such a situation may have described the Venetian ruling elite in the years immediately following the Serrata, or closing of the Great Council, which defined the principles of political enfranchisement. In his effort to assert the naturalness of a hierarchical ordering of society in both household and polity, Paolino spoke to the concerns of upper-class Venetians at the beginning of the Trecento.

A century later, another adjustment from the Serrata occurred as the contours of the Venetian ruling class were firmly drawn. In 1403 the ducal council made a momentous decision when it rejected a proposal to allow a *popolano,* or non-noble, family to join the Great Council every time a member family became extinct. And in 1423 the Arengo, the old popular assembly that formally approved ducal elections, was abolished. Within a few years new restrictions were placed on marriages between patricians and persons of low or servile status. The Venetian ruling elite had evolved into what Frederic Lane has termed a "closed caste" with an exclusive claim to political power.[22]

At the time these changes were occurring, a member of that ruling elite, Francesco Barbaro, composed a treatise entitled *De re uxoria,* which he presented in 1415 as a gift to Lorenzo de Medici, son of Giovanni de Bicci and brother of Cosimo il Vecchio, on the occasion of his marriage to Ginevra Cavalcanti.[23] Margaret King has described the treatise as "a work of fundamental importance for the understanding of Venetian humanism, of Venetian culture, and perhaps of aristocratic consciousness in Europe."[24]

Francesco Barbaro (1390–1454) was born into an old and distinguished Venetian patrician family. After his father's death, he was raised by his mother and older brother Zaccaria. Francesco studied Latin and in 1409 enrolled at the University of Padua, where he took both a master's and a doctoral degree. While in Padua he began the study of Greek with his mentor Zaccaria Trevisan. When he returned to Venice, he continued his study of Greek under the tutelage of Guarino da Verona.[25] The *De re uxoria* is filled with quotations and ideas from Greek authors. The second book of the treatise alone contains more than seventy citations from Plutarch and Xenophon.[26]

The tract is divided into two parts. In the first part Barbaro is concerned with two issues: the nature of marriage and selection of a wife.[27] According to Barbaro, marriage was instituted for the procreation of children, and the virtue of children is directly related to the quality of the parents. Noble parents produce noble children. These children naturally become the rulers of the state; indeed, Barbaro refers to the nobly born as the "walls" of the city. Given this, it is essential that the nobleman take great care in the selection of a spouse. Above all, a man should seek a wife who is virtuous and who, like him, is nobly born. As King notes, the entire treatise becomes a defense of nobility.[28] All other considerations, including wealth and political connections, are secondary to the virtue of the bride, which, as we have been told, will ensure the nobility of the progeny.

In the second part of the treatise, Barbaro turns to the duties of the wife, which are defined as "love for her husband, modesty of life, and diligent and complete care, in domestic matters."[29] Above all, a woman's love for her husband is revealed in her obedience to him, obedience that evolves into "a pattern of perfect friendship."[30] Love itself arises from the moderation a woman demonstrates in all aspects of her behavior, including her posture, gait, speech, and dress. A woman should be particularly moderate in food and drink, since "the vices of Venus and uncontrolled lovemaking do not simply follow but are the inevitable result of the delights of Alexandria and the feasts of Syracuse."[31]

When Barbaro finally takes up the third responsibility of wives, the management of households and servants, he notes that he will treat these matters as briefly as possible, discussing only those things that are absolutely essential. He begins by noting that both property and servants are necessary, for without them "family life itself cannot exist" (215). Barbaro assigns a greater role to wives in the management of household affairs than Paolino did. Although men are naturally stronger than women in body and soul, women are obliged to maintain that which men have accumulated. "What," the author asks, "is the use of bringing home great wealth unless the wife will work at preserving, maintaining, and utilizing it?" Like Pericles, who attended to the affairs of Athens, wives should attend to their households (216). In order for them to do this properly, they must be at home supervising and regimenting in the same way that generals oversee their soldiers and farmers guide their peasants. Everything must be kept in order. To this end, wives should "imitate the leaders of bees, who supervise, receive, and preserve whatever comes into their hives" (217).

Turning to servants, Barbaro observes that "provided they are not neglected," servants "can add great luster to our houses and be useful and pleasant." But for this to occur, wives must manage them carefully, again like "the leaders of the bees, who allow no one under their control to be lazy or negligent" (218). Barbaro recommends that wives adopt the ancient custom of selling or dismissing aged or useless slaves and servants. In contrast, maidservants who show themselves to be hardworking and diligent should be promoted to more important tasks.

Like Paolino, Barbaro recommends that servants be rewarded with food and clothing. Following Hesiod, he advises that servants not be separated from their families and that they be provided with good medical care, "for these acts of humanity, this solicitousness will make servants very conscientious and hardworking for the household." For a third time a comparison is made to bees, "who never desert their leader on account of his care and provision for them" (219).

The theme of gratitude and loyalty is amplified by the extended story of Xanthippus the Elder's dog. When the Athenians were embarking for the Persian War, Xanthippus's dog whined and barked and finally swam out to follow his master. Later, when the dog died, Xanthippus erected a tomb for the faithful animal. "In this way," Barbaro concludes, "Xanthippus was able to leave for posterity a perpetual monument of the mutual affection to be observed between masters and their inferiors" (219–20).

Barbaro concludes his discussion of servants by reiterating the need to assign them specific tasks. Like officers in military affairs and magistrates in civil ones, wives should regiment their underlings. Just as in a harp or the heavens themselves "one part is joined to another until all the parts fit together in a harmonious whole," in the well-ordered household wives must arrange affairs and order servants so as to ensure "the splendor, utility, and pleasantness of their homes" (220).

In the final chapter of the treatise, Barbaro addresses the education of children. He recommends that mothers nurse their children themselves, even repeating Plutarch's advice that to increase "friendship and love" mistresses should occasionally take to their breasts the infants of their servants (222–23). But if a woman cannot nurse her own children, then she should select a wet nurse of good character, since the child's impressionable nature is easily influenced by the milk and habits of the nurse. After further consideration of the virtues to be inculcated in children, Barbaro concludes with the hope that Lorenzo de Medici will accept his gift, which he terms "this wife's necklace," as a token of friendship (228).

Barbaro's discussion of household management and the oversight of servants differs in some important ways from that of Paolino the Minorite. Unlike the Franciscan, Barbaro assigns greater responsibility for maintenance of the household and servants to wives. Whereas in Paolino's view the wife's role is clearly secondary to that of her husband, in the household itself Barbaro gives the wife pride of place. It is she who supervises the maidservants and appoints the stewards. It is she who makes sure that the servants are properly fed and clothed. It is she who is compared to the marshal and the magistrate. In part this difference in emphasis can be explained by the subject matter of the two treatises: Paolino was interested in the role of rulers, Barbaro in that of wives.

Another difference concerns the care of servants. Although both authors agree that servants should be rewarded with food and clothing adequate to their needs, Barbaro avoids entirely the subject of recalcitrant or disobedient servants. Perhaps he considered the topic inappropriate for a treatise on wifely duties. But more likely he believed that if the household were properly administered, such problems could be avoided altogether. He even went so far as to advise wives not to get angry with servants, since they themselves were likely to have made many of the same mistakes (218). In Barbaro's vision of household affairs, servants would desire to serve their noble masters out of a sense of loyalty and gratitude. Through the wife's solicitude for the welfare of her servants, she would engender loyalty and obedience, in the same way that Xanthippus engendered the loyalty and obedience of his dog.

In the end, Barbaro goes further than Paolino in emphasizing the positive aspects of master-servant relations. As noted earlier, through the use of exempla Paolino made the point that the governance of servants reflected the reputation of the master. But in his view the situation was fraught with danger, since servants were just as likely to bring disgrace as they were to bring honor on a household. Barbaro goes beyond this to suggest that servants actually increase the splendor and reputation of a house. Servants become symbols of their masters' status.

In the *De regimine rectoris* and the *De re uxoria* we can already discern the distinct but related ways in which domestic service and master-servant relations were understood ideologically by members of the elite in late medieval and early modern Venice. According to the view expressed by Paolino, the relationship between master and servant served as a metaphor for politics, mimicking at the household level the civic relationship between the ruler and his subjects. The emphasis was on a natural order not to be contravened; inferiors were to be controlled through the careful manipulation of rewards and punishments.

For Barbaro, by contrast, the master-servant relationship was primarily a social metaphor and not a political one. Servants were part of a natural social order that awarded nobility and virtue to some and not to others. When properly trained, servants adhered to their natural place just as the heavenly orbs did to theirs, and conflict was avoided. What is more, inferiors helped to exalt the status of their superiors. Servants were accouterments to life that increased the pleasantness and dignity of noble households.

Of course the political and the social meanings of master-servant relations were by no means mutually exclusive; indeed, the two were mutually dependent. Nevertheless, at different times and for different reasons, various authors who considered master-servant relations chose to emphasize one understanding over another. Generally speaking, the view of the master-servant relationship as a metaphor for the relationship between ruler and subject was predominant in the fourteenth and fifteenth centuries, whereas the social reading prevailed in the sixteenth century. This was due in large part to the shifting concerns of the servant-keeping elite and to their view of themselves and their place in society.[32] By charting the fortunes of these constructs, we can better understand the elite's sense of themselves and the significance of domestic service.

## Giovanni Caldiera and the Apogee of the Political Metaphor

The fullest Venetian expression of the family as metaphor for the state, the father as magistrate, came not from a Venetian patrician but from a member of Venice's hereditarily defined class of secretaries and diplomats, the *cittadini*. Giovanni Caldiera (c. 1400–c. 1474) was born into a citizen family in Venice. After a period of study and teaching at the University of Padua, he returned to his native city, where he practiced medicine and moved in a wide circle of patrician and nonpatrician humanists. The most important of his writings is a trilogy of works composed between October 1463 and August 1464, which King has termed "a monumental summa of Venetian attitudes and values."[33]

Like Paolino, Caldiera's trilogy treats the three realms of practical philosophy: ethics, economics, and politics. The first work, *De virtutibus moralibus et theologicis,* is an exposition of the virtues and vices, with particular emphasis on the behavior of the ruling class. In the second treatise, *De oeconomia veneta,* Caldiera carefully lays out the organization and responsibilities of family members and considers such matters as the proper location and design of the house. The third work, *De praestantia venetae politicae,* includes a discussion of the seven mechanical and liberal arts and the seven virtues and concludes with a description of the Venetian governmental system.[34]

Caldiera's treatise on the household, *De oeconomia veneta,* is itself divided into two books. Caldiera describes the structure of the household as a strict hierarchy composed of the paterfamilias and his wife, children, servants, and domesticated animals. He further divides the servants or slaves into three categories. The first is made up of those servants who can supervise others and be entrusted with important tasks. These servants are intelligent creatures who serve "not by nature but by will" [non pro nature sed pro voluntate].[35] The second category comprises those who serve the household more out of honor than out of utility.[36] The final category of servants is made up of those who serve by nature. Lacking native intelligence, they provide the basic muscle power for the household and must be carefully supervised. Caldiera advises the paterfamilias to be especially diligent in the selection of servants, since a mistake in this area can lead to losses of both honor and riches for the household.[37]

The ideal household is one in which each member practices the virtues appropriate to his or her place in the complex. All members have responsibilities and obligations to other household members. Above all, the paterfamilias must be prudent and wise. The success of the household enterprise depends on his ability to put and keep everyone in their place and performing their appointed tasks. The wife must be obedient to her husband and an ornament to the household. Children, as yet imperfectly formed creatures, are the special objects of the household's attention. The primary virtues or obligations of servants are obedience and loyalty.[38]

The significance of Caldiera's treatise lies in the fact that he makes explicit an equation that his pre-humanist predecessor Fra Paolino left implicit. According to Caldiera, the household is a microcosm of the state. He writes, "And just as every economy resembles a polity, so also the home is in the likeness of the city."[39] In Caldiera's view, households are the constituent parts of the state and right rule by the paterfamilias parallels right rule by the magistrate. Management of the household is a training ground for stewardship of the republic. Indeed, Caldiera recommends that parents sometimes entrust supervision of the servants to the children so that they may become accustomed to ruling.[40]

Just as in the household, in society at large too every member has responsibilities and obligations to others. By extension, then, the primary obligation of
the *popolo,* or commoners, whom Caldiera virtually neglects, is obedience to the
regime.[41] Caldiera's vision of both household and society is hierarchical and authoritarian, though tempered by virtues appropriate to all members. Like
Paolino, Caldiera employs a physiological metaphor to describe the household
(and by analogy the "body" politic): "Hence if any of these fail in health the
whole body sickens, yet more or less depending whether any more principal part
is affected.... And indeed all should be sound, for if any one part is weak, they
all perish, and the entire household is destroyed."[42]

More than anything else, the very structure of Caldiera's trilogy accustoms
his readers to accepting the sustained "parallelism" of household and polity.[43] A
peaceful and tranquil polity depends upon virtuous rulers who have learned to
govern themselves through cultivation of virtues and avoidance of vices and who
have been apprenticed in the workshop of the household. There is no contradic-
tion between public and private; household and polity are part of a continuum.

Ideas such as these were widely current in the works of other Venetian humanist writers. For example, a few years before Caldiera published his trilogy, another Venetian humanist, nobleman Lauro Querini, wrote a spirited defense of
nobility by birth. The work was written as a refutation of the Florentine Poggio
Bracciolini's argument that nobility does not depend upon blood but upon the
cultivation of virtue. Querini followed up his defense of nobility with another
tract, *De republica,* in which he praised the aristocratic republic as the ideal form
of government.[44]

According to Querini, households, composed of the paterfamilias and his
wife, children, and servants, were the constituent "parts" of the city.[45] This hierarchical ordering, especially of masters and servants, was sanctioned by nature:

> And nature herself, that greatest craftsman of all things, teaches that lord-
> ship and servitude are naturally distinct in many things. For the soul nat-
> urally commands the body despotically, while the mind controls desire by
> a just and regal rule. Any thing is naturally a ruler which knows and pro-
> vides and for which it is rather useful to rule; that serves indeed which is
> rude in soul and strong in body, so that what the lord commands the ser-
> vant executes, and for which it is better to be ruled than to rule—which
> arrangement is beneficial both to lord and servant.[46]

Venetian humanists hammered home the idea that privilege and power were the
result of nature, not human artifice.[47]

Foreign writers who moved in Venetian circles or whose works were published or circulated in Venice also employed political metaphors in their descriptions of the household. In 1458 Ragusan merchant Benedetto Cotrugli wrote a work entitled *Il libro dell'arte di mercatura*, which Ugo Tucci has described as "referable without reserve to the Venetian ambit."[48] Cotrugli began the fourth and final book of the treatise, which was dedicated to economics, by equating the domestic and the political. He wrote that governance of the household and family was no less worthy of the merchant than "'l vivere politico."[49] He repeated Valerius Maximus's question "What can be strong outside the house if one lives poorly within the house?" [Quid opportet foris esse strenuum, si domi male vivitur?] and Aristotle's pronouncement from the *Politics* that the "paterfamilias of the house can be called the king of his household, since just as a king rules his realm, so the father of the family (ought to rule) his house."[50] And in his *Della instituzione morale,* published in 1560, the Sienese Alessandro Piccolomini, a friend of Venetian patrician Daniele Barbaro, wrote that "a house . . . is none other than a small city; and a city a big house."[51]

In all these works the primary attribute or virtue assigned to servants was obedience. Seldom did writers who emphasized the political metaphor concern themselves much with outlining the care and nurturing that fathers ought to display to those for whom they were responsible. Instead, servants, whose low and brutish nature inclined them to base activities, were to be strictly disciplined and regimented. Piccolomini wrote that "obedience is useful to servants as governing and ruling is to others."[52] Furthermore, he compared governance of servants with tyranny, the difference being that whereas the tyrant rules only for his own benefit, the tyrannical head of household rules for "the utility and benefit of all the members of the house, each according to his station."[53]

As we shall see, the tendency of early modern Venetians to read master-servant relations as a political metaphor, that is, as an analogy for relations between ruler and subject, at times profoundly influenced the ways masters and servants actually interacted with one another and also the ways masters understood and dealt with acts of disobedience. In one instance at least, the tyranny of masters was transformed into the tyranny of servants. In minds accustomed to analogues and metaphors and to thinking hierarchically, master-servant relations were an important barometer of the health of the Venetian polity.

## Giacomo Lanteri and the Social Utility of Servants

While the theme of the household as the polity writ small remained an important component of many treatises on household management and the family, during the sixteenth century the genre became less overtly political and was instead associated more and more with the growing debate over the essence of nobility. As Frigo notes, in the sixteenth century economics became "a complete guide to the *vivere civile* in all its shadings and subtleties."[54] In the early part of the century such works served as models for upwardly mobile courtiers. By the later part, again according to Frigo, they had become justifications of the entire social order.[55] The household came to be seen less as a building block or metaphor of the well-ordered polity and more as a symbol of the hierarchical and nobly dominated social system.

In 1560 Brescian nobleman Giacomo Lanteri published in Venice his *Della economica*.[56] The work was dedicated to Reneé of France, duchess of Ferrara. Unlike the works examined earlier, Lanteri's is in the form of a dialogue that extends over six days. The male interlocutors, who converse for four days, are Gioanbattista Lupatino, Pietro Antonio Lupatino, and Apotrotide, who is, as Lanteri says, "fictitiously named."[57] Gioanbattista takes the lead throughout, imparting advice to his fellow conversationists. In the second part, the interlocutors are three women, Isabella Borromeo, Deianira Comnena, and Laura Gonzaga, with Deianira leading the discussion. Their conversation lasts two days. While the men discuss the duties and responsibilities of the paterfamilias, the women concern themselves with the duties of the "madre di famiglia." Even so, Deianira tells her friends that she is repeating advice given her by her husband. Indeed, she adds that when he first instructed her, he compared their household to "una picciola Città" in which he was the supreme authority and she was his "castellan or lieutenant" [Castellano o' sia Luogotenente] (159).

In the first part of the treatise, which is dedicated to Gioanandrea Palazzo, a Brescian gentleman, the men discuss the proper disposition of the house, its furnishings, and its inhabitants, all selected according to the social rank of the owner. Gioanbattista advises that in the house of a titled nobleman the part "most healthy and pleasant" [sana et piu allegra] be reserved for the master. The women's quarters should be isolated as much as possible from other parts of the house, but the women should have access to a courtyard and garden so that they can pass time pleasurably without being seen by outsiders. By contrast, the servants' quarters are to be situated in the "most abject" [piu abietta] part of the house. Guest quarters are to be located as far away as possible from household noise so that guests will not be bothered by housekeeping activities. These rooms should be especially well appointed with tapestries and other furnishings. Above all, Gioanbattista advises his friends, the guest quarters should be placed as far as possible from the kitchen and other service areas. Gioanbattista fears that the "bustle of the family" [romore della famiglia] and the "bother of ignorant servants" [confusione de i servitori ignoranti] will lead visitors to conclude that "the head of the family [is] either negligent or of small account" [il capo di famiglia ò negligente, ò dapoco] (17–18). Pietro Antonio concurs, noting, "I believe indeed that the greatest enemies which homes have are the servants."[58]

On the second day, the men turn specifically to the subject of servants. They agree that masters should employ the number of servants appropriate to their status and needs. Yet the selection and training of servants is a particularly difficult task. Gioanbattista asks how one can possibly have any honor if one has a servant who wanders about the neighborhood all day long revealing the defects of the household. He answers his own question by noting that if one does not select one's servants with prudence, "discontent, dishonor and ruin" [discontento, dishonore, et danno] can follow (41). To avoid these problems, the master should choose servants who are "wellborn" [ben nati] and suited intellectually to their duties and who avoid all vices associated with food, drink, sleep, gambling, and prostitution. Above all, he should choose servants who fear God (42–43).

Once selected, the "patre di famiglia" should train the servants, since to be well served is a "difficil cosa" (45). When a servant first enters the household, the master should impart some general advice and admonitions. After a few days of observing the servant, the master can then proceed to more specific instructions. By offering rewards and favors for good service, and disgrace and punishment for negligence, the master will make his servants "solicitous and eager to serve well" [sollecito et curioso nel ben servire] (46). The master should carefully assign tasks to servants according to their intelligence, since he will not be well served if servants perceive injustice in the allocation of duties (55–56). If a master has done his job properly, the servants will obey and serve "lovingly, and with reverence" [amorevolmente, et con riverenza] (54). The master should dismiss any servant who habitually causes discord. "In this manner, rewarding those who in serving him do their duty, and punishing them who do the contrary, the master will spur the servants to be diligent in their duties and loyal."[59] On the third and fourth days, the men discuss the income and outlays of the household.

In the second part of the treatise, dedicated to Lucretia Bona de Lanteri, wife of Lanteri's cousin, the women converse under the rubric of the qualities and duties of the honest wife and consider many of the same topics as the men during their two days of conversations. The wife is a helpmate, or as Lanteri says, a lieutenant, to her husband. Deianira supports this division of labor by repeating the Aristotelian idea that women, who are weaker than men, conserve what their husbands have acquired (154).

The female interlocutors, like the men, are especially concerned with establishing a well-defined division of labor among servants. Deianira says that there are basically two kinds of female servants: those who serve the person of the mistress and those who serve the house. The first are called "damigelle" [ladies-in-waiting]; the second, "fantesche" [serving girls]. The fantesche are assigned the task of doing the laundry and otherwise keeping the household neat and orderly. The damigelle, by contrast, when they are not attending to the personal needs of the mistress, should be occupied in serving and keeping the house well supplied with linens.[60]

Deianira informs her friends that she herself has always employed eight female servants: two matrons, four damigelle, and two housekeepers or serving girls. One of the two matrons has charge of the damigelle. Deianira says that she has been fortunate to have a matron who was raised by her own mother, Princess Francesca Paleologa (115). Deianira notes that this woman "has excellent judgment, is virtuous and very competent in all womanly matters."[61] The other matron has charge of the household. To her Deianira has entrusted the day-to-day affairs of the house. She holds the keys to the pantry and dispensaries, reports to her mistress, and directly oversees the fantesche. To the matron in charge of the damigelle, Deianira has given care of the household's finest furnishings, especially those reserved for guests. Deianira concludes by noting that under her own guidance everything is kept in appropriate order (169–70).

When Lanteri's discussion of the household and servants is compared with those of Paolino and Caldiera, we see the great distance that has been traversed. First, the audience for the works has changed. Whereas Paolino and Caldiera wrote for the merchant patricians of the city-states, Lanteri addressed his words primarily to the nobility. At the beginning of the men's conversation, Gioanbattista makes clear that there are four kinds of nobles, including merchants.[62] Yet throughout, his remarks are directed to the first two grades of nobility: those who are noble by blood and those who enjoy honorific titles. Station is reflected first and foremost in the size of households. Paolino began his discussion of servants with a consideration of whether it was necessary to employ more than one servant. Lanteri, by contrast, assumes that the paterfamilias will employ several.[63] Deianira alone employs eight women.

Moreover, the servants are now systematically arranged in a clear-cut hierarchy of roles and responsibilities. Both Paolino and Caldiera believed that servants should be given particular tasks, but they did not elaborate on the duties of specific kinds of servants or assign them titles. In Lanteri's work, female servants are clearly ranked into three categories: matrons, damigelle, and fantesche. And the men talk of pages, menservants, and other "staffieri." Gioanbattista notes that great noblemen often employ a majordomo (55–56).

Like his predecessors, Lanteri emphasizes repeatedly that the hierarchy that exists in the household is natural and based on God-given talents, such as intelligence, and on the capabilities of household members. In Lanteri's mind, intelligence is closely linked to virtue. Those servants who are the least intelligent are also the least virtuous; they are likely to give themselves over to the animal vices associated with bodily needs. The more intelligent servants, by contrast, have learned to curb their natural desires and to cultivate virtue and good manners.[64]

Lanteri also emphasizes a theme that was important to Barbaro, namely, that the governance of servants directly affects the master's reputation and social standing. Servants can bring not only honor but also disgrace. Well-mannered servants are an indication of a master's "natural" ability to rule his household and himself; they are the very personification of the triumph of virtue over vice. They increase the master's reputation. At the same time, ill-mannered servants can destroy a master's reputation. For this reason, the paterfamilias must take every possible precaution to avoid dishonor.

These same themes are taken up even more forcefully in Stefano Guazzo's treatise *La civil conversatione,* published in Brescia in 1574 and in Venice in 1575, 1584, and 1609.[65] Guazzo (1530–93) was from a noble Piedmontese family and spent much of his life serving various princes, including the Gonzagas of Mantua. The topic of his book is conversation, which he places at the very center of civil life. Divided into four books, the work defines "civil conversation" as practiced in both the public and domestic spheres, and an example of such conversation is provided in book 4.[66]

Book 3 concerns various forms of "domestic conversation," including those between husbands and wives, fathers and sons, brothers, and masters and servants. In Guazzo's view, the key to the master-servant relationship lies in the master's ability to control his servants. The master must know how to command. A true gentleman does not reprimand his servants in front of guests or beat them. He controls his servants firmly but kindly. He is not overly familiar with them, yet he is solicitous of their welfare.[67]

A man who cannot control his servants loses face because he calls into question his own social position by revealing himself ill suited to rule. For example, a master who changes servants often shows himself to be an "huomo impatiente" (439). To the proverb "We have as many enemies as we have servants" [Tanti nemici habbiamo, quanti servitori] Guazzo responds that it is not an indictment of the servants, but of their masters, since "we do not hire servants who are enemies, we make them into enemies" [noi non habbiamo i servitori nimici, ma li facciamo] (446). By contrast, the master who knows how to command will be richly rewarded. Guazzo says that a well-trained servant "is part of his master" and that there is no greater possession in the world than a good servant. He paraphrases Ecclesiasticus (33:30), saying that if one has a loyal servant, one has a second self.[68]

In the end, both Lanteri and Guazzo emphasize loyalty over obedience. In Lanteri's view, a good servant is not secured through the ire of the master, but through a combination of gentle admonitions and rewards. If properly selected, trained, and handled, a servant will demonstrate "the love, the fear, and the reverence that he owes the master" [l'amore, il timore, et la riverenza, che quello è debitore di portagli].[69]

For Lanteri, Guazzo, and other writers of the mid- and later sixteenth century, the household was only secondarily a microcosm of the polity. For them the household stood as a model of the social order. Whereas according to the political metaphor, rule of the household was an indicator of the master's ability in the political sphere and a barometer of the health of the polity, according to writers who emphasized the social metaphor, rule of the household was an indicator of the master's social standing and a justification of nobility. Or as Frigo notes, there was no distinction between "signoria domestica" and "egemonia sociale."[70] Society, like the household, was a hierarchy based on "natural" abilities and talents. In the well-ordered society, as in the well-run household, everyone was expected to adhere willingly to his or her place. Those who were at the apex did not retain their position through repression, and those at the bottom did not covet the positions of their betters. Loyalty replaced obedience as the primary virtue of servants, and loyal servants increased the honor and prestige of their masters.

## Agostino Valier and "Christian" Economy

During the sixteenth century a subgenre developed within the larger genre of treatises on household management and wifely duties. In the wake of the Tridentine reform of the Catholic Church, a number of writers undertook the task of describing a Christian economy, in which masters had a special obligation to provide moral guidance for the members of their households. Although these treatises remain deeply rooted in the classical tradition of treatises on economics, they reflect as well the religious preoccupations of the sixteenth century.[71]

One Venetian representative of the genre is Cardinal Agostino Valier's *Della istruzione delle donne maritate*. Valier (1531–1606) was a member of a distinguished Venetian patrician family. As a young man he lectured on philosophy in Venice. In 1565 he became bishop of Verona, succeeding his uncle Bernardo Navagero. Like his friend Carlo Borromeo, Valier worked selflessly in his diocese during the plague of 1576, and like the archbishop of Milan, he was a major exponent of Catholic reform. He was made a cardinal in 1583.[72]

Valier composed four tracts, or sets of instructions, for the female members of his flock. He wrote instructions for nuns, for spinsters, for widows, and for married women.[73] Valier wrote his *On the Instruction of Married Women* for his sister, Laura Gradenigo. In the preface he states that he has composed the work "because good mothers of the family are the firm foundations of the discipline of cities, whence is born obedience, right governance, and the tranquility of the people, with honor and glory to God."[74]

As his prefatory remarks indicate, Valier believed that women had an important function to play in the family. In chapter 2 of the treatise he also assigns a political role to mothers. By their example and prayers, women help not only their husbands and sons but also "Cities, Republics, and Kingdoms" by raising "good fathers of the family, good citizens, good gentlemen, good princes." Most importantly, they serve as "Mothers of the people of God."[75]

Nevertheless, wives remain firmly subject to their husbands. Valier warns married women that they should always be alert, since "any little thing" can besmirch their honor. Wives should be virtuous in all matters, being especially careful to avoid public festivals and comedies, where "the Devil triumphs" (21). In order to avoid the snares of Satan, they should keep busy tending to their husbands' needs, overseeing their households, reading pious works, and engaging in other "honest" activities. Their free time should be spent reading devotional literature, especially a little book containing the "Christian Institution." Wives should learn it by heart so that they can instruct their children and their maidservants in it. This is especially important since at the Last Judgment mothers will be questioned about their negligence of children and maidservants.[76]

In the chapter on wives' treatment of the household, Valier recommends that they treat servants as they themselves would wish to be treated if they were the subject ones. In order for wives to better command, they should themselves be obedient to their husbands and thereby serve as an example to all of "humility, obedience, and subjection" [di umiltà, di obbedienza, e di soggezione].[77] Mothers should instruct their children with great care, discouraging their daughters from frequenting the female servants (37). Wives should be especially alert to the character of the servants they employ, since unfaithful servants have brought misery to "many fathers and many mothers." For Valier, the ideal wife is one who is the first to rise in the morning and the last to retire at night. She is always diligent and attentive to the affairs of the household. In the epilogue, Valier asks that the Holy Spirit "cascade on all of the mothers of the family of Verona, of our country, and finally on all the married women of the world" so that all homes will be "truly houses of God, lodges of peace and concord."[78]

In his *On the Instruction of Married Women* Valier repeats many of the same themes found in the works of other writers on household management. Wives should be subservient to their husbands and should teach their servants to be both loyal and obedient. But Valier expands the obligations to include providing not only for servants' physical needs but for their moral welfare as well. It is the duty of masters and mistresses to lead their servants to virtue. If this is done, society and the polity will be better off, since the practices of individual households will resonate throughout the wider world.

~

Transformations in the political organization of the Venetian republic and the social position of the Venetian nobility, as well as wider cultural currents, are subtly revealed in the treatises on household management and wifely duties that we have examined. During the fourteenth and fifteenth centuries, when Venice was at the height of its power, treatises were addressed to a politically active elite. The household was read as a metaphor of the state in which the master was born to rule, and the servant to obey. But as the sixteenth century progressed, the political power of Venice began to wane and the elite strove to retain their power not so much through the bald exercise of force as through the careful control and manipulation of social forms. Expertise in *il vivere civile* became the key to social prominence and political power. All aspects of life were now read according to this scale of values, and a well-run household became one of many indicators of nobility.[79] The household was understood as society writ small, and the primary obligation of servants within the household was loyalty.

The importance of these treatises lay precisely in that vision, more than in the practical information they imparted. Writers such as Barbaro and Caldiera did include some useful advice in their treatises, but they did so because the same advice had been included in works by Aristotle or Xenophon. There is little in these treatises to suggest a deep familiarity with the everyday problems of household management and wifely duties.[80] None conveys a sense of immediacy; rather, these treatises were intended to propagandize and legitimize a particular vision of the world as patriarchal and hierarchical.

## An Encyclopedia, a Book of Fashion, an Oration, and a Treatise on Death

During the sixteenth century the discussion of servants and domestic service was not confined simply to humanist treatises on household management and wifely duties based on classical models. Servants now became legitimate topics in other genres as well. Four especially important works in the Venetian context were Tommaso Garzoni's encyclopedic account of various professions,

Cesare Vecellio's illustrated book of costumes, Bartolomeo Spatafora's facetious defense of servitude, and Fabio Glissenti's tract on death.

These works differ from the treatises examined earlier, above all, in purpose. In treatises on the household the intention of the authors was explicitly didactic. They admonished and advised their readers concerning ways to order their households and rule their lives. They thus provide valuable clues to the familial ideals and mental constructs that shaped the patriarchal ideology of the servant-keeping elite. By contrast, Garzoni and Vecellio sought to describe rather than to teach, Spatafora to provide a pleasant diversion for his learned audience, and Glissenti to admonish readers to lead a moral life. At first reading, the works of Garzoni and Vecellio seem more "realistic," for they purport to catalogue and illustrate the professions and costumes of their world. Yet, upon closer examination we see that these works too reinforce a hierarchical view of the world and the "naturalness" of service. Spatafora's polemic unwittingly reveals the preoccupations and fears of the servant-keeping elite as they struggled to classify and control the world around them. Glissenti's admonition to seek a good death uses images of servants and gondoliers to characterize a life of dissolution and immorality.

## Tommaso Garzoni

Tommaso Garzoni was born in 1549 at Bagnacavallo to a family of middling rank. After studying law at Ferrara and Siena, he underwent a spiritual crisis and in 1566 joined the order of Canons Regular of the Lateran. As a member of the order, he made frequent trips to Treviso, Venice, and elsewhere. He died at age forty at Bagnacavallo.[81] In 1586 Garzoni published his encyclopedic *Piazza universale di tutte le professioni del mondo,* which he dedicated to Alfonso II, duke of Ferrara.[82] Garzoni announces in the dedication that his intention is to examine "the good and the evil that are found in all the professions of the world" in order that the sovereign may better know his subjects and rule his realm.[83] In nearly a thousand pages, Garzoni provides descriptions or sketches of more than 450 professions, from popes and kings to prostitutes and muleteers. On a superficial level the work is a celebration of the diversity of the world and the ingenuity of humans. But when one looks more closely, one sees that classification is subtly transformed into stratification, and diversity into conformity, according to a system based on notions of nobility and morality. Alessandro Gnavi sees the work as an "ideological instrument" in the Counter Reformation effort to create greater social discipline.[84]

In the *Piazza,* Garzoni discusses servants under several different rubrics. The work includes chapters, or "discourses," on midwives, wet nurses, and governesses (discourse 130), on cooks and other kitchen and table help (discourse 93), on stable hands (discourse 55), on boatmen, including gondoliers (discourse 144), and on other specialized servants. Yet it is best to begin with discourse 91, entitled "De servitori, paggi, et schiavi" [On servants, pages, and slaves].[85]

Garzoni lays out his view of servants in the very first sentence of the discourse. Refuting the "defense of servitude" made by Bartolomeo Spatafora, Garzoni labels service odious because in it the servant, either by his own will or predisposed to do so by a "vile nature" [natura vile], surrenders himself for money to the master and thereby loses "dear liberty" [la cara libertà], which even animals love above all else. Garzoni says that there are some unfortunate souls who cannot survive if they are not in service, since they do not know how to rule themselves.

The author makes clear that he is not discussing those whose service is involuntary, and he cites several examples of honorable ancients who, having once ruled, found themselves suddenly in servitude. He continues with a discussion of service among the ancient Greeks, Romans, Cretans, and others. This leads him to ask how masters and servants should interact. Rejecting the notion that masters and servants are incapable of being friendly, Garzoni argues that servants should be treated "humanely and piously" [humanamente et piamente]. But if servants are evil, they should be disciplined. Masters should be especially solicitous of those servants who conduct themselves "most humanely" and "most loyally." Garzoni cites several examples of faithful servants, including the handmaidens of Cleopatra, who wished to end their life when their masters and mistresses ended theirs. Servants like those should be "appreciated and held most dear" [apprezzati, e tenuti molto cari] (676).

But soon the tone changes again as Garzoni describes haughty and disloyal servants. His words reach a crescendo as he describes them as "vile kings of trickery, and scum of laziness" who are "unfaithful like the Moors, thieves like Gypsies, assassins like the Arabs, traitors like the Parthians"—people who "were created from nothing" and deserve nothing but discipline and labor.[86] Such servants were never esteemed by the ancients: Aristotle did not consider them part of the city, and jurists accorded them no legal rights. Lucian found servants well practiced in "thievery, tricks, flight, arrogance, stupidity, drunkenness, greed, sleep, tardiness, and sloth."[87] The discourse concludes with a brief discussion of slaves, who are "worse still."

If literary style is any guide to attitudes, then Garzoni feels the baseness of servants much more deeply than their goodness. When discussing loyal servants, those who know their place and are faithful, he carefully selects edifying examples from ancient history to illustrate his points. But when he discusses the vices of servants, Garzoni's language and style come alive as he piles descriptions one upon another until he has created a veritable catalogue of servants' turpitude. Gnavi suggests that Garzoni's prose reflects the cadences of popular preachers.[88]

The same rhetorical devices are employed in the discourses on factors or stewards and gondoliers and boatmen. According to Garzoni, the duty of factors is to record the income and outlays of their masters, but often they are so simple-minded that they cannot perform even that basic task. In an addition or annotation to the discourse, Garzoni notes that factors "sin" in ten different ways: they sin "in substance," because they rob and dissipate their masters' goods; in "quantity," because they never give a precise answer when asked what the master has earned and what they themselves have spent; in "quality," "because ruined and spoiled goods are the perfume of their deeds" [la robba guasta, et marcia è il profumo della loro asinità]. They also sin in place, in site, in clothing, in time, in action, and finally in passion, since they exhibit neither gentility nor courtesy.[89]

Garzoni's most vituperative and scathing remarks, however, are reserved for boatmen, including gondoliers (867–81). After discussing the beauty of boats and commenting on the origins of the names of various kinds of ships and boats, he notes that boatmen take after Charon, the oarsman who ferries souls across the river Styx. They are "gente del diavolo" who lack all sense of conscience and shame. In them the evils of the world have collected "in a pile." Boatmen exhibit, in Garzoni's words, "all the ills that a soldier exhibits, all the greed of a merchant, all the crimes of a ruffian, all the evils of a Jew, all the trickery of a scholar, all the curses of a prostitute."[90] Gondoliers are no better; they are the basest sort of people and always speak "foul words, vain oaths of all sorts, and terrible imprecations." Garzoni concludes, "In them one will not find even one truth, one will not discover even one good manner, one will not see any goodness, because they are for the most part rabble."[91]

The only good that comes of the profession of boatmen is that it allows passengers to travel about Venice in great comfort and security. Gondoliers deliver passengers to their destination and await them. Furthermore, in a gondola one travels in peace and repose (870). On board one can sing, laugh, and play. In his discussion of the sedan-chair carriers of Naples, Garzoni comments that at first glance this profession too appears "ignoble and vile" but that it is in fact an honest profession because the men who practice it are made respectable by the passengers they carry (615–17). This apparently is not true of gondoliers.

Female servants are considered in discourse 130, concerning midwives, wet nurses, and governesses.[92] Here Garzoni repeats many of the traditional complaints leveled against wet nurses: often they nurse even when their milk is "bad and pestilent"; and they "imprint" their charges "with bad customs, vices, and defects."[93] The role of the governess is an important one. According to Garzoni, children love liberty, so it is the governess's duty to apply a brake on their natural inclinations and to teach them good manners. Children are naturally vulnerable to vice; they are like "tender plants," which must be raised with modesty and fear. They are particularly at risk when their governesses and tutors do shameful things in their presence, for they learn by imitating their elders. Wet nurses are especially prone to sin, since often they beguile their masters and become pregnant by them, causing "manifest shame to the mistresses" [manifesta vergogna alle padrone]. Worst of all, they often dispose of these unwanted infants by tossing them into latrines. In a brief annotation to discourse 130, Garzoni cites Barges, who says that three things can set a house afire: "a prodigal son, an adulterous wife, or a whoring nurse."[94]

In Garzoni's view, service is inferior to most other professions. Servants have shown themselves to be weak and in some essential ways barely human, for they have voluntarily surrendered that most cherished of personal qualities—liberty. Some have done this for money, others because of a "vile nature," still others because they do not possess the moral fiber to rule themselves. The absence of self-control and intelligence makes servants especially vulnerable to all the vices that plague mankind. With no moral center, servants are like a magnet or a sponge (or as Garzoni says, a "pile"), to which are attracted all moral failings. Unlike such groups as Gypsies and Moors, who are associated with only one particular vice, servants exhibit them all. The danger for masters is that servants will contaminate their household. Masters face a terrible dilemma in that they need servants but are at the same time threatened by them. Garzoni says that boatmen are both "bassissima, et utilissima."[95]

It is their lack of any sense of honor or shame that makes servants so foul. Yet Garzoni recognizes that a curious symbiosis exists between masters and servants. Some servants, such as sedan-chair carriers, are actually ennobled by their work. Similarly, the most vile boatmen make it possible for their masters to travel about in comfort and seclusion. It is for this reason that boatmen are "utilissima." In Garzoni's strictly hierarchical and moralized view of the world, servants are an important and necessary evil.

## Cesare Vecellio

Another work laden with hierarchical notions of honor is Cesare Vecellio's *De gli habiti antichi, et moderni di diverse parti del mondo libri due,* published in Venice in 1590.[96] Vecellio (1521–1601) was a relative and follower of the painter Titian, and in this work he not only describes but also illustrates the costumes and, to a lesser extent, the character of various members of Venetian and other societies. The work begins with Rome, ancient and modern, then moves to Venice and then to other parts of Italy, Europe, Asia, Africa, and America. He includes in his work nobles, both male and female, at various stages of the life cycle, as well as merchants, soldiers, peasants, and, for Venice, boatmen or gondoliers and maidservants.

Vecellio opens his discussion of boatmen, entitled "Concerning the Dress of Boatmen and the Commodiousness of Boats" [De gli habiti de' Barcaruoli, et della commodità delle Barche], by noting, as Garzoni does, that boats are a great convenience for the elite. While the poor utilize the public ferries to cross the Grand Canal, nobles, cittadini, and other "persone ricche" have their own boats, which are manned by two servants. The first, who is actually in charge of the boat, is called the "poop man" [il fante de poppa]; the other, the "center man" or "prow man" [il fante de mezo]. While the center man often is responsible for performing other services for the master, the poop man's main task is to keep the gondola "clean, adorned, and rigged." He then describes the gondola's furnishings, including the iron or steel dolphin that adorns the prow and the *felce*, an awning made of black twill.[97] In the accompanying illustration, Vecellio shows three gondolas covered with felci (see plate 1). In two of the boats the passengers are female; in the third, male. Vecellio includes no description of the gondoliers' clothing, although in the illustration it appears that they wear a long jacket over trousers. Only the distinctive hats seem to set the crews apart.

The discussion of female servants is entitled "Serving Women and Serving Girls, or Housekeepers of Venice" [Serve, et fantesche, ò massare di Venetia] (150r). Vecellio notes that female servants have different tasks, some more important than others. According to Vecellio, wet nurses, who have charge of governing and nursing children, are "rather respected and appreciated" [assai rispettate et accarezzate] and are better treated to food, drink, and rest so that their milk will be more "substantial." Next in rank are "chambermaids" [cameriere], who hold the keys to the pantry. They normally wear an outfit of tan, tawny, or other dark-colored serge. They cover their head and shoulders with a kerchief of silk or floss silk. Other maids wear a black outfit and a kerchief. Some are "ladies-in-waiting" [donzelle], who accompany their mistress wherever she goes and keep her company at home, assuming they are "honest and not malicious" [honeste et senza malitia]. Others may be widowed matrons or spinsters. All receive a salary that is "appropriate to their duties and their competence." The women who do the cooking and cleaning often wear a colored skirt, a white or tan smock, and a white kerchief. "They attend to all the needs of the household" [attendona à tutti i bisogni della Casa] (150r).

Plate 1. Illustration of *barcaruoli* from Cesare Vecellio's *De gli habiti antichi, et moderni di diverse parti del mondo libri due* (Venice, 1590). Photograph courtesy of Museo Civico Correr, Venice.

Plate 2. Illustration of *fantesche* from Cesare Vecellio's *De gli habiti antichi, et moderni di diverse parti del mondo libri due* (Venice, 1590). Photograph courtesy of Biblioteca Nazionale Marciana, Venice.

In the accompanying illustration, simply labeled "Fantesche," Vecellio shows a matronly figure wearing a long skirt and a shawl that covers her head and shoulders. She carries a small book, probably a prayer book, and rosary beads (see plate 2). It appears that Vecellio has chosen to illustrate one of the matrons who accompany their mistresses to church.

In his description of servants, Vecellio concentrates on the tasks servants actually perform. Male servants have two essential tasks: to row their masters about the city and to keep their gondolas in good condition. Female servants have a greater variety of tasks: some are in charge of rearing the children, others escort and keep company with the mistress of the household, and still others do the actual housework. In Vecellio's view, servants matter primarily in the sense that they are useful.

In striking contrast to Garzoni, Vecellio makes no mention whatsoever of the problems that masters face with domestic servants or of servants' failings and vices, nor does he mention their virtues. Instead he sees servants largely as props or accouterments to the noble style of life. Boats and boatmen are "commodious"—they make it easy and pleasant for the elite to go on picnics and to travel about in safety and comfort. It is no accident that Vecellio spends more time describing the gondolas than he does describing the boatmen. Indeed in this book of costumes he devotes not one word to the outfits of gondoliers but goes into some detail about the trappings and riggings of the gondolas. In Vecellio's view, servants are always present but little regarded.[98]

In his engravings of boatmen and fantesche, Vecellio further reveals his idealized vision of servants. In the illustration of boatmen Vecellio shows five men hard at work at their task. All row with determination and skill. They seem ready to meet their passengers' needs at a moment's notice. The passengers, likewise, appear at ease, confident that it is in the end they, not the boatmen, who are really in charge. One sees no resemblance between these oarsmen and the foulmouthed ruffians portrayed by Garzoni. Similarly, Vecellio has chosen to represent the fantesca as a matronly figure rather than as a nubile young girl. There is no danger that this serving woman will beguile the head of the household. From her bearing and demeanor, she appears both pious and humble, an edifying example of the doubly faithful servant.

At heart Vecellio's idealized vision is even more hierarchical than Garzoni's. In his world servants know their proper place and adhere to it. They do not challenge their masters or dishonor them; rather, they confirm their masters' importance by performing their tasks with humility and alacrity. In Vecellio's illustrations we see masters who, in Lanteri's words, know how to command. The servants thereby become visual symbols of their masters' station, and their own position is revealed and confirmed by their dress. Female servants in particular dress in a very plain manner, in clothing made of common fabric and dyed drab colors—tan, white, or black. They provide an indistinct backdrop against which the richness of their masters and mistresses can shine. Vecellio presents servants as masters wished them to appear.

∽

The same is true of other depictions of servants in Venetian art. One of the most striking examples is Paolo Veronese's fresco rendering of Giustiniana Barbaro at the Villa Barbaro at Maser (see the frontispiece), which Mary Rogers has recently interpreted as a visualization of Renaissance theories of marriage, including those of Francesco Barbaro.[99] Looking across the room from a balustrade, Barbaro is the epitome of Venetian aristocratic elegance. Even here, on *villeggiatura,* her hair is well coifed and she wears a sumptuous gown and pearls. At her left stands her faithful nurse, dressed in drab green and white and showing every one of her many years of labor. The maid's crude, haggard features and leathery skin serve to highlight the refinement and nobility of Barbaro. Yet Barbaro also seems to rely upon this woman, who is eternally at her side, ready to serve her and the rest of the family. A tiny lap dog, frequently a symbol of fidelity in Renaissance paintings, sits on the balustrade directly in front of the maid.

If Veronese's portrait of Giustiniana Barbaro emphasizes the bonds that sometimes linked masters and servants together, Titian's portrait *Fabricius Salvaresius with a Black Page* demonstrates how easily and quickly relations between masters and servants could blend into and become symbols of larger political and social concerns (see plate 3). In this portrait, Titian's intent is to illustrate the sitter's power and importance. The black page (very likely a slave) provides a clue to Salvaresius's exalted station and profession. The portrait conveys no sense of an emotional bond between the two; the page merely serves by his presence and attitude to highlight the social prominence of his master.[100]

Servants also appear in a number of the painted narrative cycles for which Venice is famous. In these scenes domestics serve as symbols of the social harmony that Venice sought to project both to itself and to the outside world. In Gentile Bellini's *Miracle at the Bridge of San Lorenzo,* executed for the *scuola* (confraternity) of San Giovanni Evangelista, a black slave, stripped to his loin cloth, appears ready to plunge into the water to help retrieve the precious relic that has toppled into the canal but, miraculously, floats. A female servant dressed in common cloth and headgear is prepared to steady him as he steps out onto the land-

Plate 3. Titian, *Portrait of Fabricius Salvaresius with a Black Page,* Kunsthistoriches Museum, Vienna. Photograph courtesy of Kunsthistoriches Museum.

ing. In Mansueti's *Miracle at the Bridge of San Lio,* everyday life proceeds normally as the miracle occurs; workmen repair an *altana,* or rooftop deck, a chimney sweep chases a cat, and a maid hangs laundry on a clothesline strung from the window of an attic dormer. In the background of Vittore Carpaccio's *Healing of the Possessed Man,* executed for the same cycle, a maid on a distant altana beats a carpet, while in the foreground gaily attired gondoliers skillfully guide their boats toward the Rialto (see plate 4). As Patricia Fortini Brown has argued, these painters wanted "the narrative moment to be embedded and even subdued in a richly described environment."[101] That environment is a mythically peace-

Plate 4. Vittore Carpaccio, detail of gondoliers from *The Healing of the Possessed Man,* Galleria dell'Accademia, Venice. Photograph courtesy of O. Böhm, Venice.

ful Venice wherein nobles and cittadini attend to business and holiness, while artisans and servants attend to their chores.

## Bartolomeo Spatafora

In his defense of service Bartolomeo Spatafora shows that behind the self-confident smiles and assured countenances of the masters depicted by the painters there lurked doubts and fears. Spatafora was, as he noted in the dedicatory letter to his collection of orations, Sicilian by birth but "Venetian by election." The collection includes four orations: one presented on the death of Doge Marco Antonio Trevisan; another on the election of Doge Francesco Venier; as well as two speeches "in soggetto giocoso," one a defense of discord, the other a defense of servitude, both delivered to the Accademia degli Uniti, a Venetian academy founded circa 1551 by Pietro da Mosto. The defense of servitude, which Spatafora presented on 10 September 1552, was a response to an earlier speech by Pietro Basadonna celebrating freedom.[102]

Spatafora begins the speech by laying out his basic argument, namely, that service is "better, more useful, and more desirable than liberty" [migliore, più utile, et più desiderabile della libertà]. It is precisely this thesis that Garzoni counters. Like Garzoni, Spatafora carefully defines service: he is not referring to forced service such as that suffered by Turkish captives or galley slaves; instead, he is discussing service in which one is employed by a "da bene, et prudente patrone." Spatafora is determined to prove that under these circumstances, "it is much better to be a servant than to be a master."[103] This is true for three reasons: unlike the master, the servant has peace of mind, a healthy body, and a clear conscience.

Spatafora "proves" his first point quickly enough. While the master has to worry constantly about every little detail of the household, the servant has nothing to fret about. He does not even know if the price of grain is rising or falling. While the master lies awake at night, tossing and turning, the servant sleeps soundly. The first point is demonstrated: servitude renders the soul tranquil (97–99).

Turning to the second point, Spatafora argues that constant physical activity actually renders the body more robust. The various tasks that servants perform make them strong and healthy. The orator contrasts them with the doges, who get hardly any exercise and who quickly lose their health through lack of physical activity and worry. Even though they may enter the dogeship in good health, they quickly "change nature and complexion" (99–101).

Spatafora's third point is that servitude is superior to freedom because servants have a clean conscience. Humans must fight constantly to control their appetites, but servants, who lack freedom of action, are not faced with such temptations. "Who," the orator asks, "prohibits a servant from doing good" [chi . . . proibisse il servitore di far bene]? Speaking of monarchs, he says that they are envied for their freedom to do as they please. "But," Spatafora says "more praiseworthy is the benefit of servitude, which does not allow one to do evil—whence is born and grows the one true and healthy freedom, namely, to do good."[104]

Spatafora tells his distinguished audience that if they are not yet convinced, he can corroborate his position with the opinions of great authors, and he notes that in the Scripture men are enjoined to be servants of God. In the end, servitude is superior to freedom because it allows one to practice virtue, not destroy it. The oration ends with an exhortation to the audience to be servants of God.[105]

As Spatafora himself notes in the preface to his book, his oration was intended as a diversion, an entertainment, a "soggetto giocoso" (1). Except for the exhortation at the end, he did not intend it to be taken seriously. Hence the work cannot be understood as an actual defense of servitude, nor does it in any way reveal what those who actually were in service may have thought about their position. But it does tell us something about the elite's attitude toward servants and about their own role as masters.

From Spatafora's text, we see that at times masters viewed servants as carefree, childlike creatures who were not preoccupied with worries or a guilty conscience. The vision of servants as childlike was an especially significant one that fit readily into the patriarchal vision of the family. As "children," servants were not fully rational beings nor fully responsible for their actions; they were more susceptible to temptation, but their lack of freedom prevented them from acting on their impulses. Similarly, masters associated servants with physicality. Spatafora commented that their duties made their bodies robust. As mentioned earlier, humanists often compared servants to members of the animal kingdom. In Garzoni's view, that physicality could become threatening. Indeed, all these texts reveal a fear on the part of the male elite of the potentially violent strength of male servants and of the seductive allure of female ones.

Spatafora unwittingly reveals the mental burden and strain that go with command. Lanteri's interlocutors believed that acts of insubordination on the part of servants were not so much their fault as they were the fault of their masters, who failed to command and demand respect. Spatafora provides some insight into the masters' mindset. Overwhelmed with details, forced by circumstances to act against their conscience, masters literally make themselves sick with worry. One wonders whether Spatafora's oration was met, not just with amusement, but with the nervous laughter of self-recognition.

## Fabio Glissenti

Fabio Glissenti's *Discorsi morali contra il dispiacer del morire* includes a vivid portrayal of the activities and habits of both the servants and the gondoliers of Venice. Yet the picture of servants is subordinated to the larger theme of the work, which has to do with reaffirming traditional Catholic ideas about a good death and the afterlife. For their part servants and gondoliers, along with other kinds of "persone basse, e vili," serve as representations of the senses triumphing over reason.

Fabio Glissenti was born at Vestone in the Brescian Valle Sabbia. He studied medicine at Padua and became a leading physician in late-sixteenth-century Venice. He wrote a large number of works in both Italian and Latin, including a number of plays, and died a very rich man sometime after 1615.[106]

In 1596 Glissenti published the *Discorsi morali,* also known as the *Athanatophilia.*[107] Over eleven hundred pages in length, it is divided into five dialogues that take place over five days: the dialogues of reason, the senses, free will, opinion, and truth. The main interlocutors throughout are the Philosopher, who enjoins all he meets to desire death, since it is the highest form of liberty, freeing humans from the world, and the Courtier, who recognizes that no one eagerly seeks death.

The servant and the boatman or gondolier appear in the second dialogue, which, like all the others, takes place in Venice. During the course of their travels about the city, the Philosopher and the Courtier encounter various members of the *popolo minuto,* or lower classes, including a porter, a wine porter, a beggar, a butcher, the steward of a country estate, and a gypsy woman, all of whom the Philosopher believes must, given their lives of labor and suffering, look forward to death. Yet each relishes life no matter how difficult.

When he finally meets the servant of one of his friends, who is returning from doing the shopping, the Courtier convinces the Philosopher that they should talk to this man of "misera conditione" since perhaps *he* actually desires death. The Philosopher asks the servant if he enjoys his job; the servant responds that he serves for money, selling his services to the highest bidder, but that he has never found a master to his liking, although he has tried more than a hundred. When the Philosopher asks how this can be, the servant responds that in Venice, where every "gentleman, citizen, and merchant" wants one or more servants, it is easy to change masters. He says that all masters are terrible: they treat servants like slaves and love to give commands and be obeyed, yet are stingy with pay and food. After three or four months, the servant leaves one for another (127r–127v). The Philosopher tells him that he can be free of his servitude and live in complete freedom, that he can be "Lord and master" [Signore, e padrone] of himself, if he will desire death and seek "that happy freedom of Heaven" [quella felice libertà del Cielo]. The servant reacts angrily to this advice, saying that if he could live forever by serving, he would gladly do so. When the Philosopher asks how he can voluntarily give up his liberty, the servant responds by explaining to the Philosopher all the advantages of his position (128r–129r).

He begins with a pun, noting that especially in Venice a servant is not a "servitore" [servant] but actually a "Servito Rè" [served King], because he turns everything to his own advantage, that in fact he is the one who is served (129v–130r). He indulges all his senses without reprisal, because in Venice the demand for servants far exceeds the supply. He tells the Philosopher that he always puts on an act in the master's presence, pretending to be what he is not [mostro d'esser in presenza sua quel, ch'io non sono]. In actuality, he skims off the household funds to buy himself "qualche cosarella"; he eats the best cuts of meat, the richest broths, the tastiest soups. He never actually refuses an order, but if the task is too difficult, he says he does not know how to do it and that it would be best to hire a porter for the job. When out on errands, he visits taverns and friends, and upon returning he complains that those he was sent to find were not at home. The female servants never turn him in, because, as he says, "One wolf never eats another wolf" [Lupo non mangia mai d'un altro Lupo], and because without male servants in the house female servants are like "little widows." When the master is away, the servants have parties and meetings (130v–131v). He concludes by asking, "Now consider if this isn't the life of a King, to be cherished and preserved as long as possible?"[108] The stunned Philosopher concedes, "You are not the servant, as you say, but the master."[109]

After declining a snack of delicacies skimmed from the masters' stores, the Philosopher and Courtier discuss service, agreeing with various classical authors that one has as many enemies as one has servants and that master and servant can never be friends. Recalling the honorable servants of the ancients, they castigate those of their own time, "who do not merit the name of servants, but rather of rogues, parasites, and sluggards," and who ought to be consigned to the galleys.[110] As they continue their discussion of service, they note that a master should be "solicitous, circumspect, and good" [sollecito, circonspetto e buono] and that the good servant should exhibit three qualities as well: he should "be diligent, have patience, and exhibit loyalty" [diligente essere, patienza havere, e fedeltà osservare], but above all else he must exhibit perseverance (135r).

Riding home in a gondola, the Courtier convinces the Philosopher to engage the gondolier in conversation. The Philosopher learns how little the gondolier earns and how difficult his job is, exposed as he is to the weather and treacherous canals. The ingenuous Philosopher is impressed, as usual, and believes that "these men, whom we may call aquatic, are not as evil as other men."[111] When the Philosopher says he wishes he could practice this noble trade, the gondolier replies that he would not wish it on his worst enemy. But when the Philosopher asks if he does not desire death as a way to escape his toil, the gondolier replies that he does not, for there are advantages to his trade that he has not yet mentioned (140r–140v).

First, the gondolier notes, although there are established fares for various ferry routes, there are also ways to induce or force passengers to pay more. If the passenger is a native Venetian who knows that there are fixed rates, then the gondolier claims that it is a feast day, when higher fees are allowed, or that he is rowing against the tide, or that the weather is bad. If the passenger is a foreigner, the gondolier has it even easier. He refuses to pull up to an embankment until he is paid what he demands, or he terrorizes the passenger by making the gondola rock wildly. He notes that gondoliers are expert at all sorts of verbal insults and "dirty words" [parole sporche], which they use especially after they have deposited their passengers on shore and are safe from reprisal.[112]

If he should tire of his work at the ferry stations [traghetti], he can hire himself out by the month to a nobleman; then he, along with the other servants, can cheat the master. If the master does not want to lodge him in his house, he keeps him waiting and moonlights on the side. When he rows the mistress or the children of the household, he gets tips and treats; if not, he guides the boat recklessly until they promise him a reward. When asked to haul wood, wine, or other supplies, he steals some for himself and hides it under the poop (142v).

Returning to the subject of foreigners, the gondolier says that when he is asked to transport them to the Lido or elsewhere for a picnic, he takes his share of the delicacies they have prepared. If the passengers do not give him the leftovers, he steals a silver fork or gilded knife or some other object. He is also in collusion with the courtesans of the city, bringing them clients and receiving favors in return (143r–143v). Completely disillusioned by the evil ways of the gondolier, the Philosopher demands to be taken ashore. As he and the Courtier walk home, the Philosopher laments that "the senses rule, and reason is dead" [regnano i sensi, e la ragion è morta] (143v). The second dialogue ends with the Philosopher recounting the tale of a man who banished reason and gave himself over to the senses and who, as a consequence, found himself condemned to hell (144v–152v).

In the *Athanatophilia* Glissenti reveals a remarkable understanding of the habits and behavior of domestic servants and gondoliers in late-sixteenth-century Venice. Although it is clear from his citation of classical authors and his use of exempla from ancient sources that his opinions have been shaped and influenced by literary traditions, the inclusion of certain telling details, such as those about traghetto fares and the rowing tricks of gondoliers, indicate that much of what Glissenti records was drawn from experience. Hence his work provides a fairly accurate catalogue of the vicious practices (though not the virtues) of Venetian servants and boatmen. The image that emerges is of duplicitous rogues and rascals who feign loyalty and obedience but in the end disobey and rob their masters. They turn the world upside down and become masters of the situation themselves.

The broader significance of the work, however, lies precisely in Glissenti's placement of servants and boatmen in the dialogue concerning the senses. The message of the entire treatise is that humans should turn from the vanities of this world and seek a good death. Yet servants and boatmen, along with other "persone basse," are most tied to the sensual pleasures of this world and are least responsive to the call of reason. They take every opportunity to indulge the senses, and according to Glissenti's moralized view, they are damned. Hence Glissenti confirms the opinion both of the household economists and of Garzoni and Spatafora that servants are like animals. The physicality of servants predominates over the spiritual. Vice triumphs over virtue. Glissenti's moral hierarchy justifies the political and social hierarchy propounded by the other writers.

≈

The sixteenth century saw the publication of many works that were not part of the classical tradition of texts on household management but shared many elements with those texts. In all of the works examined, to varying degrees authors mirrored their world and created expectations and ideals for it. Through texts, members of the servant-keeping elite of Venice and the Veneto created a set of mental constructs that shaped the way masters thought about servants and may indirectly have affected the ways masters and servants interacted.

First and foremost, they saw domestic service as the household manifestation of hierarchy and order, which governed all aspects of nature and the cosmos. This hierarchy was based upon two principles: intelligence and virtue. Masters were superior beings because they excelled in both. Servants, by contrast, were closer to the animal kingdom and hence were especially susceptible to vice, especially sexual corruption.

In the household, hierarchy took the form of patriarchy. Primary responsibility and authority rested firmly in the hands of the paterfamilias. It was his obligation to affirm, assert, and perpetuate this hierarchy, which was seen as divinely ordained and natural. This obligation could take many forms. As Valier and other advocates of Christian economy asserted, masters had a responsibility to provide for the moral welfare of their servants. Masters had to show their servants the way to salvation—a way that led to the Christian faith. On the other hand, fathers also had to control vice, even when that meant the use of force. Servants could not always be tamed with education and moral suasion; fathers might have to resort to punishment or discipline.

This fixation with hierarchy and stratification revealed itself in many ways. For writers such as Paolino the Minorite and Lanteri, it involved constant effort on the part of masters and mistresses to find the natural pattern and put things in order. Every aspect of life, from the assignment of duties to servants, to the careful provisioning of the household, to the proper use of older supplies before newer ones, was a manifestation (and affirmation) of the principle of order. For Vecellio, inward patterns and virtues were revealed through outward forms, as clothing became a visual indicator of hierarchy.

This examination also shows that masters viewed service familially; that is, servants were considered part of the family. This point may seem obvious, yet it is not the way service is viewed today, nor may it have been the way all servants viewed service. In the master's view, servants were part of the household, just as the household furnishings and utensils were. Like other family members, including wives and children, servants had responsibilities; they were expected to be both obedient and loyal. At the same time, the paterfamilias had responsibilities to the servants: he was to provide them not only with the physical necessities of life but also with moral education and guidance, as Valier recalled. The master's responsibility was an especially onerous one, since servants were naturally inferior. Additionally, familial relations became models for political and social ones; loyalty and obedience became public virtues as well as personal ones.[113]

Nevertheless, all of these writers remained extremely ambivalent about servants and about master-servant relations. Garzoni summed up the prevailing attitude of masters toward domestic help when he called gondoliers both "bassissima" and "utilissima." For the elite, servants were useful in many ways; they not only performed a variety of household tasks that it was ignoble for masters to perform themselves but also, by their proximity and behavior, affirmed their masters' position at the apex of the social hierarchy. But as the lowest members of that order, servants were themselves seen as corrupt and potential contaminators of their master's households. This fear was revealed especially clearly in warnings about wet nurses, who might infect the children. Insubordinate, disloyal, and immoral servants threatened a master's reputation (and thereby the master's place in the hierarchy) by calling into question his ability to command respect.

In all these works, writers created a vision of master-servant relations and of the larger world as essentially immobile and fixed. They emphasized structure, classification, stratification, hierarchy, and morality. Yet such a vision accorded little with reality, as Spatafora's worried masters well knew. Through treatises and tracts the servant-keeping elite created their vision of the world. They then tried to formalize that vision through legal codes. And so it is to the laws and to the magistracies with jurisdiction over servants that we now turn.

Chapter Two

# The Venetian Government and the
# Regulation of Domestic Service

On 17 august 1541 the Council of Ten, the most powerful of Venice's governmental councils, voted to transfer authority over the city's domestic servants to the office of the *censori* (censors), officials already charged with oversight of electoral corruption and gambling.[1] The prologue to the law clearly states the reasons for the Ten's decision:

> There are multiplying daily so many complaints to the heads of this council concerning the ill condition, the assemblies, and the gatherings that the boatmen and servants of this city continuously form and the ill words that they publicly use, besides their other insolent and dishonorable habits, showing no respect for noblemen and noblewomen, or for men and women citizens, or for other persons, and with a most evil example and little honor for the city, that if something is not done, their insolence will grow even greater as they see that it goes unpunished. This matter is of such importance that everyone recognizes that it must be entrusted to a magistracy that has the authority summarily to expedite and put in place those ordinances that seem necessary.[2]

With this justification, the Ten then authorized the two censors, with the assistance of one of the *avogadori di comun* (state attorneys), to uncover and disband the accords and agreements that servants and boatmen had been forming among themselves, as well as to control their insolent and disgusting behavior and to put in order regulations designed to ensure honesty and morality. Furthermore, the censors were given strong enforcement authority. If two of the three were in accord on a case, they could inflict punishments up to the drawing of blood; if all three agreed, they could impose corporal punishment that drew blood, including the death penalty, "just as if it had been decided and deliberated by this council [of the Ten]."[3] The only restriction on the censors' power involved criminal cases of homicide and theft, which continued to fall under the traditional jurisdiction of the state attorneys and the *signori di notte,* one of the city's police forces.

Attempts by patricians, who monopolized political power in Venice, to prevent artisans and others among the popolo from gathering and organizing were nothing new. In the thirteenth century the government had placed the city's craft guilds under the control of the *giustizieri vecchi,* three noble officials charged with supervision of the guilds; and in the wake of popular protests in the 1260s the government had forced all the city's guilds to include provisions in their statutes forbidding unauthorized assemblies "against the honor of the doge and his council and the commune of Venice."[4] A distant echo of that earlier language was contained in the preliminary draft of the Ten's 1541 decision transferring authority over servants to the censori, which spoke of the malicious words that servants publicly used "against our state" [contra il stato nostro].[5] Similarly, during the fourteenth century the government had become suspicious of the numerous scuole in the city, voting in 1360 to place them under the jurisdiction of the Ten, which kept watch over confraternal bylaws and prohibited the scuole from assembling at night.[6] Nor were governmental attempts to regulate domestic service in Venice new. Since the late thirteenth century the Great Council had been legislating various aspects of the master-servant relationship; and from an unknown date (but certainly by the later fourteenth century) the government had authorized registration of at least part of the city's servant population. Until the transfer of authority to the censors in 1541, jurisdiction over domestic servants was the province of the *capi di sestieri,* the heads of the six sections of the city.

## The *capi di sestieri* and the Registration of Servants

According to tradition, Venice was first divided into six districts *(sestieri)* in 1171, during the dogeship of Vitale Michiel.[7] The primary officials assigned to them were the capi di sestieri. Although most of their records have been lost, some sense of the capi's organization and responsibilities can be gleaned from a Council of Ten deliberation dated 10 August 1319 and from Marino Sanuto's *De origine, situ et magistratibus urbis Venetae,* a brief description of the city and its magistracies composed in the late fifteenth century.[8] The six capi, who were elected from among the city's nobles, supervised the *capi di contrade,* the heads of the city's approximately seventy parishes. Each capo di sestiere was assisted by four guards, or wardens, who did much of the actual patrolling of the city. Like many other Venetian officials, they had offices at Rialto, where they convened three days a week to hear cases and administer justice. They were assisted by at least one notary, who recorded their decisions, kept accounts, and performed other administrative tasks. The capi were also responsible for supervising the city's inns and taverns and, indirectly, through the capi di contrade, for maintaining surveillance over foreigners. In the fifteenth century they had jurisdiction over prostitutes and pimps as well.[9]

The loss of almost all of the capi's records makes it difficult to reconstruct the composition of the office or its procedures.[10] However, records of a jurisdictional dispute between various magistracies deliberated by the Senate in April 1444 indicate that in addition to their policing powers, the capi were responsible for registering at least some domestic servants in the city. The act reads in part:

> Be it enacted that from now on no official of Venice may register any apprentice to any guild of Venice under penalty of a one-hundred-lire fine, except for the officials of the giustizia [vecchia], who ought to register them just as the rules of their office demand, excepting, however, apprentices in the silk industry, who are to be registered by the *consoli dei mercanti*. However, the capi di sestieri can and ought to register servants on contract to noblemen and other cittadini according to the custom of their office, but they are not to register those of artisans, whom the artisans take in to teach the trade.[11]

Sanuto's description from the end of the century further clarifies the issue. Writing of the capi, he notes,

> They inscribe the boy servants and girl servants who wish to work for anyone in this city, and at what salary, as seems fit to the lord capi. And when these servants have completed their time, they make the masters pay them; and if they do not complete their term, but flee, the capi find them and whip them. They have the right to detain and imprison [them].[12]

The Senate law and Sanuto's description clearly indicate that in the fifteenth century the capi di sestieri were responsible for registering domestic servants. But what exactly did that entail, and did it include all servants?

Judging from the extant records of apprenticeship registrations maintained by the giustizieri vecchi and from family account books, registration of servants involved the master's (and perhaps the servant's) going to the office of the capi at Rialto, where a notary recorded in a large notebook the master's name, the servant's name and age, and the terms of the contract, including its duration, the servant's salary, and other conditions of employment, such as whether the master was obliged to provide food, clothing, and shelter.[13] In this way an official record of the agreement was made that provided the basis for any future legal action. In their personal account books, masters usually recorded in more cryptic form the basic terms of their servants' contracts. For example, Moisè Venier noted in his accounts on 4 June 1438, "Had inscribed with the capi di sestieri my servant Luca, whom I got through my brother-in-law . . . he is obliged to serve me for six years at a salary of ten ducats. He came to my house on the first of the month."[14] Niccolò and Alvise Barbarigo were even more succinct when they recorded on 27 February 1460mv, "Gasparo, our servant, was inscribed with the capi di sestieri for five years at eight ducats by us, Niccolò and Alvise Barbarigo."[15]

As the Senate noted in 1444, registering servants was already "common practice" [segondo uxança]. The earliest incontrovertible evidence that I have uncovered for registration of servants with the capi dates from 1422. On 13 July of that year Lucia of Zagreb, the servant of Pietro Grisson of Santa Maria Formosa, acknowledged receipt of twelve ducats for eight years of service, "as it is said to appear in the office of the capi di sestieri."[16] However, registration of other kinds of workers had a venerable tradition in Venice, dating back in one form or another to the late thirteenth century.

In 1291 the giustizieri vecchi ordered all artisans employing apprentices to inscribe them with their office. The reason they gave was simple: they wanted a record of the terms of employment in the event that disputes should arise. In order to ensure compliance, the justices warned masters that if they failed to register their apprentices, they (the giustizieri) would refuse to hear claims and masters would be unable to obtain justice. Failure to register apprentices properly could place guildsmen outside the protection of the law.[17]

As will become clear in the next chapter, the line separating apprentices from servants was never very clearly drawn. A 1402 provision included in the capitulary of the giustizieri vecchi indicates just how blurry the distinctions were and suggests another reason for registering assistants. The rule prohibited notaries from drawing up pacts or agreements between craftsmen, merchants, or others and "any boy or girl, either big or small, or apprentices, male servants, female servants, workers, or other familiars." Instead agreements had to be drawn up with the giustizieri vecchi themselves in order to prevent "ignorant boys and girls" [famuli et puelle ignorantes] from being tricked into unfair work arrangements.[18] Whereas in 1291 the motive behind registration had been to protect the appellate rights of masters, it was now to prevent the deception of apprentices.

Despite the Senate's efforts in 1444 to separate the registration of apprentices by the giustizieri vecchi from that of servants by the capi di sestieri, the line continued to be indistinct, especially among artisans employing young women. As late as 1582, for example, a certain Menega was inscribed in the apprenticeship registers of the giustizieri vecchi as the employee of a cheese seller named Bernardin. According to the terms of their contract, Menega, aged thirteen or so, was "to live and serve in the house and do everything required by sir Bernardin" for the next six years. Bernardin, in turn, was to pay her expenses both in sickness and in health and give her a salary of sixteen ducats.[19] There is nothing in the contract to indicate that Menega was hired to be anything other than a servant. For example, no mention was made of any obligation on Bernardin's part to teach her his trade. By contrast, Caterina, aged thirteen, inscribed by Cesare Tomasini, was obliged to serve "as housekeeper" [pro masere] for Tomasini, who agreed in turn to train her in wool manufacture.[20] Caterina's roles as apprentice and servant were mixed. The continued appearance of what appear to be servants in the records of the giustizieri vecchi, despite the government's prohibitions, suggests the extent to which the boundaries separating servants from apprentices were ill drawn. In any event, the registration of servants may have evolved naturally out of the time-honored practice of registering apprentices.

It is more likely, however, that the registration of servants grew from governmental attempts to monitor both the slave trade and indentured service in fourteenth-century Venice. Venice, along with Genoa, served as the major entrepôt for slaves imported from the eastern Mediterranean. Although many slaves were bought by Venetians and Genoese for their own use, many others were reexported to Florence, Milan, Mantua, and other inland cities. In Venice, the slave market had its center at Rialto; in 1368 the government declared that henceforth all those wishing to export slaves had to obtain export licenses from the capi di sestieri.[21]

Along with slaves, the Venetians imported young people as servants from the Balkans, then under the threat of the Turks. Known as *anime,* they were essentially indentured servants like those imported to colonial America. In return for transportation to Venice, they had to complete a prescribed number of years of service. However, in Venice, unlike in colonial America, slavery was not closely linked to race, and it was easy for unscrupulous merchants and middlemen to sell these young people into perpetual slavery. This was perceived as especially nefarious since the anime were Christians. In order to guard against this practice, described as an "evil deed against God and the honor of our dominion" [pessime factum et contra Deum et honorem nostri dominii], the Senate decreed in 1386 that those who possessed or imported anime had to register them with the capi di sestieri within eight days. The law further stated that the term of indenture was not to exceed four years.[22]

But pressure from the employers of indentured servants forced the Senate to modify the law just two years later. Responding to employers' complaints that anime were so "rustic and simpleminded" [rustice et rudis intellectus] that it took longer than four years to train them and recoup their investment, the Senate agreed to extend the maximum term of indenture to ten years. They further justified the longer term by noting that by being brought to Venice, the anime were being done a favor, for they were thereby saved from perpetual slavery or, worse yet, massacre at the hands of the Turks. Masters were still required, however, to register them with the capi di sestieri.[23]

In light of this, it seems fairly clear that both the 1444 Senate law and Sanuto's description of the office of the capi di sestieri refer to the registration of indentured servants by the capi. This leaves open the question whether non-indentured servants, what the Venetians referred to as salaried servants, were also registered. The evidence from account books suggests that in the fifteenth and sixteenth centuries they were not, for masters were usually careful to note which servants had been registered with the capi (i.e., the indentured servants) and which had not.[24]

It is also unclear if or how this changed after jurisdiction over servants passed from the office of the capi to the office of the censors in 1541. There is, for example, a reference in the censors' judicial proceedings to a servant who was duly registered with their office ("accordium annotatum in officio Censoratus"); and when in 1548 the censors issued a ruling setting wage limits, they required that contracts be registered with them.[25] This law clearly encompassed not just indentured servants but salaried servants as well. Nevertheless, there is also evidence from the censors' own records of servants working without contracts and even of a servant who was registered with the *signori di notte al civil,* officials who took over some of the duties of the capi when that office was abolished.[26] Unfortunately, the loss of the bulk of the censors' archives makes any more definitive judgment impossible.

Although the sources leave many questions unanswered, they do indicate that registration of apprentices by the office of the giustizieri vecchi had been in place since 1291, and registration of indentured servants in the office of the capi themselves since 1386. Furthermore, it is likely that by the sixteenth century most domestic servants were being registered by the censors. The Venetian government had a long history of registering and supervising at least some portion of the service-performing population. The motive behind registration was at times to protect the interests of masters and at times to discourage the most serious abuses against servants. Regardless, registration represented only one aspect of the government's multifaceted effort to regulate domestic service.

## The *capi di sestieri* and the Capitulary of 1503

Since the thirteenth century many different Venetian governmental coun-cils, including the Great Council, had legislated various aspects of the master-ser-vant relationship. Responsibility for enforcing these regulations fell largely on the capi di sestieri, whose own decrees and rulings, like those of other Venetian magistracies, carried the force of law.[27] In July 1503 the six sitting capi, namely, noblemen Giovanni Donà, Giovanni Battista Condulmer, Domenico Minio, Vi-tale Michiel, Lorenzo da Lezze, and Giovanni Francesco Barbaro, decided to put in order not only various laws that had been passed concerning domestic service but also "good and ancient customs" in observance in the city so that "good cus-toms not change to bad ones." The resulting eight-chapter capitulary provides a convenient summary of Venetian legislation concerning domestic service to the beginning of the sixteenth century. It serves as a guide to the concerns and in-terests of those in Venetian society who kept servants (see appendix A).[28]

The first four *capitoli* (chapters) dealt in one way or another with contrac-tual aspects of the master-servant relationship. The first chapter, citing the 1388 Senate law on anime examined above, stated that no servant, whether male or female, in service in Venice or its overseas domains, could be placed under con-tract for more than ten years. No justification was given for this ten-year limit, although, as we have seen, the original thrust of the 1388 law was to protect the masters' investment in training indentured servants. However, the law as in-cluded in the capitulary can also be construed as protecting servants from con-tracts of unreasonable duration. If at the end of ten years masters and servants wished to continue their relationship, new contracts could be negotiated.

Chapters 2 through 4 were more clearly designed to protect the interests of masters, the purchasers of labor. Chapter 2 explicitly reiterated a law passed by the Great Council on 31 December 1284, the earliest extant Venetian law treating domestic servants.[29] It stated that anyone who knowingly hired a servant who had left the service of another master without that master's permission would be liable for a fine of one hundred *lire di piccoli*. The law was designed to discour-age servants from leaving their masters in hopes of finding more favorable terms of service elsewhere, as well as to prevent masters from luring away the servants of others. It may also have protected masters from engaging in bidding wars for particularly valued servants. The third chapter levied the same hundred-lire fine plus a possible jail term against anyone who incited a servant to flee from his or her master. Chapter 4 dealt with servants who fled. Servants who took flight would lose their entire salary (it was not to be prorated for the time served); and if they were caught, they were to be whipped by order of the capi "as an example to others." If, however, a master agreed to take back a servant who had fled, then the servant's salary was to be restored, even if he or she had fled more than once.

Taken together, the first four chapters of the 1503 capitulary reveal the elites' concern with securing reliable servants and holding down the costs of domestic labor and their efforts to bind servants through contractual obligations. As a reflection of the masters' point of view, they suggest a vision of the master-servant relationship that is quite different from the familial and social models explored in the preceding chapter. These rules, at least, reveal that masters viewed service as a business arrangement and were concerned with enforcing the terms of contracts and discouraging efforts by servants or other masters to break agreements. As might be expected, the law protected the buyers rather than the sellers of domestic service in the Venetian labor market. Masters were especially concerned with keeping the salaries of servants in check. Nevertheless, the ten-year limit on contracts and the requirement that salaries of servants who fled and then returned be restored secured some minor guarantees for servants.

This same concern with protecting the interests of employers was reflected in three others laws passed in the fifteenth century but not included in the capi's redaction. According to a summary of material contained in the capitularies of the giustizieri vecchi, a law of 1436 stated that servants who broke their contracts would forfeit their entire salary (including what they had already earned) and be fined fifty lire. A similar law, also passed in the 1430s, apparently extended this penalty to wet nurses who became pregnant while nursing their employers' children.[30] These laws suggest that there was a particularly strong antilabor mood during the 1430s. Whatever the case, the laws must have been repealed, for they made no reappearance, and such provisions were absent from the capi's 1503 capitulary.

Another law, dating from 1493, placed a five-year statute of limitations on servants' claims to their salaries. If servants did not claim their pay within five years of termination of service, they forfeited the sum. However, if servants contracted on a month-to-month basis, then the statute of limitations was reduced to only two years.[31]

The fifth chapter of the capitulary was one of two designed to protect the interests of servants, although it too reflected the strongly legal and contractual character of the master-servant tie. According to the capi, some masters had devised "malicious schemes and methods" to deny servants their salaries. One practice was especially pernicious. By beating or mistreating servants, masters could incite them to flee and then deny them their salaries for the time they had served on the grounds they had fled. The capi decreed that in such cases servants were to receive their pay prorated for the time they had served, and furthermore, they could keep any clothes they had been given by their masters. In cases in which servants had been severely beaten or had suffered bone fractures, the capi could require masters to pay servants the entire salary for which they had contracted.[32]

The final three chapters of the 1503 capitulary reveal the masters' concern for protecting their material possessions and maintaining the sexual honor of their households. The sixth chapter warned that servants who robbed the homes of their masters would forfeit their pay and, if caught, be whipped. It sanctioned the same penalties for maidservants who fornicated in the homes of their masters and for menservants who fornicated either with female servants of the household or with women whom they brought there for that purpose. The capi reserved the right to impose further penalties on malefactors so that the punishments would serve "as an example to others." Chapter 7 authorized monetary fines and prison terms for those who knowingly assisted servants in the theft of their masters' goods or who accepted stolen goods from them.

The sexual conduct of servants had long concerned Venetian councils. On 10 August 1287 the Great Council had passed an important piece of legislation that included all the major provisions later contained in chapter 6 of the 1503 capitulary. It legislated against male and female servants who brought others into the homes of their masters to fornicate.[33] It imposed a fine of fifty lire on men and menservants who fornicated; if they could not pay, they were to be whipped and branded. Female servants were to be whipped, branded, and banished. The legislation further authorized the signori di notte to use torture to uncover such cases. In 1374 the Great Council had returned to the issue when the signori di notte claimed that the penalties for men who fornicated with servants were not having the desired effect. In response, the council raised the penalty to include a three-month jail term. But the rule applied only to men who were not themselves servants; according to the law, menservants who fornicated were to be given other, unspecified penalties.[34]

The Great Council had also previously addressed the problem of theft. On 25 July 1490 it had passed by a vote of 1,242 to 24, with 11 abstentions, a law that servants who committed thefts would henceforth be subject to the same penalties as other members of Venetian society, including the death penalty.[35] The law opened with a detailed prologue stating that "the loyalty and goodness" of servants and other domestic familiars was in decline and that the threat of thefts by servants was increasing because servants were undeterred by the penalties currently levied on them. The council recommended increasing the penalty for those who would abstain from doing evil not out of a "love of virtue" but only out of fear of the consequences.

These two chapters of the capitulary reflect other concerns and fears of those who kept servants in Renaissance Venice. By opening their homes to strangers, masters placed their own lives and those of their kin, as well as their material possessions, at some risk. The threat became frighteningly real in the spring of 1410, when nobleman Niccolò Barbo, son of Procurator of San Marco Giovanni Barbo, was murdered in his own home by his slave. Apparently, when Barbo learned that his Tatar slave Bona was pregnant, he became furious and beat her with a shoulder harness used for carrying water. According to the avo-gadori di comun who tried the case, Bona decided to take revenge on her master and went to a pharmacy in the parish of San Pantalon, where she purchased some arsenic from a shop assistant. She put the arsenic in Barbo's food, and after two doses he died. The avogadori sentenced Bona to be burned at the stake in the Piazza San Marco.[36]

The case sent shock waves through the city and prompted the Great Council to pass a law in June forbidding apothecaries and other spice dealers whose shops were not located on the Merceria, the main street of shops between Rialto and San Marco, to sell or even stock toxic substances and poisons. The only exception applied to druggists along the two main streets of apothecary shops running from the parish of San Zulian to the Rialto bridge, who were allowed to keep toxins in their shops as long as they remained under lock and key and out of the hands of shop boys. Druggists were forbidden to sell these poisons to anyone who did not have a receipt for the drug from the giustizieri vecchi. Appended to the law was a list of the prohibited substances. As the Great Council noted, these changes were prompted specifically by the Barbo case and by masters' inattentiveness to the "threats and dangers [posed] by the servants of their own households."[37] The case was still reverberating through the city in late October, when the Great Council passed a piece of legislation authorizing the signori di notte to investigate persons, especially servants and slaves, who were mixing brews and other concoctions in order to cause mental or physical illness.[38] The purpose of chapters 6 and 7 of the capi's capitulary was to bring right order to Venetian households by sanctioning punishment of servants who jeopardized the property and lives of their masters.

The eighth and final chapter, like the fifth, on the surface at least was designed to protect servants from unscrupulous masters. It simply stated that any master or master's son who "deflowered" a servant girl inscribed with the capi had to pay her her entire salary as well as give her a dowry appropriate to her "position and status" as judged by the capi. In addition, the master was liable for a fine of fifty lire. Although the purpose of this chapter was to protect young girls from the sexual advances of masters and their male kinsmen and to provide assurance that girls who had been violated would have the means to marry, when seen in conjunction with the preceding chapters, it reveals a preoccupation on the part of masters with maintaining the sexual propriety of their households. Sexual misconduct, whether it was committed by servants who fornicated with outsiders or other servants or by masters who took advantage of vulnerable young serving girls, threatened the peacefulness of households, especially relations between spouses, which were so carefully outlined in treatises on wifely duties and household management.[39] The honor of households was ultimately at stake.

Yet the concern about sexual trafficking between masters and servants was also part of a broader patrician concern for maintaining the integrity of the ruling class. In May 1422 the Great Council passed a law that declared ineligible for council membership the issue of unions between noblemen and slave women; and in Venice denial of council membership amounted to denial of noble status. The law further extended the restriction to the children of illicit unions between members of the council and servant girls and other women of "low status" [vilis condicionis].[40] In order to protect the purity of an increasingly status-conscious elite, the council discouraged unions with servants and slaves by making the children of those unions ineligible for noble rank.

Overall, the capi di sestieri's 1503 capitulary indicates that the elite viewed domestic service as a contract, that is, as a legal, judicially binding relationship between employer and employee, a relationship governed at least in part by the rules of the labor market and enforceable by law. As employers, masters were interested in getting the most from their employees at the lowest possible cost and in guaranteeing the inviolability of contracts. Accordingly, they passed rules designed to prevent masters from competing with one another for servants (thereby driving up wages) and to force servants to fulfill all the terms of their agreements. But contracts cut both ways; they also provided some basic protection to servants, safeguarding them from the very worst abuses of masters. At the same time, the capitulary reflected the familial or household model of service found in treatises of the fourteenth and fifteenth centuries. According to that vision of service, masters and servants were bound by a moral contract, as were other members of the household. The rules in the capitulary concerning theft and fornication illustrate that members of the elite were worried about safeguarding their reputation, as based on the integrity and sexual propriety of their households. In the end, servants were employed to facilitate the smooth operation of busy households. Servants could not bring honor to their masters per se, but they could jeopardize it by calling into question their masters' ability to control their households. The capitulary reflects the belief current in the fourteenth and fifteenth centuries that stable, secure, and efficient households were the building blocks of the larger polity.[41]

## The Transfer of Authority to the *censori* and the Capitulary of 1541

When the capi di sestieri issued their capitulary in 1503 the office was already in its waning days. Never as powerful as the signori di notte, who were also organized by sestieri, the capi witnessed during the first four decades of the sixteenth century a steady diminution of their power and the eventual abolition of their office. Civil jurisdiction over servants passed to the censors.

The office of the censors was first created in 1517 to deal with the problem of electoral corruption. Although the first censors worked diligently to root out dishonesty, the office was abolished in October 1521, only to be revived in 1524.[42] The censors also regulated gambling in the city, especially wagers on elections. And, as we have already seen, in August 1541 the Ten voted to transfer authority over civil cases involving servants to the censors, while authority over criminal cases remained with the signori di notte and the avogadori di comun.

The transfer of civil authority over servants to the censors was followed three years later by the creation of another new office, that of the *signori di notte al civil,* as distinct from the *signori di notte al criminal.* Given competence over a variety of matters, including rents, pledges, and public holidays, the signori di notte al civil enjoyed jurisdiction over matters that traditionally had been the concern of the capi di sestieri. As a consequence, the capi were rendered superfluous and their office was abolished that same year (1544).[43]

For their part, the censors wasted no time exercising their jurisdiction over servants. Just eight days after being given competence to regulate servants, the censori issued a twenty-one-chapter capitulary dealing with domestic servants and boatmen or gondoliers (see appendix B). The tone, concerns, and issues contained in the censors' statutes of 25 August 1541 contrast markedly with those of the capi di sestieri's capitulary issued just thirty-eight years earlier. They highlight a major shift in the relationship between Venetian masters and servants and a change in the style of servant keeping.[44]

The capitulary opened on a note of urgency, almost of crisis. The two censors, noblemen Alessandro Foscari and Federico Contarini, in conjunction with the avogador di comun, Agostino Surian, began by stating that they intended to preserve the welfare of "all the noblemen, cittadini, and other inhabitants of the city" from the "deceitful fury, temerarious insolence, and presumption of the familiars, servants, and boatmen of this city." Invoking the authority recently ceded to them by the Council of Ten, including the power to impose the death penalty, they issued their capitulary concerning domestic servants.

The difference in tone between this prologue and that of the capi is striking. The capi justified their redaction as legislative; they were codifying long-standing statutes and "good and ancient customs." For them the compilation of the capitulary was an act of lawmaking. The censori, by contrast, chose to emphasize their judicial and penal powers: they intended to discipline, judge, and punish. In the capi's prologue, servants remained largely nondescript; the laws were passed to stop their "ill intention and will." In the censors' prologue, servants were portrayed as purveyors of deceit, insolence, and presumption, language similar to that found in Garzoni and Glissenti. With servants already under attack, the censors began their capitulary.

The censors gave prominence of place to three chapters designed to prevent servants and boatmen from organizing. The first chapter prohibited servants from congregating in groups of four or more in private homes or elsewhere. Those who violated these restrictions would have their right hand amputated and be perpetually banished from Venice and its district; and those who subsequently violated the ban would be imprisoned for a year and reexpelled. In order to encourage informers, the censors offered amnesty and a reward to participants who would reveal these meetings to the authorities within three days and a hundred-lire reward to others who knew of such meetings. Anyone who was cognizant of these meetings and did not report them within three days was to be whipped from San Marco to Rialto.

In their apparent rush to issue the capitulary, the censors did not take the care needed to craft it into a tight, well-knit document. The second and third chapters merely strengthened and clarified provisions of the first. Chapter 2 added that the penalty for participation would also include blinding in both eyes, and chapter 3 extended the prohibition to those who congregated on boats in groups of four or more while waiting for their masters, although in such cases the penalties were less severe.

In addition to discouraging servants from gathering together in groups, the censors tried to regulate and control the insolent behavior of individuals. Servants were to be branded and whipped if they insulted a man, that is, if they directed insulting words at him. The same penalties applied if they merely use "any shameful word" in the presence of a woman (chs. 7, 8). And brides received special protection. As Francesco Sansovino noted in his *Venetia città nobilissima,* it was customary for brides to be rowed about the city in order to visit friends and female relatives in convents.[45] These were important occasions for the display of family honor. The capitulary forbade servants to shout insults at brides, and it forbade boatmen to make obscene gestures toward them with their oars.[46]

As the gondolier in Glissenti's dialogue knew, masters and mistresses were especially vulnerable while in their boats, since they were at the mercy of the oarsmen.[47] To protect masters, the censors warned that gondoliers who engaged in brawls with other gondoliers while their masters were on board would be whipped and branded. The censors reserved the right to impose even greater penalties if the brawls led to physical injury or death. To keep serious injuries to a minimum, servants were forbidden to carry arms of any sort; and those who resisted an arresting officer would be whipped.[48]

Gondoliers posed other problems unique to their trade. For instance, when awaiting their masters while they attended meetings of the Great Council, gondoliers crowded and blocked the major canals, especially in front of the Ducal Palace. The censors ordered those who had delivered their masters to move away from the area until the meetings adjourned. Another chapter ordered boatmen who rented out their services to keep the *riva* (quay) in front of the palace free for arriving and departing traffic.[49]

In addition, the censors' capitulary of 1541, like the capi's earlier one, contained a number of provisions regulating contractual aspects of the master-servant relationship and controlling the economic life of servants. According to the censors, servants who received salary advances could not leave until the service had been rendered. Servants who were planning to depart had to give their masters fifteen days' notice so they would have time to collect clothes or other items entrusted to the servants and to procure the services of new ones. Servants could not take their rations out of the house, defraud their masters, or moonlight. This last prohibition was most likely aimed especially at gondoliers (although the law referred to "famegli, servitori e barcaruoli"), who could earn extra money on the side by renting out their own services or those of their masters' boats. Furthermore, boatmen were prohibited from working at any of the city's many traghetti or even from hiring out their services until they had first served at least three years in someone's personal service.[50]

The censors also made an effort to control relations between servants within households. Male servants were not to intimidate other male servants into doing a greater share of the work or to encourage them to leave their master. They were forbidden to insult one another, especially to call a *fameglio* (manservant) a *fante* (boy) (ch. 4). Male servants were not to use violence with female servants, insult them, induce them to leave their master, or encourage them to steal (chs. 5, 10). Men could be whipped for giving lodging to strangers in their master's home or for bringing prostitutes there and were forbidden to marry, or even promise to marry, a female servant without their master's consent (chs. 16, 20).

Finally, the censors included one sumptuary regulation in their capitulary. Servants were forbidden to wear clothes made of silk, especially velvet hats and shoes, or to wear other outfits not deemed "respectable." The penalty included a whipping from the Piazza San Marco to Rialto, and any official who discovered the infraction could confiscate and keep the items.[51]

In content and form the censors' capitulary represents a major shift in the attitudes and concerns of the servant-keeping classes. In this document servants appear as a more immediate threat to their masters, the chapters of the capitulary providing a veritable catalogue of their failings and crimes (and their masters' fears). Significantly, the two chapters in the capi di sestieri's statutes that protected servants, one safeguarding them from masters who beat them in order to induce them to flee, the other protecting virgins who had been violated, are both conspicuously absent in this document. Indeed, in 1520 the Great Council had made it more difficult for female servants to press claims of sexual violation against their masters.[52] Noting that in the past magistrates had had little choice but to accept the word of "an infamous woman" [una femena infame], the Great Council declared that a woman could not press suit if she had consented to sexual relations, only if she had been forced or deceived into having them. Even then she had to support her suit either with witnesses or by other "just and useful means" [altri modi iusti o convenienti]. The council provided an exception for servant girls under age sixteen who "out of either fear or obedience" had been forced into having sex. But even then judges were warned to be attentive to the character of both master and servant, and the girl had to bring suit within six months of her departure from the master's service. And although in 1529 the capi di sestieri had reiterated the need to have all contracts registered with their office in order to prevent servants from being defrauded "with no small offense to the majesty of our Lord God" [cun non poca offensione della maesta del nostro signor Idio], the censors chose not to include such a provision in this redaction of their rules.[53] Indeed, unlike the capi, the censors made no specific reference in their statutes to prior legislation.

The censors' focus on male servants, particularly on gondoliers, constitutes another notable difference between the two capitularies. Several provisions in the censors' statutes, including those against congregating in groups, shouting insults, blocking quays, engaging in brawls, and moonlighting, were aimed specifically at male servants. The increasingly masculine character of domestic service (discussed more fully in the next chapter) may in part account for the censors' severe stance. Less sure of their ability to control male servants, the censors chose to emphasize penal rather than contractual aspects of the master-servant relationship.

In trying to account for this shift in tone, it is possible to focus on both some short-term events and some long-term trends. The three chapters prohibiting servants from gathering in groups, which included the draconian punishment of blinding, suggest that some specific episode or incident like the 1410 murder of Niccolò Barbo by his slave Bona prompted the censors to act. In authorizing the censors to take charge of servants, the Ten noted the assemblies and meetings that they were holding. I have been unable to pinpoint any specific event that may have prompted their decision, but the city had been under severe strain in the preceding decade as the result of a war with the Turks that raged from 1537 to 1540. Popular disturbances against the patrician regime were extremely rare in Venice, yet two events occurred during this period that may have made the patricians uneasy. In December 1539 there was a riot among the popolo at a grain warehouse where food was distributed; and in October 1540, a popular festival, a gang fistfight in the parish of San Marcilian, degenerated into a riot.[54] Events such as these or perhaps some even more shadowy conspiracy may have frightened the Ten and the censors in turn.

Further support for this hypothesis is provided by the fact that in three subsequent redactions of the censors' rules concerning servants, dated 1556, 1569, and 1595, the censors deleted the ordinances forbidding servants to gather in groups of four or more.[55] The rule did make one more sixteenth-century appearance, however, when in 1591 the censors, responding to pressure from the Great Council, issued an order that servants were not to use foul language in front of women or to gather in groups of four or more. However, in this instance the meetings appear somewhat less sinister and may simply refer to gatherings in taverns, since the censors also reminded servants that they were not to gamble or blaspheme.[56]

Even if the censors' actions were not prompted by a specific event, they were in keeping with the general program of *renovatio* promoted by Doge Andrea Gritti (1523–38). Gritti's efforts at renewal included the withdrawal of noblemen from the more vulgar aspects of Carnival and the creation of a more decorous civic center at San Marco. The censors' special concern with keeping gondoliers away from the riva at the Ducal Palace is in keeping with Gritti's desire for dignity and propriety.[57]

Another innovation of Gritti's reign was the creation in December 1537 of a new magistracy, the *esecutori contro la bestemmia* (executors against blasphemy), who had special jurisdiction over blasphemy and morals. The establishment of this office signaled a new elite attitude of contempt for the manners and morals of the lower orders.[58] That new attitude found reflection in the 1541 capitulary in the rules forbidding servants and boatmen to use foul language and to make obscene gestures. And finally, just a few years later, in 1547, the government set up yet another magistracy, the *tre savi all'eresia*, whose job it was to investigate those suspected of heresy.[59]

In this context the censori's capitulary of 1541 may be understood as part of a larger program by the patrician government to reform and discipline the city. The lower orders of society, including servants, were now seen as different from their superiors, and their behavior would have to be supervised, channeled, and controlled. The servant keepers were trying to place distance between themselves and their inferiors. Not coincidentally, in this same period the Great Council chose yet again to discourage marriages between noblemen and servants. Noting that "the condition of our nobility is by the Grace of God of such honorable quality" [Il grado della nobilita nostra è per la divina gratia di tal honorevole qualita] that it was incumbent upon them to preserve it, the council in 1533 reiterated that children of unions between nobles and women of vile status were ineligible for membership. According to the councillors, such rules were needed in order to preserve the "decorum, dignity, and greatness" [decoro, dignita, et amplitudine] of the council.[60] The censors' capitulary of 1541 was well in keeping with Doge Andrea Gritti's program for the *renovatio urbis* and with the more general trend to see service as a reflection of the entire social order.

## Later-Sixteenth-Century Legislation Concerning Servants

Legislation governing servants did not end with the 1541 statutes. As noted above, the censors issued three more capitularies, in 1556 (1555mv), 1569, and 1595, and republished the capitulary of 1569 in 1572 and 1574.[61] Although the prologue to the 1569 statutes had little to say about the character of servants, those of 1556 and 1595 provide further evidence of masters' growing contempt for and fear of their domestics. The prologue of 1556 catalogued the crimes of male servants and condemned them for their "effrontery and insolence."[62] The prologue of 1595 was even stronger, warning of the "insolence and tyranny that male and female servants exercise in the households and against their masters."[63] Harking back to the capi's prologue, the censors in 1595 saw their task as administrative and legislative; they intended to put in order the various regulations governing servants.

The three capitularies of the second half of the sixteenth century were basically similar in content to the capitulary of 1541, except regarding the deletion of the chapters about gatherings of servants.[64] But there was one major innovation: all three included chapters setting limits on servants' wages. The censors' first effort to control wages was not, however, in the capitulary of 1556, but in a ruling they issued in August 1548.[65] It established not only limits on wages but also minimum terms of service.

The censors began the 1548 law by noting that male servants ("fameglii, et barcharuoli") had adopted the practice of receiving advances on their pay and then departing after only "four, five, or ten days," catching their masters unaware, to their great "damage, loss, and shame" [danno, iattura et vergogna]. To correct this situation, the censors decreed that servants were not to reach accords of less than six months' duration and that wages for gondoliers who lived in the households of their masters at their masters' expense should not exceed one ducat per month. This applied both to gondoliers who served in the poop and those who served in the bow. To guarantee compliance, contracts had to be registered with the censors. If servants decided to leave at the end of their contract, they had to give their master fifteen days' notice and then go to the office of the censors and have the contract officially canceled, after certifying that all the terms had been fulfilled. Servants were not to sign on with a new master until their old contract had been canceled. Those who contravened these regulations were to be whipped from San Marco to Rialto and then sentenced to two years of galley service. The censors also promised a reward to informers.[66] The capitulary of 1556 spelled out in even more detail the employment procedures to be followed by both masters and male servants. In addition, it forbade male servants from receiving more than one-month advances on their salary, under pain of having to serve eighteen months in the galleys. Masters who made such advances would be fined 50 ducats and lose the advance.[67]

The capitulary of 1595 contained much more elaborate rules governing wages, accounting for five of eighteen chapters. The censors noted that the issue of wages had become very confused. In the new rules servants were carefully distinguished according to tasks and gender. The *popier*, the gondolier who served in the poop, the more important of the two, was to get a maximum salary of ten lire per month if he lived at the master's expense. If he got rations *(marende)* that he took outside the house (and could sell), his maximum salary was to be eight lire per month. A popier who worked "outside the house at his own expense," apparently meaning that he hired out his services on a daily or monthly basis, was to receive at most 5 ducats a month, and one who worked feast days and business hours other days, 3 ducats a month.[68] The *servitor de mezo,* who stood at the front of the boat, got a maximum salary of 7 lire per month, 5 if he removed rations (ch. 7). Female servants *(massare)* were limited to 6 ducats a year and "no more," except for wet nurses, who earned 7 lire a month, the same amount as the gondolier de mezo. Wet nurses had to serve until the children they were caring for were weaned. However, if when a child was weaned a nurse was in debt to her master for advances on her salary, then she had to work "as a housekeeper" [per massare] until the debt was paid. For that work she was to be paid at the rate of 6 ducats a year "as is established for other women servants" (chs. 13, 16).

Women were treated differently from men in other ways as well. For example, they were forced into longer contracts; whereas the minimum contract for men was for just six months, for women it was for one year (chs. 8, 14). Men who received clothes from their masters (as part of their upkeep or salary) could keep the clothes after six months of service; women could only do so after a year (chs. 10, 15). Male servants who violated the statutes on wages and contracts could be sentenced to eighteen months in the galleys; if they were physically unable to serve, they were to be imprisoned for six months and then exiled for three years (ch. 12). Women could be imprisoned for six months; and if they were not physically fit for prison, they were to be exiled for two years (ch. 17).

Finally, the capitulary stated that efforts by servants to circumvent wage controls by extorting promises from their masters, either for higher wages or for gifts, would carry no legal weight and that masters could not be judicially compelled to pay wages higher than those outlined in the statutes. The censors also stated that masters who had been pressured could appear before them and have them punish the offending servants.[69]

Like the capi di sestieri's statutes of 1503, those issued by the censors in 1595 document a preoccupation on the part of masters with securing a reliable and cheap source of domestic labor. To do this, they emphasized the sanctity of contracts, created administrative procedures to guarantee compliance, and imposed penalties for their infraction. The censors' intent was to protect the employers of labor by establishing wage limits and by discouraging servants from moving from one household to another. They specifically noted that they wanted to stop practices whereby masters "are reduced to such misery that every day they have to be occupied in hiring servants."[70] As will be considered in chapter 4, the demographic catastrophe caused by the plague of 1575–77 exacerbated the shortage of labor, leading to higher wages and hence to even stricter wage controls.[71] In this age of tight labor, the censors as representatives of the servant-keeping elite included no provisions in their statutes designed to protect the rights of servants.

If an emphasis on the contractual aspects of the master-servant relationship remained a constant in all the capitularies examined, there were also differences that reflect a change in the style and purposes of servant keeping in Venice. As noted earlier, the capi di sestieri's 1503 capitulary illustrated a style of servant keeping that was typical from the late thirteenth through the fifteenth century, a style that might be termed "bourgeois." Masters were interested in maintaining efficient and honorable households as reflections of their own sagacity and esteem and as models of the well-ordered polity. In the sixteenth century a more aristocratic style of servant keeping developed.[72] In addition to their role as maintainers of the household, servants served as accouterments of a noble style of life. Servants became symbols of their masters' status. However, the actual burden of display fell primarily on male servants, who accompanied their masters about the city, rather than on female servants, who worked primarily in the household. As we have seen, masters now had artists include servants in their portraits, and the true nobleman was the one who had not one but two gondoliers to row him about.[73] Masters competed by dressing their servants in fine livery, apparently even in silk, the fabric of gentlemen. The "masculinization" of domestic service, or at least the new concern among the elite with male servants, reflects this shift.[74] Menservants were increasingly symbols of their masters' nobility.

This transformation was in part the product of a new notion of honor. Whereas in the fourteenth and fifteenth centuries honor was believed to accrue rather abstractly to the patriline and the household, in the sixteenth century it became more directly associated with self-presentation and the person of the master.[75] Books of manners, including Giovanni della Casa's *Galateo,* instructed would-be gentlemen in all forms of deportment, including their appearance, gait, and speech. In accord with this new concern for appearances, servants were not to insult their masters, mistresses were not to be subjected even to the sound of vulgar words, and brides were not to witness obscene gestures. As the censors noted in 1548, servants who abandoned their masters subjected them not only to financial loss and damage but also to shame.[76]

This shift was also part of a new vision of society as more hierarchical and stratified. The dignified master accompanied by his loyal male servant became the visible expression (in the master's eyes) of a well-ordered society in which some enjoyed a natural right to rule, while others were destined to serve. Thus we see a congruence between the changing concerns of the writers explored in the preceding chapter and the shifting preoccupations of legislators. By the sixteenth century the well-ordered household served as a replica not merely of the polity but of the larger society as well.

As a consequence of the new significance of servants as reflections of their masters' status and honor, the relationship between masters and servants took on new meaning. With the new emphasis on personal dignity, decorum, and honor, masters were now more vulnerable. The disobedient servant jeopardized the master's public image. For this reason the censors railed in their prologues against the insolence and effrontery and even the tyranny of servants. By adopting an aristocratic style of servant keeping, Venetian elites unwittingly placed themselves at the mercy of their servants. And when things went awry, they sometimes looked to the state for assistance.

## The Censors as Judges

In the Venetian republic there was no clear-cut division between the legislative, executive, and judicial areas of government. Magistrates, like the censors, regularly issued decrees, enforced regulations, and adjudicated disputes. Competence over criminal prosecution was shared by a number of councils and magistracies. Street brawls and other minor crimes were regularly handled by neighborhood patrols organized by the capi di sestieri or the *cinque alla pace,* a police magistracy. More serious offenses, including theft, rape, and murder, generally fell under the jurisdiction of the signori di notte al criminal but could be prosecuted by the avogadori di comun before the Council of Forty. The most heinous crimes, including sodomy and treason, were under the special authority of the Council of Ten.[77]

As the authorities charged with the supervision and regulation of domestic service, the censors arbitrated civil disputes between masters and servants. Although an analysis of the cases they adjudicated moves our discussion from the realm of norms to that of praxis, some consideration of the censors' judicial power is warranted here since they used that power to enforce the ideals laid out in their capitularies. In other words, judicial action served to strengthen and reinforce normative legislation.

Three registers recording the censors' decisions survive for the years 1561 to 1609. For this study I have examined all of the cases between 1569 and 1600 involving disputes between masters and servants.[78] I have not included cases of gambling or electoral corruption, the other juridical responsibilities of the censors, or the miscellaneous cases not directly concerning masters and servants.

Between 1569 and 1600 the censors heard 416 disputes between masters and servants, or an average of approximately 18 cases per year. Of the 416 total cases, 412 were disputes in which masters brought suit against servants, 3 involved servants prosecuting masters, and 1 concerned a servant who, apparently with the assistance of his master, prosecuted another servant. (These latter 4 cases have not been included in the aggregated data presented below but are analyzed separately in chapter 6.)

The profile of the plaintiffs shows that in the overwhelming majority of cases (349 of 412) it was current or former masters who brought suit against servants. Occasionally a group of masters would join forces to prosecute; generally this occurred when a servant broke a contract with one master and then signed on with another. In 21 cases charges were brought by someone other than the master. For example, in 1584 nobleman Fantino Dandolo prosecuted Giovanni

Battista Fiorito, famulus of nobleman Girolamo Orio, for "making love" [facesse d'amor] to Dandolo's maid.[79] In other instances servants were prosecuted by the master's kinsmen. The records for 42 cases do not clearly indicate who brought the charges, although judging from the accusations, it seems likely that in most instances it was the masters and that the notaries simply neglected to note that fact. The office of the censors served overwhelmingly, then, as a vehicle for current or former masters to bring unruly servants to heel.

The majority of the persons who brought charges against their servants came from the ranks of the city's nobility: 268 cases were brought by one or more current or former masters or by other noblemen. Commoners, that is both cittadini and popolani, were plaintiffs in 82 cases. Ecclesiastics or their representatives were involved in 4 cases; foreigners, including the Vicentine architect Vincenzo Scamozzi, in 12.[80] In the remaining cases the status of the plaintiffs cannot be identified, since the notaries did not specify who brought suit. As for the sex of the plaintiffs, all but 4 were male.[81]

Plaintiffs charged servants and their accomplices with a variety of offenses mirroring the judicial competence of the censors and the concerns and preoccupations delineated in the capitularies. Often they accused servants of more than one offense. For instance, nobleman Tommaso Lion's complaint against his servant Battista da Lemesanis contained a veritable catalogue of crimes. Lion charged Battista with using indecent language in front of the women of the household and exposing himself to them. "What is worse still" [quod peius est], he had sex with Giovanna, a maidservant in the household, and talked back to his master, refusing to follow orders. Finally, he left Lion's service without permission, thereby breaking the four-year contract to which they had agreed.[82]

Often it is difficult to untangle and categorize the charges brought against servants. In tallying the offenses of which servants were accused, I have used the following thirteen categories: (1) breaking contract, for which servants were prosecuted if they left without first obtaining permission or license from the master (often they were in debt to their masters for salary or clothing advances); (2) *malam servitutem* (rendering "bad service"), a vague charge that seemed to encapsulate masters' frustrations; (3) theft of goods; (4) destruction of property; (5) leaving the house vulnerable, usually by leaving doors open or unlocked; (6) allowing strangers (often prostitutes or lovers) inside the house. Five categories involved interpersonal relations, either between masters and servants or among servants: (7) refusal to take orders; (8) verbal abuse; (9) harassment; (10) physical attack or threat thereof; and (11) corruption of other servants, which generally involved one servant trying to persuade another servant to leave the master's service or commit some other crime. The final two categories are (12) sexual activity among servants in the household or with outsiders; and (13) miscellaneous, which serves as a catchall for other offenses (e.g., fencing stolen goods), many of which were committed by accomplices.

Table 2.1 records the number of accusations leveled in each of the categories outlined above in the years 1569–1600. By far the most frequent charge leveled against servants was that of breaking their contracts. In 258 instances this appeared as the sole accusation or as one of a series of accusations. Some servants made a habit of this; gondolier Andrea da Verona was charged with breaking his contracts with four different masters, members of the Sagredo, Valaresso, Morosini, and Pizzamano families.[83] As noted above, servants often left after receiving salary advances or suits of clothing. Francesco Buzzuola from Treviso left nobleman Niccolò Michiel's service after only two days, taking some small change Michiel had entrusted to him for making purchases.[84] In addition to the financial loss involved and the inconvenience of having to find other servants, there was some loss of honor as well when servants quit. In 1573 Vittore Dandolo charged his servant Francesco with abandoning him without permission, leaving him "without service" [absque servitutem].[85] Noblewoman Cristina Donà, widow of Vincenzo, claimed that Sebastiano da Montagnana had broken

Table 2.1
Accusations in Censors' Trials, 1569–1600

| Type of Accusation | Number of Accusations Against | |
|---|---|---|
| | Servants and Accomplices | Servants Only |
| Breaking contract | 258 | 258 |
| *Malam servitutem* | 24 | 24 |
| Theft of goods | 146 | 145 |
| Destruction of property | 19 | 19 |
| Leaving house vulnerable | 18 | 18 |
| Strangers in house | 11 | 11 |
| Refusing orders | 9 | 9 |
| Verbal abuse | 32 | 32 |
| Harassment | 15 | 15 |
| Physical attack or threat | 25 | 25 |
| Corruption of servants | 23 | 21 |
| Sex crimes | 135 | 128 |
| Miscellaneous | 63 | 41 |
| Total | 778 | 746 |

Source: ASV, Censori, busta 3, registers 1–3.

his contract, leaving her "sine famulo."[86] Like the capitularies, prosecutions reflect the masters' concern with the inviolability of legal contracts.

Theft was the second most frequently prosecuted crime. In March 1571, for example, nobleman Giovanni Gritti charged his servants Valerio and Battista with using counterfeit keys to enter his storehouse and steal provisions.[87] In 1585 Francesco and Paolo Gasparini Bortholuzzi, servants of nobleman Girolamo Tiepolo, were prosecuted by two German merchants who claimed the two servants had stolen goods from their storeroom in the Tiepolo house. Also implicated were two perfumers, Antonio Michael and Bartolomeo, as well as a certain Stefano à Coloribus, who purchased the stolen goods.[88]

Sexual activity was the third most common charge; sometimes this involved servants of the same household. Bartolomeo and Marina, servants in the household of nobleman Giulio Michiel, were charged with having sex "in the house, damaging the morals and reputation" [in ipsa domo, contra bonos mores, et honestatem] of the household.[89] Servants were also prosecuted for sexual relations with outsiders. Paolina, ancilla of nobleman Andrea Valier, was accused of allowing Bettino, apprentice to a sausage maker, into her master's home and having sex with him.[90] Ioseph, gondolier for the household of nobleman Giovanni Battista Capello, was charged with bringing prostitutes into the home and fornicating with a maid.[91]

Verbal abuse and physical attacks were not unknown; there were 32 charges for the former crime and 25 for the latter. In 1571 Andrea Gritti's gondolier Francesco, nicknamed Rizzo, disobeyed orders by not waiting to pick up Gritti after a meeting of the Great Council and by talking back to his master. When Gritti fired him, Francesco got a sword and actually threatened his master.[92]

As the aggregated data show, plaintiffs charged and the censors tried servants for a variety of offenses, ranging from infraction of contracts to sex crimes, vandalism, disobedience, insults, and threats. Like the capitularies, the registers of the censors' cases reveal a strong concern for the sanctity of legal contracts and the reputations of households and persons, especially when threatened by unlicensed sex.

Turning from plaintiffs and their accusations to defendants, the 412 cases involved the prosecution of 523 individuals, of whom 491 were servants, and 32, accomplices. The gender breakdown of the defendants is as follows: 380 male servants, 111 female servants, 27 male accomplices, and 5 female accomplices. With regard to the nationality of defendants, 49 were native Venetians, 343 were immigrants, and in 132 cases the information is unclear.

When the accusations against defendants are broken down by gender, some telling differences appear (see table 2.2). Women were most likely to be accused of allowing strangers into the house, leaving the home of the master vulnerable, or engaging in illicit sexual activity. This may partly be explained by the fact that female servants' activities, unlike those of male servants, tended to center around the household, but it also indicates that masters especially feared the unlicensed sexuality of their female servants and feared that that sexuality would damage their households. By contrast, masters feared direct confrontation with male servants. All of the charges of refusing orders, harassment, and rendering bad service were directed at them, as were the overwhelming number of accusations of physical attack and verbal abuse. All this suggests that masters' fears for the honor and reputation of their households were generally directed toward female servants, while fears for their personal safety and dignity were centered on males.[93]

When rendering their decisions and fixing penalties, the censors exhibited a great deal of flexibility. Several scholars, notably Gaetano Cozzi, have remarked the tendency of Venetian magistrates to judge cases on their individual charac-

Table 2.2
Accusations, by Gender of Defendant, 1569–1600

| | Number of Accusations against | | | | |
| | Males | | Females | | |
| Type of Accusation | No. | % | No. | % | Total |
|---|---|---|---|---|---|
| Breaking contract | 212 | 82.17 | 46 | 17.82 | 258 |
| *Malam servitutem* | 24 | 100.00 | 0 | 0.00 | 24 |
| Theft of goods | 119 | 81.50 | 27 | 18.49 | 146 |
| Destruction of property | 17 | 89.47 | 2 | 10.52 | 19 |
| Leaving house vulnerable | 9 | 50.00 | 9 | 50.00 | 18 |
| Strangers in house | 4 | 36.36 | 7 | 63.63 | 11 |
| Refusing orders | 9 | 100.00 | 0 | 0.00 | 9 |
| Verbal abuse | 31 | 96.87 | 1 | 3.12 | 32 |
| Harassment | 15 | 100.00 | 0 | 0.00 | 15 |
| Physical attack or threat | 24 | 96.00 | 1 | 4.00 | 25 |
| Corruption of servants | 21 | 91.30 | 2 | 8.69 | 23 |
| Sex crimes | 91 | 67.40 | 44 | 32.59 | 135 |
| Miscellaneous | 48 | 76.19 | 15 | 23.80 | 63 |

*Source*: ASV, Censori, busta 3, registers 1–3.
*Note:* Data are for 523 defendants, of whom 407 (77.82%) were males and 116 (22.17%) were females. Information for servants versus nonservants is not included here since few significant variations appear. All 5 female accomplices were charged with crimes in the "miscellaneous" category. Among male accomplices, 17 were charged with "miscellaneous" crimes, 7 with sex crimes, 2 with corrupting servants, and 1 with theft.

teristics rather than to adhere strictly to statutory requirements.[94] Like other Venetian officials, the censors considered the gravity and circumstances of crimes and the character and position of plaintiffs and defendants when adjudicating disputes. Unfortunately, in most cases the notaries did not record the rationale for the censors' decisions.

In the vast majority of cases, the censors found for the plaintiffs. This is not surprising, for two reasons. First, the censors themselves came from the ranks of the city's servant-keeping elite and thus were predisposed to sympathize and identify with the accusers. Second, when a master decided to take a servant to court, there was a good chance that he had a fairly strong case, since he would lose face if the suit was unsuccessful. Of the 523 individuals prosecuted in the cases examined, 445 were found guilty by the censors. In the cases of the remaining 78 defendants, the suits were either withdrawn by the plaintiff or dismissed or prorogued by the censors, or the defendants were actually acquitted.

In the 445 instances in which servants were found guilty, the penalties varied considerably. The censors fixed punishment according to several criteria, including the penalties established by the capitularies, the sex of the defendants, and most importantly, whether the defendants were actually present or were tried in contumacy. Defendants were present in 299 instances, in contumacy in 215; and in 9 cases the information is unclear. For those tried in contumacy, a common form of punishment was banishment from Venice and its territories for a prescribed number of years. Violation of the ban would incur galley service or a jail term and, upon completion of that sentence, rebanishment. The censors regularly offered bounties for those who broke the terms of their banishment. For defendants who were present, penalties often included galley service for men, if they were physically fit for service, and jail time for women. In cases in which servants broke their contracts, taking with them salary advances or clothes, the censors usually declared that the punishment would not begin until the master had been fully compensated for his loss. Other punishments included whipping, branding, and public humiliation by being placed in the public stocks at San Marco or Rialto with a miter on which the offense was spelled out.

The aggregated data concerning punishment are difficult to interpret for two reasons. First, since servants were often tried for more than one offense, it is impossible to determine how the judges weighed the various offenses in establishing their sentences. Second, since the judges often issued sentences involving a mixture of punishments as well as conditions that could reduce or change the punishment, the sentences are nearly impossible to quantify. Table 2.3 presents the data for the most common forms of punishment, namely, banishment, jail terms, and galley service, for all defendants and by gender. When defendants were tried in contumacy, males were banished for nearly twice as long as females. But when the defendants were actually present, then women received longer banishments and longer jail terms than men. This was because men who were present for their trials and convicted were likely to be condemned to the galleys if the gravity of their crimes so warranted.

Table 2.3
Average Penalties Expressed in Years, 1569–1600

| Presence/Absence at Trial | Penalty | All Defendants | Males | Females |
|---|---|---|---|---|
| Absent | Banishment | 6.654 | 7.352 | 3.707 |
| Present | Banishment | 2.634 | 1.357 | 3.105 |
| Present | Jail | 0.309 | 0.232 | 0.571 |
| Present | Galley | 2.012 | 2.012 | 0.000 |

Source: ASV, Censori, busta 3, registers 1–3.

More informative in some ways than the aggregated data is an examination of some of the punishments meted out to individual defendants. The most severe punishment for those tried in contumacy was perpetual banishment from Venice and its territories. This penalty was levied in only two instances. In the first case, Giovanni di Tomasi da Castrignano, famulus of non-noble Gaspare Marino, was found guilty of breaking contract with his master and stealing two hundred ducats that he had received from another person in his master's name.[95] The censors attached a long series of conditions to the sentence; for instance, if caught, he was to serve four years in the galleys. One of Marino's relatives even offered some of his own money in order to increase the reward for Giovanni's capture. The other case of perpetual banishment from Venice and its territories involved Natalino Permuta, who had broken contract and taken a salary advance of thirty-six ducats. If caught, he was to spend six years in the galleys; however, the censors added the proviso that if he repaid his master within four months, his banishment would be reduced to only two years.[96] Both crimes involved the loss of significant sums of money.

Francesco da Sibenico, servant of Antonio Emo, committed a similar crime. He not only broke contract with his master but also used "many tricks" to defraud people of their money. He was sentenced to twenty years' exile from Venice and its territories, as was Leonardo di Purliliis, who was banished for theft, breaking contract, and fornicating with a maid.[97] The other two individuals who were banished for twenty years were convicted of different sorts of crimes. When

Philipo da Conegliano was fired by his master, he entered his former employer's house to engage in dishonest acts with one of the maids.[98] And Quintiliano Polangelo, servant of Vincenzo di Garzoni, was banished for corrupting a female servant.[99] For those tried in contumacy, the harshest penalties were leveled against men who had defrauded their masters, stolen significant sums of money, corrupted other servants, or engaged in sex crimes.

Among servants who were actually present for their trials, the most severe punishment for males involved galley service. The longest sentence was a ten-year term meted out to Giacomo, famulus of nobleman Francesco Longo, for quitting service and stealing. Before beginning his galley service, he had to spend three hours in the stocks at Rialto with a miter on his head. Furthermore, if he was physically unfit for galley service, he would have to spend fifteen years in jail and afterwards be banished in perpetuity.[100] Bartolomeo di Gobbati da Padova, servant of noblemen Marcantonio and Pietro Gritti, stole from a series of nobles using his masters' names; he also forged their names to certain documents. For this, the censors ordered him whipped from San Marco to Rialto, placed in the stocks, and branded, after which he was to serve five years in the galleys. The used-clothing dealer who purchased the stolen goods from Bartolomeo was sentenced to two hours in the stocks at Rialto and one month in jail, and he had to restitute everything he had bought from Bartolomeo.[101] Other servants who received sentences of five years of galley service were accused of theft and trying to corrupt a female servant.[102] The final case involved Enrico, servant of nobleman Francesco da Molin, and Mattea, ancilla of nobleman Francesco Priuli, who were accused by Priuli of having carnal relations. They confessed to the crime but stated that they planned to marry. Despite their confession, the censors sentenced Enrico to an hour in the stocks at Rialto and five years of galley service; if he was physically unfit for the galleys, he would have to spend three years in jail and afterwards be banished from Venice and its lands for ten years. Mattea was sentenced to an hour in the stocks, a year in jail, and a ten-year banishment.[103]

This last sentence highlights the different kinds of punishments assigned to males and females. Since women were ineligible for galley service, they were more likely than men to receive jail time. However, they often got lighter sentences than men, especially in crimes of illicit sexual activity. Venerando and Caterina, servants of the Civran household, who were tried in contumacy got different sentences. He was banished for eight years, and if caught, he was to serve two years in the galleys; she was banished for four years, and if caught, she was to spend six months in the women's prison and then be rebanished.[104] Bernardino and Caterina, servants of the Foscarini household, married after

Caterina became pregnant. Tried on 3 July 1570, Bernardino was sentenced to spend the balance of the month in jail. Since Caterina was pregnant, the censors decided not to prosecute her for the time being.[105] The outcome of this case, so different from that of Enrico and Mattea, who claimed they wished to marry, illustrates the ability of the censors to be flexible.

Although the censors usually found in favor of the plaintiffs, they sometimes recognized extenuating circumstances and meted out very mild punishments to servants. Such was the case of Pietro da Cividale, who was accused by his master of leaving without permission and taking with him a salary advance and other money entrusted to him by his master's wife to buy food. Pietro did not deny the charge but explained that when he returned from shopping, he tried to return the money to his mistress, but she was too busy to see him. Later that same day, when Pietro was stopped by some officials for debts he gave them his mistress's money to keep from going to jail. He testified that out of fear and shame he did not return home, but tried unsuccessfully to secure another loan to cover his mistress's money. After much discussion, the censors decided that if he repaid his master and covered the costs of the case, he would be released from jail.[106] Apparently the censors were convinced by his story and the master agreed to the sentence.

In another case the censors sentenced Francesco Buzzuola, servant of Niccolò Michiel, to fifteen days in jail and court costs for breaking his contract. Since Francesco had only been in Michiel's service for two days before leaving, the censors must have reasoned that Michiel had not suffered much loss.[107] An identical sentence was levied on Galeatio, former servant of Tiberio Barbaro, who broke his contract, deserting the master who had raised and cared for him. In this case the censors ruled that in light of his age (just fifteen years) and "other unspecified factors fully considered" [allis in dictu caso maturè consideratis], Galeatio would not be severely punished. It is also possible that his new master, nobleman Lorenzo Lombardo, intervened on his behalf.[108] When nobleman Pietro Corner prosecuted his servant Liberale for breaking his contract and stealing some bread, the censors ordered Liberale to spend just two months in jail, "considering his youth" [habita consideratione eius minori aetate]. But he was not to be released until he had repaid his master; and at that time he was to complete his contract with Corner.[109] Overall, in fixing punishment the censors showed extraordinary flexibility. They did not follow a rigid formula but took into consideration a variety of factors, including the sex and age of the defendants, the circumstances and gravity of the crimes, the position and prestige of the plaintiffs, and in some instances the impact of a public punishment.

In seventy-eight instances the censors did not convict. These cases were resolved in one of four ways: the defendant's release from jail, which often amounted to a kind of arbitrated settlement; dismissal of the case by the censors; withdrawal of the charges or forgiveness by the plaintiff; or actual acquittal. In thirty-four instances the censors ordered the defendants released from jail (the term they used was *relaxatur ex carceribus*), although in some instances they reserved the right to prosecute in the future. The censors usually reached this decision when the charges were very minor, when the damage done the master could be easily repaired, or when the time the defendant had already spent in jail seemed sufficient punishment. In 1586, for instance, Cristoforo Centoni accused the wet nurse Andriana, wife of a cobbler, of taking some items of little value. The censors ordered her released from jail with the proviso that she return the items to Centoni.[110] In 1591 nobleman Francesco Trevisan accused his famulus Gaspar of theft. Gaspar was convicted, but the censors ordered him released because of his ill health and the time he had already served. He was, however, ordered to pay the court costs.[111]

Ten defendants' cases were dismissed by the censors. The term used was *licentiatus ab offitio*. This solution, like release from jail, was utilized by the censors when the charges were minor and some sort of agreement between the master and servant could be easily found. In 1585, for instance, the censors dismissed the case against Alexander, servant of Francesco Ricio, who had been accused of breaking his contract and taking some clothes made for him. The censors did so with the proviso that he complete his contract.[112]

Seventeen individuals were acquitted of the charges leveled against them. It is clear that in these cases the censors simply did not believe the plaintiffs or were convinced by the defendants of their innocence. For instance, in 1573 the censors absolved Francesco, famulus of nobleman Vittore Dandolo, of the charge that he had broken his contract, leaving service without the required fifteen days' notice. Francesco defended himself against the charge, claiming that he had in fact notified his master twenty days before he left.[113] In 1584 Vittore Paparoto, famulus of nobleman Alvise Morosini, was acquitted of fraud, theft, and opening some sealed caskets. Normally, charges such as these elicited a severe response from the censors.[114] When the censors acquitted Ursa, servant of nobleman Leonardo Barbaro, of theft, they even ordered Barbaro to pay Ursa her salary.[115] Certainly the most spectacular acquittal involved nobleman Niccolò Bernardo and his two male servants, gondolier Gerolamo Scorzoni and famulus Francesco di Madiotis. Bernardo claimed the two had conspired to kill him while he slept and to rob his house of its plate, very serious charges indeed. The censors detained and interrogated the servants, who denied everything. The censors agreed, acquitted them, and ordered Bernardo to pay the court costs.[116] Something in

Bernardo's story or perhaps his reputation within the patriciate made it clear to the censors that the charges against the servants were patently false. Although the censors were generally predisposed to rule in favor of the servant keepers, in some instances they chose to dismiss cases, to arbitrate disputes without a clear-cut condemnation, and in a few cases where the evidence was unequivocal actually to absolve the servants. While the system of Venetian justice was clearly stacked in favor of the elites, individuals from the lower class occasionally saw justice served. Overwhelmingly, however, the office of the censors served as an instrument to protect the interests of masters against what they perceived to be unruly servants. Masters prosecuted before that office servants who had violated the norms established by the censors' capitularies. The full weight of the law was most likely to fall upon male servants who had violated contractual obligations or disrupted licit business practices; female servants were prosecuted for sex crimes, which threatened the honor of their masters' households.

Although flexible, the censors also utilized their judgments to publicize the normative behavior expected of servants by making an example of disobedient servants in order to discourage others from following their example. They did so through the selective use of the stocks and other ritualized punishments. When Domenico, servant of Alvise Foscarini, was convicted of theft, the censors ordered him whipped in the parish where he committed the crime and jailed for a year.[117] In 1576 Pietro da Carrara and Santa, servants of nobleman Raimondo Gritti, were accused of engaging in sexual relations and other crimes. The censors had them whipped "egregiously" around the house of their master.[118] Slogans hung around the necks of condemned criminals further publicized official notions of improper behavior. For example, when Gaspar da Venezia and Maddalena da Este were sentenced to the stocks in 1602, they were forced to wear a slogan that read, "For having committed dishonest acts in the house of their master" [Per haver commesso disonesta in casa del Patron].[119]

≈

By a variety of means, then, including the registration of servants, the creation of magistracies with competence over domestic service, the issuance by those magistracies of capitularies establishing guidelines for master-servant interaction, the adjudication of disputes between masters and servants, and the selective use of ritual punishments, the government, through the agency of its servant-keeping members, established norms and expectations concerning master-servant relations and flexibly enforced them. In so doing, the elite articulated their vision of the proper relationship between masters and servants, and by extension of the larger society and polity. They saw the relationship as a legal and contractual one. This was a constant feature of the changing capitularies and the primary concern of masters who took their servants to court. Yet the master-servant relationship was more than that, and we detect in the evolution of the capitularies and in some of the charges leveled against servants an increasing concern with servants as symbols of their masters' status and reflections of their honor. To this extent, the evolution seems to parallel the changes noted in chapter 1, namely, an increasing emphasis on the social as opposed to the political model of master-servant ties. Together, writings on master-servant relations, legal codes, and administrative and judicial actions created a series of guidelines that to some extent governed the ways in which masters and servants interacted within households. But before examining that interaction in detail, we need first to explore the structure of households, the mechanics of domestic labor, and the social world of servants in Renaissance Venice.

# Part II
# Structures

# Chapter Three

# Servants in the Venetian Household

In his will dated 1562 the future doge Alvise Mocenigo roundly condemned a common Venetian household practice. According to Mocenigo, patrician families were destroying the beauty and architectural integrity of their palaces by subdividing them into individual apartments. He asked that his "casa nova grande" at San Samuele remain "open and spacious and be enjoyed as it currently exists."[1]

Mocenigo's injunction signals the importance the palace and domestic establishment held for members of the Venetian elite. Yet knowledge of the actual structure and composition of households remains the single largest gap in our understanding of Venetian family life.[2] This lacuna is understandable given the lack of sources such as census data for the period prior to the late sixteenth century and the haphazard survival of account books and family diaries, but it is particularly frustrating for the historian whose focus is on servants, who, as we have seen, were closely associated with household activities.[3]

In an effort to begin filling that gap in Venetian family history, this chapter focuses on households and explores several aspects of servant keeping, including the relationship between servant keeping and the family life cycle, the differentiation between servants and their role in various kinds of households, and the connections between servant keeping and social status. I shall approach these topics by examining the official household of the doge, as well as the households of leading patricians, cittadini, artisans, and even a courtesan. At the end of the chapter, I shall consider some quantitative evidence of servant-keeping and households.

## The Ducal Household

The doge, or duke, occupied a unique position in the Venetian government and in society. In the early and central Middle Ages he enjoyed nearly exclusive power, but over the course of several centuries his authority was hemmed in by councils and magistrates as Venice evolved from a dukedom into a commune.

With the death of each doge, additions and corrections were made to the ducal *promissione* (oath of office). In the late thirteenth and early fourteenth centuries, when most Italian city-states were succumbing to the lure of signorial rule, the promissioni were designed to limit that threat by restricting the personal prerogatives and powers of the doges. The councillors were especially wary of dynastic ambitions and sought to curtail the influence of members of the ducal family. The doge, for instance, was forbidden to contract marriages with foreign rulers for kinsmen, and residence in the Ducal Palace was limited to all but his most immediate relatives. In addition, ducal patronage rights were restricted, as was the doge's ability to grant favors and pardons. Among his fellow patricians, that is, among other members of the Great Council, the doge was ideally to be simply *primus inter pares*.[4]

But this ideal did not correspond to reality or to the exigencies of international diplomacy. Despite limitations on his authority, the doge remained the single most powerful figure in the Venetian government. He presided over all the most important councils, and he was one of the few officers of state to hold office for life. Furthermore, for ceremonial and diplomatic purposes, the doge had to function as the personification of the state. All Venetian claims on the international stage were predicated on the notion that the city recognized no suzerain other than God, that among emperors and popes the doge was *par inter pares*. For this reason, Venice zealously guarded the symbols of ducal power; and it was essential that the doge be surrounded by the aura of authority.[5] The Ducal Palace, then, had to function not only as the venue of the councils of government but also as the residence of a sovereign.

It is difficult to define the precise limits of the ducal household, for in one sense the entire structure of Venetian government was but an extension of ducal authority. Rejecting that notion as ultimately too unwieldy to be meaningful, we are still left with the daunting problem of defining the limits of the ducal household. Fortunately, the promissioni provide a fairly reliable guide to the composition and evolution of the official ducal staff and a consistent index of the doge's official household.[6]

The earliest extant ducal oath and perhaps the first written oath is that of Enrico Dandolo, conqueror of Constantinople, who took office in 1192. Dandolo's oath, however, contains no references to the ducal staff.[7] For that we must proceed to the promissione of Jacopo Tiepolo, who ascended to the ducal throne in 1229. Tiepolo swore to maintain twenty "servitores," including the kitchen staff, and he agreed to replace within one month any servant who left. Furthermore, he vowed to select the keeper of the ducal seal from among the "worthiest" [legalioribus] of these servants.[8] Little more can be gleaned from the oath about the household, but Tiepolo's promissione does suggest that in its earliest form the ducal household resembled in some respects those of feudal rulers in northern Europe, in which household positions and government functions were mixed, for one of the doge's household members was to serve as keeper of the seal. In addition, the choice of the word *legalioribus* to describe the keeper suggests that these were not men of humble status.

The next extant promissione, that of Doge Marino Morosini, dated 1249, contains a crucial addition to the clause requiring the doge to maintain twenty *servitores*. Morosini promised to outfit them with "iron weapons" [arma ferrea].[9] Three years later, Ranieri Zeno's oath of office added age and residence requirements. The twenty *servitores* had to be between twenty and sixty years of age and residents of the *dogado,* the lagunal zone between Grado and Cavarzere.[10] The requirement that they be able-bodied men furnished with weapons indicates that one of their functions was to serve as bodyguards for the doge.

The doge was not the only member of the elite at this time to maintain bodyguards. During the thirteenth century other Venetian magistrates were keeping armed retainers as well, and this came to pose a serious threat to the stability of the government. In 1276 the Great Council passed a law prohibiting the bringing of weapons into the Ducal Palace while the council was in session. And once members of the council had deposited their weapons, no squire *(scutifer)* was allowed to bring other weapons into the building.[11] A law passed ten years earlier had forbidden any Venetian, either "small or great" [parvus vel magnus], to bear the coat of arms of any magnate on his shield or on any other sort of weapon.[12] These laws were designed to minimize growing divisions within Venetian society by prohibiting outward displays of loyalty to particular individuals or families. The councillors feared that, as had happened in other cities, public offices would be used for private ends, specifically that officeholders would transform subordinates into personal retainers. To prevent this, in February 1266 the Great Council forbade underlings *(pueri)* in government offices to display the personal arms of officials. They were to bear instead the insignia of Saint Mark, the city's patron saint, on either their sleeve or their shield.[13] The Querini-Tiepolo conspiracy of 1310 justified these fears, for it revealed the dangerous potential of magnate families' acting in collusion with non-noble followers. Yet for a variety of reasons, including constitutional reforms and an element of luck, Venice survived the conspiracy, retaining and strengthening its republican orientation.[14]

During this period the ducal household staff continued to expand. By the time Pietro Gradenigo ascended to the ducal throne, in 1289, the official household had grown to at least twenty-nine persons.[15] Gradenigo's promissione required him to maintain two "esquires or knights" [sotios sive milites], who were to lodge in the palace.[16] The doge was to pay their salaries and outfit them as well. These two men apparently functioned as masters of the bedchamber, which gave them ready access to the doge and possibly some control over who received an audience with him. For this reason, the doge had to swear that they would not receive any gifts.[17] By the time Gradenigo became doge the number of servitores had risen to twenty-three, three of whom were to supervise the kitchen. Additionally, Gradenigo continued to maintain a notary and a keeper of the seal and had to keep a priest and acolyte on the staff so that Mass could be performed within the confines of the palace.[18] Although impressive, the doge's personal staff did not rival either in size or in scope those of the royal households of northern Europe, which sometimes numbered in the hundreds.[19]

Gradenigo was the doge who presided over the Serrata of the Great Council, the act that gave Venice its form as an aristocratic republic. Thenceforth, the path to power in Venice lay, not in positions on the ruler's staff, as it did in northern Europe, but rather with seats in the councils of government.

The promissioni of Francesco Foscari, dated 1423, and of Agostino Barbarigo, dated 1486, indicate that the ducal staff remained basically the same as it had during the dogeship of Gradenigo.[20] However, a number of changes were instituted when Pietro Lando ascended to the throne in 1538. Both as an economy measure and in order that the servitores (now known as *scudieri*) be better paid, the doge was absolved of responsibility for maintaining a notary and paying the expenses of the keeper of the seal. In place of two cavaliers (successors of the knights), Lando was required to maintain just one at sixty ducats a year and a steward *(scalco)* at forty ducats. Furthermore, the number of scudieri was reduced from twenty to eighteen (at a salary of twenty-four ducats each). The oath added that the baker, chef, sous-chef, wine steward, and gondolier were not to be included among the scudieri.[21]

By 1538 the requirements to be a scudiere had changed somewhat as well. Incumbents had to be citizens of Venice or one of the subject territories or else residents of the city for at least fifteen years.[22] These positions provided the doge an important pool of patronage jobs. According to Vecellio, the cavalier normally was selected from among the corps of scudieri, although from time to time a doge might select a personal servant who had shown special devotion to the doge's family.[23] The jobs were held for life; hence a sitting doge was often served by men selected by his predecessors.

By the mid-sixteenth century the official household was actually a bit smaller than it had been at the end of the thirteenth. According to an anonymous treatise entitled *Il modo che debbe tener il Seren.mo Principe di Venezia. . .* , written in 1559, during the reign of Doge Girolamo Priuli, the ducal "court" comprised one cavalier, one steward, two chamberlains, sixteen shield bearers, a baker, a chef, and a second baker. Promissioni from the period indicate that the doge still maintained a priest and cleric as well.[24]

As the dangers of factionalism and civil unrest subsided, the court evolved from an actual bodyguard into an honorific corps designed to enhance the prestige of the ducal officeholder. According to Vecellio, the cavalier served as head of the scudieri, but his primary responsibility was to remain close to the doge, ready to serve his every need. One of his functions was to bodily support the doge, especially as he descended the stairs of the Ducal Palace.[25] Given the propensity of the Venetians for electing especially aged men to the city's highest honor, this support was often a necessity (see plate 5).[26] The duty of the scudieri was to gather every morning at the Ducal Palace and accompany the prince into the Collegio. In public processions they played an important role as bearers of the various insignia of ducal authority, including the ducal chair and cushion and the ducal umbrella. They also showed visitors about the palace.[27] Every week two of the scudieri lodged in the palace and stood guard over the doge's bedchamber.[28] The steward's primary job was to coordinate and supervise the four banquets that by custom the doge offered annually to members of the patriciate (see plate 6).[29]

Over time, posts within the ducal household themselves evolved into honorific positions that carried both healthy stipends and a degree of prestige. In addition to their prescribed salaries, members of the court received a variety of gifts throughout the year. On All Saints' Day the cavalier and steward each received a goose; the other members of the staff, including the scudieri, the baker, and the chefs, each received half a goose. In February each received twelve soldi in order to purchase gloves.[30] The highest officials, including the cavalier and the steward, had apartments in the palace; and all must have taken some meals there. In an age obsessed with status distinctions, members of the court enjoyed the additional privilege of wearing distinctive uniforms. The cavalier wore a long crimson gown and a beret similar to that of the admiral and the capitano grande. The steward was distinguished by his baton.

All of these positions were held by popolani of fairly modest circumstances. In the early 1380s one of the doge's two *milites* was a certain Andrea di Varnarussiis of Conegliano, whose wife's dowry of 250 ducats indicates that Varnarussiis occupied the middling ranks of society.[31] Of perhaps more humble origins were Guglielmo da Peraga, *camerarius* of Doge Francesco Foscari, who married a freed slave with a dowry of 100 ducats in 1441, and Ventura di Circulis da Verona,

CAVALIER DEL DOGE.

Plate 5. Illustration of *cavalier del doge* from Cesare Vecellio's *De gli habiti antichi, et moderni di diverse parti del mondo libri due* (Venice, 1590). Photograph courtesy of Museo Civico Correr, Venice.

Plate 6. Illustration of *scudieri del doge* from Cesare Vecellio's *De gli habiti antichi, et moderni di diverse parti del mondo libri due* (Venice, 1590). Photograph courtesy of Museo Civico Correr, Venice.

squire of Doge Andrea Gritti, whose wife, Franceschina, was the daughter of a sailor.[32] Silvestro di Vidali, ducal cavalier at the beginning of the 1570s, owned shares in a brokerage in the Ghetto and provided his son Zuanne with an office "for maintenance of our family" [per sustantation della nostra fameglia].[33] And a scudiere at the end of the sixteenth century himself employed a serving woman.[34] In 1578 the Great Council voted to make the former Turkish slave of the late Doge Sebastiano Venier a scudiere.[35]

The cavaliers, squires, and others formed the official ducal household. Yet each doge and dogaressa also brought with them to the Ducal Palace a number of personal servants who met their private as opposed to their public needs. As Vecellio noted, the doges sometimes rewarded their personal servants with official positions, but they maintained private staffs as well.

The will and codicils of Doge Alvise Mocenigo (1570–77) provide a glimpse into both his official and his unofficial household. In his will of 1562, before he became doge, Mocenigo made no bequests to servants. However, in a first codicil, dated 1574, after his ascension to the ducal throne, he included a number of bequests both to his own and to his deceased wife's personal male and female servants. The female servants were given money to assist them to marry or join a convent; for example, his massara Lucia, who had served him for many years, was bequeathed fifty ducats, and the housekeeper at his home on the Giudecca, twenty-five. He left no bequests to his two camerieri, Tommaso and Carlo, since he had already procured offices for them; he did, however, note that they could keep some money he had loaned them. In a final codicil, dated 1576, Mocenigo disinherited a servant Lucia for whom he had provided a house owned by the Cà di Dio, a hospital for women under ducal patronage, and passed the legacies instead to his servant Lucia da Portogruaro. And for the first time, Mocenigo mentioned his official household. Wishing that "those who are in our service here in the house at the time of our death" enjoy "some small benefit from this our codicil," Mocenigo bequeathed ten ducats to the cavalier, eight to the steward, and five each to the scudieri, the two cooks, and the baker; the second baker received three ducats. The contrast between the carefully crafted bequests to personal servants and the simple monetary gifts to the official ones, none of whom were mentioned by name, suggests that the official public household was just that, official and public.[36]

During the later sixteenth century, ducal families tried to enhance the position of the dogaressa as a way to increase the prestige of the ducal office itself.[37] This included efforts to augment her "court." In June 1559 a proposal was placed before the Senate suggesting that the dogaressa be given fifty ducats of public monies per month to support a staff of no fewer than eight donzelle in order to increase the "decorum and honor of Our Republic." The measure was defeated.[38]

But only eight months later, in February 1560, former dogaressa Zilia Dandolo, widow of Doge Lorenzo Priuli, wrote to the government that she was in a quandary about how she was to appear in public now that she was a widow. Specifically, she was concerned that she not appear to be a "donna privata." In response, the Senate voted to give her three hundred ducats a year to support four ladies-in-waiting, who would accompany Dandolo and be dressed in an appropriate manner. These donzelle were to serve in addition to any "fantesche et servitori" she already employed.[39]

And in April 1578 the Senate voted to give former dogaressa Cecilia Contarini, widow of Doge Sebastiano Venier, four hundred ducats a year in order for her to employ four cameriere, maintain a gondola with two gondoliers, and dress herself and four ladies-in-waiting in the same manner as had Zilia Dandolo. All this was done so that both in clothing and escort Contarini would appropriately "represent" the memory of her husband, who was esteemed "not only by our [Republic], but by all Christendom."[40]

In addition to the official ducal household and to the doge's and dogaressa's personal servants, there must have been other members of the household staff who maintained the palace. There were almost certainly servants of even more humble status, perhaps including some women, who scoured kitchens, emptied latrines, laundered linens, and swept halls and chambers. And of course the *arsenalotti*, the workers at the state-run shipyard, maintained the doge's official barge, the *bucentoro*.[41] Unfortunately, the rest of this staff is hidden from our view, as it was from the diplomats and dignitaries who visited the Ducal Palace to pay their respects to the doge.

All in all, the ducal household, like the doge himself, was an anomaly in Venetian society. It supported a prince, yet functioned in a republic; it was, as we shall see, larger than the average patrician household, and it was staffed exclusively by men who were selected and rewarded by the doges themselves. The ducal court exemplified the unique position of the doge as the princely head of an aristocratic republic.

## The Patrician Household

In the centuries following the Serrata, members of the Venetian ruling elite, the patricians, became linked to one another through a complex web of ties, so that the aristocracy as a whole formed a kind of great interlocking kinship group. Marriages often were used to cement alliances forged for economic and political purposes. On one level at least, Venetian politics can profitably be examined from the vantage point of families, that is, as a contest between kinship groups vying with one another for shares of governmental spoils.[42]

One of the most distinguishing characteristics of patrician family life was the institution of the *fraterna,* which had both a restricted legal meaning and a broader social one. According to Venetian law, brothers who did not go through the formal process of legal separation were treated as a financial and legal unit. Economic historians, notably Frederic Lane, have viewed the fraterna as a kinship arrangement well adapted to the needs of a maritime republic. Undivided fraternal patrimonies provided a reliable source of investment capital for trading ventures during the period of Venetian commercial expansion.[43]

In addition to its narrow legal definition, fraterna also referred to a certain kind of household arrangement characteristic of some patrician families. Sometimes brothers, even when legally separated, continued to live under the same roof, dividing the family palace into a variety of smaller apartments suitable for nuclear family units, the practice Mocenigo condemned. James C. Davis, who has studied the Donà family, finds a functional explanation for the custom of living *in fraterna* as well. He argues that by sharing the same living quarters, brothers were able to save money on food and other living expenses. The fraterna as a family institution was thus also ideally suited to the conservation of wealth. Davis notes, however, that the motive for living in fraterna extended beyond purely financial considerations. Patricians viewed having the extended family under one roof as a particularly appropriate and esteemable living arrangement that expressed their vision of themselves.[44] But how and where did servants fit into these patrician household arrangements? The ledger book of nobleman Lorenzo Priuli and his sons provides a glimpse into the workings of one important patrician household.[45]

The Priuli family was one of the most powerful patrician families at the beginning of the sixteenth century. Lorenzo Priuli (1446–1518) had a distinguished government career that included stints as captain of Vicenza, avogador di commun, member of the Council of Ten, and podesta of Cremona. He married Paola Barbarigo, niece of the two Barbarigo doges of the later fifteenth century, Marco and Agostino. Together Lorenzo and Paola had four sons, three of whom (Vincenzo, Francesco, and Girolamo) lived to adulthood. The Priuli were also very wealthy. In 1504 they had more than ten thousand ducats invested in the Flemish galleys. Vincenzo and Girolamo were especially active in business and commerce. Vincenzo was heavily involved in the English wool trade; and Girolamo, following emancipation from his father in January 1507, set up a bank at Rialto. He is best known, however, for the diary he kept between 1498 and 1512, which constitutes a major source for the period of the League of Cambrai. In their social connections, financial resources, and political influence, Lorenzo Priuli and his sons stood near the very top of the Venetian patriciate.[46]

Despite their wealth and influence, Lorenzo and his sons did not inhabit their own family palace; instead they rented a "caxa grande" in the parish of Santa Fosca belonging to the Lippomano family. Renting accommodations was common practice among Venetian patricians. In 1525 the Priuli's rent was eighty ducats per year, and at one point Lorenzo deducted the expense of improvements on the property from the rent.[47] Throughout their father's lifetime and for some time after his death the sons lived together, even though Girolamo at least, and perhaps the other sons as well, had been formally emancipated.[48] During the period 1505–35 Lorenzo and later his sons maintained a large ledger of income and outlays. Lorenzo kept the book from 1505 until his death in 1518, and it is for this period that it is most valuable for studying servants. Although many of the family's interests, including records of Girolamo's bank, were not included in this register, Frederic Lane described it as "the central record" of a large family fortune.[49]

For the family's living expenses at least, Lorenzo's entries appear to resemble more closely a budget than an actual record of expenditures. Each year, on the last day of February (the last day of the year according to the Venetian calendar) Lorenzo recorded the expenses for each member of the family and for each servant. The figures were not based on actual outlays, however, but on estimated figures that presumably could be used if and when the family's resources had to be divided. For example, the annual figure for the maintenance of Girolamo and his male servant was set by Lorenzo at forty ducats for each year from 1505 to 1514. Almost certainly Lorenzo kept other books in which the actual expenditures for food, fuel, and clothing were recorded, but as long as the father and sons lived together amicably, there was probably no need for a more precise accounting system.[50] Instead the ledger provides a somewhat idealized financial account and a changing image of the household from 1505 to 1518. It also illustrates how the maintenance of servants was closely tied to the rhythms of family life as well as to the status demands of gender and class.

The ledger opens in 1505. On 28 February of that year Lorenzo compiled his first year-end summary of expenses.[51] As noted above, he calculated the "living expenses" [spese di boca] for Girolamo, aged twenty-nine, and a manservant at forty ducats.[52] The expenses for Francesco totaled ninety-eight ducats; but unlike his brother Girolamo, who never married, Francesco had a wife and two children in 1505.[53] Lorenzo calculated the spese di boca for Francesco and his wife at twenty-five ducats each. They also had four servants: a young male servant, a female servant, and two wet nurses. Lorenzo calculated the expenses for the servants at forty-eight ducats, sixteen ducats each, not including those for the wet nurse of newly born Marina. Lorenzo's third son, Vincenzo, was not included in the 1505 tallies, because he was not resident in Venice. Perhaps he was in England supervising the family's business interests there; from 1493 to 1498 Girolamo had been in England practicing trade.[54] Lorenzo also listed fifty-eight ducats as spese di boca presumably for himself, his wife, and a fourth son, Antonio (who died in 1510), in his 1505 accounts.[55]

Little changed in 1506, except that a third nurse was added when Francesco and his wife had another child. However, in 1507 the number of nurses dropped back to two. This was also the first year for which Lorenzo more specifically mentioned expenses for himself and his wife, Paola, including expenses of their servants, medical and clothing costs, and charitable gifts.[56] Unfortunately, Lorenzo did not actually list his own servants, as he did those of his sons, until the years 1515 to 1517.

The next major change, other than the birth of more children to Francesco and his wife, occurred in 1511 with Vincenzo's return to Venice. Lorenzo had quarters prepared for him and his wife, so that the father and all three adult sons were now reunited under the same roof.[57] Although it is difficult to keep track of the infants who were born and died, it appears that there were now as many as thirteen Priuli in the household: Lorenzo and Paola, the bachelor Girolamo, Vincenzo and his wife, and Francesco and his spouse, who may have had six children. Serving the Priuli were at least ten servants. When he compiled his ledger Lorenzo was very careful to group servants with each of the smaller nuclear family units to which they were attached rather than to list them all as servants of the entire family. Girolamo, as usual, had one male servant. The newly returned Vincenzo and his wife had one male servant and one female servant. Francesco, his wife, and their children were served by five domestics, including a male servant, a female servant named Zuana, Catarina (probably an indentured servant), a wet nurse, and the wet nurse's daughter, Isabeta.[58] Lorenzo and his wife Paola were assisted by an unspecified number of servants, but at least two, since he used the plural "mei famegli." One was a certain Zaneto da Bergamo, who, as we learn later in the ledger, served as Lorenzo's servitor from 1505 until Lorenzo's death in 1518.[59]

By 1517, the final year for which Lorenzo kept the ledger, the family had changed considerably in composition, if not in size. There were now about thirteen Priuli under the roof: Lorenzo and Paola, their three sons, and their sons' children. However, both Francesco and Vincenzo had lost their wives; Vincenzo had only one child, a daughter, Laura; and Francesco may have had as many as seven children.[60] The household was served by eleven domestics. Lorenzo and Paola employed four male servants during the year, although it is unlikely that all four served simultaneously. Vincenzo and his daughter Laura had one male servant and one female; Francesco and his brood were assisted by one male and two female servants. Finally Girolamo, who for years had had only one male servant, was now assisted by two male servants, Domenego and a certain Niccolò, whose job it was to "row the boat" [vuoga la barca].[61]

Several points should be noted from this analysis of the Priuli family ledger. First, servant keeping was at least partially connected to the rhythms of life, particularly to changes in the family life cycle. This is most evident in the hiring and release of wet nurses. As Francesco's nuclear family grew in size, he hired more wet nurses, so that at one point in 1506 there were three, one for each child. In fundamental ways servant keeping was tied to biological cycles and especially to the need to care for children. In the year following the death of his wife, Chiara, Vincenzo no longer needed all three of his servants—a male servant, a female servant, and a nurse. In 1513 his nuclear family, which now consisted solely of himself and his infant daughter, Laura, were able to get along with a male servant and a wet nurse.[62] As the family shrank in size, then, the need for staff diminished as well.

The second point that emerges is that cultural factors were also important in determining the patterns of servant keeping.[63] Despite constant fluctuations in both family size and the number of servants during the period 1505–17, one feature of servant keeping remained constant: at no time during the twelve-year period did any adult male lack a male servant specifically assigned to him. This tends to confirm that it was considered essential for elite males to have a manservant at all times. The patriarch Lorenzo had at least two male servants, as did Girolamo after his return from Rome in 1517.

By contrast, women were not always aided by a particular servant. Surprisingly, there is no mention of any female servants for Paola, matriarch of the family.[64] Instead, female servants were clustered around the offspring of Francesco and around Vincenzo's wife and daughter. The bachelor Girolamo never had a female servant assigned to him.[65]

In the actual day-to-day operation of the Priuli household, the specific assignment of servants to particular individuals may have counted for little. It is easy to imagine that one of the female servants or nurses was sent to clean Girolamo's quarters and to launder his clothes. And from time to time one of the male servants must have been ordered to row Paola to a convent to visit a kinswoman or to the bedside of a convalescing friend. Lorenzo's neat and orderly ledger, with its estimated rather than actual expenses and its compartmentalized nuclear family units and servants, is an idealized representation of a patrician household in which the realities of life were made to accord with Lorenzo's own notions of noble status and honor and the purposes of domestic service.

Different aspects of servant keeping in a patrician family emerge from another set of account books, those maintained by the merchant Andrea Barbarigo and his heirs. These books, which cover most of the period 1431–1582, illustrate the evolution of servant keeping in a patrician family over the course of the fifteenth and sixteenth centuries.[66]

Frederic Lane studied the journals and account books of Andrea Barbarigo in order to illustrate the business practices of a fifteenth-century man of affairs. Beginning in 1418, with a total capital of only two hundred ducats, Barbarigo accumulated, through a combination of hard work, family connections, and some luck, an estate valued at more than ten thousand ducats by the time of his death in 1449. Unlike many patricians who dedicated themselves to a political as well as a business career, Barbarigo single-mindedly pursued his goal of rebuilding the fortune lost by his father. He preferred to keep most of his capital in liquid assets, where he could get to it quickly. For this reason, he rented rather than purchased a house in the parish of San Barnaba; and for some years he hired the services of a slave from his future mother-in-law, Coronea Capello.[67]

In February 1439 Barbarigo married Cristina Capello, who brought to the marriage a dowry of four thousand ducats. And on the first page of his ledger, Andrea duly recorded the births of their two sons: Niccolò, born on 6 October 1440, and Alvise, born on 28 July 1443.[68] At about the time of his marriage, Andrea purchased three slaves, Agnese, Catarina, and Jacomo (nicknamed Ungaro), for a total price of 147 ducats, a modest sum for a man now worth about ten thousand ducats.[69]

To some extent at least, Barbarigo treated his slaves as an investment like any other. Perhaps he did not feel that his modest household, consisting of himself, his wife, and possibly his mother-in-law, needed three servants. Whatever his reason, he rented out the services of Agnese to Nadal Corner for sixteen ducats a year.[70] However, with the birth of his son Niccolò, Barbarigo found himself in need of more help, so he hired the wet nurse Stana at a salary of nineteen ducats a year.[71] In 1442 the slave Agnese was rented to Piero Paxeto for eight ducats a year and a pair of shoes; and the birth of Barbarigo's second son, Alvise, necessitated the hiring of yet another wet nurse, again at nineteen ducats per year.[72]

Andrea Barbarigo, the sensible businessman intent on building his fortune, tried to maintain the minimum staff that necessity and respectability required. He had one male slave to serve him, a female slave to assist Cristina with the household chores, and the requisite wet nurses for the children. More staff was not needed, so the third slave, Agnese, was hired out to others.[73]

Barbarigo's reliance on slaves instead of free servants is notable. The first half of the fifteenth century probably represented the high point of the Italian slave trade, and Barbarigo's own experience as a merchant in this human traffic may have led him to utilize this particular form of domestic labor.[74] Given his propensity for saving money, it is safe to assume that Barbarigo calculated that in the long run the initial purchase price and maintenance cost of slaves would be cheaper, or at least more efficient, than hiring other servants.

Andrea Barbarigo's death in 1449 brought a retrenchment on the part of his heirs. The trustees of Andrea's estate moved much of his capital out of commerce and into safer investments in government bonds and land; and his widow, Cristina, made the decision to purchase the house they had been renting in San Barnaba.[75] Upon their coming of age, his sons Niccolò and Alvise began to keep the family ledgers. One ledger begins with a brief summary of servants' contracts registered with the capi di sestieri and ends with a list of offices held by Niccolò from 1467 to 1499. The other begins with a record of the births and deaths of Niccolò's children.[76] Carefully synchronized, these data present for one particular point in time a strikingly complete picture of the Barbarigo household.

The year was 1469 (according to the Venetian calendar, March 1469 to February 1470). The household consisted of Andrea's widow Cristina and her two sons, Niccolò, aged twenty-nine, and Alvise, aged twenty-six, living together in fraterna. In the meantime, Niccolò had married Elena Lippomano, who in February 1469 had given birth to a son, Andrea, and in January 1470 gave birth to a daughter, Paola. A number of servants also resided in the household. First and foremost was Lena, the former wet nurse of Niccolò, who now apparently served as a companion to the widow Cristina. In her will written four years earlier, in June 1466, Cristina had expressed her intention to provide for Lena by promising her a bequest of twenty ducats and requiring that she be maintained at her sons' expense "according to her station" [segondo suo grado].[77] There was one male indentured servant, Niccolò da Liesna (Lesina?), and two indentured fantesche, Catarina da Sibenico and Petrussa da Cattaro.[78] Tragedy struck on 29 August, when Petrussa fell in the courtyard of the palace and died.[79] But within two months she was replaced by another fantesca, also from Cattaro, a certain Maddalena.[80] The infants Andrea and Paola required the services of the wet nurses Lena and Margarita.[81] It is also likely that there were one or two slaves in the household. Certainly in 1479 Niccolò had a male slave named Marco.[82]

Alvise died in 1471, and the estate became concentrated in his brother Niccolò's hands. Together Niccolò and his wife, Elena, had eleven children, four of whom, all boys, survived to adulthood. The ledger shows the coming and going of nurses (as befit a family with eleven infants), teachers (for Andrea and Paola), and a cook (appropriately called Lucia the Fat).[83] The ledgers of Niccolò and Alvise provide another glimpse into a busy and ever-changing patrician household.

From the next generation, account books survive for two of Niccolò's four sons (and Andrea's grandsons), Giovanni Alvise and Andrea.[84] Giovanni Alvise's books include entries from the years 1496–1528, while those of Andrea cover the period 1517–28. Giovanni Alvise married in 1518. His wife gave birth to two sons, one in 1519, the other in 1522, but the second son died two and one-half years later. Giovanni Alvise moved out of the family palace and established himself in a separate residence in the parish of Sant'Agnese. Much of his energy was spent in pursuit of political office.[85]

During the years 1501 to 1518 Giovanni Alvise was aided by a male servant called Zorzi Turcho. He referred to him at times as "mio schiavo" and at other times as "Zorzi fante." The account for Zorzi ends in 1518, the same year that accounts begin for Giovanni Alvise's wife.[86] Perhaps Zorzi was manumitted as part of the wedding festivities. Curiously, after his departure there is no mention of other male servants.[87]

Both before and after his marriage Giovanni Alvise employed a number of female servants. Over thirty serving women came through his household between 1506 and 1528. Payments were recorded as well for six wet nurses.[88] This independent household, consisting of Giovanni Alvise, his wife, and, from 1524 on, one son, regularly employed one or two female servants.

The final set of books belonged to Antonio Barbarigo, son of Giovanni Alvise and great-grandson of Andrea the merchant. These registers, including two journals, a ledger, and several special account books, cover the years 1537 to 1582.[89] Antonio was born in 1519, and in 1552 he married Elena Marcello, who brought him a dowry of four thousand ducats. The couple remained childless. In 1565 Antonio abandoned the house his father had bought in Sant'Agnese and returned to the traditional family center at San Barnaba. In addition, he sold off the last Cretan estate still in the family's hands and purchased more land on the terraferma. In many ways, Antonio was as typical of his generation as his great-grandfather had been of his. He made no investments in international commerce, preferring instead to put his money in real estate and government bonds. As Lane noted, "With this representative of the fourth generation the shift from maritime to territorial interest was completed."[90]

Like Lorenzo Priuli, Antonio Barbarigo calculated yearly living expenses and recorded them in his books on the last day of the year, 28 February. In most years he simply listed a figure for "salarii de servitori e massere," but in two years (1559mv and 1560mv) he listed the servants. The first year he listed nine servants, seven of whom were men. These included three *servitori di pope* (Andrea da Murano, Isepo, and Zuane di Martin) and two *servitori di mezo* (Bortolomeo da Sacile and Bortolomeo da Lendinara). The seventh male employee was a certain Ludovico, steward of Barbarigo's estates near Padua. In addition, there were two massere, Catarina da Vicenza and Diamante.[91]

The following year, Barbarigo listed only five servants, three men and two women. He paid two servitori di mezo (Piero da Sibenico and Gratiadio da Salò) and a certain Rado da Custoza, as well as the massere Maria da Pordenone and Catarina da Vicenza.[92] The turnover of servants is noteworthy; only Catarina had been in his employ a year before. The decline in numbers can probably be attributed to the natural turnover in servants during the course of the year. That is, it is unlikely that Antonio ever employed nine servants simultaneously; rather, during the course of the year a total of nine servants were in his employ. In 1569 Barbarigo again appears to have employed five servants, two male gondoliers and three female housekeepers.[93]

The Barbarigo family account books covering most of the fifteenth and sixteenth centuries suggest an evolution in servant-keeping practices as the family shifted from being entrepreneurs to rentiers. First, it appears that the ratio of servants to masters increased slightly. While Andrea Barbarigo, his wife, and two sons got by with three slaves (and various wet nurses), his great-grandson, who was childless, needed no fewer than five servants.[94] Second, there was a steady shift away from slaves to free labor. Andrea Barbarigo had relied almost exclusively on slave labor, and his grandson Giovanni Alvise had a slave attendant, Zorzi Turcho; however, there is no evidence that Antonio utilized the services of slaves. Third, during the fifteenth and sixteenth centuries the ratio of male to female servants increased. Antonio's accounts are the first in which the distinction between the servitori di pope and the servitori di mezo appears (indicating the use of more than one gondolier), and he was the first adult male of the family to be served consistently by two men. The Venetian patricians' new consciousness of status, illustrated in part by their turn to landed estates, demanded a larger and more masculine staff. It is not coincidental that the new legislative concern with male servants explored in chapter 2 occurred during the lifetime of Antonio Barbarigo. Although the Barbarigo account books provide information for only one family, they are suggestive of trends occurring in the upper ranks of the Venetian patriciate as a whole.

Before we turn to an examination of non-noble households, a brief consideration of servant housing is in order. The living arrangements for servants were as varied as the households in which they served. Some servants did not actually live with their masters, but found accommodations elsewhere and came daily to serve. This practice was probably more common for male than for female servants, especially gondoliers.[95] For example, in one large tenement owned by nobleman Francesco Bernardo in the parish of Santa Maria Maggiore there were twelve "houses" [case] and five "apartments" [mezadi], rented for twelve to fourteen ducats. The tenants in the five mezadi included a servant named Paolo, two boatmen named Matteo and Santo, a boatman's widow, and a certain Francesco di Andrea.[96] In 1531 noblewoman Marina Barbaro sold to her brother Zaccaria a "little house" [domunculam] in which the boatman Luca della Braza had lived.[97] Zuan Simon Donà rented a small house attached to his own to his servant Menego for six ducats a year.[98] And Pietro Bembo listed in his *decima* (tax declaration) of 1582 a house valued at fifty ducats that included "some storerooms and little houses underneath for porters and similar types—all of it most old and falling apart."[99] Parish registers too indicate that servants sometimes found separate housing.[100]

Some servants got use of houses or apartments as part of their terms of employment or as testamentary legacies. Marina Mocenigo made such provisions for Maria, her son Pietro's wet nurse. She requested that Maria be supplied with one of the "little houses" [domibus parvis] owned by her or by her husband, Lazzaro.[101] Bernardo da Molin granted his slave Caterina the use of a "domum parvam" for eight years; the house had formerly been inhabited by Molin's slave Valens.[102] And Diana Michiel bequeathed use of a "caseta" in her courtyard to her maid Marina for life.[103]

Other servants lived in the palace or house proper. Mezzanines and garrets, the small floors tucked between and above the main floors of palaces, were commonly used for servants' quarters.[104] The 1603 inventory for Palazzo Dolfin, designed by Jacopo Sansovino, refers to two servants' "mezadi" located next to the room used to store firewood.[105] Included in the 1561 inventory of the merchant Pierantonio Gentili's house was a mezzanine "where the boy slept" [dove dormiva il garzon].[106] In his will of 1536 Girolamo Dolfin spoke of a room "on the ground floor" [à pe pian] used by his servant Iacomo da Correzzo.[107] And in Marino Contarini's Cà d'Oro, servants were to be housed in a ground-floor room.[108]

In other instances servants did not have separate rooms but were accommodated as necessity required. A 1569 inventory of a house rented by nobleman Paolo Malipiero refers not only to a "camera de servitori" and a "caseta del barchariol" but also to two sawhorses or benches in the dining room "for the bed of the housekeeper."[109] Often servants' beds were extremely simple and could be assembled and disassembled quickly. Margarita from Mantua, the former housemaid of Alvise Negro, asked that the "bedframe on which I sleep with a sack of straw" [la Cariola in la qual dormo con el sacco de paia] be given to some poor girl as a pious bequest.[110]

As noted in chapter 1, Giacomo Lanteri advised that servants be relegated to the "most abject part of the house," hidden from the view of visitors.[111] Although this was advice masters wished to follow, many were unable to do so as the realities of family life challenged the ideal constructs of architects and theorists.

## The *cittadino* Household

Patricians were by no means the only Venetians to employ domestic servants. Service extended to all levels of society, including the very lowest. Exploring the place and role of servants in non-noble households enables us to see the various uses to which servants were put and to gain a better understanding of the social significance of servant keeping.

The cittadini constituted a distinct status group in Venetian society immediately below the nobility. There were two categories of cittadini: *cittadini originarii,* who enjoyed citizen status as a birthright, and *cittadini de intus et de extra,* who petitioned for and received the privileges of Venetian citizenship. Citizens enjoyed a monopoly over many positions in the chancery, including the post of grand chancellor, and enjoyed social prestige as rectors of the most prestigious confraternities in the city, the *scuole grandi*. The cittadini were closely linked to patricians by a variety of kinship, friendship, and patronage ties.[112]

The most important cittadino was the grand chancellor, whom Gasparo Contarini dubbed "the prince of the common people."[113] Elected for life, he had two primary responsibilities: to supervise the chancery and to officiate at meetings of the most important state councils. Around 1500 his salary was three hundred ducats per year, and electoral competition for the office was intense.[114] To date no household account books for a grand chancellor have come to light, but at least one grand chancellor's household can be glimpsed through the *status animarum* (status of souls) records maintained by the parish clergy at the end of the sixteenth century. In 1593 the parish priest of San Giovanni Novo surveyed and recorded the inhabitants of his parish. Among the residents was Grand Chancellor Andrea Surian, who lived in the Michiel palace. Surian headed an unusually large household, with twenty-four members, including his widowed daughter-in-law, eight children ranging from adults to a two-year-old, a certain Piero Basalu, described as a "parente," and the priest Giovanni Simbaldi. Twelve of the household's twenty-four members were servants, four male servants and eight female servants. Unfortunately, the priest did not identify the tasks these servants performed; he simply referred to the men as "servitori" and the women as "massere." Nonetheless, we can see that at the end of the sixteenth century the household of a grand chancellor, the most important citizen of Venice, could rival in size the households of the greatest patricians.[115]

A very different picture of a cittadino household emerges from the account book of Agostino Spinelli, whose household was much more modest. Various members of the Spinelli family held government secretariats, one was the grand chancellor of Candia, another secretary of the Senate.[116] In 1567 Agostino married Angela Lupini, who brought him a dowry valued at twelve hundred ducats, including two baker's shops. This was a second marriage for both, for Agostino had been married to a certain Polissena, and Angela had earlier been the wife of Zuane di Comin, a soap seller from the parish of San Pantalon. Both Spinelli and his wife came from prosperous, if not especially wealthy, families. Spinelli had no children by either of his wives, so he bequeathed the bulk of his estate to his nephews.[117]

Spinelli's account book for the period 1566–93 shows that at any particular time he and his wife were served by one female domestic.[118] The accounts suggest that Spinelli was especially solicitous of his servants, and perhaps for this reason they tended to remain in his employ for fairly long periods of time. During the twenty-seven years for which records survive, only five female servants passed through his household.

The first was a certain donna Agatha Furlana, who contracted with him in December 1566 to work for five ducats a year. In her will Spinelli's first wife, Polissena, asked that twenty-five ducats be given to a certain Gratia to help her marry and that if Gratia could not be located, the money be used to marry some other "poor and respectable girl." In 1567 Spinelli set out to fulfill the terms of the bequest but was unable to locate Gratia, so he promised ten ducats to Agatha, the daughter of boatman Domenego Trevisan, and the other fifteen ducats to Maddalena, the daughter of his servant Agatha, with the proviso that the girl's mother "continue to serve me faithfully." Agatha remained in his service only until 15 September 1570, but even after that date Spinelli continued to make loans to her and her daughter.[119]

Agatha was replaced three days after her departure by Veronica, daughter of a boatman. With the help of Spinelli and his friends, she married; and in 1572 yet another massara, Maddalena Feltrina, joined his service. Maddalena remained with Spinelli until her death in January 1578.[120] During her final illness, Spinelli took good care of her, procuring chickens and eggs for her to eat, medicines of various sorts, and the services of a barber, who bled her. When she died, two women kept vigil over her body, and she was given a proper burial at the convent of Sant'Alvise, performed by a priest and a sacristan.[121] In April 1578,

Lucieta Trevisana joined Spinelli's service, and she remained until July 1583.[122] The last of his servants was Gironima da Gorizia, who contracted in September 1583 at eight ducats and a pair of clogs per year.[123] On Easter Sunday 1586, as a reward for her excellent service, Spinelli promised Gironima twenty-five ducats beyond her salary to help her marry, similar to the bequest his first wife Polissena had made to Gratia. She was still in his service when the account book ends; and a receipt written on the original promissory note indicates that Paolo Cimador, Gironima's new husband, took possession of the twenty-five ducats on 26 September 1598, one year after Spinelli's death.[124]

This account of Spinelli's household calls for two comments. First, the absence of male servants is notable. Unlike the patricians or even Grand Chancellor Surian, Spinelli never employed a male servant. In all likelihood, he did not have enough income and prestige to require the services of a manservant. Second, the accounts illustrate that a master who was solicitous of his servants was himself rewarded with their loyalty and long service.[125] By treating his servants well, as indicated by his treatment of Maddalena Feltrina, Spinelli spared himself the arduous task of continually finding and training new servants. It is tempting to speculate that his solicitude grew out of deep-felt religious convictions, for Spinelli named the governors of the hospital of San Zanipolo and the Incurabili as his executors, and in a codicil to his will he reinstated a nephew whom he had earlier disinherited, "knowing that it is the duty of a Christian to repay evil with good."[126]

A very different kind of cittadino household was that of Julia Lombardo, one of the city's renowned courtesans. Contemporaries liked to believe that "La Lombardo" was of peasant origin, but in fact her father, Zuane Leoncini, was a draper from Lombardy and her grandfather, a Venetian physician. In a document dated 1559, Julia's invalid sister Angelica described herself as a "cittadina vinetiana" and used the honorific title *magnifica*, usually associated with the cittadini.[127]

The two sisters, the courtesan and the invalid, maintained a joint household and were buried together in a tomb adorned with the family crest in the church of San Francesco della Vigna. Their house, located in the parish of Santa Maria Nova, contained three bedrooms, a receiving room, a kitchen, an attic, a pantry, and other rooms, all quite well furnished. In addition, Julia owned property on the terraferma, including 154 *campi* at Brenta Secco.[128]

When she prepared her tax declaration in 1542, Julia naturally emphasized her liabilities rather than her assets, including the need to prepare for her own future and to sustain her sister with "two women servants who have always cared for her" [con due massere che sempre lhan governata].[129] Six weeks later Julia was dead, but for the next twenty-five years Angelica continued to live with the aid of two servants. In her own will, dated March 1569, she remembered Julia, the daughter of her servant Lucia, as well as Ursetta, her "garzona di casa";[130] Ursetta had come into Angelica's service just ten months earlier.[131] Angelica also employed a steward for her property at Brenta Secco.[132]

Julia Lombardo, the "somtuosa meretrize," was somewhat unusual in that she enjoyed citizen status and had the responsibility of caring for her sister; but it was not uncommon for courtesans, the elite among Venetian prostitutes, to have female servants.[133] Indeed, the practice of servant keeping by prostitutes became an object of government concern and regulation. Rightly or wrongly, the government feared that servant girls would be lured or forced into the profession by their mistresses. Accordingly, in 1539 the Ten and the *proveditori alla sanità*, the city's health commissioners, issued orders forbidding courtesans or prostitutes, as well as procuresses, from hiring female servants under thirty years of age. The penalty for contravention was two months in jail and a fine of two hundred lire di piccoli. To encourage enforcement, the authorities promised that servants who reported their mistresses would receive their entire salary as well as half of the fine; a servant who failed to denounce her mistress could face whipping, banishment, and a twenty-five-lire fine.[134]

The proveditori also worried that servant women were renting rooms from procuresses, becoming corrupted by them, and then spreading the corruption to households of "persons of honest life and station" [persone de bona vita et conditione]. To prevent this, the authorities forbade anyone from letting rooms to wet nurses, servants, or immigrant women without a special license from the proveditori alla sanità. The government feared that young servant girls housed in the homes of prostitutes would become apprentices in the trade.[135]

The government showed similar concern for servants employed by Jews in the Ghetto. Servants or porters who wished to be employed in the Jewish quarter had to obtain special permission to do so from the *ufficiali al cattaver*, officials who had jurisdiction over the Jews. Christian servants were forbidden to eat, drink, or sleep in the homes of their employers, and generally licenses were granted to mature men and women. According to Brian Pullan, these regulations were designed to reduce close contact between Christians and Jews, especially among the young, who were perceived as especially impressionable and vulnerable.[136]

The Surian, Spinelli, and Lombardo households indicate that among the wealthiest and most prestigious non-noble families there were a variety of servant-keeping styles. At least some powerful cittadino men, like Andrea Surian, imitated nobles and were assisted by large households with male servants. More modest cittadini, like Agostino Spinelli, either could not afford or did not feel the need for the assistance of menservants and contented themselves with that of serving women. Finally, courtesans, like Julia Lombardo, employed female servants, a practice that especially disturbed the government, which feared that young girls would be drawn into the profession by their mistresses.

## The Artisan Household

Service permeated all aspects of Venetian society and encompassed a bewildering variety of tasks and ranks. Yet nowhere were the lines surrounding service more blurry than in artisan households, where the roles of servants, apprentices, salaried assistants, and even kin were indistinctly drawn. The households of three well-known Venetian painters provide illustrative examples of servant keeping in popolano households.

Iacobello del Fiore (d. 1439) was the foremost practitioner in Venice of the International Gothic style of painting. Iacobello's father, Francesco, himself had been a painter of some distinction and a leading figure in the painters' guild. Iacobello was selected as the official painter of the Ducal Palace, and he was elected as gastaldus, or warden, of the painters' guild in 1415. He married twice; his first wife brought him a dowry of two hundred ducats, his second wife the larger sum of five hundred ducats. And according to his will, Iacobello owned two female slaves. He had no sons but adopted two boys, Ercole and Matteo.[137]

Adoption was a fairly common practice in fifteenth- and sixteenth-century Venice, but determining what exactly it signified is difficult. In some instances at least, adopted children were considered little more than servants; indeed, when a certain Lucia acknowledged receipt of a bequest left to her by the mason Bartolomeo, she referred to herself as his "servant or adopted daughter" [serviciales sive filia adoptiva].[138] And in 1467 the state attorneys prosecuted a barber for violating his "pedisequa" or "filia adoptiva" Eufemia da Pola.[139]

Parents or kinsmen put children up for adoption when they could not support them themselves. In 1409 the widow Bona da Istria gave up her three-year-old daughter Lucia to Philippo da Polonia, a cook at the Fondaco dei Tedeschi, the German merchants' warehouse. Philippo agreed to treat Lucia as his own child and to marry her off as best he could. The contract stipulated that if Lucia left Philippo, her mother was to reimburse him for his expenses.[140] The tailor Niccolò allowed Caterina, widow of Antonio di Mercatello, to adopt his sister Lucia. Like Bona da Istria, he agreed to reimburse the adoptive parent if the child left. Furthermore, he agreed that if he were able to recover funds left to Lucia by a "certain lady of Corfino," he would add them to his sister's dowry fund.[141] Notarial records contain dowry receipts in which girls were married off by their adoptive parents, almost certainly as a reward for years of service.[142] The story of three-year-old Lucia had a happy ending. In 1420 the cook Philippo da Polonia married her to Giorgio da Scutari with a dowry of one hundred ducats.[143] Parents who could not afford to take care of their children themselves sometimes put them up for adoption as a way of assuring their future well-being.

At least one extant adoption agreement for a boy closely resembles an apprenticeship contract. In 1415 Helena, widow of Marco Morosini from Capodistria, gave up her seven-year-old son to master Giovanni da Francia, a furrier in the parish of Santa Maria Formosa. Francesco agreed to treat the boy as his own, to send him to school, and to teach him his craft. He also agreed to clothe him according to his means. As in the agreements for girls, the mother agreed that if the boy left his adoptive father's service, she would reimburse him for his expenses.[144] On one level at least, adopting children was considered as little more than a means of acquiring service or labor.

Yet adoption was not only a means of securing extra hands; it could also be a charitable and pious act. One linguistic indication of this is that the expressions for "adopted" and "spiritual" children, *figliuoli d'anima,* could be used interchangeably.[145] Through the adoption of a child, a spiritual bond was created. Adoption was also used to cement emotional bonds that had already developed between masters and servants. According to her will dated 1417, Lucia, widow of Iacobello Virilis, adopted her slave Natasha.[146] And in 1527 Giovanni Vittore Belino, who had no sons, adopted his twenty-five-year-old servant Giovanni as a reward for the loyalty and service Giovanni had rendered over the past nine years.[147]

The practice of adopting or at least supporting orphans housed in the city's foundling hospitals grew increasingly popular during the fifteenth and sixteenth centuries.[148] Orphans could be taken into the household proper. Marieta, daughter of a sailor, was an "arlieva" in the home of Francesco Trevisan, and a certain Diana was raised in the Contarini household.[149] Elisabeta, daughter of a silk-maker, was raised in the household of noblewoman Laura Gritti. When she married in 1567, Gritti supplied her with a dowry "because she was a good, loyal, and honest young girl in her house." In return, Elisabeta agreed not to sue Gritti for a salary, suggesting again that adoption and service were very closely connected.[150]

It is difficult to unravel the motives behind boatman Agostino Buranello and his wife Hippolita's adoption of an orphan child. Hippolita had been nursing the child at the behest of the girl's brother-in-law and guardian. According to the contract, Buranello and his wife, who were childless, had grown quite attached to the baby. Therefore, "moved by the zeal of piety and for the glory of

God," they wished to raise the infant as their "adopted daughter" [fiola d'anima et adottiva]. The guardian agreed, stating that he would not take the child back without just cause and that if he did do so, the couple would be compensated for their trouble at the rate of twelve scudi per year. The child's paternal inheritance was to be invested and used to support her eventual marriage; if she were to die before marrying, however, then it was to go to her adoptive parents. The brother-in-law was to keep the accounts, but he agreed to show them to Buranello and his wife on request.[151] Love, piety, and profit all seem to have figured in the agreement to adopt the infant orphan Lucia.

Returning to Iacobello del Fiore, given the fragmentary nature of the sources, it is impossible to say with certitude what motivated him to adopt two sons. Perhaps he did so in order to acquire service or apprentices or as an act of charity and piety. Another possibility is that since he was childless, Iacobello wanted to perpetuate his name and the artistic tradition established by him and his father. We know that in his will dated 1439 he bequeathed his drawings and pigments to Ercole in case he should wish to practice the painter's trade.[152] Whatever his motives, the phenomenon of adoption illustrates the flexible nature of kinship ties, especially among the popolani, and the often hazy distinctions between kinship, apprenticeship, and servanthood.

Thanks to the fortuitous survival of his account book, a much more complete picture emerges of the life of the painter Lorenzo Lotto (c. 1480–1556). Lotto was born in Venice but spent time in Treviso, Recanati, Rome, and Bergamo before returning to Venice for an extended stay from 1525 to 1549, a stay interrupted by some time in Treviso. In 1549 Lotto left Venice for good and spent his final years in the Marches.[153]

Lotto never married, never owned a house, and, according to his will, had few close relatives.[154] He adopted a variety of living arrangements. In 1545 he lived in the parish of San Matteo di Rialto, where he shared a house owned by Giovanni dalla Volta with a tailor named Battista. In 1547 he moved to the Ruga dei Botteri, and in 1548 he was splitting the annual rent for a house in San Giovanni Degolado with a godson.[155] For a time in the early 1540s he lived in Treviso in the large household of his *compare* Giovanni dal Saon. He had been encouraged to go there by a mutual friend, the jeweler Antonio Carpan, since by Lotto's own admission he was "lacking adequate care and was mentally distressed" [senza fidel governo et molto inquieto dela mente].[156] Saon did not want payment for the hospitality, since Lotto intended to instruct his sons. Nonetheless, Lotto calculated that his maintenance would cost Saon about twenty-five ducats per year. On his departure the painter recorded that he owed Saon sixty ducats as recompense for the expenses he had incurred caring for Lotto.[157]

Back in Venice and on his own again, Lotto hired the services of a house-keeper. In March 1546 he agreed to take on donna Lucia, whom he identified, even though she was more than sixty years old, as "raised in the Venier household" [alevata in chà Venier]. Her salary was to be four ducats a year, and she was to do some spinning. But Lotto had to let her go within a month of her arrival, since she could not perform her duties on account of her advanced age.[158] In August he found a new female servant, Maria da Montagnana, who also received a salary of four ducats per year. She remained in his service until October 1547.[159] In the autumn, Lotto became ill and stayed for a while in the household of Bartolomeo Carpan, brother of Antonio, a jeweler at Rialto. In his accounts, Lotto recorded that he promised four ducats to help marry Carpan's servant Menega, "who served me during my illness in the house of the said sir Bartolomeo."[160]

In January 1547 Lotto took on as an *disepolo* (apprentice) Piero da Venezia, son of the widow Orsola of San Giovanni in Bragora. The agreement registered with the giustizieri vecchi was for three years, and Lotto was obliged to maintain the boy as well as pay him fifteen ducats in three installments, four the first year, five the second, and six the third. In September 1548 Lotto dismissed the boy because they could not get along.[161] In 1549, the year he left Venice for good, Lotto hired another apprentice, Paolo Bressano, son of a medical doctor from Brescia. Paolo accompanied him to Ancona.[162]

Upon arriving in Ancona, Lotto employed several apprentices. In July he hired Giovanni Matteo Pozzo, who remained only until November.[163] In September he added Marco da Fiume, son of the late Zorzi Catalenich, aged fourteen. According to Lotto, he hired Marco "for household service, to pick up and keep [the house] clean, and to cook and do the shopping, and to learn my craft." The agreement was to last six years. During the first three years the majority of Marco's time was to be spent in Lotto's personal service; during the second three years he was to concentrate on learning the trade. At the end of the time Lotto was to give him ten scudi, but Lotto discharged him in December of the first year.[164] In the same month, Ercole della Rocha Contrada became Lotto's next apprentice. According to the terms of their agreement, Lotto would not pay the boy a salary, but he would feed, clothe, and shoe him. In return, Ercole was to perform "all household tasks" [ogni servimento de casa], as well as those associated with painting. At the end of the year they renewed the pact for three years, but Ercole was let go in November 1552.[165] In 1551 Lotto hired Ercole's grandmother Caterina della Rocha Contrada as his housekeeper at an initial salary of four scudi per year.[166]

During the final four years of his life Lotto continued to be assisted by a succession of young men, including Antonuzo "pittor de Jesi"; Paolo, son of a Lombard mason; and Bastian, son of the late painter "mastro Baptista da San Jenese." Battista was "to serve me in all the duties of a servant and to learn the craft," but like so many others, he left after just three days, taking with him a variety of items.[167] Lotto spent the final two years of his life as an oblate in the Santa Casa di Loreto.

Art historians who have studied Lotto have made much of his difficult personality.[168] Certainly his own admission of distress, together with the frequent departure of his apprentices under less than amicable circumstances, suggests that he could be a difficult taskmaster. But the disagreements with apprentices should not necessarily be taken as evidence of instability. Many other artists had difficult relations with apprentices. Benvenuto Cellini's autobiography is filled with disagreements between the master and his assistants and with a bewildering passage of artisans from shop to shop.[169] Given the freewheeling and flexible family life of the popolo, this is not altogether surprising.

Lotto is a good example of a rootless artisan who commanded some fairly important and moderately lucrative commissions. Single and childless, he nevertheless required (and could afford) the services of female housekeepers, although two of them, Caterina della Rocha Contrada and Lucia, were older women who may have had difficulty finding employment elsewhere. Lotto also employed apprentices and assistants, whom he expected not only to assist him in the trade but also to meet his personal needs, that is, to serve him.

The peripatetic life of Lorenzo Lotto stands in stark contrast with that of a painter of the next generation, Giacomo Negretti, better known as Palma il Giovane (1548–1628), to distinguish him from his uncle Palma il Vecchio (c. 1480–1528). Palma, who almost certainly apprenticed in Titian's workshop, was a leading exponent of Venetian Mannerism. He worked mainly in Venice, where he completed several major works during the redecoration of the Ducal Palace.[170]

Around 1582 Palma married Andriana Fondra, and in the 1590s his household included thirteen persons: Palma and Andriana, their seven children (three boys, Marcio, Belisario, and Settimio; and four girls, Giulia [or Iulia], Verginia, Cretia [or Cleria], and Antonila), Palma's sister Ortensia, and three servants (two massare, Zuana and Mattia, and one servitor, Iseppo).[171] It is impossible to say exactly what Iseppo's role was. He may have been an apprentice or a servant, although generally the term *garzon* was used to indicate an apprentice. Regardless, this large and prosperous artisan household had three employees.

By the time Palma drafted his will, in April 1627, his family had been decimated. Andriana had died in 1605, and the only children mentioned in the will are his daughters Giulia and Cretia. To Cretia and her son, Palma bequeathed three thousand ducats. He expressed the hope that his grandson would follow in the profession and that he would take the name Palma as a way of memorializing both himself and Palma il Vecchio. Palma also bequeathed two canvases, thirty drawings, and one hundred ducats to his "allievo" Giacomo Alborello. The term *allievo* is very ambiguous; it may simply indicate that Alborello was an apprentice, or it may signify an orphan who had been adopted and raised in the household. Palma spoke of the love and "service" [servitù] Giacomo had shown him for some time and lamented that he could not better demonstrate "the great love that I feel for him."[172] The painter also remembered a certain Maria Miona with one hundred ducats. Apparently, Maria was a servant in the household, in return for whose service Palma maintained her son and taught him the painter's craft.[173] This relationship is reminiscent of that of Lotto's servant and apprentice in Ancona.

It is difficult to say how representative of their fellow painters, much less of the entire artisan population of Venice, Iacobello del Fiore, Lorenzo Lotto, and Palma il Giovane were. Certainly Iacobello and Palma were well off by popolano standards and had connections to some of the most powerful members of Venetian society.[174] The question is further complicated by the uncertain position and status of artists in the sixteenth century, a subject of much debate at the time.[175]

But given the workshop organization of artistic production, the servant-keeping practices of Iacobello, Lotto, and Palma il Giovane are probably illustrative of their popolano counterparts, that is, of those members of the popolo who were wealthy enough to employ servants.[176] What emerges from this analysis of their households is that the lines separating masters from servants were much less clearly demarcated than among patricians and even among cittadini. Apprentices performed many of the tasks associated with servants, servants were drawn from the same status groups (and in some instances from the same kinship groups) as apprentices, and through either formal or informal adoption apprentices and servants became part of the kinship circle. In popolano households, going into service was a way to survive, and acquiring service was a way to preserve what had been attained.

The overlapping functions of apprentices and servants, the mixture of motives leading to the adoption and hiring of young people, and the often ill-defined boundaries of popolano families could also lead to misunderstandings and legal entanglements. To guard against financial liabilities, certain masters or benefactors required those they assisted to certify that no financial obligation was involved. For instance, when in March 1561 Domenego Taia agreed to take into his home Pasqua, the eleven-year-old daughter of his massera Altina, he made Altina agree to a notarized statement that the girl would never seek a salary for the time she stayed in his home. Instead Altina certified that Taia took the girl in as an act of charity and courtesy.[177] In 1564 Marin Valentin had his step-daughter, whom he had kept in his home for six years, agree that she would not seek any money from him "on account of the salary she could ask of him for the service she performed in his house while she lived there."[178] And when in 1566 Bartolomeo di Francesco Patento and Isabella, who had had a child together out of wedlock, decided to separate "in order no longer to live in sin and to be able to live more freely as Christians" [per non star piu in peccato, et per poter piu liberamente viver da Christiani), they agreed that Bartolomeo would keep the child and pay Isabella twenty-three ducats in cash and kind. In return, Isabella declared herself satisfied and agreed that she would not sue him for compensation for housekeeping or wet-nursing services.[179]

The flexible, ill-defined attitude of artisans toward service may be explained in part by the fact that service in one form or another constituted an essential aspect of the artisan's education. Whether as apprentices or as actual domestic servants, most popolano men and women spent some part of their youth in service to others. Serving was part of learning, as the Tuscan Paolo da Certaldo reminded readers in his *Libro di buoni costumi:* "One cannot be a master who has not first been an apprentice: do not disdain serving in the craft you wish to practice, for by serving, one learns."[180] Like the ambiguous term *allievo,* the terms *famulus* and *discipulus* could be used interchangeably or in tandem.[181]

Service could even extend to the very lowest levels of society. For brief periods of time, perhaps after childbirth, during illness, or as residents of hospitals, even servants enjoyed the assistance of others. For instance, when she drafted her will in 1426, Cita, a former servant of noblewoman Clara Sanuto, asked that one ducat be given to "the one who will serve me in my illness."[182] Giorgio, a servant in the household of Niccolò Foscari, left several bequests to present and former servants of the Foscari household, including four ducats to "Maddalena, who served me."[183] When Lucia, wife of a boatman, drafted her will in 1408, she left a couple of items of clothing to Uliana, "who serves me."[184] And in her will dated 1540, another Lucia, a servant in the home of Matteo Armelino, left all her savings and salary, amounting to forty-six ducats, to Armelino's daughter Pelegrina, who nursed her while she was ill.[185] Among the very poor, it is often difficult to determine where assisting friends ended and providing service began.

Servant keeping extended throughout Venetian society, from the princely household of the doge to the humble homes of artisans. Yet the practices and purposes of servant keeping varied considerably with wealth and status. Patricians kept servants not only to facilitate domestic living but also as symbols of their status. Among patrician men, maintaining male servants was seen as a necessary sign of noble rank. Cittadini also utilized servants and perhaps tried to emulate and imitate patricians. Among the popolo, servants fit naturally and somewhat indistinguishably into the patterns of work associated with artisanal production. Finally, the poor enjoyed service as acts of charity or friendship. Domestic service was thus a phenomenon that in one way or another seems to have touched the lives of nearly all Venetians.

## Toward a Quantitative Analysis of Servant Keeping: Census Data

The foregoing exposition of households attempts to convey the extent of domestic service in Venetian society, the various forms that service took, and variations in servant keeping among different status groups. What it does not do is provide a means of gauging whether the practices observed in particular households were typical. For the later years of the sixteenth century and the seventeenth century, however, records exist that provide some tentative means of assessing quantitatively the extent to which practices and customs observed in particular households were characteristic of others as well.

Although the Venetian republic was among the first European states to compile information about its population for tax and military purposes, no complete census data survive from before the sixteenth century.[186] And data that survive from after that date present a number of interpretive problems. Table 3.1 shows the population of the city during the sixteenth century and first half of the seventeenth century.

These figures show that the city's population reached one peak during the third quarter of the sixteenth century and was then decimated by the plague of 1575–77. Estimates of the city's population before the plague range from the 195,863 inhabitants suggested by Aldo Contento to the 120,000 posited by Rocco Benedetti.[187] Andrea Zannini has recently uncovered some statistics that indicate that the population made a dramatic recovery by the first decade of the seventeenth century, when the city reached another peak, of 188,970 souls.[188] This

Table 3.1
Venetian Census Figures, 1509–1642

| Year | Population | Year | Population |
|------|-----------|------|-----------|
| 1509 | 115,000 | 1586 | 148,637 |
| 1540 | 129,971 | 1607 | 188,970 |
| 1552 | 158,069 | 1624 | 141,625 |
| 1555 | 159,467 | 1633 | 102,243 |
| 1563 | 168,627 | 1642 | 120,307 |
| 1581 | 134,871 | | |

*Source:* Beltrami, 59; Zannini, "Censimento," 108.

increase in turn was cut off by the devastating plague of 1630–31, which it has been calculated claimed at least 30 percent of the populace.

None of the population figures for the first half of the sixteenth century are broken down into social categories, hence it is impossible to calculate how many servants there were and what percentage of the total population they constituted. The first data that include a category for servants are those of 1563.[189] The city's population was divided into five general categories—nobles, cittadini, artisans, the poor, and the religious, including Jews—and was further subdivided into men, women, boys, girls, male servants, female servants, and other categories. Table 3.2 presents the 1563 census data.

The data in table 3.2 present a number of interpretive problems. Most obviously, only the categories for nobles and cittadini contain subcategories for servants. Writing almost a century ago, Aldo Contento argued that the lack of a subcategory for servants among artisans was easily explained, so easily explained, in fact, that he did not elaborate. Presumably he assumed that artisans did not employ servants, an untenable conclusion in light of the preceding discussion.[190]

Table 3.2
Population of Venice, 1563

| *Nobles* | | *Artisans* | |
|---|---|---|---|
| Men | 2,435 | Men | 41,244 |
| Women | 2,257 | Women | 36,695 |
| Boys | 1,487 | Boys | 27,045 |
| Girls | 1,418 | Girls | 22,762 |
| Male servants | 2,877 | Total | 127,746 |
| Female servants | 4,696 | | |
| Total | 15,170 | *Poor, Beggars* | |
| | | Men | 251 |
| *Cittadini* | | Women | 181 |
| Men | 4,714 | Boys | 53 |
| Women | 4,120 | Girls | 54 |
| Boys | 2,550 | Total | 539 |
| Girls | 2,220 | | |
| Male servants | 1,797 | *Religious* | |
| Female servants | 3,538 | Friars | 1,196 |
| Total | 18,939 | Nuns | 2,134 |
| | | Hospital inmates | 1,479 |
| | | Jews | 1,424 |
| | | Total | 6,233 |

*Source:* MCC, Ms. Donà dalle Rose, 53, fol. 157r.

One possible explanation is that the sixteenth-century compilers and recorders of the data simply could not conceive of servants in artisans households if, as suggested earlier, servant keeping was closely linked to their notions of status. This impression is born out by some seventeenth-century census forms preserved in the Museo Civico Correr. The office of the Sanità, the health commissioners who were in charge of compiling census data, provided instructions for the parish priests, who were to survey their parishioners. The commissioners specifically instructed the census takers to place a "0" in the box for "male servants" [servitori] in artisan households.[191] Some of the completed forms show that the priests did not read the instructions carefully, for they listed servants in artisan households. They then had to go back and change the entries to accord with the instructions.[192] But this still would not explain the absence in the 1563 census data of servants among the religious, many of whom did employ domestics. Even with these difficulties, the data are informative.

According to the data, in 1563 there were 12,908 servants in Venice, comprising 7.65 percent of the city's total population of 168,627 inhabitants. Female servants outnumbered men 8,234 to 4,674. Nobles, numbering 7,597 souls and making up 4.5 percent of the population, maintained 7,573 servants, whereas cittadini (13,604 souls), constituting 8.06 percent of the total population, kept only 5,335 servants. Put another way, the statistics show that there was virtually one servant for every noble man, woman, and child, compared with one servant for every two and a half cittadini. With regard to the gender distribution of servants, there was one male servant for every adult nobleman and two female servants for every adult noblewoman.

Censuses from the later years of the sixteenth century and the mid-seventeenth century likewise included categories for servants. Table 3.3 presents these figures, as well as, for purposes of comparison, those of 1563. These statistics show that the total number of servants declined during the latter years of the sixteenth century, as did the general population. Servants as a percentage of the total population also declined. What is more striking still is that while by 1607 the absolute number of servants had dramatically rebounded (as had the total population), servants as a percentage of the total population continued to decline. However, by 1642 the percentage of servants as part of the total population reached a new high of 8.5 percent. One possible explanation for the decline in the percentage of servants in the last third of the sixteenth century is the devastating plague of the 1570s. The precipitous decline in the population opened up job possibilities in guilds and other sectors of the economy. As a consequence, young people could find work in areas other than domestic service. What is more, the prosperity of the economy continued into the first two decades of the seven-

Table 3.3
Servant Population of Venice, 1563–1642

|      |     | Servants | | Total | Total |
|------|-----|----------|---------|----------|------------|
|      |     | Males    | Females | Servants | Population |
| 1563 | No. | 4,674    | 8,234   | 12,908   | 168,627    |
|      | %   | 2.77     | 4.88    | 7.65     | 100.00     |
| 1581 | No. | 3,722    | 5,663   | 9,385    | 134,871    |
|      | %   | 2.75     | 4.19    | 6.94     | 100.00     |
| 1586 | No. | 3,861    | 6,122   | 9,983    | 148,637    |
|      | %   | 2.59     | 4.11    | 6.70     | 100.00     |
| 1607 | No. | 3,592    | 8,560   | 12,152   | 188,970    |
|      | %   | 1.90     | 4.52    | 6.42     | 100.00     |
| 1642 | No. | 3,681    | 6,554   | 10,235   | 120,307    |
|      | %   | 3.05     | 5.44    | 8.49     | 100.00     |

*Sources:* Beltrami, 213; MCC, Ms. Donà dalle Rose, 53, fol. 157r; Zannini, "Censimento," 113–14.

teenth century.[193] By the 1630s, however, with the general depression of the Venetian economy, this was no longer the case, so that the plague of the 1630s was accompanied by a decline in the number of jobs.[194] The decline in the number of people seeking service positions in the 1570s would also help explain the heightened concern over wages expressed in the capitulary of the last years of the century, discussed in chapter 2 above. With fewer young people looking for domestic work, masters were forced to pay higher wages and tried to limit the damage by tightening wage controls.[195]

Table 3.4 presents an analysis of servants by gender. These data show that the proportion of male to female servants reached a peak in 1581, when nearly 40 percent of servants were male. The rise in the percentage of male to female servants in these years is difficult to explain, since it seems reasonable to assume that men would have been better able than women to take advantage of new nonservice job opportunities created by the plague. It may be that it took some years for the economy to recover fully. By 1607, however, when the economy was in full swing, the percentage of male servants reached a low point and then grew to nearly 36 percent in the mid-seventeenth century.[196]

Table 3.4
Gender Distribution of Servants, 1563–1642

|  | Males | | Females | |
|---|---|---|---|---|
|  | No. | % | No. | % |
| 1563 | 4,674 | 36.2 | 8,234 | 63.8 |
| 1581 | 3,722 | 39.7 | 5,663 | 60.3 |
| 1586 | 3,861 | 38.7 | 6,122 | 61.3 |
| 1607 | 3,592 | 29.6 | 8,560 | 70.4 |
| 1642 | 3,681 | 35.9 | 6,554 | 64.1 |

*Sources:* Beltrami, 213; MCC, Ms. Donà dalle Rose, 53, 157r; Zannini, "Censimento," 113–14.

Overall the census data suggest two general conclusions: first, that male servants were closely linked to noble status; and second, that the plague of 1575–77 and the economic prosperity of the first decade of the seventeenth century made servants relatively more scarce and allowed them to demand, if not always to receive, higher wages. Again, the twin uses of domestic service (in a labor relationship and as a cultural symbol) come into focus.

Although sparse, the census data deepen our understanding of the place of service in Venetian society. But there are many things that these aggregated data cannot tell us, such as the distribution of servants throughout the city and the character of Venetian households. Another group of documents, the registers of souls maintained by the parish clergy, do provide some tentative answers to these and other questions.

## *Status animarum* Records

Following the Council of Trent in the mid-sixteenth century, the Catholic Church tried to reorient the lives of its followers toward parishes and away from supraparochial institutions such as mendicant houses and confraternities. As part of this effort, it enjoined the parish clergy to keep better track of the spiritual life of their parishioners by making regular surveys of the "status of souls." The Venetian government also utilized the parish clergy as census takers.[197]

In the typical Venetian register of souls, the priest listed the inhabitants of his parish by household, beginning in a particular palace or block of apartments and proceeding through the entire parish. He recorded each inhabitant of the household and noted the condition of his or her soul, that is, whether or not the parishioner had communicated and been confirmed. Those following the Greek rite were listed as living "alla greca." Although the intention of the priests was to evaluate the spiritual condition of their parishioners, the registers can be used today to explore certain aspects of Venetian household and family life in the sixteenth century and, especially for the purposes of this study, to evaluate servant keeping.

Fifty registers of souls from the late sixteenth and early seventeenth centuries survive in the Archivio Curia Patriarcale, and there are one or two others in parish archives.[198] In this period there were approximately seventy parishes in the city. Many of the registers in the patriarchal archives are undated, but the earliest dated register is from 1584, and the latest from 1609, with the majority dated 1593 and 1594.

What follows is based on a detailed examination of four of these registers: for San Benedetto (San Benetto), 1593; San Giovanni Degolado (San Zan Degolà), 1591; San Basilio (San Basegio), 1592; and San Provolo, undated.[199] Although none of these parishes was especially large, they were located in different areas of the city. San Provolo was located in the eastern reaches of the city, beyond San Marco and fairly close to the Arsenal, the center of shipbuilding. San Benetto, in the sestiere of San Marco, was located near Rialto, the center of wholesale and retail merchandising. San Zan Degolà, in the sestiere of Santa Croce, was near the Rio Marin, an ancient center of textile production. And San Basilio, in the far reaches of the sestiere of Dorsoduro and near the fishermen's parish of San Niccolò dei Mendicoli, was an area where cargos from the mainland were delivered by *zattere* (rafts).

Table 3.5 shows the population of these four parishes, as well as the number and percentage of parishioners who were servants living in households headed by others.[200] Not surprisingly, these numbers illustrate that servants were not evenly distributed throughout the city. San Benetto, directly on the Grand Canal and near the commercial center at Rialto, had the highest percentage of servants. San Zan Degolà, which also bordered the Grand Canal, the most prized location

Table 3.5
Parish Populations and Servant Populations, 1590s

|  | San Provolo | | San Benetto | | San Zan Degolà | | San Basilio | |
|---|---|---|---|---|---|---|---|---|
| Population | No. | % | No. | % | No. | % | No. | % |
| Total | 869 | 100.00 | 504 | 100.00 | 625 | 100.00 | 1,645 | 100.00 |
| Servants | 82 | 9.43 | 94 | 18.65 | 76 | 12.16 | 109 | 6.62 |

*Source:* ACPV, CP, buste 1–3

for patrician palaces, also had a sizeable servant population. In San Provolo and especially San Basilio, which were located in more humble sections of the city, the percentages of servants were lower.[201] Generally speaking, the density of servants increased as one moved toward the centers of political and economic power, along the Grand Canal and in the zone from San Marco to Rialto.

As noted above, the priests who compiled the status animarum records organized their censuses by household. Table 3.6 shows the total number of households in each parish as well as the number and percentage of households employing one or more servants. At first glance, these figures appear to modify significantly the conclusions based upon the previous data. For although the number of servants as a percentage of the population was the highest in San Benetto, both San Zan Degolà and San Provolo had more households with at least one servant. The discrepancy may be explained by the fact that the wealthiest inhabitants of San Benetto employed a larger number of servants per household. In fact, when the total number of servants in a parish is divided by the number of households in the parish employing servants, San Benetto regains its privileged position. The average number of servants per servant-keeping household was 2.76 in San Benetto, 2.53 in San Basilio, 2.30 in San Zan Degolà, and only 1.50 in San Provolo.

The average size of households in the four parishes varied considerably. San Provolo and San Zan Degolà had an average household size of 5.1 persons and 5.2 persons, respectively, and San Benetto and San Basilio had an average of 3.4 persons per household. The average household size for all four parishes combined was 3.99 persons. There are several possible explanations for the discrepancies. One is that economic activities determined size. Many in San Basilio were immigrants; they were more likely to be living alone, thereby lowering the average household size. Another explanation is that the housing stock in particular

Table 3.6
Total Households and Servant-Keeping Households, 1590s

| Type of Households | San Provolo | | San Benetto | | San Zan Degolà | | San Basilio | |
|---|---|---|---|---|---|---|---|---|
| | No. | % | No. | % | No. | % | No. | % |
| Total households | 167 | 100.00 | 146 | 100.00 | 122 | 100.00 | 478 | 100.00 |
| With servants | 42 | 25.14 | 34 | 23.28 | 33 | 27.04 | 43 | 8.99 |

*Source:* ACPV, CP, buste 1–3.

parishes (i.e., the number and size of houses and apartments) helped determine the composition of households, as did the perceived social prestige of the parishes. Another, more likely explanation is that the parish priests were not entirely consistent in their definitions of households. This may have been especially true when they surveyed rooming houses, where many single persons boarded. For example, the priest of San Basilio several times listed in succession a number of solitary men and women, many of whom were engaged in the textile industries.[202] By contrast, the priest of San Zan Degolà often grouped together or with their employers large numbers of "homeni à mese."[203] Only an analysis of all the extant registers could provide a definitive figure for household size.

As table 3.7 shows, household size varied considerably in all four parishes. The largest household, containing twenty persons, was in the parish of San Basilio. This was the fraternal household of the noble brothers Bartolomeo and Francesco Lippomano. It comprised Bartolomeo, his wife, and three sons, one of whom was married and had three children of his own; and Bartolomeo's brother Francesco, who was not married. In addition, there were ten servants, three males and seven females, one of whom, a certain Maria, was a wet nurse.[204] The next largest household, belonging to a cittadino or perhaps a merchant, was also a fraternal one; the domestic establishment of Giovanni Battista Albinoni and his brother Battista in the parish of San Provolo contained nineteen persons. Both men were married, and between them they had eleven children. In addition, there were two "garzoni" [apprentices or shop boys] and two "massere."[205] The third largest household, that of nobleman Santo Venier from San Benetto, comprised himself, his wife, his two sons, a niece, and a daughter-in-law. The household also included six male servants, or two for each adult noble male, and six female servants, two for each of the three women.[206] A few households in other parishes were larger than these. The twenty-four-person household of Grand Chancellor Andrea Surian, with his four male and eight female servants, has already been noted.[207] As Surian's example illustrates, nobles by no means monopolized large households. Of the forty-six households in the four parishes having ten or more members, only twenty-two were headed by nobles.[208]

Two other factors need to be considered: the distribution of servants according to social class and by gender. Table 3.8 shows the number and percentage of noble households in the four parishes and the number and percentage of servants in the parish they employed. These data clearly illustrate the importance of servant keeping to noble status. In three of the four parishes examined, noble households, which never constituted even 10 percent of the total households, employed at least half of the servants. In the poor parish of San Basilio, the seventeen noble households, constituting only 3.55 percent of the total house-

Table 3.7
Distribution of Households by Size, 1590s

| Persons per | Number of Households | | | |
|---|---|---|---|---|
| Household | San Provolo | San Benetto | San Zan Degolà | San Basilio |
| 20 | 0 | 0 | 0 | 1 |
| 19 | 1 | 0 | 0 | 0 |
| 18 | 0 | 1 | 0 | 0 |
| 17 | 0 | 0 | 0 | 0 |
| 16 | 0 | 0 | 0 | 2 |
| 15 | 0 | 0 | 1 | 0 |
| 14 | 2 | 0 | 1 | 3 |
| 13 | 0 | 2 | 0 | 0 |
| 12 | 0 | 2 | 2 | 2 |
| 11 | 5 | 2 | 2 | 1 |
| 10 | 7 | 0 | 3 | 7 |
| 9 | 6 | 1 | 4 | 7 |
| 8 | 8 | 1 | 10 | 6 |
| 7 | 21 | 2 | 11 | 20 |
| 6 | 21 | 9 | 16 | 26 |
| 5 | 22 | 4 | 9 | 39 |
| 4 | 18 | 26 | 22 | 69 |
| 3 | 27 | 30 | 23 | 84 |
| 2 | 14 | 49 | 12 | 104 |
| 1 | 15 | 17 | 6 | 107 |
| Total | 167 | 146 | 122 | 478 |

*Source:* ACPV, CP, buste 1–3.

holds, employed 69.7 percent of the servants. Only San Provolo is an exception. There the six noble households employed only about a third of the parish's servants.[209] Of the forty-four noble households in all four parishes, all employed at least one male or female servant.[210]

The difficulty of determining the distribution of servants among the population is complicated by the problem of identifying who enjoyed cittadino status. Although the term of address *magnifico* was commonly used to denote cittadini, it was not used consistently by the four priests whose registers were examined. One very approximate measure of citizen status, or at least of some kind of social distinction, is the attribution of any term of address other than *clarissimo*, which was used for nobles.[211] Table 3.10 shows the number of households headed by someone with an appellation indicating other than noble status.

Table 3.8
Servants in Noble Households, 1590s

| Households/ | San Provolo | | San Benetto | | San Zan Degolà | | San Basilio | |
|---|---|---|---|---|---|---|---|---|
| Servants | No. | % | No. | % | No. | % | No. | % |
| Total households | 167 | 100.00 | 146 | 100.00 | 122 | 100.00 | 478 | 100.00 |
| Noble households | 6 | 3.59 | 9 | 6.16 | 12 | 9.83 | 17 | 3.55 |
| Total servants | 82 | 100.00 | 94 | 100.00 | 76 | 100.00 | 109 | 100.00 |
| Servants in noble households | 25 | 30.48 | 48 | 51.06 | 39 | 51.31 | 76 | 69.72 |

Source: ACPV, CP, buste 1–3.

Table 3.9
Non-Noble Titled Households, 1590s

| Type of Households | San Provolo | San Benetto | San Zan Degolà | San Basilio |
|---|---|---|---|---|
| Total households | 167 | 146 | 122 | 478 |
| Non-noble titled | 108 | 48 | 25 | 37 |
| Non-noble titled with servants | 35 | 23 | 18 | 20 |

Source: ACPV, CP, buste 1–3.
Note: Non-noble titled households are households in which the head of household is distinguished by a term of address.

The distribution of servants among the three kinds of households, namely, non-noble households headed by persons identified with a term of address, households headed by persons with no term of address, and noble households, is shown in table 3.10. These data show that the overwhelming majority of servants were maintained in noble or non-noble households headed by persons whom the parish priests chose to distinguish by some term of address. Only thirteen servants in all four parishes were employed in homes of persons who did not enjoy some distinction from their fellow parishioners. These servants were employed by, among others, a glassmaker, a used-clothing seller, a boatyard

Table 3.10
Distribution of Servants by Household Type, 1590s

|  | Number of Servants | | | | | | | |
| --- | --- | --- | --- | --- | --- | --- | --- | --- |
| Type of | San Provolo | | San Benetto | | San Zan Degolà | | San Basilio | |
| Households | No | % | No | % | No | % | No | % |
| Non-noble titled | 56 | 68.3 | 44 | 46.8 | 32 | 42.1 | 28 | 25.7 |
| Nontitled | 1 | 1.2 | 2 | 2.1 | 5 | 6.6 | 5 | 4.6 |
| Noble | 25 | 30.5 | 48 | 51.1 | 39 | 51.3 | 76 | 69.7 |
| Total servants | 82 | 100.0 | 94 | 100.0 | 76 | 100.0 | 109 | 100.0 |

*Source:* ACPV, CP, buste 1–3.
*Note:* Non-noble titled households are households in which the head of household is distinguished by a term of address.

owner, and a water seller. These data reconfirm the close correlation between servant keeping and social status in late sixteenth-century Venice.[212] Servant keeping set the middle and upper classes off from the rest of the populace.

Table 3.11 shows the distribution of servants by gender among all households and among noble households. These figures reconfirm the close relationship between noble status and the maintenance of male servants. In all four parishes, nobles employed nearly 50 percent of the male servants, and in the parish of San Basilio the figure was an astonishing 95 percent. In that parish at least, employing a male servant was almost synonymous with noble status.[213] We should remember, however, that artisans often employed and housed male apprentices and laborers who could be called upon to perform service duties.

Before concluding this analysis of parish registers, two other points should

Table 3.11
Gender Distribution of Servants, 1590s

|  | San Provolo | | San Benetto | | San Zan Degolà | | San Basilio | |
| --- | --- | --- | --- | --- | --- | --- | --- | --- |
| Servants | No. | % | No. | % | No. | % | No. | % |
| Total males | 23 | 100.0 | 34 | 100.0 | 19 | 100.0 | 23 | 100.0 |
| Males in noble households | 11 | 47.8 | 19 | 55.8 | 13 | 68.4 | 22 | 95.6 |
| Total females | 59 | 100.0 | 60 | 100.0 | 57 | 100.0 | 86 | 100.0 |
| Females in noble households | 14 | 23.7 | 29 | 48.3 | 26 | 45.6 | 54 | 62.7 |

*Source:* ACPV, CP, buste 1–3.

be remarked. First, the parish clergy also employed servants, especially female housekeepers. The household of the parish priest of San Zan Degolà consisted of the priest, his mother, a maternal aunt, a niece, and Maria, a massara.[214] Second, the registers indicate that Julia Lombardo, the "somtuosa meretrize," was hardly unique among prostitutes in employing servants. On one of the last pages of his register, the priest of San Zan Degolà listed three "meretrice," Lodovica Gonzaga, Isabella Vesentina, and Camilla. Lodovica and Isabella each employed two massere, and Camilla, one.[215] In the parish of San Basilio, Laura Malipiera and her sister Lucietta, whom the priest labeled "cortesane," employed a widow named Lucia as their maid. In San Basilio, madonna Andriana Obici, meretrice, and madonna Isabetta Furlana employed domestics, while other prostitutes in the parish did not.[216] A 1565 catalogue of Venetian prostitutes designed for foreign visitors informed customers that many of the women could be contacted through their servants.[217] The government was probably justified in its concern that young girls would be drawn into the profession if they were employed as domestics by prostitutes.

Finally, in the register for the parish of San Benetto four servants appear as heads of independent households. A certain Santo "servitor" lived with his wife, Marina, and daughter, Franceschina; Paulo "servitor" lived with his wife, Simona; Vizenzo "servitor" lived independently with his wife, Betta; and Gasparo "servitor" lived with the widow Elena.[218] There are also many barcaruoli in these parishes. As noted earlier, servants, especially gondoliers, sometimes lived on their own and hired out their services on a yearly, monthly, or even daily basis. There is no way of knowing where or for whom these men worked. It is certainly possible, even likely, that other servants, especially wet nurses, lurk in the lists of the parish priests, hidden by their roles as wives, widows, and mothers.[219]

The foregoing examination of individual Venetian households and of some aggregated population statistics provides valuable information about the composition of Venetian households. Throughout this analysis two general conclusions have held up consistently under the scrutiny of various sources. First, the Venetian household was a surprisingly flexible institution. Venetians adopted a bewildering variety of living arrangements determined in part by the exigencies of economic life and the biological life cycle. Second, servant keeping was also closely related to the demands of status and gender. It was first and foremost, although not exclusively, the prerogative of the nobility. What most distinguished noble from non-noble servant keeping was the presence of male servants. But while the analysis of normative literature, legislation action, and household structure highlights the cultural uses of service, it reveals little about the other face of service, that is, as a labor relationship. And so it is to the mechanics of household labor that we now turn.

Chapter Four

# Recruitment, Contracts, and Wages
## The Mechanics of Labor

At the end of his account book Andrea Barbarigo, son of Niccolò, copied out
the following list of aphorisms:

> Chi a moger a pensier
> Chi a fioli a dolori
> Chi a danari ia ale
> Chi a posesion a chustion
> Chi a chaxe mai sta in paxe
> Chi a pani a afiani
> Chi fa marchadantia sta in fantaxia
> Chi fa marchadantia di formenti sta sempre in tormenti
> Chi a tere a quera
> Chi a molini a stele
> Chi a piegore a pele

> [He who has a wife has worries
> He who has children has sorrows
> He who has money has wings
> He who has possessions has litigations
> He who has houses never is at peace
> He who has cloth has worries
> He who practices business lives in worry
> He who practices the grain trade is always in torment
> He who has land has wars
> He who has mills has stars
> He who has sheep has hide][1]

It was common for merchants in Renaissance Italy to express through aphorisms
and proverbs the accumulated wisdom of the centuries, by which they tried to
live their own lives and to educate their sons.[2] Through these sayings and

mnemonic devices, they expressed their vision of the world and gave voice to their hopes and fears. Coming at the end of his accounts, one particular aphorism—"Chi a chaxe mai sta in paxe"—may have had special meaning for Barbarigo, since page after page of his ledger is filled with notices of male and female servants who entered his service and then took their leave after only a short time. The entries are testimony to the tribulations that Barbarigo faced as an employer: Lunardo Padoan "was always ill"; Franceschina, daughter of Isabeta Feltrina, "took off from our house and took with her all her clothes"; Romana da Asolo "left with her husband without saying a word"; Lucia da Treviso "fled from us," taking with her "a new blouse, ten bunches of thread, and two new tablecloths."[3] The servants who entered Barbarigo's service in good faith and then broke their contracts surely had their own version of what transpired in the household, but their view of things has not survived.

Andrea Barbarigo's household "mai sta in paxe," yet it was not altogether atypical. Managing a household required recruiting domestic help, drawing up contracts, agreeing to wages, training servants, making payments, and settling accounts. Masters were forced to view master-servant ties in the context of contractual, business relationships, a view that, as we have already noted, clashed with their vision of domestic service as a metaphorical expression for the political and social orders. This chapter examines the domestic labor market in Renaissance Venice.

## Finding Work

The first requirement of any labor market is to bring together those seeking employment and those seeking workers. The exact mechanisms by which this was accomplished in Renaissance Venice are often quite difficult to trace. It is unclear, for example, whether there was a designated slave market or, as in Siena at the Piazza del Campo, a site in the city where those who were seeking domestic servants could examine and negotiate with potential employees.[4] Perhaps the general precinct around Rialto played this role; or the corridors of the capi di sestieri and later the censori's offices may have served this function. Those seeking figliuoli d'anima may have gone directly to the various hospitals, such as the Pietà, to negotiate with the wardens.

One clue to the recruitment of servants is provided by attempts by Isabella d'Este, the marchioness of Mantua, to procure a Negro child to add to the Gonzaga family's famous collection of dwarfs and jesters. She wrote to her agent in Venice that she wanted a "little Moor" [moretta] between one and one-half and four years of age "as black as possible" [più negra che possibile]. On 21 June 1491 her agent wrote that he had "searched with great diligence" and had located a small child "very black and well formed," the daughter of a boatman, but that the child's parents were not willing to sell her.[5] Ten days later he wrote again to inform her that he had "looked up and down the city to find a *moretta* for Your Excellency" and that he had located a two-year-old at the hospital of the Pietà. He noted that the price was right: "some sort of alms to the hospital will suffice."[6] Although the marchioness's special requirements made this search somewhat unusual, the agent's letters suggest that there were some established as well as less formal ways of searching for and recruiting servants and other retainers.

There is also some evidence of professional brokers who matched masters and servants. Marino Sanuto reported an incident involving a corrupt broker. In August 1513 the avogadori di comun tried a certain Gasparo d'Arquà and sentenced him to death. According to Sanuto, d'Arquà had engaged in a "traffic" of wet nurses and female servants. He lured country girls to the city, and city girls to the country, with promises of good money. Then, while they were on the road, he robbed the unsuspecting women. He was caught when he was recognized on a street in the parish of San Fantin by one of the women whom he had defrauded.[7] Glissenti's fictional servant also refers to "brokers" [sensali] who match masters and servants.[8] Professionals may also have operated the regular trade in indentured servants that linked Venice with Dalmatia and Albania. In their account book, Niccolò and Alvise Barbarigo recorded payments to Zuan da Sibenico and Zorzi da Dolzego, the latter described as a "paron de barcha," who transported servants to them.[9]

Women too served as both formal and informal brokers, matching employers and employees. Lorenzo Lotto recorded in his accounts that his massara, Maria da Montagnana, had come to him "by means of donna Lucia da Cadore, laundress of cloth in the courtyard of cà Barozzi at San Moisè."[10] In 1521 Francesco Priuli, son of Giacomo, made a small payment "per Cortesia" to a woman who had helped him secure the service of a massara named Margarita da Colalto.[11] And Laura, daughter of Andrea, a wine porter, was placed as a massara in the home of mercer Zaccaria Fondra through the efforts of donna Pasqua, the widow of Francesco di Corte.[12]

Masters and mistresses sometimes found servants through their own contacts. Many servants came from Venice's terraferma dominions, and the estates owned by the Venetian elite provided a convenient recruiting ground for at least some domestic help. Giovanni Francesco Bragadin owned a villa called Roncha in the Veronese. When he bequeathed the villa to his nephews Alvise and Francesco Tron, he asked them to be especially solicitous of the villa, noting that he himself "was favorably disposed to the men of the said villa de Roncha." Indeed, two of Bragadin's male servants, Francesco di Bereti and Domenego di Zamboni, were described as being "da Roncha."[13] Venetian landowners and the peasants who worked their estates were already linked by formal contractual ties and in some instances by ties of affection. When Marcantonio Barbaro wrote his will in 1594, he left thirty ducats "to the poor contadini of Maser" and recommended them to his heirs and successors.[14] It is certainly possible that such ties led to agreements by which the children of peasants traveled to the capital to work as servants. Administrative stints on the terraferma provided still other opportunities to locate and recruit domestic help. While serving as the podesta of Montagnana in 1554, nobleman Zorzi Morosini reached an accord for twelve-year-old Francesca, daughter of the deceased Zuanalvise di Damiani da Montagnana, to serve as massara to his mother, Elena.[15] Through a variety of mechanisms, then, masters were able to locate the domestic help they needed.

For their part, servants were interested in finding favorable terms of employment and reasonable masters and had their own informal but effective methods of finding work. Kinsmen and friends from the same village or district could help recent immigrants find employment. Among the most trusted confidants of Marcantonio Morosini, procurator of San Marco, was his servant Zuan Terzo, whom Morosini named one of the executors of his estate. At some point, Morosini also took Terzo's nephew *(nepote)* Gasparo into his service.[16] There are other examples of masters employing servants who were related to one another. Nobleman Giovanni Alvise Barbarigo employed both donna Laura Veronese and her daughter Dorotea.[17] And as noted in the preceding chapter, in 1550 Lorenzo Lotto took on as his apprentice Ercole della Rocha Contrada and then six months later hired Ercole's grandmother, donna Caterina, as his housekeeper.[18] While in Venice, Lotto employed a certain donna Lucia as his massara; both Lucia's niece Maddalena and the wife of Lotto's landlord, Giovanni dalla Volta, were present when the accord was reached. It is possible that one of these two women brought employer and employee together in much the same way that the laundress Lucia da Cadore brought Lotto and Maria da Montagnana together.[19] When Andrea Barbarigo took on the servant Zanetto da Ragusa in October 1519, a fellow Ragusan, the barber Zuane, was present.[20] Immigrants who had already made the journey to Venice were in a position to help their more recently arrived compatriots find work.

Kinsmen and countrymen not only helped relatives and friends find work but also counseled them about the reputations of various masters and gave them advice about the practices of particular households, as well as about wages and other matters. In October 1518 Andrea Barbarigo reached an accord with Zuane da Salò, which he registered with the capi di sestieri. They agreed that Zuane would work for Barbarigo for five years in return for twenty-four ducats and that Zuane would pay for his own shoes and clothes. But later Zuane asked to change the terms, and they agreed that he would work for six years for twenty-six ducats and that Barbarigo would pay for his clothes and shoes. As Barbarigo noted, the new terms followed those of Zuane's cousin Antonio, a servant of cà Lion.[21] It is possible that the two cousins had compared contracts, prompting Zuane to seek the changes. When Battista di Zuanne di Constantin reached an accord to serve nobleman Niccolò Priuli, his brother Simon, a servant of nobleman Leonardo Giustinian, stood pledge.[22] And when Constantin da Flambro in Friuli hired on as a servant of Virgilio Serena, a fellow Friulan, Gironimo, servant of nobleman Giacomo Morosini, was guarantor.[23] Talk among servants made them better bargainers with their masters. Certainly servants broke contracts and moved from master to master with great frequency. When gondolier Sebastiano da Pordenone left the service of nobleman Alvise Michiel for that of Francesco Correr, he convinced his fellow servant Giovanni Maria to do the same.[24] The continual search for better pay and working conditions may help explain governmental efforts to limit wages and to enforce minimum terms of service on servants.

## Recruitment of Servants

While individual masters might utilize various methods to recruit servants, the Venetian labor market as a whole was subject to a variety of forces, including war, plague, and famine, that affected both the supply and the geographic provenance of servants. Unfortunately, the same problems that make a reliable count of Venice's servant population impossible apply as well to a thoroughgoing analysis of servant origins. But the extensive Barbarigo family account books provide evidence for the geographic recruitment of servants for one patrician family.

As we have seen, the books cover, with gaps, the period 1431–1582 and thus allow us to trace changes in recruitment patterns over time. The most obvious drawback of the books is that they provide data for only one family; therefore, any peculiarities of Barbarigo family recruitment (e.g., a tendency to recruit from mainland estates, particularly intense servant networks, etc.) may skew the data and render broader generalizations invalid.[25] Nevertheless, the data provide a basis from which to compare information from other account books, testaments, and court records.

The account books of Andrea are by far the least informative, for they mention only four servants by name, three of whom were slaves. Furthermore there are no indications of where these slaves came from, except that Andrea's male slave Jacomo was nicknamed "Ungaro," perhaps referring to Magyar origins.[26] From the account books kept by Andrea's sons, grandsons, and great-grandsons, however, I have compiled a list of 252 servants, only one of whom was a slave. For 215 of these 252 servants, or 85.31 percent, there is some indication of geographic origin. Provenance was indicated in one of two ways: either by an adjective describing the ethnic or geographic origin of the servant (Schiavona, Veronese, etc.) or by the preposition *da* (from) or *di* (of) followed by the name of a particular town or region (da Zara, di Friuli).

Using these phrases as indicators of geographic origins raises two problems. First, we cannot be entirely sure that these adjectival and prepositional descriptions were not in some cases surnames rather than descriptions of origin. The name Trevisan, for instance, was common in Venice and was even the name of a patrician family. Someone with the surname Trevisan may have been the descendant of a long line of Venetian natives or, just as plausibly, a recent immigrant from Treviso. Yet two factors make the former possibility unlikely, especially for servants. First, in the few instances in account books for which there is independent corroboration, it is clear that adjectival descriptions of origin were just that. In his account book Andrea, son of Niccolò Barbarigo, for example, recorded one Lena Schiavona da Sibenico, who entered his service in 1525.[27] Lena, who was from the Dalmatian town Sibenico, was called in the household Lena "the Slav" (Schiavona). Similarly, in his account Agostino Spinelli listed a Maddalena Feltrina. Elsewhere in the book, Spinelli noted that Maddalena made trips to Feltre to visit relatives; and after her death, he settled accounts with her brother-in-law in that town.[28] Masters frequently used descriptive terms or nicknames for servants, perhaps even when the servants had surnames. Andrea, son of Niccolò Barbarigo, referred to Lucia Saraxina as "Granda."[29] Adjectives derived from ethnic or geographic origin were also used to distinguish servants having the same first name.

The second difficulty with these indicators is that they do not inform us how recently servants had immigrated to the city. In 1526 Andrea, son of Niccolò, hired a female servant described as "Luzia Vexentina," who came to him from the Contarini household.[30] As her name indicates, Lucia was of Vicentine origin, but she came to the Barbarigo household via that of the Contarini. In other words, she had not just arrived in the city. An old woman who had come to Venice at age twelve might still be described as "Veronese" or "Bergamasca," in the same way that Lotto referred to his sixty-year-old housekeeper Lucia as "alevata in chà Venier."[31] Yet it is arguable whether such persons, who had spent virtually a lifetime in Venice, should be considered outsiders or foreigners. With these difficulties in mind, let us proceed to an analysis of the Barbarigo family servants.

Table 4.1 presents the data for all servants in the account books, except those of Andrea (the regional boundaries are the modern ones). Not surprisingly, the majority of servants came from Venice's mainland dominions or from the maritime domains over which Venice enjoyed either political or economic control, or both. The coasts of Dalmatia and Albania provided a hefty share of servants, as did the Veneto.[32] If we remember that during much of the sixteenth century Brescia, Salò, and other towns (listed under Lombardy in the table) were under Venetian rule, the impression is even stronger that the Venetian state's political borders and economic sphere of influence provided the catchment area for the Barbarigo family servants. With the exception of Dalmatians and Albanians, the absence of non-Italians is quite notable. The Barbarigos employed only one servant from Germany and one from Crete, an island where the family had long had holdings.[33] At least as far as domestic help is concerned, the Barbarigo evidence suggests that Venice was not a magnet for labor from beyond the Alps. Of course it may be that German and Austrian immigrants gravitated to the homes of German merchants and artisans resident in the city.[34] Also notable is the small number of native Venetians and other residents of the lagoon. Even if all those

Table 4.1
Origins of Barbarigo Family Servants, 1460–1582

| Place of Origin | No. | % |
| --- | --- | --- |
| Dalmatia and Albania | 53 | 21.03 |
| Moslem-held lands[a] | 10 | 3.97 |
| Crete | 1 | 0.39 |
| Germany | 1 | 0.39 |
| Trentino | 4 | 1.59 |
| Lombardy | 22 | 8.73 |
| Friuli | 11 | 4.37 |
| Romagna | 2 | 0.79 |
| Veneto | 91 | 36.11 |
| Venice and lagoon | 9 | 3.57 |
| Unidentifiable[b] | 15 | 5.95 |
| No indication | 33 | 13.10 |
| Total | 252 | 100.00 |

Source: ASV, RPC, RBG.
[a]Servant called Saraxina.
[b]Meaning towns that cannot be found on a map today or town names found in more than one region, making sure identification impossible.

for whom no origins are given were counted as Venetians, native-born servants would still account for only about 18 percent of the Barbarigos' domestic help.

Table 4.2 breaks down the data in table 4.1 chronologically, allowing us to note changes in the recruitment patterns of Barbarigo family servants. There were some significant shifts in Barbarigo recruitment from the mid-fifteenth to the mid- and later sixteenth century. Over this period, the number of servants coming from Dalmatia and Albania declined steadily and dramatically, from 54.2 percent to 9.6 percent. The most likely explanation for this shift is the incursion of the Turks into the Balkans (in 1479, for example, the Venetians ceded Scutari in Albania to the Turks). As Dalmatia and Albania declined as recruitment areas, the Italian mainland, especially the Veneto, replaced them, although the significantly higher number of servants in the account book of Niccolò and Alvise with no indication of geographic origins makes a definitive conclusion on this point difficult. In general, however, the shift in servant recruitment seems to have paralleled broader changes in Venice's political and commercial interests from the Adriatic and Mediterranean basins toward the terraferma.

Table 4.2
Geographic Origins of Barbarigo Family Servants, by Time Period and Account Books, 1460–1582

| | Niccolò and Alvise 1460–1482 | | Giovanni Alvise and Andrea 1506–1528 | | Antonio 1543–1582 | |
|---|---|---|---|---|---|---|
| Place of Origin | No. | % | No. | % | No. | % |
| Dalmatia and Albania | 13 | 54.17 | 35 | 19.89 | 5 | 9.62 |
| Moslem-held lands | 0 | 0.00 | 10 | 5.68 | 0 | 0.00 |
| Crete | 0 | 0.00 | 1 | 0.57 | 0 | 0.00 |
| Germany | 1 | 4.16 | 0 | 0.00 | 0 | 0.00 |
| Trentino | 0 | 0.00 | 2 | 1.14 | 2 | 3.85 |
| Lombardy | 0 | 0.00 | 18 | 10.23 | 4 | 7.69 |
| Friuli | 0 | 0.00 | 7 | 3.97 | 4 | 7.69 |
| Romagna | 0 | 0.00 | 2 | 1.14 | 0 | 0.00 |
| Veneto | 1 | 4.16 | 71 | 40.34 | 19 | 36.54 |
| Venice and lagoon | 0 | 0.00 | 4 | 2.27 | 5 | 9.62 |
| Unidentifiable[a] | 0 | 0.00 | 8 | 4.54 | 7 | 13.46 |
| No indication | 9 | 37.50 | 18 | 10.23 | 6 | 11.53 |
| Total | 24 | 100.00 | 176 | 100.00 | 52 | 100.00 |

Source: ASV, RPC, RBG.

[a]Meaning towns that cannot be found on a map today or town names found in more than one region, making sure identification impossible.

Table 4.3
Geographic Recruitment of Barbarigo Servants, by Gender, 1460–1582

| Place of Origin | Males | | Females | |
|---|---|---|---|---|
| | No. | % | No. | % |
| Dalmatia and Albania | 16 | 22.22 | 37 | 20.56 |
| Moslem-held lands | 1 | 1.39 | 9 | 5.00 |
| Crete | 0 | 0.00 | 1 | 0.56 |
| Germany | 0 | 0.00 | 1 | 0.56 |
| Trentino | 2 | 2.78 | 2 | 1.11 |
| Lombardy | 5 | 6.94 | 16 | 8.89 |
| Friuli | 1 | 1.39 | 9 | 5.00 |
| Romagna | 0 | 0.00 | 2 | 1.11 |
| Veneto | 23 | 31.94 | 69 | 38.33 |
| Venice and lagoon | 5 | 6.94 | 4 | 2.22 |
| Unidentifiable[a] | 5 | 6.94 | 10 | 5.55 |
| No indication | 14 | 19.44 | 20 | 11.11 |
| Total | 72 | 100.00 | 180 | 100.00 |

*Source:* ASV, RPC, RBG.
[a]Meaning towns that cannot be found on a map today or town names found in more than one region, making sure identification impossible.

As Table 4.3 indicates, approximately the same proportions of male and female servants came from various regions to work in the Barbarigo family households. If the data are broken down chronologically, they indicate that there was very little variation in recruitment over time. Over the course of the fifteenth and sixteenth centuries, fewer and fewer male and female servants came from Dalmatia and more and more came from the Veneto and other mainland dominions.

Some sparse data from other account books seem to confirm the general recruitment pattern observed in the Barbarigo records. Estate accounts for nobleman Zaccaria Giustinian dating from the third quarter of the fifteenth century show that he employed at least five servants between 1468 and 1472 and that all five (four women and one man) came from the Balkans.[35] As we have seen, Lorenzo Priuli was not in the habit of listing the names of his servants in his accounts; he generally recorded simply "a female servant" or "a male servant." However, between 1515 and 1517 he listed six servants by name, all males. Of these, two were from Dalmatia or Albania, three were from Lombardy (two from Bergamo and one from Salò), and one was from Friuli.[36] And as we noted in the pre-

Table 4.4
Geographic Origins of Servants Based on Testaments, 15th and 16th Centuries

| Place of Origin | 15th Century | | 16th Century | |
|---|---|---|---|---|
| | No. | % | No. | % |
| Dalmatia and Albania | 11 | 17.19 | 10 | 15.62 |
| Moslem-held lands | 0 | 0.00 | 2 | 3.13 |
| Crete | 0 | 0.00 | 1 | 1.56 |
| Cyprus | 1 | 1.56 | 0 | 0.00 |
| Germany | 1 | 1.56 | 0 | 0.00 |
| Greece | 0 | 0.00 | 1 | 1.56 |
| Cefalonia | 0 | 0.00 | 1 | 1.56 |
| Black Sea region | 3 | 4.69 | 0 | 0.00 |
| Trentino | 0 | 0.00 | 0 | 0.00 |
| Lombardy | 0 | 0.00 | 8 | 12.50 |
| Friuli | 1 | 1.56 | 2 | 3.13 |
| Romagna | 0 | 0.00 | 2 | 3.13 |
| Piedmont | 0 | 0.00 | 1 | 1.56 |
| Veneto | 0 | 0.00 | 13 | 20.31 |
| Venice and lagoon | 1 | 1.56 | 1 | 1.56 |
| Unidentifiable[a] | 0 | 0.00 | 4 | 6.25 |
| No indication | 46 | 71.88 | 18 | 28.13 |
| Total | 64 | 100.00 | 64 | 100.00 |

*Sources:* ASV, CI, Notai; NT.
[a]Meaning towns that cannot be found on a map today or town names found in more than one region, making sure identification impossible.

ceding chapter, Agostino Spinelli employed five female servants between 1566 and 1583. The origins of four of these servants can be identified: two came from Friuli, and two were from the Veneto.[37]

Better comparisons can be made with the evidence in the wills of 128 servants (113 females and 15 males), garnered from various sources. In some instances the origins of the servants can be determined from the way they described themselves. The data, presented in table 4.4, suggest a less dramatic decline in recruitment of servants from Dalmatia and Albania than the Barbarigo data do, but they confirm the rise in recruitment from the terraferma.

Finally, we can examine the geographic origins of servants tried by the censors. Table 4.5 presents the evidence for 200 servants brought before the censors between January 1569 and May 1579. Two points are especially worth noting here. First, the evidence of the censors' trials provides the best evidence of the decline

Table 4.5

Geographic Origins of Servants Based on Censors' Trials, 1569–1579

| Place of Origin | No. | % |
|---|---|---|
| Dalmatia and Albania | 9 | 4.5 |
| Moslem-held lands | 0 | 0.0 |
| Crete | 1 | 0.5 |
| Cyprus | 2 | 1.0 |
| Greece | 2 | 1.0 |
| Africa | 1 | 0.5 |
| Germany | 0 | 0.0 |
| France | 1 | 0.5 |
| Trentino | 3 | 1.5 |
| Lombardy | 10 | 5.0 |
| Friuli | 17 | 8.5 |
| Romagna | 0 | 0.0 |
| Piedmont | 0 | 0.0 |
| Veneto | 82 | 41.0 |
| Venice and lagoon[a] | 26 | 13.0 |
| Tuscany | 2 | 1.0 |
| Unidentifiable[b] | 12 | 6.0 |
| No indication | 32 | 16.0 |
| Total | 200 | 100.0 |

*Source:* ASV, Censori, busta 3, registers 1 and 2.

[a]Including Chioggia.

[b]Meaning towns that cannot be found on a map today or town names found in more than one region, making sure identification impossible.

of Dalmatia and Albania as recruiting grounds for Venetian servants. Only 9 of 200 servants, or 4.5 percent, were from those areas. Second, these data show both the highest level of servant recruitment from Venice and the lagoon (including Chioggia) and the lowest percentage of servants who are unidentifiable or for whom no place of origin is indicated, further evidence that at least some of the servants for whom no indication was given in the preceding data, and perhaps a hefty percentage, were from Venice.[38]

The material we have examined indicates that a significant shift took place in the recruitment of Venice's service-providing population. If we recall that especially in the first half of the fifteenth century a fairly substantial portion of Venice's domestic help was provided by slaves, then the shift was even more pronounced. During the fifteenth century much of Venice's domestic help was provided by Tatar, Russian, Bulgar, Turkish, or Saracen slaves and by indentured labor from the Balkan Peninsula, whereas in the sixteenth century the shift was toward more free labor from Italy, especially the Veneto, Friuli, and Lombardy.[39]

## Contracts

Once master and servant reached an informal agreement of employment, they then recorded in a contract the basic terms of the relationship that legally bound them and that, to some extent, laid the groundwork for all future inter- action. In their account books, Venetian masters recorded in cryptic form what they considered to be the essential aspects of these agreements—the name of the servant, the date when service was to begin, and the wages to be paid. In the few extant notarized contracts and presumably in the volumes of servant regis- trations maintained by the capi di sestieri and later by the censori, masters and servants laid out more detailed agreements concerning not only wages and the duration of contracts but also other obligations and responsibilities.[40] Even then many conditions were left unstated.

In his will dated 1509, Marcantonio Morosini wrote, "I have in my house- hold male and female servants on salary and in indenture" [Io me truovo in casa famegli e femene a salario e scriti].[41] Morosini distinguished between indentured servants, that is, servants who signed on for multiple years of service in return for upkeep and who might or might not receive a lump-sum payment at the end of the contract, from salaried servants, who contracted on a monthly or yearly basis and expected regular payment on that schedule.

An early contract following the inscribed pattern was the agreement be- tween Giacomo, an immigrant from Cremona, and Clara, widow of Pietro di Avanzo, made on behalf of Giacomo's daughter Francesca in March 1407. The text is worth quoting in full:

> I, Giacomo from Cremona now an inhabitant of Venice in the parish of San Paternian, make manifest with my heirs and successors that I give and af- firm to you, lady Clara, widow of sir Pietro di Avanzo of the parish of San Lorenzo, my daughter named Francesca such that from now on at your free will she must live and remain with you and in your service (and) serve you loyally and that she must maintain and keep your possessions to the best of her ability, without fraud or evil intent. For your part, you must give her food, clothing, and shoes in good measure according to your means. The girl must not leave you or your service without your consent. And if at any time I cause the girl to leave your service, then I promise and obligate my-

self to pay you all the expenses that you have incurred up to that day on which she is removed by me or by some other person acting on my behalf from your service. If, however, I ever try to act against this agreement, then I, with my heirs and successors, am obliged to pay you or your heirs and successors five gold lire. And this agreement remains in force.[42]

Giacomo consigned his daughter to Avanzo and obligated her to remain in service. Giacomo promised that his daughter would act in good faith, that she would not leave without permission, and that she would carefully administer Avanzo's possessions. To back this up, he pledged himself and his heirs as guarantors of the agreement. For her part, Avanzo agreed to feed, clothe, and provide shoes for the child. For all this, the contract was vague on two points: the length of the commitment and Avanzo's exact financial obligations to the child. Concerning the length of service, no term was set on the contract. As we have seen, in 1388 the Senate established a ten-year limit on contracts for indentured servants from Dalmatia, and that same law may have applied here.[43] The contract does not state Francesca's age. Avanzo also agreed that she would maintain the child at her own discretion, although the contract did stipulate that it was to be done "in good measure." Most surprising of all is that there is no mention of a salary. Unlike an agreement made between Matteo da Spalato and Catarina Arimondo in 1403, in which Arimondo agreed to dower and marry off Matteo's daughter at age twenty according to her "discretion and means" [discretionem, et possibilitatem],[44] the contract between Giacomo and Avanzo contained no specific provisions for a salary or dowry for Francesca. The best she could hope for was that at the end of her service Avanzo would out of charity reward her with a payment, presumably to go toward a dowry. Necessity appears to have driven Giacomo to make such a potentially disadvantageous agreement, for on that very same day he placed another daughter, named Lucia, in the service of Georgina, widow of nobleman Andrea Zeno, under the same terms.[45] In effect, this immigrant from Cremona consigned his daughters to two elite widows for upbringing and relieved himself of that burden.

One hundred and sixty-four years later, on 18 April 1571, an inscription contract was drawn up between Francesco Feltrin, acting on behalf of his daughter Maria, and Zuan Battista Pizzuol. The contract states,

> In the apothecary shop at the sign of Saint John in the parish of San Salvador. Sir Francesco Feltrin, son of the late sir Zuan Domenego of Feltre, inhabitant at Guia, below Treviso, for the next five years beginning on the third of March, recently passed has agreed to place as housekeeper with his Excellent physician, sir Zuan Battista Pizzuol, his daughter named Maria,

seventeen years of age or thereabouts. And the said Excellent sir Zuan Battista promises to give as a salary to the said Maria sixty lire di piccoli at the end of the said five years; and if during this time she needs some money to clothe herself, he consents to give her some money in good account from the said sixty lire. And sir Francesco himself promises that the said Maria will serve loyally, and he constitutes himself pledge and principal payer both for her good administration and for her bad administration or theft from the house of the said Excellent sir Zuan Battista, obligating himself in all places and personally and all his goods present and future.[46]

In this contract the father, this time an inhabitant of the terraferma, obligated his seventeen-year-old daughter to five years of service to the physician Pizzuol. In return, Pizzuol agreed to pay her a salary of sixty lire di piccoli (about ten ducats) at the end of the service. Presumably Pizzuol was to feed and house the girl. But he was not obligated to clothe or shoe her. Any money she received from him for that purpose was to be deducted from her salary. Like Giacomo from Cremona, Francesco stood pledge for his daughter's good behavior and obligated himself and his possessions for any damage or theft she might cause. Unlike the earlier agreement, this contract contained no provisions regarding what would occur if it were broken.

These two contracts are broadly typical of the indentured, or inscribed, pattern of service, in which servants obligated themselves or, since many were minors, were obligated by their parents or guardians to multiple years of service. Although most would receive payment at the end of their term, provisions of food, shelter, clothing, and shoes constituted important elements of the agreements. Such contracts became a way for the poor to pass the responsibility of raising and maintaining their offspring to those who were better off. The servants (or their guardians) swore to provide loyal service and to protect their masters' goods; and to back up this promise, they pledged as collateral their property or that of their kin.[47]

Inscription contracts shared many characteristics with apprenticeship contracts. Like indentured servants, apprentices were obligated to serve their masters in return for food, clothing, and shelter. Yet apprenticeship contracts differed in one fundamental way from inscriptions, for in addition to maintaining apprentices, masters agreed to teach them a trade. For example, in an agreement between fifteen-year-old Zuan Giacomo Spada and the tailor Battista di Michiel da Bari dated 1565, Battista agreed to teach the youngster how to cut fabric and "to do all that pertains to the art of tailoring" [far tutto quello, che aspetta all'arte del sartor].[48] When they completed their contract, apprentices had acquired not only a salary and maintenance but also skills they could use throughout their lifetime.

This was also the case in at least a few master-servant contracts. Occasionally masters agreed to do more than simply maintain children. In August 1563, Pasqua, a widow from Asolo and a servant of the physician Flaminio da Modena, placed her twelve-year-old son, Francesco, in service with the ambassador from Famagosta. For the next thirteen years Francesco was "to serve your lordship as a real and true servant in everything that will be required." In return, the ambassador agreed to feed and clothe the boy and at the end of the term to give him a salary of fifteen gold scudi. In addition, he agreed "to teach the boy good manners and to treat him as one ought to treat good and loyal servants."[49] In 1564 Battista Fornasier, another terraferma native, placed his nine-year-old son, Bastian, with the lawyer Francesco Trevisan "per garzon" for nine years. Battista promised that his son would lend "good and loyal service" to Trevisan; in return, Trevisan agreed to feed, clothe, and shoe the boy and to give him ten ducats in salary. He also pledged "to teach the boy to read and write and to treat him well."[50]

The similarities between these two contracts and apprenticeship contracts are striking, for the children were not only to receive maintenance and money but also to be taught some skills. One boy was to learn good manners, the other to read and write. Christiane Klapisch-Zuber has noted that in Tuscany young boys between the ages of seven and fourteen were often put out as servants. Some received instruction in reading, writing, and arithmetic. When they completed this service, the boys were then ready to be apprenticed into a craft.[51] The same may be true in the case of these contracts. It is also possible that as the Venetian elite became more conscious of social graces during the sixteenth century, they wished to hire better-mannered servants. Accordingly, parents sought skills for their children that later would translate into more gainful employment as trusted menservants or even as factors. It is also noteworthy that both contracts involved boys. Most girls who entered into domestic service had already learned at home many of the skills they would be required to perform for as long as they remained in service.[52]

The other kind of contract involved servants who worked for a salary that was figured on a regular (monthly or yearly) basis. But in this kind of agreement as well, upkeep and clothing often figured as part of the accord. In September 1456, Niccolò da Patras reached the following terms with Francesco Loredan:

> Niccolò da Patras obligates himself to live with noble lord Francesco Loredan, son of the late lord Giorgio, for the next three years, with these

conditions: that the aforesaid Niccolò must perform all deeds and services for the said Francesco and must clothe and shoe himself for the entire aforesaid period at his own expense. Lord Francesco himself must keep and pay the expenses for Niccolò and for his salary or wage must give him every year three and one-half ducats and two pairs of clogs. If [the contract is broken], there is a penalty of five gold lire and the contract remains in force.[53]

This contract differs in some important respects from the preceding ones. First, Niccolò was legally an adult and so acted for himself in this agreement. Second, although the contract was to last for three years, it made clear that Niccolò was to be paid a yearly salary of three and one-half ducats and two pairs of clogs. As in some inscription contracts, the two parties clearly spelled out their obligations regarding food, clothing, and shelter. Niccolò would receive food and shelter from Loredan, but he was responsible for his own clothing and shoes, except for the clogs.

But masters and servants were not always explicit about all of the terms. On 30 December 1557, Rado, a recent immigrant from Montenegro, made the following contract with the Memo family:

At the chancery. Sir Rado, son of the late sir Niccolò d'Andrizza of Montenegro, above Cattaro, in the presence of me the notary and of the witnesses written below, has agreed and agrees to serve as servant the most Illustrious sir Zuan Maria Memo, Doctor and Knight, son of the most Illustrious sir Niccolò, absent, but in his place present, stipulating and promising [the terms], sir Niccolò Memo, his son, for the next five years beginning on the first of January upcoming. He promises to serve his most Illustrious Magnificence well and loyally as is required of a good servant. And the said sir Niccolò by name as above on behalf of his father promises to give him for his salary twenty-eight ducats at 6 lire, 4 soldi, per ducat in this way, that is, four ducats the first year, five the second year, six the third and fourth years, and seven the fifth year. They obligate themselves to one another, with Rado placing all his goods present and future under obligation according to the law of the signori di notte al civil. The same not knowing how to speak Italian very well, sir Zorzi di Paulo Zentil da Nadin, sailor and inhabitant of Venice in the parish of Castello in the houses of sir Marco Frizzier, was his interpreter word for word.[54]

Memo agreed to pay Rado on a sliding scale; his salary was to increase from four to seven ducats over the course of the five-year contract. But there was no mention of food, shelter, or clothing, some or all of which the parties may have understood to be included in the agreement. The pact does contain some familiar language. Rado agreed to serve loyally and pledged his own goods as security.

Attempting to distinguish between inscribed and salaried servants is not always easy, as the following contract dated 7 September 1461 illustrates:

> I, Andrea da Mugla, formerly the servant of lord Niccolò di Conte, being of legitimate age, make manifest that I obligate myself to stand and live with you, noble lord Michele Salamon, son of the late honorable lord Niccolò of Venice, of the parish of Santa Maria Formosa, for the next four years beginning on the first day of October upcoming. With this condition, that I must perform all honest and licit deeds and services for you and your house that you assign me day and night for the entire period. And you must pay my expenses for food and clothing and maintain me in your house for the entire period. And at the end of the time you must give me for my salary ten gold ducats. Of which I now acknowledge that I have gotten and received as part four gold ducats, which in my name you have disbursed and paid to the aforesaid lord Niccolò di Conte, to whom I am obligated for the said money. Declaring between us that if I leave you, lord Michele, before the expiration of the said time of my own will and defect, I am to forfeit the entire aforesaid salary. And I will be obliged to restitute to you the four ducats that you paid for me. If, however, I leave on your account, then I am to receive my entire salary, regardless of whether or not the four years have been completed.[55]

In this rather complicated arrangement, Andrea da Mugla, an adult, pledged himself to serve Salamon for four years at a salary of ten ducats. Food, clothing, and shelter, all of which Salamon was required to provide, constituted important elements of the arrangement. But because Salamon immediately disbursed four ducats to pay Andrea's debt to his former master, Andrea found himself already indebted to Salamon, thereby constituting a kind of indenture. The contract did, however, contain provisions in the event that either party chose to break the agreement. It is difficult to categorize this arrangement, for it has elements of both inscribed and salaried contracts.

One reason why it is difficult to categorize arrangements between Venetian servants and masters is that a wide variety of motives underlay these arrangements. In some cases, parents placed their children as servants in order to relieve themselves of the burden of supporting them. In other cases, the parents of young boys saw service as a way for their sons to acquire potentially valuable skills. Adults sometimes pledged themselves to service as a way to guarantee food and shelter, while others, such as Andrea da Mugla, may have done so in order to relieve themselves of other obligations.

For their part, masters usually hired servants in order to acquire needed domestic help. But in some cases at least, masters had other motives. Occasionally they took on young people and maintained elderly servants as acts of charity. Such was the case with the Locadello family, who agreed to shelter and maintain in sickness and health Tonina, widow of Simon da Lovatina, "gia vecchia, et impotente," who had already been in their care for four years. But to protect themselves from future legal action, they made Tonina agree never to seek payment for past or future service to the family.[56] As this example illustrates, service agreements cannot always be reduced to a simple calculation of the cost of wage labor, for other factors applied as well. Contracts bespeak the myriad desires, aspirations, realities, and expectations that brought masters and servants together.

## The Length of Contracts

Specific contracts reveal the kind of conditions and terms to which particular masters and servants agreed. But when analyzed together, contracts, as well as other sources, such as testaments and account books, provide evidence for evaluating more generally the conditions of the domestic labor market in Venice. Specifically, they allow us to chart broad changes in the length of contracts and in wages.

From a wide variety of sources, I have gathered data on the terms of employment of 320 different servants during the fifteenth and sixteenth centuries. The data include both the wage and the period of service, so that a yearly wage rate can be calculated. Many more incomplete data exist, such as wage receipts, but since most receipts give no indication of the amount of time served, they cannot be used to calculate annual wages.

The length of service to which masters and servants agreed depended to a very great extent on the kind of contract they signed, that is, on whether it was for inscribed or salaried service. Table 4.6 gives the average period of contracted service for male and female indentured servants, broken down by century. Although the evidence is sparse, one general observation can be made, namely, that girls generally were inscribed for longer periods than boys. On average, boys and young men agreed to inscriptions of almost six years, whereas girls and young women were inscribed for about seven and one-half years. The longest period of inscription was the thirteen years that donna Pasqua pledged her son Francesco to the ambassador from Famagosta. Since Francesco was twelve years old at the time, he would have been twenty-five when he completed the con-

Table 4.6
Average Length of Indentured Service Contracts, by Gender,
15th and 16th Centuries

| | Males | | Females | |
| --- | --- | --- | --- | --- |
| Time Period | Average Years | No. of Observations | Average Years | No. of Observations |
| 1400–1499 | 5.81 | 11 | 7.88 | 17 |
| 1500–1599 | 6.20 | 10 | 7.27 | 18 |
| Total | 5.95 | 21 | 7.55 | 35 |

*Sources:* ASV, RPC, RBG; PSM, Commissarie; NA; and NT.

tract.[57] The shortest contracts were for two years.[58] The longest contract for a female was the eleven-year contract between Matteo da Spalato and Catarina Arimondo concerning Matteo's nine-year-old daughter, Bona.[59] The shortest contract for a female was four years; that was in the somewhat unusual case in which Cristina, wife of notary Marco di Raphanellis, freed her Circassian slave Cita and then had Cita pledge to work for her for four more years in return for upkeep, clothing, and shoes.[60]

The length of inscription contracts can be compared with the length of apprenticeship contracts made by young men entering Venetian guilds. According to guild statutes from the late thirteenth and fourteenth centuries, apprenticeship in Venice generally lasted from 4 to 8 years, depending on the trade.[61] According to Richard Rapp, who studied Venetian guilds in the late sixteenth and seventeenth centuries, the average duration of apprenticeship contracts was 5.1 years in 1591 and 4.9 years in 1606. He noted that the length of contracts was closely related to the age of the apprentices, with younger boys serving longer terms.[62] The same may have been true for servants, especially young males.

Yet the contracted length of inscription service was one thing, and the actual amount of time served quite another. Some references to inscription, especially those found in account books, in which masters recorded when servants entered and left their service, allow us also to calculate how long indentured servants actually stayed with their masters. Table 4.7 presents data on contracted and actual indentured service in the fifteenth and sixteenth centuries. These data show that on average, male indentured servants stayed about one and one-half of a contracted five and one-half years, whereas females stayed approximately half of the seven years they were obligated to serve. The amount of time that an inscribed or any other servant chose to stay depended on a variety of factors, including the character of the servant and his or her master and the practices of

Table 4.7
Contracted and Actual Length of Indentured Service, by Gender,
15th and 16th Centuries

| Indentured Servants | Contracted Service | | Actual Service | |
|---|---|---|---|---|
| | Years | No. of Observations | Years | No. of Observations |
| Males | 5.4 | 10 | 1.50 | 10 |
| Females | 7.6 | 18 | 3.51 | 18 |

Sources: ASV, RPC, RBG; PSM, Commissarie.

the household. For instance, Niccolò and Alvise Barbarigo saw their indentured servants through their contracts quite successfully. Caterina da Sibenico and Maddalena da Cattaro both completed their terms of nine and eight years, respectively; another inscribee, Petrussa da Cattaro, died in the sixth year of her seven-year contract, and Agnese da Scutari left after five of her eight years; and the male inscribee Manoli da Modon completed three years and five months of his four-year contract.[63] On the other hand, Niccolò's son Andrea (who copied out the aphorisms found at the beginning of this chapter) had a household constantly in flux. The longest that any of his indentured servants stayed was one year, nine months.[64] Others stayed a few months, some just a few days: Zanetto da Ragusa stayed six days, and Piero da Bardolino left the day after he agreed to serve as Andrea's fante.[65] The five-year contract between Rado da Montenegro and Zuan Maria Memo that we examined earlier was canceled by mutual accord nine months after they first agreed to it. The cancellation noted that "sir Rado ought and may go freely to attend to his own affairs."[66]

The same irregular pattern seems to have held for salaried servants. Some remained with their masters all their life. In 1518 Leonardo Raimondo hired donna Marro da Lepanto as his "servitrice et massara" at a salary of five ducats per year; thirty years later she was still in his service.[67] In her will dated 1559, Menega, daughter of Francesco di Calegari, was identified by the notary as "now for thirty years the housekeeper" [gia trenta anni massara] of the late nobleman Priamo Malipiero and currently housekeeper for Priamo's grandson Piero.[68] Lucia da Trau served as nobleman Federico Ferro's footmaid for fifty years.[69] But it was much more common for servants to remain with masters for a few years or even for a few months. Servants left for many reasons: some were harassed by their masters; others sought better terms of employment elsewhere; still others became pregnant or were fired. Some, like Rado da Montenegro and Zuan Maria Memo, simply parted company by mutual accord.

The fairly rapid turnover of servants, even among inscribees, aggravated and disturbed masters. As one ruling by the censors stated, the coming and going of servants subjected masters to "damage, loss, and shame." Such concerns prompted the government to impose minimum contracts on both male and female servants. As we have seen, in 1548 the censors set a six-month minimum on contracts since, as they said, servants were leaving after only "four, five, or ten days." And in the 1595 capitulary the minimum contract was set at six months for men and one year for women.[70] Servants' willingness to break contracts forced masters into the unpleasant task of finding and training new employees. It also revealed to masters and to prying neighbors that their households were not the well-ordered microcosms of the polity and society that humanist treatises said they should be.

## Wages

Most important of all to both servants and their masters was the wages paid for service. Yet it is nearly impossible to calculate the actual wages paid, since food, shelter, and clothing often constituted significant aspects of the agreements but were not always explicitly listed among the terms, especially in the account books maintained by masters or even in formally notarized contracts. Since most servants, especially females, lived with their masters, food and shelter were generally assumed to be part of the arrangement, whereas provisions of clothing and shoes were much more likely to be determined by negotiation.

Another factor complicating the wage picture is tips. It was customary for masters to tip servants at the New Year and at the feast of the Ascension, or Sensa, as it was known in Venice. Although tips *(bonaman)* were just that, voluntary increments to the agreed salary, they were important. Marino Contarini carefully recorded in his accounts that the two wet nurses of his son Piero, Ruossa and Lucia, each received a salary of nineteen ducats per year plus one ducat "per bona mano."[71] For masters, tips figured as one more component of the servants' wages.

Remembering that monetary wages constituted only one part of servants' compensation (and not necessarily the most important part), we can examine the average wage paid to male and female salaried and inscribed servants. These data are summarized in table 4.8, which also provides information on wet nurses and a factor. For purposes of comparison, the established wage rates for ducal scudieri and the limits placed on servants' wages by Venetian law are also included. First, let us examine the differential in wages paid to salaried and inscribed servants. During the fifteenth century, male inscribed servants made on average 1.5 ducats per year in addition to the food, shelter, and any clothing their contracts provided; female inscribed servants made just over 1 ducat. In the sixteenth century the rate of compensation for males increased to nearly 3.5 ducats per year, whereas that of females rose to almost 1.75 ducats. But these rates remained well below the wages paid to salaried employees.

The transition out of inscribed labor into salaried labor increased a servant's compensation considerably. Two examples nicely illustrate this point. In May

Table 4.8
Servants' Wages in Ducats per Year, 15th and 16th Centuries

| Indentured and Salaried Servants | Men Wages | No. | Women Wages | No. | Nurses Wages | No. | Factors Wages | No. | Scudieri | Limit by Law |
|---|---|---|---|---|---|---|---|---|---|---|
| 1400–1499 | | | | | | | | | | |
| Indentured | 1.50 | 11 | 1.10 | 19 | | | | | 18.0[a] | |
| Salaried | 7.06 | 4 | 7.13 | 6 | 15.58 | 12 | | | | |
| Total | 2.98 | 15 | 2.55 | 25 | | | | | | |
| 1500–1549 | | | | | | | | | | 12.0[b] |
| Indentured | 3.58 | 7 | 1.57 | 12 | | | | | 24.0[c] | |
| Salaried | 7.08 | 22 | 3.91 | 130 | 9.3 | 3 | | | | |
| 1550-1599 | | | | | | | | | | 12.0[d] |
| Indentured | 2.66 | 3 | 2.03 | 6 | | | | | | |
| Salaried | 15.78 | 36 | 5.40 | 35 | 13.75 | 12 | 20.0 | 1 | 48.0[e] | |
| 1500-1599 | | | | | | | | | | |
| Indentured | 3.31 | 10 | 1.73 | 18 | | | | | | 19.3[f] |
| Salaried | 12.48 | 58 | 4.23 | 165 | | | | | | 6.0[g] |
| Total | 11.13 | 68 | 3.98 | 183 | 12.86 | 15 | 20.0 | 1 | | |
| Total No.: | 320 | | | | | | | | | |

*Sources:* ASV, RPC, RBG; PSM, Commissarie; NA; and NT.
[a]As set by the 1423 law.
[b]Annual salary of a gondolier as reported by Sanuto.
[c]As set by the 1522 law.
[d]Annual salary of a fameglio di pope according to 1548 law of the censori.
[e]As set by the 1559 law.
[f]Annual salary of a fameglio di pope according to the 1595 capitulary.
[g]Annual salary of a massara according to the 1595 capitulary.

1422 Caterina da Lesina made a receipt to her employer, Giovanni Bonacorsi. First she acknowledged receipt of "ten ducats, which are for my salary for the eight years I was required to live with you at your expense for food and clothes." According to that agreement, she was compensated at the rate of 1.25 ducats per year, in addition to food, clothing, and shelter. Then she acknowledged receipt of "twelve ducats, which are for my salary for the two years I stayed with you beyond the aforesaid eight years."[72] Once her inscription ended, she was compensated with a salary of 6 ducats per year. Similarly, in their account book Niccolò and Alvise Barbarigo recorded payment to Maddalena da Cattaro, who, when she was inscribed as their fantesca, received 10 ducats for eight years of service (1.25 ducats per year) but received 4 ducats for the extra year that she served them "per masara."[73]

The marked difference in compensation paid to inscribed and salaried employees indicates that inscription, or indenture, represented a significant exploitation of child and immigrant labor. Most inscribed employees were children or very young adults who agreed to long terms of employment. Within a year or two of their acceptance they probably had acquired many of the same skills as other servants, yet their rate of pay remained considerably less. Of course, placing children in service represented a way for poor families to pass at least part of the burden of raising children onto the shoulders of the more fortunate, but the benefit accrued to the children's parents, not to the children themselves.[74] Since many adult salaried workers also received food and shelter, the inescapable conclusion is that masters benefited monetarily from hiring inscribed domestic help.

Another striking variation was in the wages paid to male and female domestics. With one exception (the wages of salaried workers in the fifteenth century), women consistently earned less money than men. What is more, the gap between men's and women's wages widened during the course of the sixteenth century. Whereas in the first half of the sixteenth century female salaried employees made almost 4 ducats per year, compared with 7 for men, in the second half of the century women made on average 5.4 ducats per year, compared with almost 16 ducats for men. Men's salaries rose 129 percent, while those of women rose only 37.5 percent. Given that wheat prices doubled during the last quarter of the century, the real wages of female servants may actually have declined.[75] According to the censors' 1595 capitulary, the maximum salary that a male servant could earn was the 19.3 ducats allotted to famegli di pope; for massare the legal limit was set at less than a third of that amount—6 ducats.[76]

The one exception to this pattern was wages paid to salaried domestics in the fifteenth century, when men and women were compensated at nearly the same rate. The very small number of observations (a mere ten for the entire century) makes conclusions hazardous. Yet another small data set, the wages paid to wet nurses, suggests that during the fifteenth century female domestics were paid fairly well relative to men but that their earning power (again relative to men) declined sharply in the sixteenth century. The data for wet nurses show that their salaries peaked in the mid-fifteenth century and then declined dramatically, only to recover in the 1580s and 1590s (see table 4.9). At the end of the sixteenth century the legal limit of 13.5 ducats meant that wet nurses were earning about the same amount that they had earned a century and a half earlier, although some masters were ignoring the law. The dramatic decline in wet nurses' compensation raises the possibility at least that the parity that salaried women enjoyed with men in the fifteenth century and its subsequent decline in the sixteenth was not an aberration of the small data base. But further study is needed before this can be confirmed.[77]

The decline in salaried women's wages stands in marked contrast to the rise in salaried men's wages during the sixteenth century. Men's wages rose from 7 ducats per year in the first half of the century to nearly 16 ducats per year in the second half. At the end of the century the censors set the upper limit on gondo-

Table 4.9
Wet Nurses' Wages in Ducats, 1438–1598

| Year | Wages | Year | Wages |
|------|-------|------|-------|
| 1438 | 14 | 1524 | 10 |
| 1439 | 18 | 1569 | 14 |
| 1439 | 16[a] | 1571 | 12 |
| 1440 | 19[b] | 1572 | 12 |
| 1440 | 19[b] | 1573 | 12 |
| 1440 | 19 | 1578 | 12 |
| 1440 | 19 | 1580 | 12 |
| 1453 | 14 | 1580 | 14 |
| 1456 | 14 | 1581 | 15 |
| 1473 | 12 | 1583 | 14 |
| 1477 | 12 | 1586 | 18 |
| 1482 | 11 | 1595 | 13.5[c] |
| 1521 | 9 | 1596 | 14 |
| 1524 | 9 | 1598 | 16 |

*Sources:* ASV, RPC, RBG; PSM, Commissarie; NA; and NT.
[a]Plus a shirt.
[b]Plus a tip of 1 ducat.
[c]The legal limit.

liers' wages at nearly 20 ducats, although again masters were exceeding these limits. For example, in his will dated 1585, Paolo Contarini recorded the salaries of his "camarier" and his "servitor" at 2 ducats per month each, while his "popier" earned 3 ducats per month.[78] The sharp rise in wages at the end of the century was almost certainly due to the shortage of labor caused by the devastating plague of the 1570s and the opening of employment opportunities in other sectors of the economy.[79] We will recall that Glissenti's fictional gondolier boasted that he could easily find employment since the city need twenty thousand servants but only had five thousand.[80] The shortage of labor may explain new governmental efforts to limit wages.[81]

The wage data also suggest additional reasons for the shift in legislative concern from female to male servants, as evidenced by the capitularies of the capi di sestieri and the censors. The new concern with male servants may reflect the fact that they now cost masters significantly more in wages than their female counterparts. Furthermore, the desire to employ male servants for purposes of display, combined with the labor shortage (especially of males, who could find employment elsewhere), may have fueled the inflation in their wages.

Two final points about salaries need to be noted. First, the wage for a factor employed in 1559 was 20 ducats, among the highest compensations paid to any privately employed servant, although again very close to the wages of wet nurses in the mid-fifteenth century.[82] Second, the wage rates of ducal scudieri illustrate the special position of these servants, although their wages also evidence the rise in men's wages, for between 1522 and 1559 their salaries doubled.

A comparison between the wages paid to servants and the wages paid to other laborers in Venetian society is also instructive. Table 4.10 gives the annual wage rates of various categories of workers in Venice, some of whom (e.g., oarsmen and stevedores), like servants, formed part of Venice's pool of unskilled or semiskilled labor. As a comparison with Table 4.8 makes clear, domestic servants were paid substantially less in cash than many unskilled laborers. For example, according to Marino Sanuto, an unskilled laborer in the Arsenal about 1500 received about 20 ducats a year in pay, yet the pay of salaried male domestics in the same period was about a third of that amount.[83] Whereas stevedores in the Arsenal were earning about 23 ducats per year around 1560,[84] salaried male servants were making about 16 ducats per year in the period 1550–99. And whereas female sailmakers in the Arsenal received about 11 ducats per year (and their mistress about 16 ducats),[85] female servants in the years 1550–99 were earning about 5.5 ducats, and in 1595 the legal limit for them was set at 6 ducats.

These comparisons further illustrate the importance that food, shelter, and in some instances clothing played as part of servants' compensation. If unskilled

Table 4.10
Wage Comparisons in Ducats per Year, 1407–1580s

| Year | Profession | Wage |
|---|---|---|
| 1407–47 | Master shipwright | 48 |
| 1420 | Oarsman | 28 |
| 1425 | Stonecutter | 60[a] |
| Late 15th century | Unskilled worker, Arsenal | 20 |
| 1504 | Oarsman on galleys | 15 |
| c. 1560 | Foreman caulker, Arsenal | 100[b] |
| c. 1560 | Female sailmaker, Arsenal | 11[c] |
| c. 1560 | Stevedore, Arsenal | 23 |
| 1560s | Master builder | 63[d] |
| 1560s | Builder's laborer | 40 |
| 1580s | Master builder | 87 |
| 1580s | Builder's laborer | 54 |

*Sources:* For 1407–47 and 1420, Lane, *Andrea Barbarigo,* 33; for 1425, Goy, 94; for the late fifteenth century, Luzzato, *Storia,* 234; for 1504, Tucci, *Mercanti,* 189; for c. 1560, Lane, *Venetian Ships,* 161–62; and for the 1560s, Pullan, "Wage-Earners," 158.

[a]Assuming an average daily rate of pay of 25 soldi and 250 days of work per year (Luzzatto, *Storia,* 234), we arrive at 6,250 soldi per year. Divided by 104 soldi, the rate for the ducat in 1425 (Goy, xxiv), this comes to 60 ducats.

[b]Plus housing.

[c]Female sailmakers were paid 5 soldi per day in winter and 6 soldi per day in summer. Assuming 250 days of work per year, this comes to 625 soldi and 750 soldi, respectively; dividing by 124 (the official rate for the ducat in the later sixteenth century) gives us 5 ducats and 6 ducats, respectively.

[d]Based on 250 work days.

laborers such as oarsmen and stevedores made more than servants, then in many instances the salaries servants received would have been inadequate for survival if they had not been supplemented with housing and food. As we have seen, in his account book Lorenzo Priuli estimated the yearly "spese di boca" for adult members of the family at twenty-five ducats per year, and that for servants, both male and female, at sixteen ducats per year.[86] If such a figure bears any relation to the actual cost of living, then servants' total compensation, including food, shelter, and salary, would have placed them about on par with other kinds of unskilled laborers in Venice, who had to provide for their own food and housing from their wages.

Conversely, we may ask what it cost masters to maintain and pay their servants, especially as a portion of their annual income. Precise answers to this question too are very difficult to arrive at for several reasons. First, very few data are available on the cost of living in Venice. Second, it is impossible to determine what portion of the stores of food and fuel listed in account books was consumed by servants. Third, we lack accurate information on the actual income of most masters since, as Richard Goldthwaite notes, "no amount of digging around in the accounts—including those dedicated only to business activities—will reveal how much money they were earning."[87] All we can do is provide some general indications.

Gino Luzzatto studied the patrician Guglielmo Querini, a merchant active in the mid-fifteenth century. Querini never married or had children, but he seems to have regularly been served by one or two slaves. In 1439 the officials in charge of the *estimo* (tax assessment) valued his patrimony at 4,900 ducats. Nine years later Querini reported that in the interval he had spent 362 ducats on rent, 1,200 on food and clothing, and 48 on the purchase of a slave, for a total of 1,610 ducats, or about 179 ducats per year.[88]

According to Frederic Lane, the merchant Andrea Barbarigo spent about 400 ducats per year maintaining his family. Lane also calculated that Barbarigo's successors could easily have sustained his standard of living if they received an annual return of approximately 5 percent on his estate, which was worth between 10,000 and 15,000 ducats.[89] In 1440 Andrea purchased three slaves (two females and one male) for 147 ducats, a rather modest investment given his income. After that he simply had to maintain the slaves. Even so, as we have seen, for a time at least, he rented out the services of one of the female slaves and so recovered at least some of the expense of maintaining the others.[90]

The account books of Andrea's great-grandson Antonio provide some indication of what it cost a moderately wealthy patrician to maintain his household in the mid-sixteenth century. In an entry dated 28 February 1557mv, Antonio wrote that he had not kept good records of his household expenses that year—"per piu spese delle quali non ho tenuto conto minuto il presente anno"— but that he calculated the "spese di casa" at 140 ducats, clothing at 20 ducats, and "estraordinarii" at 200 ducats, for a total of 360 ducats.[91] Two years later, under the "spese di casa" account he listed all of his servants and the salaries they had been paid; the nine servants received in total just over 37 ducats in pay. In the same year Antonio spent 21 ducats for his wife's clothing, and six months later he spent 70 ducats for his mother's burial.[92] In February 1560mv Antonio recorded that he had disbursed 21 ducats in cash for the salaries of five servants. Again, these figures do not include the expenses he incurred for food, shelter, and clothing, which would have been included in the overall "spese di casa" accounts, but not itemized for each servant.[93] It seems fairly safe to conclude that the cost of paying and maintaining servants represented a small to very moderate portion of Antonio's total annual expenses.

The same was probably true for the painter Lorenzo Lotto. Lotto calculated the yearly cost of his own maintenance while he was living in the house of a friend in Treviso at 25 ducats per year.[94] In March 1546 he hired as his massara the aged donna Lucia at 4 ducats per year. But apparently Lotto was not obliged to pay anything else to Lucia, since he recorded "promessoli ducati quatro a l'anno de salario, senza altro obligo mio." In August 1546 Lotto hired Maria da Montagnana at the same salary, but unlike Lucia, Maria seems to have lived with him, since when she left a porter was hired to remove her trunk.[95] In the same year (1546), Lotto received 8 ducats for a portrait of friar Gregorio da Vicenza.[96] Four years earlier, a major commission, the *pala* (altarpiece) of Saint Antoninus for San Zanipolo (see plate 8), had garnered him 125 ducats.[97] Evidently Lotto could recoup the yearly salary and maintenance of a female servant by producing two or three fairly standard canvases per year.

The evidence suggests that it cost Venetian masters between 15 and 20 ducats per year to pay and maintain female servants in the mid-sixteenth century. The comparatively small cost of keeping a female servant, particularly if she did not reside with the master, explains their presence in households of even modest income. Indeed, as we have seen, the employment of a serving girl served to mark the middle ranks from the rest of Venetian society.

The expense of servants grew as their number increased and if they were males. In the late sixteenth century, a "fameglio di pope" would have cost a master at least 20 ducats per year and perhaps as much as 40 if he received maintenance. A household staff of two male and two female servants would probably have cost something in the vicinity of 112 ducats per year (based on 20 ducats' maintenance for each and a salary of 6 ducats for women and 20 for men). But even this would have been easily manageable for many patricians.

## Payment Schedules

While contracts often stated the salary that was to be paid on a monthly or yearly basis, the actual amount of money that a master disbursed in any given year could vary widely. Even wealthy patricians were sometimes strapped for ready cash. In 1442, for instance, Andrea Barbarigo had to pawn a ring for 10 ducats.[98] Some masters may have tided themselves over times of cash shortage by delaying payments to their servants. Lorenzo Priuli's accounts illustrate the irregular flow of payments to his domestic laborers. In 1515 Priuli recorded that expenses for himself and his wife, Paola, including costs of clothing and charity, amounted to 57 ducats. That same year he paid out 74 ducats in salaries to his four servants: 50 ducats to his fante Matteo, 16 to Philipo da Salò, 7 to Jacomo Furlan, and 1 to another fante, Zaneto.[99] Neither Matteo nor Philipo was recorded in the following year, and so the fairly substantial payments of 50 and 16 ducats, respectively, probably represented major disbursements at the end of their employment. In 1516 Priuli recorded payment to only two servants—Jacomo Furlan and Jacomo da Sibenico—of just over 5 ducats total.[100] In 1517 Priuli paid out 17 ducats in salaries to four servants, including just over 1 ducat to Zaneto da Bergamo, the Zaneto who was listed in 1515 but not mentioned in 1516.[101]

In May 1523 Lorenzo's sons recorded that this same Zaneto had died. They also noted that he had entered their father's service in June 1505 and that he had still been in his service when Lorenzo himself died in September 1518, a total of thirteen years and three months. Since his agreed-upon salary was 1 ducat per month, his total earnings were 159 ducats, but during Lorenzo's lifetime Zaneto had received only 55 ducats, leaving a balance of 104. In the years following Lorenzo's death, Zaneto remained in the household but did not receive a salary. After apparently deducting the cost of his funeral, Lorenzo's sons made a payment of 53 ducats to Zaneto's father and brother.[102]

The case of Lorenzo Priuli and Zaneto da Bergamo was not the only one in which a servant spent years in service without receiving payment of his or her salary. In 1548 Leonardo Raimondo acknowledged that he owed 150 ducats to his servant donna Marro da Lepanto for her thirty years of service.[103] In 1604 donna Marina da Cadore sued the executors of Scipione Rini in order to recover what they owed her. The case was quite extraordinary. Marina had entered Rini's service in August 1548 under an indenture contract according to which she was to receive 10 ducats in August 1554. Yet she had remained in Rini's service, working without a contract from the end of that initial contract in August 1554 until Rini's death in 1590. After Rini's death she had continued in the family's service until May 1604. Eventually it was decided that Marina would be compensated at the rate of 7 ducats per year for her service from August 1554 to May 1604. And in the final settlement, Marina received just over 380 ducats as payment for her salary, for bequests left to her by various family members, and for expenses she had incurred for the family.[104]

There are several possible explanations for this and similar cases in which servants passed years, sometimes even a lifetime, in service without compensation. In some instances they probably mask illicit relationships between masters and servants. Given the Venetian practice of fraterna, it was not uncommon for patrician males to remain bachelors; and some developed long-term sexual and emotional relationships with female servants.[105] Since in such cases master and servant lived together as a couple, there was no need for the servant to be paid until the master died, when the servant had to sue for compensation in order to survive.

In other cases, the attachment was not sexual and quasi-conjugal but paternal. Servants who became part of the family often were not paid on a regular basis. Such appears to have been the case with Lorenzo Priuli and Zaneto da Bergamo. After Lorenzo's death, his sons continued to maintain Zaneto, but without a salary. The relationship between nobleman Federico Ferro and Lucia da Trau may have been sexual or purely sentimental. Lucia entered Federico's father's service, and after his death she remained in Federico's service for the next fifty years. When at age eighty Federico was threatened with eviction from his house, Lucia gave him 105 ducats to purchase the property, which he then donated to her.[106]

At other times delays in payment may indicate that masters were short of cash, so that the delays really represented a kind of loan from servants to their masters. Nor were actual loans unknown. In 1567 the wife of Marcantonio Rimondo, who described herself as a "povera gentildonna," acknowledged that she owed 150 ducats to Marco di Gregorio partly as repayment of a loan and "in part for his salary for the service he has given her for many years."[107] In his will Zuane da Cattaro recorded that he had loaned 22 ducats to his "patron" Marco Grimani.[108] And in July 1548 friar Galeatio da Venezia, a priest at San Marco, acknowledged that he owed his servant Laura 60 ducats for her ten years of service, as well as 100 ducats that she had extended to him as a free loan.[109]

A final possibility is that servants were not paid on a regular basis because they asked their masters to retain their earnings for them "in salvo," that is, in safekeeping. For example, Girolamo Donà recorded in a memorial that his massara Agnola had asked him to keep "in salvo" her salary for the past year.[110] Since their expenses were usually provided for, servants had little need of large amounts of cash. Additionally, the rooms they shared with other servants allowed for little privacy or security. Hence servants may simply have asked or expected their masters to keep their money for them in a strongbox. Such a system again benefited masters, who only had to disburse cash on demand and who could use the debt to bind servants to them. Legally, however, a servant's claim to his or her salary enjoyed legal precedence over most other claims to the master's estate, apparently even over a widow's claim to her dowry.[111]

Although some servants went for years without payment, others were paid on a regular basis. Paolo di Massimi, a cittadino, stated as much in his will:

Concerning the salary of donna Zuana, wife of sir Marco di Vivian Cinganetto, silkworker, who serves me at present and who has served me continuously for almost sixteen years, as she knows, I do not need to say anything about her salary because ordinarily I pay her every month courteously and sometimes I make advances to her according to her greater or lesser need, as she knows very well and as one can see in her account in a certain of my [account] books.[112]

In this instance, since she was married, Zuana almost certainly lived apart from her master; and regular payment probably allowed her and her husband to meet their housing and other expenses.

An example of semiregular payments to a servant is the case of donna Caterina, daughter of the late Leonardo Giovanni Leon of Vicenza. On 8 November 1534 she hired on to live and serve as a maid for Sebastiano di Pace at a salary of 4 ducats per year (1 ducat being worth 6 lire, 4 soldi). She remained in his service for twelve years, until 8 November 1546. In January 1547 she and Pace had the notary Vettor Maffei prepare a final receipt for the balance of her pay. They recorded that during those twelve years she had received in cash 125 lire, 12 soldi, and 60 lire, 14 soldi, worth of goods and clothes, for a total of 192 lire, 6 soldi. Since her salary of 48 ducats equaled 297 lire, 12 soldi, Pace still owed her a balance of 105 lire, 6 soldi; and it was for that amount that she now acknowledged receipt. In addition, the notary copied into his protocol Caterina's account from Pace's books. It shows that every year between 1534 and 1546 she received between two and five disbursements of petty cash. In 1537, for example, she received 3 lire, 4 soldi, on 3 June; 2 lire, 8 soldi, on 4 September; and 1 lire on 19 December. In 1544 she received 2 lire, 10 soldi, on 13 June; 2 lire on 2 August "per zocoli" [for clogs]; and 2 lire, 8 soldi, on 3 October. Of the 66 lira, 14 soldi, spent on clothes, Caterina had bought two sheepskin furs, worth 8 lire; four blouses, worth 10 lire, 4 soldi; and a cloak, worth 21 lire. During her twelve years of service she had spent just over 31 ducats, leaving her a final payment of almost 17 ducats.[113]

Another example of payment patterns appears in the account book of Agostino Spinelli. In 1572 he hired Maddalena Feltrina as his massara at a salary of 5 ducats per year. Each year he carefully recorded that the 5 ducats equaled 31 lire and then deducted any cash disbursements he had made to her. In 1575, for example, he advanced her part of her salary so that she could buy salted eels and rice to send to relatives in Feltre; in 1577 he docked her fifteen days' pay when she traveled to Feltre. When in the same year Maddalena became mortally ill, Spinelli recorded all the expenses of her final illness and funeral, including 4 soldi for a syrup made of radicchio, parsley, borage, and other herbs; 1 lira, 16 soldi, for a barber to bleed her; and 1 lira, 10 soldi, for a chicken. After her death, Spinelli sent 69 lire, 7 soldi (about 11 ducats), to the beneficiaries of her estate in Feltre. Included were the 11 lire, 7 soldi (1.8 ducats), that she had asked him to keep for her "in salvo" and the 2 lire, 3 soldi (.34 ducats), she had in her purse at the time of her death.[114] After a lifetime in trade, the merchant Andrea Barbarigo left an estate worth more than 10,000 ducats to his heirs; Maddalena Feltrina bequeathed her heirs a bit more than 10 ducats. These sums speak volumes about the conditions of domestic labor in fifteenth- and sixteenth-century Venice.

~

The Venetian domestic labor market operated through a series of both formal and informal means. While some domestics were supplied by professional brokers and dealers in indentured servants, many servants came to their masters through less organized methods. Servants themselves played an active role in finding jobs for friends, relatives, and fellow immigrants. The bulk of domestic labor was performed by immigrants to the city, the vast majority of whom came either from Venice's Adriatic catchment area or from the Italian terraferma lands directly under Venetian control. Immigrants gravitated to domestic service because it required little skill and was one of the few areas not controlled by the guilds. Masters and servants agreed to a bewildering variety of conditions and clauses, and there was a major distinction between inscribed, or indentured, and salaried labor. Domestic service represented a significant exploitation of child labor; and masters faced the problem of rapid turnover among their servants. Wages remained fairly stable during the fifteenth century and the first half of the sixteenth century but then rose significantly, especially for male servants, in the second half of the sixteenth century. Servants were paid about on a par with other unskilled workers in Venice, if one takes into account the food, clothing, and shelter they received. Finally, servants were paid on an irregular basis, indebtedness between masters and servants further binding them together.

Overall, the picture that emerges is not of a labor market geared to the efficient recruitment and training of a disciplined work force, like the one the government was trying to create at the Arsenal.[115] The reason for this seems fairly clear; domestic service was based on the performance of service, broadly defined, rather than on the production of tangible goods. It often had more to do with the moral economy than with the market economy. Labor relations between masters and servants were complicated by the fact that both endowed the relationship with broader moral, social, and political significance. The hiring of servants required more than determining whether they could perform the tasks required; masters also had to judge whether servants would project the proper image of the household. This was not an easy task. As Leone Zambelli wrote in his 1635 treatise *Il Savio Industrioso,* "The ability to divine which servants are good, true, and loving is a gift from God."[116]

# Chapter Five

# The Lives of Servants

On 12 April 1567 Giorgio, son of Michele Cosmo da Brazzo di Maina, *falconier* of King Philip of Spain,[1] called the notary Rocco di Benedetto to his residence in the vicinity of San Francesco della Vigna to record the story of fourteen-year-old Africo Negro, a Cypriot lad whom he had taken under his care "per l'amor di Dio." Africo's story was a complicated one. Son of a Cypriot caulker named Flori, Africo had first entered the service of Venetian nobleman Girolamo Contarini. But Contarini had dismissed Africo and consigned him to Tomà Zane Stauri of Famagosta, captain of a galley, who planned to take the boy with him to Cyprus. Not wishing to return to Cyprus, when they reached the island of Zante, off the coast of Greece, Africo had taken his leave of Stauri and entered the service of Michelin Scandori. Within twenty days Scandori had grown tired of Africo and dismissed him. "Having no master" [non havendo patrone] ,the boy had begun begging. It was at this point that he had come under da Brazzo's care. Since da Brazzo had first had to complete duties elsewhere, he had entrusted Africo to some "persone da bene," and upon his return four months later, he had settled accounts with them for Africo's expenses. The two then had traveled to France before finally returning to Venice. Now in Venice, da Brazzo wanted the notary to record that he intended to maintain Africo "for the glory of God" [à laude de Dio] as long as he behaved. Indeed, before Africo had come under his care, he had been "going to ruin" [andava à ramengo]. Africo confirmed that all that had been recorded about him was true.[2]

Four years earlier, on 26 March 1563, Isabeta, wife of Zanmaria di Constantin, had gone before the same notary to ask him to prepare a *protesto,* in which she recounted her life story.[3] Orphaned at a young age in Rome, Isabeta was taken under the care of a certain Madonna Cesarea, who maintained her as her "figliola adottiva." When she reached adulthood, her mistress married her to Zanmaria, a fisherman from Pesaro. Upon arriving in Venice, Isabeta thought that she had reached "the promised Land" [in terra di promissione] and found a god-fearing husband. Instead, she had fallen "into the hands of a Pharaoh" [nelle mani d'un Faraone], for even though she was "loving, loyal, obedient, and

Servants came from a wide variety of social backgrounds. Many of the servants who immigrated to Venice from the terraferma must have been from peasant families. In some instances, the censors' trial records record the profession or trade of the defendants' fathers;[18] these data are presented in table 5.1. As the table shows, some servants came from families in which the fathers practiced respectable, if humble professions. Many of the fathers for whom data are available were engaged in the leather and footwear trades as cobblers or tanners; a significant number were also engaged in the construction trades, as carpenters, stonecutters, or masons. Among those engaged in the production or sale of wine and victuals, two were millers and three were fishermen. Four were active in various sectors of the textile industries or as tailors. Not surprisingly, seven servants were the children of boatmen, most of whom worked at the city's traghetti, but only one was listed as the child of an unskilled stevedore. Two were the children of stewards of country estates (listed under small managers). A few even came from families engaged in luxury trades, including goldsmithing and goldbeating, perfumery, and mirror making. None were the children of civil servants.

Table 5.1
Professions and Trades of Servants' Fathers, 1569–1600

| Father's Profession or Trade | Number of Servants |
| --- | --- |
| Boatman | 7 |
| Servant | 0 |
| Sailor | 0 |
| Professional or higher civil servant | 0 |
| Luxury trades, books, jewelry | 4 |
| Groceries and drugs | 1 |
| Trader, broker, or unspecified merchant | 0 |
| Arsenal worker | 0 |
| Textiles and clothing | 4 |
| Footwear and leather | 5 |
| Wine and victuals | 5 |
| Building construction and furnishing | 5 |
| Wood and metal | 2 |
| Household utensils | 2 |
| Barber, surgeon, or dentist | 0 |
| Clerical worker or small manager | 2 |
| Minor government employee | 0 |
| Porter, warehouseman, or heavy laborer | 1 |
| Total | 38 |

*Source:* ASV, Censori, busta 3, registers 1–3.

Unfortunately, the records do not indicate what led the children of skilled artisans to become domestic servants. It is possible that an oversupply of labor in certain fields forced offspring into service jobs. It is also possible that some fathers encouraged their slow-witted sons into domestic service. What the data do indicate is that there was not necessarily a steady progression of families out of service and toward more respectable jobs as artisans. Often servants themselves moved between service and other occupations as the circumstances of their lives changed. This was especially true at the time of marriage.

## Marriage

As our knowledge of the family life of artisans in late medieval and early modern cities develops, it is becoming increasingly clear that for the urban working poor marriage represented the most important transition in the life cycle. For males, it signaled their entry into respectable adulthood, for many artisans did not marry until they had achieved the rank of master and secured their own shop or at least found steady employment with another master. Marriage was to some extent a public expression of their new status as responsible, economically independent adult members of the guild community. For women of artisan background as well, marriage marked a major change in status as they passed from the power of their fathers, uncles, or brothers to that of their husbands. Many of these women now began to work beside their husbands and, at the same time, to raise children. The transformation from maiden to matron offered artisan class women new freedom of movement and association.[19]

The same was true for domestic servants. Marriage signaled their entry into adulthood and for many their passage, temporarily at least, out of service and into other forms of employment. Even for those who remained in service, marriage often earned them new status and respectability and the prospect of better-paying and more responsible jobs within households. Their new status as adults could transform significantly their relationships with their masters and mistresses.[20] Now clearly identified as husbands and wives, fathers and mothers, servants fit more comfortably into the households of their employers. It is only a slight exaggeration to say that marriage marked the transformation of servants from potential "domestic enemies" into domestic allies.

Female servants are more visible in the documents, and their transformation is easier to trace. As we have already noted, one reason for placing girls (as well as boys) in service was to pass the expense of raising them from their kinsmen to those better able to do so. Accumulating a dowry was a powerful incentive for girls to go into service. It was even written into some contracts that masters were responsible for marrying off their servant girls.

Table 5.2
Dowries of Servants, Boatmen, and Others, 1400–1599

| | Dowries of | | | | | |
|---|---|---|---|---|---|---|
| | Servants | | Boatmen | | Others | |
| Period | Amount | No. | Amount | No. | Amount | No. |
| 1400–1449 | 71.3 | 18 | 80.0 | 5 | 138.1 | 20 |
| 1450–1499 | 59.9 | 25 | 65.3 | 12 | 141.7 | 70 |
| 1500–1549 | 103.7 (107.5) | 4 | 95.5 (100.4) | 8 | 141.9 (157.6) | 62 |
| 1550–1599 | 97.6 (114.4) | 35 | 113.2 (169.2) | 19 | 244.3 (269.0) | 106 |

*Sources:* ASV, CI, Notai, and NA.
*Note:* If either the husband or the wife was labeled a servant, the dowry has been included in the "servant"category. The ducat amounts in parentheses are the amounts of the dowries and counterdowries combined.

Ioseph Basello, described as a "master" [magister] as well as a discipulus of Titian, who got a dowry of 66.5 ducats from his wife, Regina, daughter of a boatyard owner or worker (he offered a counterdowry of 133.5 ducats); and Giovanni Domenico Colona, a caulker who received a dowry of 125 ducats from his wife, Peregrina, daughter of a barber.[31] Members of the Venetian elite, those specifically identified as cittadini or nobles (except for those who married artisans), are not included.[32]

These comparative data prompt several observations. First, the comparable status of domestic servants and boatmen is richly illustrated by the close correspondence between the amounts of the dowries they gave and received. During the later fifteenth century, the dowries of both servants and barcaruoli declined, only to recover in the sixteenth century and hover around 100 ducats.

It is not easy to account for the decline in dowries in the second half of the fifteenth century. It may reflect a decline in the status of servants, especially female servants as evidenced by the relative decline in their wages during this same period. The influx of servants from Dalmatia and Albania may also have caused a drop in servants' earning power. It is likely that these immigrant women, many of whom were indentured servants, could not rely on inheritances from their families to augment their dowries. But during the first half of the sixteenth century the dowries of servants and boatmen rose fairly sharply, especially in comparison with the stability of dowries for other groups. This was followed by their own period of stability. During the second half of the sixteenth century, when the dowries of other occupational groups rose dramatically, those of servants and boatmen changed little.

Although the value of dowries was expressed in ducats, many dowries, indeed most, were made up of some combination of cash and goods. Furthermore, the value of the goods portion of the dowry often exceeded that of the cash component. For example, the dowry of Caterina, a servant of the Morosini brothers, who married a boatman at the traghetto of Santa Maria Zobenigo, comprised goods worth eighty ducats and forty ducats in cash.[33] The dowry offered by the Grimani for Ruosa da Budua was evenly divided between cash and kind.[34] On the other hand, Benedetta Paduana, former ancilla of nobleman Giovanni Maria Bembo, offered her husband, Carolo, a fritter seller, a dowry of forty ducats, entirely in goods.[35]

Few dowry receipts specified the items that made up the goods portion of dowries. Generally speaking, notaries simply recorded the estimated cash value of the items without listing them. Yet evidence from bequests to marriageable girls found in women's wills indicates that trousseaux often included personal items such as clothes, shoes, and furs; household goods, including cooking utensils and linens; and even large pieces of furniture, such as beds.[36]

At least one list of items in a servant's trousseau has survived, that of Maddalena, one-time servant of Niccolò Foscari. Her dowry included 11 ducats in cash, 56 in goods; the counterdowry was 13 ducats. Her trousseau consisted almost entirely of clothes. Among the items were several dresses, including one of new cloth worth 10 ducats; two furs, worth 4 ducats; blouses valued at 6 ducats; handkerchiefs; other "little things" [cose menude], worth 6 ducats; and seven yards of plain wool cloth, valued at 7 lire.[37] The dowry Lucieta Tron provided for her servant Maria included not only goods valued at just over 77 ducats but also a piece of property at the villa of Roncadelle, near Oderzo, worth 110 ducats.[38]

As even a quick comparison of tables 4.8 and 5.2 indicates, the average female salaried servant in the latter half of the sixteenth century, making just under 5 ducats per year, would have had to work almost twenty years to earn the 98 ducats that dowries averaged in that period. Even if a girl began work at age ten, she would have been thirty years old before she could marry if she depended solely on her salary to accumulate a dowry. Furthermore, most servants did not save their entire salary, but spent part of it during their years in service. Clearly, for many servant girls, their earnings constituted only one part of their dowry.

Another important source of money was a girl's inheritance from her parents and other relatives. For example, Lucia, daughter of the late Francesco Ballota of the villa Marano, had interests in the Vicentino.[39] Marieta, daughter of the late Biagio Bartolani of the villa of Cessalto in the *podesteria* of Motta, was left goods at the villa by her sister.[40] And Benedetta, widow and servant in the home of Giovanni Corner, sold a house in Conegliano and applied the 65 ducats she received to the dowry of her daughter Orsa.[41]

Yet another source of dowry money was gifts and bequests from other working and serving women. A few examples will suffice to illustrate this widespread practice. Maria, widow of a boatman and a servant in the house of Procurator of San Marco Lorenzo Giustinian, left bequests to three serving women of the Giustinian household: she bequeathed a small bed to Cornelia and blouses and aprons to Benetta and Agnola.[42] Anna, former servant of Lorenzo Bernardo, who drafted her will before setting out on pilgrimage to Loreto, named noblewoman Isabeta Valaresso as her executor. She asked that the balance of her estate be divided "among Orsa and Pasqua, massere of sir Lorenzo Bernardo, donna Pasqua and her daughter from Gambarare, massera of domina Marieta Venier, Lucia and the cook, who now serve in the house of domina Isabeta of cà Valaresso, my executor, donna Caterina who lives in the courtyard of cà Capello, who must go to get the indulgences for me, and the gastalda of the Trinity, who must get the indulgence of the Trinity for me."[43] Bequests such as these were given as tokens of friendship—"in segno d'amor"—or as charity. Whether given to help young girls build a dowry or to assist older married or widowed women financially, they reflect the strong affective ties and friendship networks that sometimes linked working women within and between households.

Members of the elite, both women and men, were also important benefactors of unmarried girls trying to accumulate dowries. Nobleman Paolo Morosini left a whole series of items, including beds and linens, to his fantesche Lena and Stana, in the case of Stana "so that she can marry and expect to live honorably" [azo le se posi maridar e atender a far ben].[44] Sometimes the sums provided were quite substantial and represented a large increment to the dowry. Giovanni Francesco Bragadin singled out his fantesca Orsa da Schio for special treatment. Whereas most of his other servants were bequeathed small sums over and above their salary, Orsa received 100 ducats. The bequest was to go into effect "in the case that during my lifetime I have not [had the opportunity to] marry and dower her" [in caso che lo in vita mia non lavesse maridada e dotada]. The sum was given "for the honor of God and for her good behavior in the house and for her salary" [a honor di dio e per el suo bon portamento fato in caxa e per mercede de quella].[45] Providing dowries for poor girls to marry was a popular form of charity in Venice.[46] By so doing, benefactors could rest comfortably, knowing they had saved girls from the dangers of prostitution (hence Morosini's expressed concern that Stana be able to live honorably). Nobleman Angelo Morosini was "spontaneously moved by Christian piety" to give 80 ducats to Franceschina, daughter of a boatman, so that she could marry and live as a "donna da bene."[47]

Yet as Bragadin's bequest to Orsa indicates, masters and mistresses had another important motive in providing dowries to servant girls. They used the promise of dowry assistance as a way to control the behavior of their female servants. For example, Luca Vendramin wanted his slaves to be freed after five years of additional service, and he wanted the female slaves to be provided with beds and other "cossete," as three previous slaves had been. But he included a proviso: these bequests were only to be executed if "during the said five years they show good comportment in service to my sons, and if they show bad comportment, they are to be neither rewarded nor freed."[48] The promise of help with the dowry provided a powerful incentive for servant girls to obey their masters and mistresses.

Other members of the elite may have provided dowries for their servants as a way to illustrate their own magnanimity and importance and to increase their honor.[49] The ancilla Francesca, daughter of the late Andrea di Toniolis, had a dowry valued at 50 ducats, 40 of it in goods and 10 in cash. In the dowry receipt it was recorded that 5 ducats had been given to her by her mistress as the balance of her salary; the other 5 had been donated by her mistress "out of pure urbanity" [ex mera urbanitate].[50]

Still another source of dowry funds was the scuole and charitable endowments, such as those administered by the procurators of San Marco. When Franceschina, daughter of master weaver Domenico, married Santo Giovanni Alborante, a carpenter in the Arsenal, she brought him a dowry of 92 ducats, 82 of which she received in goods and cash from her mistresses, noblewomen Priula and Lucretia Priuli; the scuola of Santa Maria Maggiore provided the additional 10 ducats.[51] In November 1462 Elena, daughter of a boatman, acknowledged receipt of 8 ducats toward her dowry from the scuola of San Giovanni Evangelista.[52] Santa, former ancilla in the home of Bernardino Bentio, had a dowry of 164 ducats, 84 in goods, 68 in cash as payment of her salary, and 12 in cash from the scuola of Santa Maria della Carità.[53] While he was procurator of San Marco, future doge Leonardo Donà diligently distributed the charitable funds entrusted to his office. Among the many charities he oversaw was a fund to be used for the distribution of dowries to deserving girls. Between 1591 and 1593 he bestowed amounts ranging from 5 to 15 ducats on many poor girls, some of whom were almost certainly employed as servants. Among the recipients were Vittoria, daughter of the late Niccolò di Bertoldi, described as "da ben et senza alcuno"; and Tadia, daughter of the mariner Marco, called "poverissima."[54] In order to qualify for these funds, girls had to meet prescribed criteria. Generally speaking, they had to be honest and honorable young girls who could be saved from a life of shame through marriage.[55]

Two final examples illustrate how female servants were able to piece together dowries from many different sources. On 24 October 1422 Philipo da Alemanea, a master weaver from Treviso, acknowledged receipt of a dowry worth 30 ducats from his wife, Constantia da Trau. On that same day Constantia had herself acknowledged receipt of 16 ducats owed her by her former master, Antonio Alberegno, "as appears in the register of the capi di sestieri for the time I was required to serve the aforesaid sir Antonio Alberegno." In November, Philipo received 16 ducats that domina Domenica Condulmer had promised to him in Constantia's name at the time of the marriage contract. And in the dowry receipt itself, Philipo recorded that if Constantia were able to recuperate goods worth 100 lire di piccoli that she claimed to have in Trau or if she were able to secure funds from the procurators of San Marco, then those amounts were to be added to her dowry as well.[56] Constantia's dowry thus included her salary and a gift from a noblewoman, and she hoped to augment it with an inheritance and funds from the procurators.

In 1564 Mattea, daughter of the late Leonardo Bettino Cristoforo da Monzambano, a gardener on the Lido, brought a dowry of 89.5 ducats, 43 in goods and the balance in cash, to her husband, Antonio di Martin di Zotis da Rovado, a grain measurer. She got 15 ducats from her father's estate as her share of her mother's dowry (the other half went to her sister); in addition, she got 1.5 ducats from the estate's executor "ex sua urbanitate." The balance (73 ducats) she received from her former employer, Ventura Brombilla, a grain broker, partly as recompense for her salary.[57] She was promised a counterdowry of 10.5 ducats. Five years later, in January 1568, Brombilla's own daughter married a grain merchant employed at the grain warehouse at Rialto. Her dowry was 410 ducats, and she had a counterdowry of 50 ducats.[58] In all likelihood, Brombilla arranged both marriages through his connections with those involved in the shipment and storage of grain. It is even possible that Mattea first came into Brombilla's household through a connection between her father (a gardener) and Brombilla. Whether or not this was the case, Mattea's example illustrates how servant girls were able to piece together a dowry that would allow them to marry. It also leads to the next issue for consideration, namely, the professions of the men that servant women married.

Of the eighty-two dowry receipts under consideration, forty-eight allow us to identify the professions of the men whom female servants married and thereby to judge the degree of professional endogamy and exogamy exhibited by servants. Table 5.3 gives the breakdown of these professions.[59] The data in the table show that there was a fairly strong tendency for female servants to marry other servants or boatmen, who also performed service jobs. It is likely that crossing paths and networks among servants brought these men and women together. In 1449, for instance, Marco Donà da Sclavonia, servant of nobleman Antonio Donà of Sant'Agata, married Franceschina, the servant of Michele Donà of Santi Apostoli.[60] The two may have been met at a Donà family function, or the marriage may have been arranged by the Donà. In 1579 Giacomo di Francesco Gabia, a boatman in the service of the censor Paolo Contarini, made a dowry receipt to his wife, Paolina, daughter of Antonio di Bello, a boatman at the traghetto of San Tomà.[61] Shared duties in households and physical proximity certainly provided opportunities for servants to meet and develop relations. It

Table 5.3
Professional Endogamy and Exogamy of Female Servants, 1416–1589

| Husband's Profession or Trade | Number of Servants |
| --- | --- |
| Boatman | 10 |
| Servant | 9 |
| Sailor[a] | 6 |
| Professional and higher civil servant | 1 |
| Luxury trades, books, jewelry, etc. | 0 |
| Groceries and drugs | 0 |
| Trader, broker, or unspecified merchant | 2 |
| Arsenal worker | 1 |
| Textiles and clothing | 2 |
| Footwear and leather | 0 |
| Wine and victuals | 3 |
| Building, construction, and furnishing | 4 |
| Wood and metal | 3 |
| Household utensils | 3 |
| Barber, surgeon, or dentist | 2 |
| Clerical worker or small manager | 0 |
| Minor government employee | 2 |
| Porter, warehouseman, or heavy laborer | 0 |
| Total | 48 |

*Sources:* ASV, CI, Notai, and NA.
[a]One man labeled a "marinarius et barbitonsor" is included under barbers.

will be recalled that both the capi di sestieri and the censors, as well as authors of treatises on household management, warned masters about the possibility of servants' forming licit or illicit unions and thereby disrupting the operation of the household. In two of the nine cases in which servants married other servants, they were employed in the same household.[62]

We know from testamentary evidence that masters and mistresses took an active role in placing their female servants in marriage. This was to be expected given their parental attitude and since, especially if they were furnishing part of the dowry, they wanted to be sure that the husbands would be responsible men who would not squander the funds. Accordingly, masters sometimes used their own connections to find suitable spouses for their servant girls. In 1416 Cita, the slave of the coppersmith Toma, married the coppersmith Stefano di Climento da Alemania.[63] Toma may have been instrumental in arranging this match. In one particularly revealing case from the late fourteenth century, the ducal esquire, or cavalier, Andrea di Varnarussiis made provision in his will for the eventual marriage of his slave Catarina. He warned that she was to marry only a "good man who is not a slave" [unum bonum hominem qui non sit sclavus]. If she did otherwise, the bequest was to be canceled.[64] And in his will dated 1523, Matteo, a boatman from Murano, left the residue of his estate to his son with the proviso that he marry an "upright wife" [probam mulierem] of good reputation.[65]

A further examination of table 5.3 suggests that when servants married beyond the ranks of other servants, boatmen, and sailors, they tended to marry into the middle level of Venetian artisan society. Few married men of much status or wealth. One exception was Ruosa da Budua, whose masters, as we have seen, arranged for her to marry a citizen of Bassano. Another is Paola, daughter of a master barber (and cameriera of nobleman Aurelio Condulmer), who married a mercer with a shop in the Piazza San Marco.[66] Additionally, it appears that servants did not marry men for whom literacy and learning were high priorities: none married workers in the luxury trades, such as goldsmithing or printing, nor did they marry clerical workers. Only two female servants married men in the textile industries (one a linen worker, the other a weaver); this is somewhat surprising given the importance of the industry in sixteenth-century Venice and the likelihood that their own training in sewing and weaving would have made serving women likely helpmates to men in these professions. Among other categories, three servant women married men in hostelry and food selling, activities in which domestic skills would come in handy. And several women found husbands engaged in a variety of skilled trades involving construction and the production of tools and utensils of various sorts.

As the will of the ducal cavalier di Varnarussiis indicates, there may have been some effort on the part of servant women (or those responsible for them) to avoid men involved in the lowliest professions, at least those that did not involve personal service or work as boatmen or sailors. None married porters, warehousemen, or men engaged in other heavy labor. On the whole, female servants seem to have tried to marry into the ranks of Venice's respectable working poor.

Indeed, marriage signaled that servants were themselves "da bene," and the married state led to a change in their own status. Once taken in marriage, female servants were no longer under the direct care of their masters; instead they became, from the masters' point of view, the wives of other men and hence less susceptible to sexual exploitation.[67] Because married servants were more likely to live in their own households, there were also fewer opportunities for sexual encounters. And if servants' marital status alone were not sufficient cause for disinterest on the part of the masters, the possibility of being taken to court by the women's husbands further discouraged sexual entanglements.[68]

The transformation of female servants from potential objects of sexual exploitation into the wives of other men gave married women a more respectable and better defined place in both household and society, very unlike that of their unmarried counterparts. With this new respectability came new responsibilities and a measure of prestige within the household. Some married female servants became wet nurses and governesses and as such had responsibility for the most prized possessions of elite households, namely, the children. This responsibility was reflected in part in the higher salaries paid to wet nurses. In addition, wet nursing and raising children fostered strong emotional attachments between servants and their nurslings. Many wet nurses took special interest in and developed lifelong attachments to their "milk children."[69] Shared concern for the children could also lead to closer relations between mistresses and nurses. As a consequence of all this, the faithful nurse held a special place in many elite households. With marriage then, many serving women were transformed not only in the eyes of their masters but also in those of their mistresses. For the lady of the household, the servant woman could be changed through marriage from a wanton rival for her husband's affections into a treasured co-mother of her children.

For other servants, marriage meant the end of their term in service. Some women left service to assist in their husbands' shops.[70] Male servants moved on to new careers as well. Marcantonio Morosini's former servant Matheo da Trau obtained a position as a guard in the court of the captain of Padua.[71] Large numbers of former personal gondoliers filled the city's traghetti; at least one, a barcaruol at the traghetto of San Trovaso who had first served twenty-two years in the personal service of Tomà Michiel of Camponogara, was described by diarist Marino Sanuto as "rather wealthy" [assa ricco di danari].[72] Since the license required for membership in a traghetto could be passed from father to son (with the approval of the traghetto chapter), it is likely that initiation into the traghetto and marriage occurred at about the same time.[73]

As was the case with female servants, marriage could lead to new and greater responsibilities for those males who decided to remain in service. Important positions such as those of factors of terraferma estates or stewards of urban palazzi had to be entrusted to responsible adults.[74] For men just as for women, marriage could transform relations with their masters and mistresses. Employers recognized and esteemed the roles of husband and father that menservants now played in their own households. Marriage had the potential to transform male servants, in the eyes of their employers, from disruptive youths without roots or loyalty into stable, responsible upholders of family principles.

Although marriage meant the end of personal service for some servants, often it was merely a temporary cessation, as men and especially women returned to domestic service when the circumstances of their lives changed. During times of economic downturn when their husbands' shops were idle, women would return to service in order to supplement the family income. Widowhood was another time when many women returned to service. Since guild statutes prohibited widows from maintaining their husbands' shops, many had no choice but to return to service jobs.[75]

Men too, especially boatmen, passed back and forth between personal and nonpersonal service as financial circumstances required. In 1559, for example, when Marin d'Albona, a boatman at the traghetto of Sant'Eufemia of the Giudecca, bought a gondola from nobleman Francesco Querini for fifty ducats, he agreed to serve as Querini's personal gondolier in order to pay off the purchase price.[76] Alessandro Bergamasco, a boatman at the traghetto of the Beccaria and formerly a servant of nobleman Marco da Molin, reentered personal service, this time in the service of nobleman Girolamo Basadonna, in order to get a salary advance to pay for the gondola he had purchased from Zaneto Garabaldo, a boatman at the traghetto of Cannaregio.[77] Boatmen were not the only ones to take up service as their personal circumstances changed. In 1591 Gaspare da Serravalle was described by the censors as "former mercer and currently the servant" [olim merciarius, et ad presens famulus] of nobleman Francesco Trevisan; and in 1589 Natalino, formerly a ship's scribe, was serving nobleman Andrea Zane.[78] Former painters, furriers, and wool shearers all found work as servants.[79] For Venice's working poor, domestic and personal service remained options throughout their working lifetime.

All in all, marriage was the most important transition in the lives of servants, for it changed not only the circumstances of their lives but also their status. It allowed them to be identified as something other than servants. Now they were husbands and wives, fathers and mothers, in their own right—in other words, "persone da bene." Conversely, for some servants failure to marry meant that they would remain at the margins of society. The authorities feared that unmarried younger women would fall into prostitution, and this fear was the impetus for charitable giving to dowry funds. And unmarried older women were forced to eke out miserable lives, dependent on public and private charity. Unmarried men as well were seen as unstable and dangerous, given to dissolute lives of drinking, gambling, and crime. Often, then, the unmarried were feared and marginalized.

## Work and Associative Life

The social world of servants—the contacts they made, the circles and institutions they frequented, even their degree of mobility about the city—was determined largely by the duties and responsibilities assigned to them by their masters and mistresses. Since the duties of male and female servants differed markedly, so did their social contacts and associations.

Male servants had two major responsibilities. The first was to escort their masters about the city. As Venetian noblemen and other elites made their way through the town, they were accompanied by one or more male servants. By day these servants cleared a path for their masters through jostling crowds; at night they illuminated the way down dark and narrow streets with torches. When their masters died, they attended their funeral processions.[80] Male servants were dispatched to collect bills, receive goods, deliver messages, and to perform any number of other tasks for their masters.

Male servants were also supposed to protect their masters from danger and frequently became entangled in their quarrels. In March 1425, for example, nobleman Giovanni Trevisan and his servant were attacked by nobleman Fantino Zorzi and his famulus. The two were thrown into a recently dredged canal and nearly drowned.[81] Servants also helped their masters carry out vendettas and other crimes. Paolo, famulus of nobleman Giovanni Donà, assisted Donà in the theft of goods from a warehouse belonging to the Contarini.[82] And Giovanni da Segna, nicknamed Barbato, helped his master, Giovanni Pietro Bugatto, insult and abuse Brunori da Martinengo.[83] When attacked or attacking, male servants became extensions of their masters. In many ways this was their primary obligation.[84] For this reason, some masters may actually have sought servants who were aggressive and belligerent.[85] As public symbols of their masters' status and prestige, swaggering, roughneck gondoliers could, under the right circumstances, enhance their masters' image.

The second major responsibility of male servants was to care for their masters' boats and to provide transportation about the city for them and their families. In his treatise on costume Vecellio wrote,

> The nobles of Venice and other citizens, as well as rich and well-off people, maintain their own boats or gondolas with many servants, one of whom, who has charge of the boat, is called the poop man; the other is called the center man. The latter is often occupied in other services to the master, whereas the former has the sole responsibility of keeping the boat clean, rigged, and adorned as needed.[86]

And he added that "it is of the greatest import that the matrons and gentlewomen, when they leave their homes, have the luxury of arriving by boat at the doorstep of the palaces and churches where they are going and by similar means of returning to their own homes."[87] Hence the rhythm of the male servant's daily life was determined by the transportation needs of the master and his family. Some contracts for gondola service carefully specified the hours that boatmen, who were not resident in the homes of their employers, were required to be on duty.[88] Gondoliers spent countless hours idly waiting for their masters and mistresses to complete their business or social visits and return home. As noted earlier, the idleness of boatmen waiting for their masters concerned the Venetian government on two grounds: first, because they posed a potential threat to security, and second, because they tarnished the decorous image of the civic center at San Marco.

The duties and responsibilities of male servants pulled them both geographically and socially into the wider world of male sociability. In the company of their masters, servants traveled to Rialto and San Marco, the centers of Venetian business and politics, where they themselves could make contacts, especially with other servants. As boatmen, gondoliers were also well acquainted with the network of canals that snaked through the city and with the navigable channels that linked the Rialtine center to other islands of the lagoon and to the mainland.[89] As a consequence, male servants were drawn into the world of boats and boatmen, a rough-and-tumble subculture with its own institutions, customs, and jargon.

The traghetto stations dotting the Grand Canal and the periphery of the city provided the institutional focus of boatmen's culture. The traghetti were organized much like guilds, with their own statutes, chapter meetings, and elected officials. They were also closed corporations, admission being dependent on the favorable vote of the members. The major responsibilities of the traghetti included election of new members, scheduling of work shifts, protection of the station from encroachment by neighboring stations, and maintenance of the *cavana* (mooring station) and *casoto* (hut) from which they operated. Like artisan guilds, the traghetti also maintained scuole, or religious confraternities. These scuole erected altars in local churches or at other sites and applied themselves to charitable tasks such as burial of the dead (see plate 7).[90]

Plate 7. Tabernacle of the *traghetto* of the Ponte della Paglia. Photograph courtesy of Alinari/Art Resource, New York.

Male servants aspired to acquire boats, leave personal service, and join one of the traghetto stations. In 1565, for instance, Innocente da Salò, servant of nobleman Silvano Capello, spent twenty-two ducats to purchase traghetto rights from Pasquale Trevisan, a boatman at the traghetto of San Felice.[91] By joining traghetti, servants could participate actively in the corporate life of the city and thereby gain a degree of respectability. Indeed, the statutes of one traghetto station at Rialto specifically stated that all candidates had to be "uomini da bene."[92] When, in 1514, members of the same station were litigating with another group of ferrymen, their gastaldo was a certain Giovanni the Ethiopian, formerly a slave of the noble Capello family.[93] Giovanni's advancement from personal slave to gastaldo illustrates the kind of mobility the traghetti offered to some providers of domestic service.

Access to boats, contacts at Rialto, and knowledge of the lagoon's backwaters and channels also provided excellent opportunities for male servants to engage in illegal activities, including theft, smuggling, and rape. Both male and female servants stole from their masters, but males had an advantage over their female counterparts in that it was easier for them to remove goods from their masters' homes or offices and dispose of them through mercers and pawnbrokers.[94] In 1461, for example, Alegreto da Cattaro, servant of Simone di Castellane, a scribe at a grain warehouse, took his master's keys, went to his office, and stole money and a jeweled cross worth more than eighty ducats.[95] Similarly, the use of boats and a knowledge of the waterways made trafficking in contraband feasible. In 1568 the avogadori di comun prosecuted a group of fourteen men— four ship caulkers, nine boatmen, and one fisherman—for smuggling. Included among the boatmen was Antonio Grando, a boatman at the traghetto of cà da Mosto at Rialto, and Giovanni da cà Priuli, gondolier of nobleman Marco Giustinian.[96] Finally, servants sometimes used the isolation of boats in the lagoon to commit rape. For example, in 1414, the retainers of nobleman Giovanni Zane (a freeman and two slaves) sexually assaulted an old woman.[97]

The mooring stations of the traghetti, the quays at San Marco and Rialto, and the *squeri* (boatyards) where small vessels were made and repaired also provided foci for the sociability of boatmen. Here they joked, gambled, and gossiped. As we have seen, one aspect of their behavior, namely, their cursing and blaspheming, received special attention from Tommaso Garzoni in his *Piazza universale*.[98] Garzoni's reaction was not that of an overly sensitive individual; even the government made a special effort to curb the foul language and obscene gestures of boatmen and gondoliers. It seems likely that boatmen used this language (or, more properly, this "anti-language") as a means of promoting a sense of group identity or, alternatively, as a way of subtly challenging the value system of their superiors.[99] The culture and identity of male servants was very much tied to the boats of which they were in charge.[100]

Female servants had three major responsibilities: to maintain the home and its furnishings, to care for the children, and to serve as companions for their mistresses. The social world of female domestic laborers was therefore much more circumscribed geographically than that of male servants and revolved around different centers of sociability—the household, the neighborhood, and the church.

Vecellio distinguished three kinds of female servants: *balie* (wet nurses or governesses), cameriere (chambermaids), and others. The job of the wet nurses and governesses was to care for the children of the family. For this reason, according to Vecellio, they were offered the most respect and were better fed and housed than others. Chambermaids had primary responsibility for the provisions of the house; they held the keys to the pantry and canteen. Again according to Vecellio, chambermaids were unmarried girls who also had the responsibility of accompanying their mistresses whenever they went abroad. The rest of the female servants were occupied in the maintenance of the household and performed tasks such as cooking, cleaning, and similar chores."[101] The degree to which particular households could institute this kind of specialization depended to a great extent on their size and wealth. Many households had only one female servant, who performed all of these tasks.

Nonetheless, Vecellio's analysis illustrates that female servants were occupied in what were regarded as particularly female activities: the preparation of food, the production and maintenance of clothes and linens, and the care and upbringing of babies and small children. All this meant that the female servant's sphere of activity was largely centered on the household and its courtyard, where the well and latrines were located. When she left these confines, it was to run errands in the immediate vicinity or to accompany her mistress as she went to church or to visit friends in other homes or convents.[102]

Accordingly, female servants and slaves often developed friendships with other popolano women, both domestics and nondomestics, in their immediate neighborhood. They turned to these women for comfort, aid, and advice. Zanina Greca, wife of Pietro da Mestre of Santa Maria Formosa, commiserated with Uliana Carchassa, slave of Conforte and Gaudenzi Morosini, about Uliana's heavy labors. (Uliana eventually poisoned the family.)[103] When Cita, the Tatar slave of nobleman Pietro Morosini of San Giovanni Crisostomo, complained to her neighbor Margarita Vercia about her poor treatment, Vercia agreed to help her and Daria, the slave of Morosina Morosini, poison their mistresses. The three concocted various brews and poisons and even made a small wax statue that

Margarita "baptized" [baptizavit] in the parish church of San Giovanni Crisostomo and placed in Pietro Morosini's wife's bed.[104] Servants were peripherally involved, generally as witnesses, in several witchcraft trials.[105] Although such cases were exceptional, they illustrate that circles of women based on neighborhood ties provided emotional support and helped serving women and slaves overcome the isolation they experienced in their masters' households.

Bequests in female servants' wills are further testimony to the importance of neighborhood-based friendships. In 1458, for instance, Caterina, former slave of nobleman Marino Malipiero, left three ducats to donna Antonia, her "neighbor" [vexina] with the proviso that Antonia go to the churches of the Trinity and Santa Croce to obtain indulgences for her soul.[106] Occasionally local attachments extended beyond particular individuals to the larger community. In her will also dated 1458, Maria, of the parish of Santa Maria Maddalena, former slave of Giacomo Franco, left the residue of her estate to her executor, Antonio Ferrante, with the proviso that first he pay for nine *caritade* (love feasts), or "nine alms for nine poor people in my parish for my soul."[107] And Margarita da Caffa, former massara of the late Fra Niccolò, prior of San Cipriano on the island of Murano, also endowed a caritade of bread and wine in her will, to be distributed to every massara on Murano.[108]

The *scuole piccole,* the religious confraternities located in parish churches and monasteries, provided institutional foci for the sociability of other female servants. Of 115 wills of female servants that I examined, 21, or 18.26 percent, contained at least one bequest to a scuola.[109] Some servants left bequests to several different confraternities. Franceschina Formento, widow of a rock crystal worker and servant of the priest Marco Ferro of Santa Marina, left twenty soldi di piccoli to each of the scuole to which she belonged, including Sant'Ursula, San Venerando, Sant'Eufemia (located in the church of San Canciano), Santi Apostoli, and Santa Maria al Capo Broglio.[110] The scuola of Sant'Ursula, dedicated to the virgin Ursula and the eleven thousand virgin martyrs, elicited the greatest support. It was mentioned in 8 of the 115 wills.[111] What is more, although the scuola of Sant'Ursula was located at San Zanipolo, the servants who made bequests to the scuola lived in parishes scattered throughout the city.[112] The confraternity's strong associations with women, especially virginal women, may help explain the attachment servants felt to this particular religious establishment. Bartolomea, former servant of Doge Antonio Venier, even asked in her will dated 1427 to be buried in the scuola's tomb.[113]

Scuole dedicated to the Blessed Sacrament located in various parish churches were also frequently remembered with bequests.[114] By contrast, the large, well-endowed, and powerful scuole grandi were almost completely ignored. Only one woman, Margarita, servant of a goldsmith, left a bequest to a scuola grande—two ducats for the building fund of San Rocco.[115] As Brian Pullan has shown, very few servants belonged to the scuole grandi.[116] The scuole's associations with the powerful were perhaps too strong for them to elicit much support from female domestics. The scuole piccole, by contrast, provided female servants with an opportunity to participate in the corporately organized religious life of the city, and a number took advantage of the opportunity.

In addition to the scuole piccole, parish churches, convents, and monasteries provided other foci for female servants' associations, as they did for male servants'. But one religious tradition appears to have had especially strong associations for women, namely, the garnering of indulgences at churches throughout the city. Over the course of the centuries, many Venetian churches were granted indulgences by the popes. The faithful enjoyed the benefit of these indulgences by visiting the churches on appointed days. In 1278, for example, Pope Nicholas III granted an indulgence of forty days to anyone who visited the church of San Marco any day of the year.[117] There was also a regular weekly schedule of indulgences: pilgrims visited San Lorenzo on Wednesdays, San Pietro di Castello on Sundays, and Santa Croce on Fridays.[118] It was not necessary to go in person to receive the indulgences, and the living could accrue the benefits for the dead. It was common for testators to leave legacies to support those who would seek these benefits for their souls.[119]

Much of the spiritual work of garnering indulgences was done by poor women, especially by present or former servants. Bartolomeo da Mestre broke into the home of his master, ducal secretary Marcantonio Novello, on a Sunday because he knew that the family was not at home and that the maid had gone to seek an indulgence at San Pietro di Castello.[120] According to Francesco Sansovino, the churches were very crowded on the days on which indulgences were available—on Fridays during the month of March the popolo visited Santa Croce "con più frequenza."[121] The schedule of indulgence gathering provided an opportunity for poor women to move about the city. At regular intervals throughout the week, month, and year, they traveled from church to church and saw other women going about the same task. These visits provided opportunities for women to escape the narrow confines of their homes, to socialize with other women, and to garner spiritual benefits (see plate 8).

Testamentary evidence confirms the importance of this spiritual and social activity for women. Of the 115 testaments of female servants examined, 29, or 25.2 percent, included at least one bequest for someone to visit one or more churches in the city in order to seek indulgences. By contrast, only 1 of 15 male servants, or 6.66 percent, made such a bequest.[122] Thus while boats and the work

Plate 8. Lorenzo Lotto, *Pala di Sant'Antonino*, Church of Santi Giovanni e Paolo, Venice. Photograph courtesy of O. Böhm, Venice.

associated with them provided foci for men's associations, women's spiritual work provided foci for theirs.

It was around the household that the worlds of male and female servants conjoined, and within these confines rich ties and associations between men and women often developed. Sexual entanglements were frequent, but they were only one of many kinds of relationships between servants. Servants became fast friends (or bitter enemies), and older servants developed parental feelings toward younger colleagues.

Two testaments illustrate the complex networks linking domestic laborers. In September 1475, Giorgio, famulus of Niccolò Foscari, drafted his will.[123] He named his master as his executor and made a large number of bequests to religious institutions, including the scuola of San Francesco at the Frari, monasteries and churches scattered throughout the city, and the hospitals of the Pietà and the Nazareth. Among individuals, Giorgio left four ducats to "Madalena, who served me"; one ducat each to Anna and Lucia, described as "famulae domus"; one ducat to Cita, formerly a famula domus and currently a resident of the hospital of Santa Maria in Cannaregio; and two ducats to his godson, the son of Gregorio, formerly the servant of Andrea Bernardo. The other individuals named in his will included Bonaventura, who lived with Cita at the hospital of Santa Maria; Benvenuta, "wife of the boatman Marco"; and a certain Peregrina, otherwise unidentified. Giorgio's largest single bequest was twenty-five ducats, which he left to his niece Caterina. Additionally, he left one ducat for the man "who will row my . . . executor when he goes to dispense my legacies."[124] This male servant, who had some living kinsmen, chose to remember present and former servants of the household as well as others related to people engaged in service. He even looked ahead to reward the boatman who in the future would row his master.

The other will, dated May 1502, is that of Giacomina, from the parish of Santa Margarita, widow of the Milanese Niccolino and massara of nobleman Luca Civran.[125] She named Civran her sole executor and asked to be buried in the church of the Carmelites. She bequeathed eight ducats toward the dowry of her niece, who was living near Mantua, and some clothes to her sister, Domenica. Among her fellow servants, she left two ducats to Marco, the famulus of Civran; blouses to Civran's famula Maria; and shoes to donna Margarita, Civran's other massara. Other individuals who received legacies included "Cristina, daughter of the painter Constantin in the house of the aforesaid lord Luca [Civran]"; Madalena, wife of the woolworker Francesco; Zanina, mother of the barber Francesco; Giacomo, son of Pietro Bono of the Mantovano; and donna Francesca, who lived in the house of Girolamo Vendramin. Like the famulus Giorgio, Giacomina remembered her fellow servants as well as other working poor, including neighbors. These two testaments, selected for the richness of the legacies, illustrate the associations male and female servants forged in both the household and the neighborhood.[126]

The same forces that created amicable ties among servants could under different circumstances lead to enmity. Physical proximity and shared responsibilities led to arguments over the division of labor and precedence. Crafty servants tried to avoid work and cowed others into doing their will. Female servants, junior male servants, and slaves were especially subject to intimidation by older males.[127] Young girls were lured into sexual entanglements and theft by promises of marriage.[128] And young male servants were forced to do more than their fair share of the work.[129]

Slaves were in an especially precarious position since they could be sold at any time. Giorgio, Ethiopian slave of nobleman Andrea Zane, was terrorized by Giovanni di Broylo, a resident in Zane's house. Broylo told Giorgio that if he did not obey his commands, he would see to it that Giorgio was sold.[130] Gene Brucker has published records of a poignant case from fifteenth-century Florence in which a slave girl was persuaded with promises of marriage by a young man to steal from her mistress. She reluctantly agreed, only to be abandoned after carrying out the deed.[131]

Enmities, jealousies, and intimidation among servants sometimes led to violence. One day in 1565, for example, Salvatore Zamengo, gondolier of Grand Chancellor Gian Francesco Ottobon, quarreled with the chancellor's other male servant, Pietro. The cause of their quarrel is unknown, but the next day, when Salvatore went to his master's house "to prepare the boat," he entered Pietro's room and demanded that he take back the words he had spoken the day before. When Pietro told him to get out, Salvatore attacked and wounded him.[132] At other times violence escalated to murder. In 1596 Battista Furlan, famulus of the noble Emo brothers, was prosecuted for murdering Giovanni, the "steward" [spenditor] of the household. Baptista testified in his defense that Giovanni had insulted and hit him.[133]

Two registers of the signori di notte of those condemned in contumacy for homicide covering the years 1471–1507 and 1523–59 provide valuable evidence about intrahousehold servant violence.[134] The first register contains 1,189 legible cases of which 9 involved servants who murdered servants employed in the same household; the second contains at least 16 such cases out of 1,344. Usually the violence occurred between male servants (23 of 25 cases), and 6 of the 25 cases involved servants employed in ambassadorial households. Given the cryptic nature of the entries, it is impossible to determine with certainty the motivations behind these murders, although some almost certainly involved disputes over precedence and authority within the household. The steward of the ambassador from Milan, for example, killed another of the ambassador's servants. And the gondolier of nobleman Bartolomeo Morosini murdered the overseer of the Morosini villa at San Martino di Stra.[135] It may well be that the perpetrator resented being given orders by the overseer. In two cases, female servants murdered their male counterparts. In 1487 Rada, servant of a fruit seller, killed the master's male servant, Michele da Spalato; and in 1500 Maria da Padova, housekeeper at the hostel known as the Corona, murdered Giovanni, a famulus at the hostel.[136] Tensions, rivalries, or jealousies may have contributed to these crimes.

While much can be learned about the work and associative lives of servants, it is more difficult to gather information about their leisure time and entertainment. We do not know, for example, whether servants had a lighter schedule on Sundays and feast days.[137] But some evidence suggests that two annual holidays had special significance for servants and represented a time, if not of leisure, then at least of festivity and merrymaking. These were the Christmas season, running through New Year's Day, and the Sensa, the feast of the Ascension, in the spring. It was at these times of the year that masters gave their servants tips. Antonio Barbarigo entered in his account book under 1 January 1570 a sum for his wife to pay the bonaman to the servants.[138] In his will dated 1571 Pietro Calbo left twelve ducats a year to his servant Lucieta. She was to get an additional half-ducat "al tempo di bonaman" and another half-ducat "al tempo della Sensa."[139]

The Sensa combined a religious holiday with a major fair that was held in the Piazza San Marco and lasted for fifteen days. Various merchants, especially goldsmiths and mercers, set up stalls in the piazza. According to Gino Luzzatto, the Sensa fair was not an occasion for major international trading as the Champagne fairs of France were. Instead, it was an opportunity for shoppers to purchase small gifts and various other ornaments. Many of the merchants at the Sensa fair peddled household objects.[140] The festival seems to have had particularly strong associations for women. They were the only ones allowed into the church of San Marco to view the relics on the eve of the Sensa.[141] The fair also provided an opportunity for them to purchase household items and objects of personal adornment. Female servants in particular, especially girls who were trying to accumulate items for their trousseaux, seem to have looked forward to and attended the Sensa. Masters often gave cash advances to servants at this time; for example, Agostino Spinelli gave Gironima da Gorizia four lire "per spender in Sensa," and Giovanni Alvise Barbarigo advanced cash to Lucia da Este "per andar in Sensa."[142] In her will dated 1508, Catarina da Scutari, servant of Giacomo Morosini, asked that "a dress that I bought at this Ascension" be given to a poor woman of her executor's choosing.[143] One of the major events of this spring festival was the doge's ceremonial marriage of the sea. The Sensa's strong associations with matrimonial rights may have made the festival particularly meaningful to young women of marrying age, such as servants.[144]

Other annual festivals provided further opportunities for servants to escape their normal routine. Lorenzo Lotto recorded in his account book that he gave small coins—"bagatini e bezi"—to the children and servants of his friend Giovanni dal Saon's household in Treviso so that they could use them "to play with during Carnival" [da zugar el carneval].[145] According to Giuseppe Boerio, the Venetian expression "zornada [giorno] de le massere" signified a holiday, usually during Carnival.[146] Festive occasions in particular households, especially weddings, were other opportunities for servants to celebrate. Niccolò and Alvise Barbarigo distributed two ducats' worth of gifts to their servants when Niccolò married Elena Marcello.[147] Marriages were also occasions when gondoliers received a new set of clothing. They had to be properly decked out in order to row the bride in a procession through the city. The magistrati alle pompe tried to limit the bestowal of these marriage gifts to the "two menservants, namely, those who [actually] row the newlyweds."[148]

Daily forms of recreation and play are the most difficult leisure activities to uncover. We know that one male servant played soccer with other youths in Campo San Stae, that another owned a lyre, and that some boatmen, and perhaps servants as well, participated in *mattinate,* or charivaris, and in the gang fistfights that were popular in the city.[149] In his diary Sanuto reports that in February 1525 a group of noblemen's servants held a ball. Each contributed a ducat and brought his girlfriend—Sanuto says "la sua putana"—to dance and dine. Sanuto was displeased, commenting, "In competition with the nobles, the servants make merry"; and he urged the Ten to guard against such events.[150] It is possible that some of the lullabies that have come down to us were the compositions of the wet nurses and governesses who cared for the children of the rich.[151] But most forms of servant play are as irretrievably lost to us as are the melodies servants plucked out on their lyres, danced to at fêtes, and sang to their nurslings.

## Old Age

As already observed, many servants, especially women, who left service to work in other areas or to assist their husbands with their labors found that they were forced back into service as the circumstances of their lives changed. Widows in particular sought work as domestic servants because it was one of the few forms of labor they were trained to perform and one in which they did not meet institutional resistance to women's work. Hence many women who had begun their lives in service as young girls ended them in service as well.

Old age presented various challenges to servants because, despite their housekeeping or ship-handling experience, their basic asset was their ability to perform hard physical labor.[152] As their bodies wore out, servants found their situation increasingly precarious. We have already noted the case of donna Lucia, who at sixty years of age was fortunate to find work as Lorenzo Lotto's massara at a salary of four ducats per year but was dismissed after only one month because she could not perform her duties on account of her age.[153] Stella Trevisana, former massara of Emilia Catena who was tried for witchcraft, claimed that she was one hundred years old and that she had quit service when she went blind.[154] Andrea Alesio, a former boatman at the traghetto of San Gregorio, stated in his will that he had been confined to bed for the past eighteen years and blind for the past fourteen. A widower who lived in a house owned by the Misericordia, Andrea depended on a certain Caterina (apparently his adopted daughter), herself a resident of the hospital of San Giobbe. Caterina made his bread and brought it to him daily. It is not difficult to conjure up the image of this blind old man lying in his bed waiting for his daily visit from Caterina. In his will, Andrea left his "few things" [poche de robizole] to Caterina, and when the notary made the obligatory inquiry about charitable bequests to hospitals, he replied, "I have nothing to leave" [non ho da lassar].[155]

Aged former servants met the challenge of old age as best they could. Some no doubt begged for a living, while others tried to earn income by taking boarders or by selling fritters and other foodstuffs.[156] Still others scraped together a meager living by seeking indulgences, washing and keeping vigil over corpses, selling candles, reciting prayers, and performing other forms of physically nontaxing "spiritual labor."[157]

Some aged servants sought refuge in convents as *converse* or associated themselves with third orders. Noble and elite widows sometimes spent their later years in convents, and some took their aged servants with them. Girolamo Priuli remembered in his will Archangela and Girolama, nuns at the convent of Ognisanti, as well as Cristina, "formerly my massara, a conversa in the monastery."[158] As members of third orders, servants sought the spiritual benefits of association with the religious and received material benefits such as alms.[159]

The city's many hospitals provided another form of relief for the aged. In the fifteenth and sixteenth centuries alone more than fifty hospitals were established in Venice.[160] Many of these were founded to assist the elderly, especially aged mariners. A number of former servants populated these institutions. Doge Agostino Barbarigo placed his servant Ruosa Schiavona in the hospital of the Cà di Dio and another servant, Giacoma da Vicenza, in the hospital of San Marco.[161] Donna Lena, former servant of the Donà family, was a resident of the hospital of cà Dolfin in the parish of San Marcuola.[162] And Caterina da Zara, former mas-sara of nobleman Niccolò Michiel, lived in the hospital of the Crociferi (see plate 9).[163] Often, servants had to rely on the influence of their masters in order to re-ceive these benefits. When Lorenza, widow of Tommaso di Matteo of Florence, reconfirmed the establishment of a hospital for poor women endowed by her husband in the parish of Sant'Agata, she stipulated that her slave Ursa was to be freed and serve as rectoress of the hospital for as long as she lived.[164] Nicolosa Pa-leologa wanted her massara Susanna to be provided with one of the rooms in the hospital she intended to establish.[165] While he was a procurator of San Marco, the future doge Leonardo Donà used his position to provide Pascha di Rossi, a former servant, whom he described as "povera et vecchia de anni 70 in circa," with a "caseta" maintained by the procurators.[166]

But hospitals could not accommodate all the city's aged servants as well as other deserving poor, and so most servants had to hope that their masters and mistresses would provide for their old age. Some masters did so by providing annuities. In her will Lucrezia, widow of Sebastiano Venier, bequeathed two bushels of "good grain" annually to her former nena Caterina, wife of Stefano Fauro.[167] Doge Andrea Gritti made provision for his "serva" Marta to receive a house or money for rent, as well as a yearly allowance of grain and wine for as long as she lived.[168]

Other masters actually maintained elderly servants in their homes. Andrea Rizzo and his wife, Maria, provided for their aged servant Francesca da Vicenza but did not give her a salary.[169] In 1559 Zuan Giacomo Locadello agreed to con-tinue to keep his servant Tonina, widow of Simon da Lovatina, "già vecchia, et impotente," for as long as she lived, just as he had been doing for the past four years, and Tonina agreed to a notarized statement declaring that neither she nor her relatives would seek a salary for the past four years' service or for any future service.[170] When the notary Domenico Baldagara wrote his own will in 1552, he noted that his massara for the past twenty years, donna Anzola, had gone blind and that he received no service from her. Nevertheless, he continued to keep her in his house. In his will he declared that if he predeceased his sister, he wanted her to maintain Anzola "out of charity and out of love of the Lord and of me."[171] Alvise Macipo stated in his will that he wanted a servant named Menega to be maintained in his house and that she was not to be forced to perform any ser-vice, but was to be free to go about her devotions and prayers.[172] Laura Trevisan enjoined her husband and sons not "to abandon in old age or sickness nor to dismiss from the household" her servant, Angela Bonzanina.[173]

Trevisan's very injunction suggests that some masters did discard servants when they grew too old to perform their duties or became ill. Servants' lives were

Plate 9. Palma il Giovane, *Pasquale Cicogna Assists at the Mass,* Hospital of Santa Maria dei Crociferi, Venice. Photograph courtesy of O. Böhm, Venice.

always precarious but became more so as old age advanced and their physical powers diminished. Then they had to rely on their wits and resourcefulness, on charitable institutions such as hospitals, and on the goodwill and affection of their masters. Fears for their old age must have provided a powerful incentive for servants to obey their masters and to display loyalty through years of service. Conversely, these same fears of poverty and abandonment provided powerful weapons for masters. In old age, the drama of relations between masters and servants continued to be played out. The final act, in a double sense, included death and burial.

## Death and Burial

In their testaments, servants could leave explicit instructions about the amount of money to be spent for their funeral, the degree of pomp, and the burial site. These decisions reveal a great deal about the testators' sense of self and about their allegiances and loyalties. The selection of burial site is particularly significant, for in this servants revealed the company they wished to keep in death.[174]

At times death came quickly and unexpectedly, and these decisions had to be left to the discretion of masters. In August 1469, for example, Niccolò and Alvise Barbarigo's fantesca Petrussa da Cattaro fell in the portico of their palace and died. Late in the year, the brothers recorded that they had spent about 9 ducats for her funeral and alms for her soul: 3.5 ducats on bushels of Veronese grain, which they had distributed "per anema de Petrussa," and just over 5 ducats for her burial and for "masses and other alms."[175] When in January 1577 Agostino Spinelli's massara Maddalena Feltrina died after a two-week illness, Spinelli spent a little more than 8 lire on her funeral. The breakdown was as follows:

| | |
|---|---|
| Candles for the burial | lire 1 soldi 0 |
| For a priest and custodian from the parish | lire 1 soldi 8 |
| For the sacristan for the catafalque | lire 0 soldi 12 |
| For the chaplain of Sant'Alvise and a custodian | lire 1 soldi 2 |
| For the nuns of Sant'Alvise for the burial | lire 1 soldi 0 |
| For those who carried the body to burial | lire 0 soldi 8 |
| For two women who kept vigil over the body and clothed it after death | lire 2 soldi 10[176] |

We do not know whether Maddalena had left instructions for her funeral or whether Spinelli made the arrangements himself.

The amount of money that Spinelli spent on Maddalena's funeral was small, not unlike that which some servants bequeathed for this purpose. Caterina da Patras left four ducats to the chapter of the parish of Santa Maria Formosa for burial in the tomb of the scuola of the Madonna in that church, but it is unclear whether that figure included the expenses for other things she requested, such as a procession by the children of the hospital of San Zanipolo.[177] Giorgio, the famulus of Niccolò Foscari examined earlier, left four ducats to his scuola for burial in their tomb, as well as three ducats for candles and four ducats for the priests of his home parish, San Pantalon, to be present.[178] Many servants left the details and expenses of their funeral to the discretion of their executors, who often included their masters and mistresses.[179]

Some servants left no instructions at all about the amount of funeral pomp they desired, whereas others went into some detail. Maria, servant of Gironimo di Capi, wished to be buried at the Frari "accompanied by a priest and sacristan and by the children of the hospital of San Zanipolo and the Incurabili."[180] In her will dated 1430 Marta, servant of Giovanni Marcello, left fifteen ducats to the convent of Corpus Christi and asked to be buried in the nuns' tomb but stated that she wanted only two candles to be used.[181] Anna, the Turkish former slave of Giovanni Pasqualigo and at the time of her will the wife of Giorgio Greco, asked to be buried at the monastery of Sant'Alvise in the habit of the Servites. In addition, she wanted members of her scuola (Sant'Ursula) present, as well as four priests from her parish, San Marcuola. Four candles were to be used.[182] Ciprian di Gibelino, factor for nobleman Vittore Pisani, asked to be buried in the cemetery of San Giovanni dei Furlani "without pomp" but accompanied by the chapter of San Paternian.[183] Several female servants wished to be buried in the habit of a religious or third order. Agnes, servant of Niccolò Aldioni, left ten ducats for burial at the Augustinian church of Santo Stefano in the habit of the third order and an additional two ducats for the tertiaries to attend her funeral.[184] None of the fifteen male servants whose wills I examined asked to buried in a habit.

The choices of burial site are also revealing. Parochial churches were popular because they were familiar places where servants might have special attachments to a particular priest who served as their confessor. Maria, former slave of Francesco Arbusani, named the parish priest of San Silvestro as one of her two executors and asked to be buried in his church.[185] By selecting monasteries and priories, servants hoped to gain spiritual benefit by association with those sacred precincts, but they did not favor one order overwhelmingly over another. Servants sought burial in churches associated with the Franciscans, the Dominicans, the Augustinians, the Carmelites, the Benedictines, the Servites, and other orders. In certain instances, servants seem to have formed attachments to particular houses because members of the elite families they served patronized those houses or because they themselves had relatives in them. Dorothea dalla Cefalonia, an orphan raised in the Contarini household, asked to be buried at San Giacomo della Giudecca, a Servite foundation, where her nephew was a friar.[186]

A number of servants sought burial in the tombs of scuole to which they belonged. Three female servants (of the 113 examined) asked to be buried in the tomb of the scuola of Sant'Ursula.[187] Others specified burial in the tombs of scuole associated with their parish churches, often with scuole dedicated to the Madonna or the Eucharist. Francesca da Vicenza, ancilla of Andrea Rizzo, wished to be buried in the tomb of the scuola of Corpus Christi in San Giovanni Crisostomo.[188] Giorgio, famulus of Niccolò Foscari, chose the tomb of the scuola of San Francesco at the Frari.[189] Boatmen and their wives occasionally specified burial in the tombs of their traghetti. Niccolò da Negroponte, a boatman at the ferry station of San Gregorio, wished to be buried in the tomb of the scuola associated with the traghetto; and Martha, wife of a boatman at the traghetto of the Beccaria at Rialto, stated that she wished to lie "in the cemetery of San Geremia in the tomb of the scuola of the traghetto of the Beccaria."[190] The tomb of the traghetto of San Barnaba, located in the church of San Sebastiano, was adorned, appropriately, with a relief of a "barchetta."[191] Scuole, which provided support to servants in life, continued to be important to them in death. Through burial with their brothers and sisters, servants sought spiritual benefit for their souls and memorialization at the one place where they were treated as spiritual equals rather than as social inferiors.[192]

None of the servants whose wills I examined asked to be buried with kinsmen. There are at least three possible explanations for this. First, most servants did not specify where they wished to be buried and may simply have assumed that they would be buried with other family members. A second and more likely explanation is that, as immigrants to Venice, most servants did not have kinsmen or a family tomb in the city and could not afford to have their body transported back to their place of origin. A third possibility is that burial with relatives was not important to them, but this seems unlikely.[193] Failure to specify burial with kinsmen is more probably testimony to the isolation of servants from kith and kin.

By contrast, four female servants asked to be buried in the tomb of their masters or mistresses. Giacoma, former slave of donna Clara Aperlis, asked to be buried "apreso mia madona" at the church of Sant'Andrea de Zirada.[194] Margarita Mantoana, former massara of Alvise Negro, wished to be buried in the parish of San Geremia in the habit of the Servites and "in the tomb of the said late sir Alvise Negro."[195] Lucia Morosini, former slave of Michele Morosini (she took his last name), wanted her body to lie "in the monastery of madonna Saint Anne, where today rest the remains of the late Magnificent Madonna Maria Morosini, my most loving patroness and mother."[196] Finally, Menega, for thirty years the massara of Priamo Malipiero, stated, "I want my body to be buried in the tomb of my master at San Lorenzo [in the tomb] of cà Malipiero."[197] Some servants, like Menega, dedicated their lives to the service of particular families and came to see themselves (and to be seen) as part of the family. Hence it was appropriate for them to wish to be buried alongside those with whom they had spent their lives. The remains of other servants may lie nameless under the great funeral monuments that adorn Venetian churches.

Finally, although for practical reasons no servants asked that their remains be returned to their place of origin, some did leave pious bequests to religious establishments in their native towns. Lucrezia, a widow and servant of the physicians Marco and Francesco Alcherio, asked that her niece Nicolina have three masses said for her soul at the church of the Madonna in her hometown, the village of Lonigo in the Vicentino.[198] Maria, widow of Antonio Colbigot and servant of Gironimo di Capi, left four fields at Monfumo, near Asolo, to her cousin with the proviso that he give ten ducats to the scuola of the Madonna of Asolo.[199] Domenichina da Caravaggio, domicella (lady-in-waiting) of Anastasia, wife of Ludovico del Afeita, left four pieces of land in Caravaggio to her nephew with the proviso that if the family should become extinct, half the land was to be given to the chapel of Corpus Christi in the church of San Firmo of Caravaggio, and half to the church of Saint Mary of Caravaggio, "for my soul and the souls of my dead [relatives]."[200] Lastly, Lucia, an immigrant from Lorgia, near Castelfranco, asked to be buried in Venice at Santa Croce in the tomb of the scuola "del sagramento." But she bequeathed her property in Lorgia, including "half a walled house with a thatched roof and a field of vines," to her nephews and to their male heirs for "as long as the world will endure" [finche durera el mondo].[201] But if the male line became extinct, then she wanted the land to be given to the church of San Bartolomeo di Lorgia so that the priest would pray for her soul and those of her parents. At the end of their lives, some servants recalled the villages and hamlets whence a lifetime earlier they had set out to the great metropolis of Venice in search of work as domestic laborers.

～

Studies of domestic service in the eighteenth and nineteenth centuries have emphasized that domestic servants stood largely apart from their working-class peers. For instance, according to Sarah Maza, servants, who were easily identified by their livery, were despised as lazy, unmarried transients who did not fit into the "mainstream of the artisanal world." Caught between the upper-class world of their employers and the lower-class world of other laborers, stationed between celibacy and marriage, they stood on a "threshold," not quite fitting in anywhere and not developing a distinct or "coherent" subculture of their own.[202] Theresa McBride believes that servants occupied a similarly indeterminate place in the nineteenth century, since service functioned as a "bridging occupation" between the rural world whence many female servants had come and the urban, working-class world they would occupy when they married and left service.[203]

The evidence presented in this chapter suggests that in Renaissance Venice at least (and apparently in many other late medieval and early modern societies as well), servants fit comfortably into the world of artisans and laborers, that is, into the mainstream of popolano life.[204] This examination of the professions of servants' fathers and of professional endogamy and exogamy among servants indicates that service was not an occupation from which young men and women necessarily climbed as they became better established in the city. While it is true that many servants were the children of peasants and that servants often married one another or persons in allied professions, such as boatmen, others were the children of artisans and married into the ranks of the city's respectable poor. What is more, service did not represent a distinct stage of life through which men and women passed on the journey to more secure and stable professions. Instead, it was a profession that women and men entered and left as the circumstances of their lives changed.

In one aspect of working-class life only, namely, in their lack of guilds, did servants stand distinctly apart from Venice's artisans. Yet here too we must not rush to conclusions, since servants were not the only unskilled laborers in the city who lacked corporate organization; many occupations were not organized into guilds. And the extent to which journeymen and apprentices actually felt they belonged to the master-dominated guilds remains debatable.[205] Additionally, we should not forget that some male servants eventually did join the corporately organized traghetti. In fact, it could be argued that the required three years of service as a personal gondolier before one was allowed to join a traghetto constituted a kind of apprenticeship. Finally, although excluded from guilds, servants were not excluded from scuole, arguably the most vibrant and vital component of Venetian corporate life.

In their work and associative lives as well, both male and female servants moved in circles that linked them not only to other servants but also to persons of both high and low status. As gondoliers, male servants had frequent contact with the city's elite, as well as with boatmen, stevedores, artisans, shopkeepers, and others who frequented the centers of male power and activity. Female servants were more confined than males, but they had opportunities to socialize with other women at churches and convents, scuole, wellheads, weddings and parties of their masters, and at the annual Sensa fair.

Although there were distinctive features to life in service and individual circumstances could vary considerably, the overall impression is that domestic servants in Renaissance Venice were largely indistinguishable from their popolano counterparts who earned their livelihood in other ways. Even the ties of personal dependence were not all that unique, for, like servants, most Venetians found themselves subject to the will of others, whether as journeymen to their masters, clients to their patrons, or, in many households, children and wives to their fathers and husbands.[206] As we shall see in the next part of this study, the methods servants developed both to accommodate and to resist their masters were typical of power relations between social unequals. Far from being marginalized, domestic servants were often at the center of social struggles in early modern Venice.

# Part III
# Practice

Chapter Six

# The Dynamics of
# Master-Servant Relations

Non può esser mai pace in una famiglia, quando vi capita qualche Fantesca
di cattiva conditione.

[There can never be peace in a household when there arrives a servant girl
of bad reputation.]

Giovanni Battista della Porta, *La fantesca*

Patrona mi no vogio
più viver in sto imbrogio
come che vivo adesso,
sotto fido commesso
de tante intrighi, e affanni . . .

[Oh Mistress, I don't want to live any more like I now do in this imbroglio,
under entail to so many intrigues and worries . . .]

*L'ultima licenza della buona massara dalla cattiva patrona*

The preceding parts of this study have examined the ideological foundations
and the structural elements of domestic service in Renaissance Venice. We have
seen that writers of treatises on household management and authors of works
in other genres viewed the household and master-servant relations as metaphors
or analogues for the larger political and social orders. Masters created a patriarchal and paternalistic ideology according to which they had an obligation to protect, nurture, and morally guide their servants, whom they compared to children or even animals. Simultaneously, they saw service as an affirmation of a
hierarchical social order in which they, as virtuous superiors, were required to
discipline and control their vicious underlings. They expected servants to love
and obey them and in so doing demonstrate their assent to the political and social order.

Yet the master-servant relationship was also a contractual and legal agreement between employer and employee. At that level, the bond was little more than an economic arrangement that could be canceled or nullified at any time. This calculated attitude toward the costs and benefits of service explains the minute recording of the expenses associated with servant keeping in account books and the emphasis on contractual obligations apparent in governmental regulation of service and at least partially in the preponderance of suits charging servants with the breaking of contracts in the censors' trial records. The mechanisms of the labor market and servants' own goals of marriage or independence kept economic realities before their eyes as well.

Domestic service rested, then, on assumptions and expectations that could not be easily reconciled one to another. The elite in particular took what was essentially a contractual and labor relationship and invested it with broader social and political significance and in so doing created affective standards that they expected servants to meet. Masters wanted servants to be loyal and obedient at the same time that they wanted the freedom to exploit their labor, dismissing them as their financial resources or family interests required. Occasionally they gave unwitting testimony to these contradictions, such as when Giacomo Lanteri wrote in his dialogue on domestic economy that servants owed their masters "love, fear, and reverence."[1] He failed to see, as others who kept servants did as well,[2] that they could not make servants love someone they feared or display loyalty to employers who made a public show of concern and yet were ready to cashier them at a moment's notice. Nor did masters take adequately into account the impact of their sexual exploitation of servants, which again made a lie of the paternal, caring role they claimed for themselves.

At the same time, servants had to decide how to behave toward their masters. Many acted as their masters wished them to, demonstrating both loyalty and obedience. Some, having internalized the value system of the dominant, may have done so sincerely. Others, after having calculated the costs and potential benefits, pretended to do so. Still others refused to comply, chafed at their exploitation, and waged a nearly continuous struggle against their masters. Given the danger of such resistance, the forms it took were often quite subtle. A gondolier might be late in returning to pick up his master at a meeting of the Great Council, or a maidservant might do a sloppy job of the cleaning. At other times servants were openly defiant and disobedient.[3]

When this occurred, masters had to determine how to react. They could try to beat the servants into submission or dismiss them. Or they might prosecute them before the censors. At that point, the ideal solution, from the master's point of view, was for the servant to admit his guilt and seek mercy. In this way, the right order of things could be reestablished.

This chapter explores these strategies and demonstrates that relations between masters and servants in Renaissance Venice were characterized by myriad expectations, behaviors, and attitudes.[4] All this is telling for what it reveals about efforts to create and enforce a patriarchal vision of politics and society and leads to a consideration of the broader significance of service, the subject of the final chapter.

## Loyalty and Obedience

On 14 July 1542 donna Lucretia, daughter of the late Luca Leono of Venice, reached an accord with Girolamo Scodra, a citizen of Zacinto. Lucretia agreed to accompany Scodra to Zacinto, where she would be employed "pro servitrice." She promised to cook and wash for him and to perform all her other duties "in good faith, loyally, and without fraud" [bona fide, fideliter, et sine fraude]. For his part, Scodra agreed to transport Lucretia to his home, to dress her decently, and to care for her if she took ill. He added that if he died and she wished to remain in service, his relatives would be responsible for raising and clothing her. And if she remained in his service for ten years, she would receive fifteen ducats. Additionally, Scodra agreed that during the term of Lucretia's service he would pay for her expenses just as "if she were his own daughter" [si filia propria sibi esset].[5]

In this agreement Scodra expressed the hope that future relations with his servant would be familiar and familial, that he would assume the role of parent and treat Lucretia as if she were his daughter. He also agreed that his relatives would treat her the same if he were to die. Similar sentiments were expressed in an agreement drawn up a few years later between Lucia, a massara from Asolo, and Zuan Vetor, a founder at the mint. Lucia affirmed that she received "company in the said house not like a housekeeper but like a daughter."[6] Statements such as these, found in agreements of those from the middling ranks of society, indicate that the view of master-servant relations as profoundly familial stretched well beyond theoretical tracts and provided a working standard by which many Venetian masters tried to govern their households.[7]

There is abundant evidence that many masters and mistresses accepted these standards and, in their view, treated their servants as "children" for whom they were responsible. This attitude found expression in a number of ways, many of which have been touched upon in preceding chapters. Often it was revealed in efforts by masters to provide for the future welfare of their servants, in the same way that parents sought to provide for the future well-being of their children. For young women this most often took the form of placing them in marriage through provision of a dowry and trousseau.

For young men the pattern was somewhat different. Masters and mistresses who wished to secure their male servants' future provided them with the means to make a modest but honorable living. Sometimes this involved furnishing them with a boat, which they could use either to continue in personal service or perhaps to join one of the traghetti. For instance, in his will dated 1538, nobleman Marin da Lezze bequeathed a boat to his servant Antonio "so that he will have the means to live honorably" [azo ce habi cauxa de far ben].[8] In 1524 nobleman Pietro Soranzo bequeathed to his manservant Agnolo Visentin and his wife Lucia "uno batelo da navegar." Soranzo stated that he was making the bequest partly as a "reward for his good service" and partly "for the love of God."[9] Other male servants might be provided with government sinecures or places in the traghetti or guilds. Bernardino Giova stated in his will that he wanted his sons to purchase a traghetto post for his Ethiopian slave Marco.[10] Luca da Lezze announced in his will that he had bought tools for his servant Zorzi to practice the trade of carpentry and that if Zorzi was still in his service at the time of his death, he would receive his "barcha."[11] Doge Alvise Mocenigo noted in a codicil to his will that he had secured "officii" for his camerieri Tommaso and Carlo.[12] And according to an agreement between the painter Palma il Giovane and his servant Maria Miona, he was to maintain her son in his home and teach him "la professione della pitura."[13] Other masters left bequests for their male servants or slaves to be taught to read and write.[14]

Sometimes masters demonstrated concern by binding servants directly to their families through fictive kin ties or by otherwise protecting them through the exercise of patronage rights. A good illustration is the relationship that linked the household of nobleman Francesco Priuli to the gondolier Stefano and his wife, Ruosa. Priuli and Stefano did not agree to a formal contract for service; instead Priuli hired the boatman on an ad hoc basis, recording in his account book the locations to which Stefano rowed him and other members of his family. Ruosa also helped out the family from time to time. Sometimes she served as housekeeper. Priuli recorded that she was present when he settled accounts with another female servant by the name of Lucretia. Another time she nursed Priuli's son Domenego when the infant was ill and a permanent wet nurse could not be found.[15]

In return for their service, Priuli assisted Stefano and Ruosa in various ways. When, in 1536, Stefano's boat needed repair, Priuli loaned him the money to have the work done. Earlier that year Priuli gave some money to the couple, "for the love of God," to help marry their daughter Paola. When Ruosa agreed to nurse Priuli's son Domenego, she asked in return that Priuli have her own son, Perin, educated. Accordingly, Priuli recorded payment to "maistro Girolamo Adriatico . . . for having taught Perin, son of donna Ruosa, barcharuola." The relationship was capped in January 1537 when Priuli agreed to be godfather to Stefano and Ruosa's son Zuanantonio. A month later, Priuli duly referred to Stefano in his account book as "my co-father" [mio compare].[16] Evidently, Priuli took seriously his obligation to Stefano and his wife.

The motives behind masters' concerns for servants were often extraordinarily complex. The will of Procurator of San Marco Marcantonio Morosini drafted on 19 March 1508 underscores the curious admixture of objectives that prompted his legacies to his servants. In his will Morosini selected eight executors, including his wife, various male kinsmen, and Zuan Terzo, "mio fedelissimo e carissimo servidor."[17]

After enumerating bequests to various charitable institutions and to his wife, Morosini took up the subject of his servants, observing that "it is reasonable for me to remember my servants, and especially those who have long served me with faith and love."[18] The first servant he discussed was Zuan Terzo, one of his designated executors. He bequeathed him 150 ducats "per uno segno de amore" and noted that the other executors were to accept Zuan's word concerning other gifts and favors Morosini had bestowed upon him. The will then continued: "beyond which I leave [him] all the filigree pieces with the ebony inkwell that I keep for the use and adornment of my study. In addition, I leave [him] all the bronze casts in the said study, the globe, the small painting of Saint Jerome, and the small mosaic picture, and all my gold, silver, bronze, and copper medals."[19] He also bequeathed him his collection of books.

Next, Morosini remembered two other male servants: Antonello, a young man whom Morosini had taken into his care and raised "a honor de Dio," and Gasparo Terzo, Zuan's nephew. Morosini created an annuity fund for Antonello (which he was prohibited from managing personally) and also provided for his future housing and maintenance. In addition, he bequeathed him a bed and other household furnishings as well as his musical instruments (a monochord and a harpsichord), at the same time encouraging him to live virtuously and as a "homo da ben."[20] To Gasparo, Morosini left 150 ducats cash as well as "my missal and breviary of good paper written by hand and my printed breviary so that he will remember to pray to God for me." In addition, Gasparo was to have any duplicates of the books left to his uncle Zuan so that he could study.[21] After leaving additional bequests of shoes and clothes to all three men, Morosini included an important caveat: "The said bequests and legacies made to the said three, that is, to Zuan, Antonello, and Gasparo, I intend to be executed so long as they are living in my house and continuing to serve me, but if any one of them departs [from my service], then I intend that he be deprived of the bequests and legacies made to him and that they be returned to my estate."[22]

Morosini's will is notable not only for the content of the bequests and the value of the gifts he made to his male servants but also because in it he offered six different motives for the legacies. First, he stated that he was making the bequest to Zuan as a "sign of love." Clearly, he intended the 150-ducat legacy and the luxury objects at least in part as tokens of the close, affectionate bond between the master and his "carissimo" servant. Like the masters examined above, Morosini also wished to provide for the future welfare of the younger Gasparo and Antonello. Gasparo's access to the secular books bequeathed to Zuan would allow him to study and thereby better himself. In a slightly different vein, the annuities and gifts, including the musical instruments, left to Antonello would allow him to lead an honorable life as a "homo da ben." Like a good father or patron, Morosini wished to underscore his ties to his servants by providing for their future.

By making these bequests, Morosini also affirmed his own place in the familial and social hierarchy and asserted his elevated status. Often when masters wished to emphasize this aspect of the master-servant relationship, they used the term *urbanitas,* which encapsulated the qualities to which noblemen and other members of the elite aspired. When, for example, Marieta, an arlieva in the noble Trevisan household, made receipt for 12.5 ducats pledged to her dowry by the scuola of the Carità, she noted that the Trevisan brothers had pledged her 63 ducats above the 300 originally promised "per urbanitatem ipsorum fratrum."[23] When the lawyer Michiel Galasso remitted a loan he had made to his servant, the widow Marieta, the notary who recorded the remission noted that this was done "per sua urbanità, e cortesia."[24] And when Antonia Morosini made a bequest to her ancilla Cassandra, it was done "ex mea urbanitate."[25] Providing for one's loyal servants became an expression of the master's position and good manners.

A fourth motive behind the bequests was religious. Morosini left his missal and breviaries to Gasparo so that he would "pray to God for me." The performance of charitable deeds was another expression of a master's social status. It was also, of course, an effort to ensure the prayers of the poor on his behalf. When Donata, a Morosini widow, left her boat with all its rigging to her gondolier, Theodoro, she requested that Theodoro's wife, Iacoba, make pilgrimage to the church of San Lorenzo to get an indulgence for her soul.[26]

As the preface to the bequests to all his servants indicates, Morosini viewed these legacies first and foremost as rewards for loyal service. He was hardly alone in this regard. Loyalty was the quality masters most demanded of their servants. Humanist treatises repeatedly advised masters to secure only loyal servants; and the wills of the servant-keeping elite were filled with legacies given in gratitude for faithfulness. As noted in the preceding chapter, Isabeta and Vetor Grimani's generous bestowal of a dowry of two hundred ducats on their servant Ruosa da Budua was given as remuneration for "the loyal service and exemplary life of the said chambermaid."[27] Doge Agostino Barbarigo's bequest to his servant Battista di Santa Sofia was reward for Battista's "always having been most loyal in all our dealings."[28]

At heart, masters believed that servants were by nature untrustworthy and disloyal, and it was this fear, coupled with concern for their own honor, that led masters to undermine further the very trust they so desperately wanted to instill in servants. At the end of his bequests to Zuan, Antonello, and Gasparo, Morosini revealed his sixth and final motive. He disclosed that, in addition to all the preceding expressions of gratitude, love, and concern for the three, a further purpose lay behind the legacies, namely, his desire to secure their future service. The legacies were also an inducement for Zuan, Antonello, and Gasparo to remain with him. The master thus revealed his hand; and on that level the legacies can be considered little more than bribes.[29]

Again, Morosini was hardly exceptional. Luca Vendramin offered in his will to manumit and provide for the future of his male and female slaves after each performed five additional years of service. If, however, they showed "bad behavior" [cativo portamento] during that period, then they were to be neither "rewarded nor freed" [benefiziati ni liberi].[30] Barbarela, widow of nobleman Andrea de la Fontana, wanted her maid Maddalena to complete her contract under her "comater" Margarita, at the end of which she would receive her salary as well as a furnished bed for her dowry. But if she refused to serve the co-mother, then she was to receive nothing.[31] Even Doge Agostino Barbarigo hoped that his bequests to his loyal servant Battista di Santa Sofia would impel Battista to assist his executors.[32] And in a codicil to his will, Agostino Spinelli stated that he had promised twenty-five ducats to Gironima da Gorizia to marry or enter a convent not only as a reward for her service but also so that she would continue to serve him "con buon'animo."[33] Such attitudes indicate that expressions of parental solicitude were almost always dependent upon the demonstration of certain behaviors. And so, unwittingly, masters undercut the very loyalty that they tried to foster by making expressions of their concern contingent upon obedience and loyalty.

To this extent, then, servants were able to set the tone of relations if, out of either genuine loyalty and affection for their masters or cold calculation of benefits, they chose to play the role of faithful and obedient subordinates. The only nonkinsman to interpose himself in Leon Battista Alberti's *I libri della famiglia* is Buto, the loyal servant, who opens book 4. He enters, like a good servant, bearing gifts of fruit. Members of the family praise Buto for his loyalty and submissiveness; and he serves as a comic foil to Giannozzo's advice about training new brides when he describes his inability to control his wife. The narrator notes that the Alberti "thoroughly enjoyed these and other absurdities which Buto uttered amusingly and with appropriate gestures."[34] Buto brings to mind the familiar image of Uncle Tom, the obsequious American male slave who bowed to his master's whims. However, the narrator of *I libri Della famiglia* voices masters' fears when he notes that Buto, like other servants, may have been putting on an act, for he is described as one "who had learned, through constant poverty and the resultant necessity of living submissively and cheerfully in the houses of various people who supported him, to act the clown and to be a fine jester."[35] Buto disarms the threat of his own masculine presence by playing the fool and keeping his place. On the surface at least, he subsumes his own identity under that of his masters.

The servant in Fabio Glissenti's dialogue also admits to dissimulating, to pretending to be honest, loyal, and obedient, when in fact he is dishonest and deceitful. He says that "in the presence of the master I'm on guard and this rather pleases me, for he doesn't really come to know me, and in his presence I put on a show of being that which I am not."[36] We must remember that both of these servants were fictional creations of the elite. Nevertheless, even if these works do not faithfully record the actions of actual servants, they illustrate that masters worried about whether servants' demonstrations of loyalty and obedience were genuine or feigned.

Whether these demonstrations were sincere or calculated, many servants adopted the behavior expected of them and took their place within their master's family. One indication of this is the selection of fiduciaries found in servants' wills. Table 6.1 demonstrates how heavily servants, especially female servants, relied upon their masters and mistresses as executors. Almost 40 percent of the persons female servants chose as executors were their masters and mistresses, compared with 16 percent for male servants. More striking still is servants' reliance on their masters and mistresses' families: 101 of the 178 executors selected by female servants (56.7%) were their employers or their employers' kin. Since the category of other noble executors may contain former masters and mistresses who were not so identified, the reliance was perhaps even greater.

Table 6.1

Executors Selected by Servant Testators, 15th and 16th Centuries

| | No./% of Executors Chosen by | | | |
| --- | --- | --- | --- | --- |
| | Male Servants | | Female Servants | |
| Executors | No. | % | No. | % |
| Master or mistress | 4 | 16.0 | 69 | 38.7 |
| Former master or mistress | 3 | 12.0 | 5 | 2.8 |
| Son or daughter of master | 1 | 4.0 | 18 | 10.1 |
| Other relative of master | 0 | 0.0 | 9 | 5.1 |
| Spouse | 3 | 12.0 | 8 | 4.5 |
| Other kin | 3 | 12.0 | 9 | 5.1 |
| Godparent/co-parent | 1 | 4.0 | 5 | 2.8 |
| Other Servant | 1 | 4.0 | 5 | 2.8 |
| Other (non-noble) | 4 | 16.0 | 24 | 13.4 |
| Other (noble) | 4 | 16.0 | 17 | 9.6 |
| Clergy | 1 | 4.0 | 9 | 5.1 |
| Total | 25 | 100.0 | 178 | 100.0 |

*Sources:* ASV, CI, Notai, and NT.

*Note:* Data are for 15 male testators and 115 female testators.

Among male servants, 32 percent of their executors were present and former masters and their kin.

Another notable feature of the data is the relatively small number of their own kin chosen as executors. Among female servants, only 22 of their 178 executors were spouses, kin, or god- or co-parents, compared with 7 of 25 executors of male servants. None of the male servants and only 1 female servant named a parent as an executor: Caterina da Venezia, a servant in the household of Vito di Giovanni da Ferrara, named her mother in her will of 1405.[37] The absence of kin, especially parents, from the testaments of servants both male and female suggests the extent to which acceptance into service represented the transfer of children or young persons from the care of their parents to the care and jurisdiction of their masters and mistresses. Judging from the evidence of fiduciaries, servants were isolated from their kin. Procurator Morosini reported in his will that his deceased former servant Zaneto had named him and Zuan Terzo as his executors and that Zaneto had especially entrusted him with the responsibility of marrying off his natural daughter, Andriana. Morosini enjoined his executors to place Andriana in marriage as soon as possible and left an additional fifty ducats for her dowry.[38] It is not surprising that many servants, thrown into a strange environment with few means of emotional support, looked to their masters (and their former masters) to guard their interests, manage their estates, even to marry off their children. We cannot peer into their hearts to know whether they did so out of a genuine sense of belonging or simply because they calculated that their masters were in a better position than most to safeguard their interests.

Although it is easy to assume that servants played the role of subordinates, of "children," to their masters, the mix of generations within households—the presence of young servants and older masters or older servants and younger masters and their kin—vastly complicated the possibilities for relations between masters and servants. Calling to mind the possible plurivocality of cultural forms, that relations and symbols can have different meanings for different groups, the roles of parent and child were in some instances reversed, with servants assuming the parental role.[39] This is most clear in the case of milk children and parents.

The relatively elevated status of wet nurses in Venetian households has already been remarked. As mothers themselves, wet nurses were looked upon as stable persons whose role in the household and matronly status gave them some moral authority and made them less likely victims of their masters' sexual advances. Wet nurses enjoyed precedence among servants precisely because they were commonly believed to transmit to their nurslings certain qualities of character through their milk.[40] As governesses, they were to a certain degree responsible for the upbringing of their charges. It was not unusual for long-term, extremely intense emotional bonds to develop between wet nurses and their nurslings. In her will dated 1519, Antonia, widow of a shoemaker and servant in the household of Michele Malumbra a cittadino, named Michele's wife, Mattea, as her sole executor and left three ducats to be distributed among the couple's seven children "as a sign of love, since I raised and cared for them from infancy" [in signum amoris, quia ipsos ab Infantia citra rexi et gubernavi].[41] Margarita, from Ragusa, wife of a miller in San Trovaso, named Augustin Balanzan, "fio mio da latte carissimo et observandissimo," her sole executor and recipient (along with his children) of the residue of her estate upon the death of her husband.[42] Anna, another immigrant from Dalmatia, left the residue of her estate to Carlo Querini, "mio carissimo fiol da latte."[43] For their part, masters and mistresses sometimes found the means to provide for the old age of servants who had long served their households. When Leonardo Donà secured an almshouse for his family servant Pascha di Rossi, he wrote that he had done a "cosa condecente."[44]

The point here is a simple one: the image of master-servant relations as familial could be interpreted in a variety of ways.[45] While humanist writers advised, and masters imagined, that servants would fit into their households like children, in fact, given the extraordinary mix of ages and generations, servants could assume the role of parents, although in old age the roles might reverse again (as occurs in biological families), with the children becoming responsible for the welfare of the parents. Servants who took little or no satisfaction in subordinate roles might, under the right circumstances, find that in fact they wielded a degree of moral and persuasive power over their "masters." Additionally, the presence in certain households of children and servants who were nearly the same age may have contributed to long-term commitments not dissimilar to those between siblings. The image of masters and servants as family had within it a number of possibilities for the creation of bonds between them.

Still another variant involved the joining of male masters and female servants or slaves in long-term sexual and emotional relationships or, in a few instances at least, in clandestine marriages. As already noted, at least three times between the fourteenth and sixteenth centuries the Great Council warned noblemen about the legal consequences of marriage to women of low or servile status; children of such relationships would be ineligible for council membership. At the same time, family strategies for the preservation of wealth forced at least some men to remain bachelors. Not surprisingly, some of them became involved with their servants.[46] For example, in his will dated 1518, Antonio Zorzi, one of several sons of Paolo Zorzi, left his house and all its furnishings, as well as the profit from his shares in the mint, to "my most loving wife, who was not my wife but my slave, who always struggled to make a living with me and who nursed all her children."[47] Pietro Barbo, son of Benedetto, was in a similar situation. One of at least four brothers, Pietro was unmarried but cohabited with Maria from Padua, by whom he had a natural daughter, Angela, to whom he left the residue of his estate.[48] Zuan Antonio di Bianchini, a wood merchant in Sant'Agnese, made it clear in his will that Santa, whom he described as "mia di casa," was "my wife truly taken [in marriage] to the honor of God" [è mia moglie vera tolta à laude di Dio in fede].[49]

Another example, the extraordinary case of nobleman Pietro Soranzo, illustrates the complicated ways in which family and marriage ties could shape relations between masters and servants. In the first of three extant wills, dated 4 March 1524, Soranzo named several noblemen to be his executors, along with his sister, Isabeta, his son, Zuane, and his daughter Chiara. Soranzo was especially concerned about Benetto, son of his steward, Baldisera di Francesco da Montello, and Baldisera's wife, Lucia. Soranzo stated that he wanted to pay Lucia's dowry and that if the couple wished, their son Benetto could be raised in his household by Zuane and his daughters until he reached the age of twenty-five. Piero wished for the boy to be well schooled, as befitting the son "of such a notable woman and such a respectable father" [de una si notabil femina, et da ben padre]. Soranzo was also solicitous of Fior, nurse of his daughter Cecilia. She was to be provided with food and clothing, given one-half ducat per year, and cared for in illness. He even offered to have her buried in his tomb.[50]

In his next will, made almost two years later, in January 1525mv, Soranzo named several noblemen as his executors, as well as his daughters Cecilia and Verde. His son, Zuane, who was unmentioned, must have died in the interim. The factor, Baldisera di Francesco da Montello, was also named as an executor. The bequest to the nurse Fior was largely identical to the one in the previous will, and Soranzo continued to be concerned with Baldisera's son, Benetto, insisting on the boy's education. In the final will, made four months later (12 May 1526), Soranzo revealed the precise relationship between himself and Benetto, having been "constrained by the confessors that he ought to tell the truth" [astreto dali confessori che debia dechiarir la verita]. Soranzo disclosed that when Baldisera's wife, Lucia, was in service to him, he violated her and got her pregnant. He then married her to Baldisera, assuring him that she was a virgin. Soranzo now asked their pardon and asked that Baldisera show Lucia "good company . . . because she has neither guilt nor sin" [bona compagnia . . . perche lei non ha colpa ne peccado]. He bequeathed his "casa grande" in Feltre to Benetto and left thirty bushels of grain to Baldisera if he would stay in Feltre "with the said Benetto and his family, and if otherwise, not" [cum el dicto Benetto et la fameglia, et non altramente]. This case illustrates not only the familiar story of a master taking sexual advantage of his servant but also his concern that his illegitimate son be raised in a proper family setting. For Soranzo, paternal and patronal feelings were inseparably linked in a complicated four-way relationship involving himself, Baldisera, Lucia, and Benetto, a relationship that both was modeled on and modified the familial view of master-servant relations.

While the mix of generations within households and sexual liaisons provided opportunities for the reversal or complication of roles between masters and servants, the pietistic system of early modern Catholicism allowed still others. Late medieval and early modern theology emphasized that the poor were closer to God than the rich and that the wealthy could garner spiritual benefit through the distribution of their riches as alms to the poor.[51] As Morosini's will indicates, one of his many motives in bequeathing religious books to Gasparo Terzo was so that Gasparo would pray for his soul. Although many bequests in wills were given "pro anima," that is, for the good of the soul of the testator, those bequests that had special spiritual significance were the ones in which the recipient was charged with the task of saying prayers or garnering indulgences for the soul of the testator. As we have seen, this was primarily women's work, often entrusted to female servants, especially aged nurses.

When Doge Agostino Barbarigo wrote his will in 1501, he provided accommodation in the Ospizio San Marco (also known as Ospizio Orseolo) for his servant Giacoma da Vicenza, in return for which he asked that she visit the churches of Santa Maria dei Miracoli and San Fantin "per l'anima nostra."[52] Donata, widow of Marco Antonio Morosini, left several items to her servitrix Margarita and asked that she go to Santa Trinità for the indulgence, for which she was to get the "usual alms." It was this same Morosini widow who left her boat to her gondolier Theodoro, but it was Theodoro's wife, Iacoba, whom Morosini asked to visit San Lorenzo for the indulgence.[53]

The obligation of servants, especially women, to pray for the souls of their masters is another example of the extremely complex and plurivocal quality of master-servant relations. With the common perception of their greater capacity for spiritual merit (a direct result of their poverty), servants were positioned to serve as the patrons and matrons of their masters and mistresses, pleading for intervention on behalf of their souls. Whereas in this world masters could use their patronage rights to secure positions for their servants in traghetti or almshouses, servants could exercise their privileged moral position in attempting to secure places among the saved for their masters. All of these relationships involved variations in which masters and servants formed a "famiglia" linked by mutual ties of obligation and responsibility.

Although masters and mistresses most commonly left their servants legacies in the form of cash, annuities, household utensils, or linens, a few, like Marcantonio Morosini, left them luxury items, including silver forks, paintings, medals, and other *objets d'art*. Morosini bequeathed his painting of Saint Jerome and another "small mosaic picture" of an unknown subject to Zuan Terzo.[54] Other masters left their servants similar objects. In 1414 Beta Malipiero, widow of nobleman Marco Malipiero, left a variety of objects, including a bed and coverlet and "two painted coffers and a panel on which is depicted an image of the Blessed Virgin Mary," to her servant Clara.[55] Agnesina, widow of Francesco dal Oro, left many things, including silver forks and spoons, to her massera Orsa. She also bequeathed her "a Madonna that is in my bedroom" [una Madonna che e in la mia camera]. The items were given "for my soul and for her [Orsa's] merits and labors."[56] Lucia, wife of Zorzi da Zara, left two paintings, "un quadro della Madonna, et un'altro quadro d'un Cristo," to Stana, "who lives in the house with me and cares for me for her salary."[57]

In all likelihood, these paintings were relatively undistinguished works produced by the *madonneri*, artisans of Cretan origin who produced large quantities of religious paintings in the traditional style of Byzantium.[58] Nonetheless, their display in the households and rooms of servants provided tangible proof of the bond linking masters and servants together. No doubt masters hoped that images of the Madonna, the most important intermediary between God and the souls of the dead, would remind servants of their obligation to the souls of their benefactors and further instill the Marian virtues of humility and acceptance. We shall never know exactly how servants viewed these pictures and other luxury objects; however, it is easy to imagine that they "appropriated" them as tokens of their connection to great families, objects of personal devotion, signs of their own piety and appreciation of art, or even as reserves to be pawned in times of need.[59] What seems clear is that images of the Madonna and Christ in particular had the capacity to reflect in multiple ways the constellation of familial relationships and feelings binding masters and servants together.

Masters were not the only ones to bequeath luxury objects. Servants also made a point of leaving as legacies to their "superiors" particularly valuable or treasured objects. For instance, in her will dated 1461, Caterina, a servant in the household of the noble Da Canal family, bequeathed a coffer made of cypress wood as well as an "agnus dei" (possibly a cross or medal or a wax figurine) to the daughter of her executor, noblewoman Cecilia Bragadin.[60] Zuane da Cattaro, formerly a boatman at the ferry station of the Maddalena and at the time of his will a servant of the noble Grimani family, bequeathed "five forks and two silver spoons" as well as several other objects and cash to his master and mistress.[61] Agnese, widow of Pantaleone da Scutari and housekeeper for Doge Francesco Foscari, wrote her will in November 1425 as she prepared to set out on pilgrimage to the Holy Sepulchre. Agnese, who appears to have been childless, left bequests to various kinfolk, to other servants of the Foscari household, and for alms. Among her bequests was one in which she left a silver cup to each of Foscari's sons, Niccolò and Jacopo. A third cup she left to her sister, whom she designated, along with her nephew, as her executor.[62]

The servants who made such bequests may have had a number of motives for doing so. Some may have made them in order to perpetuate ties to their masters, in the same way that masters used legacies as inducements for future relations. Others made such legacies purely as tokens of the affection that existed between them and their masters. Still other bequests were made in gratitude for the care they had received. When she drafted her will, Franceschina, widow of a baker and servant of maistro Bortolo di Zuane da Bergamo, a silkworker, left her master ("mio patron et santolo") the balance of her estate in recognition of "the good company I had from him and because he treated me like a daughter."[63] Even an adult like Franceschina was, or wished to appear, grateful to a master who cared for her as if she were his child.[64]

Like objects bequeathed as legacies, livery was another tangible sign of the bonds linking masters and servants. Specially designed outfits adorned with insignia or family colors identified servants as retainers of particular families. But the extent to which livery was actually used in the fourteenth and fifteenth centuries remains uncertain.[65] Sumptuary legislation regulating servants' apparel did not begin until 1562; however, the censors' 1541 capitulary did prohibit servants from wearing silk shoes and other garments.[66] Evidence from the censors' records indicates that male servants were given new outfits on special occasions such as weddings, when they were called upon to appear in important public festivities.[67] In her study of domestic servants in Old Regime France, Cissie Fairchilds has argued that servants had a weak sense of self-identify—that their displaced condition led them to identify with their masters—and that it was reinforced by the donning of livery.[68] Certainly masters wanted servants to subsume their own identity under that of their masters. And there is evidence that some, but by no means all, Venetian servants acted in that way.

Servants' identification with their masters was especially apparent when masters were under attack. Then servants closed ranks to defend masters and their families. In his chronicle, Domenico Malipiero recorded an episode in which a man from Corfu who was owed money by the Lippomano bank went to the home of Geronimo Lippomano to collect what he was owed. Lippomano put him off, responding that he would be paid in time. At that point the man pulled a knife on the banker, who was instantly defended by his servant.[69] It was not uncommon for servants also to assist their masters in acts of violence. The male servants of Jacopo Foscari, son of Doge Francesco, were interrogated and sentenced as accomplices to his misdeeds.[70]

Some of the violence between male servants of different households may have originated in disputes or feuds between their masters. The registers of those condemned in contumacy for homicide by the signori di notte contain at least forty-three cases involving servants employed by different masters. One was the condemnation for murder of a servant of the English ambassador by a servant of the Spanish ambassador.[71] When in 1604 the censors heard the case against the boatman Zaneto, a traghetto operator at San Lorenzo who was accused of insulting the manservant of nobleman Pietro Corner, they noted that injury was also done to the Corner family.[72] Masters may well have encouraged servants to interpret such offenses in this way.

The degree to which servants might identify with and internalize the values of their masters is richly illustrated by an incident that occurred in 1422 when Francesco Venier and his famulus Antonello encountered Antonio Zancarolo and his familiar Manolo. When Venier threatened Zancarolo, Manolo grabbed him, exclaiming, according to the Latinized records of the avogadori di comun, "Lord Francesco, it isn't urbane for a nobleman to wish to kill another nobleman" [domine Francisce ista non est urbanitas nobilis velle interficere alium nobilem]. Nevertheless, Venier was able to wound both Zancarolo and Manolo.[73] In this case, it appears that Manolo's identification with his master was nearly complete; he saw an attack on his master as an attack on himself. At the same time, he gave expression to the elite's sense of social order by reprimanding Venier for his dishonorable behavior. As Manolo knew, *urbanitas* was supposed to distinguish the elite from others. Manolo's acceptance of his own position blended imperceptibly into acceptance of a highly stratified social hierarchy in which the elite were expected to display certain qualities not shared by their inferiors.

To summarize, masters idealized relations in which they displayed parental concern for their servants and servants responded with demonstrations of obedience and loyalty to their masters. In masters' minds, such relations not only guaranteed the smooth operation of their homes but also, according to the analogy of the household to the polity and society, affirmed the rightness of the larger political and social orders. The elite believed that the city would remain peaceful if their "inferiors" accepted and internalized their value system.

And on the surface at least a good many servants did just that. For instance, Giacomina, a widowed massara in the home of Luca Civran, named her "most singular" [singularissimus] master the sole executor of her estate and asked that he arrange her funeral "honorably according to her station" [honorifice iuxta conditionem suam].[74] So too did the widow Ursula, an "ancila domestica" in the home of the physician Giovanni da Carrara. In her will Ursula warned her kin not to seek her salary from her "patron" since Carrara had "dowered my daughter partly with my salary, and has cared for me in my illnesses, and has more than compensated me for my salary and [because] I have had good company from him."[75] Ursula amply demonstrated her gratitude for good treatment, while Giacomina willingly accepted her social position.

From the master's point of view, the ideal servant was one like Lucia Morosini, former slave of nobleman Michele Morosini. As was frequently the custom among slaves, she took her master's surname as her own, a powerful indication of her identification with the family. She named as the executors of her estate "my most honored benefactors and masters" [li mei honoratissemi benefatori e patroni] Zuane, Marcantonio, and Piero, sons of the late Michele, as well as Laura, wife of Francesco Priuli, and Orsa, wife of Piero, "my most singular mistresses" [mie singularissime patrone]. Perhaps recognizing the incongruity of naming five nobles as her executors, Lucia acknowledged that "my insignificance does not merit the many and innumerable benefits I have received from them" [la picolezia mia non merita tanti et inumerabili beneficii riceputi cusi da loro]. Lucia even asked, as noted in chapter 5, to be buried at the monastery of Sant'-Anna with her "most loving mistress and mother," Madonna Maria Morosini.[76] Lucia clearly saw herself as part of the Morosini family; not only did she take the family name as her own but she referred to her former mistress as her mother. What is more, Lucia accepted her place in society, contrasting her own "picolezza" with the "grandezza" of her masters. Her obsequious tone and gratitude for favors received rendered Lucia and others like her pliant dependents of elite households and humble subjects of the Venetian ruling class.

## Disloyalty and Disobedience

Nothing better illustrates just how precarious the position of servants was within households and how dependent they were upon the goodwill of their masters than the codicils masters attached to their wills disinheriting them. The attitude of masters toward their servants could change suddenly. Servants who were lauded one day for loyalty and obedience were excoriated the next for their bad faith and ingratitude.

When, for example, Angelica, wife of Blanchino di San Vito da Salvacono from the parish of San Geremia, wrote her will in February 1522, she bequeathed a bed and all her *interulas* (shirts) to her ancilla, Lucia, wife of Jacopo Vedregnano, "because she served me faithfully" [quia michi fideliter inservivit]. Angelica even promised that if Lucia predeceased her, in place of the legacy, one hundred masses would be said in Lucia's name. But in a codicil dated two years later, Angelica revoked the legacy and left the bed instead to Elisabeta, Lucia's sister and Angelica's current ancilla. Then in another codicil, dated 15 June 1526, Angelica disinherited both women "so that Lucia and Elisabeta may have none of my goods" [ita quod ipse Lucia et Helesabet nihil de bonis meis habere possint]. According to Angelica, she did this because the two maids "treated me badly" and, "what is worse, they fled my house, to my greatest disgrace and distress to my spirit."[77]

In his will of 4 June 1534, Piero Tron, son of the late Alvise of the parish of Sant'Agata, left, contingent on their comportment, five ducats beyond their salary to "tuta la mia fameglia," including his male servants Roberto Todesco, Anzolo da Peschiera, and Julio da Brescia. He also provided for his female servant Orsa. But just a few weeks later, on 30 June, Tron added a codicil disinheriting Roberto and Anzolo for not conducting themselves properly. Tron noted that he was not motivated by hatred in this action but stated that he expected all servants whom he rewarded "to serve their masters continuously, remaining in their households."[78]

In a codicil dated 10 November 1574, Doge Alvise Mocenigo left fifty ducats to donna Lucia, his massara, who "for many years has served me in the household" [che già molti anni me serve in casa]. He also left fifty ducats to help marry or place in a convent Lucia's daughter, who apparently was serving in the house of a certain Francesco di Niccolò. But in another codicil, dated 15 September 1576, Mocenigo revoked the bequests to Lucia and her daughter and repossessed an apartment that he had assigned to them in the Cà di Dio, the ducally controlled hospital. He did this because "she brought shame upon herself and upon our household" [havendo lei fatto vergogna à lei et à casa nostra].[79]

And in his will dated 3 October 1571, Pietro Calbo raised the salary of Lucieta, whom he described as "a youth of most honest character and loyalty" [giovene de honestissimi costumi e fedele alla casa] who had once served his deceased wife, from seven to twelve ducats per year, plus a tip of one ducat. He did this as an enticement for her to remain in charge of his children until the youngest of them reached age fifteen. But on 16 May 1572 Calbo revoked the legacy "for just and reasonable causes, as she well knows" [per giuste e convenienti cause a lei benissimo note].[80]

In these codicils masters and mistresses offered various explanations for their change of opinion. Angelica, wife of Blanchino, was offended by her servants' behavior and angry because they left her service. Likewise, Pietro Tron was outraged by the ill behavior of his male servants. Doge Mocenigo condemned Lucia for the disgrace she brought upon herself and his household; most likely she became pregnant. And Pietro Calbo disinherited Lucieta for the "just and reasonable causes" that were well known to the two of them but remain a mystery to us. Relations went sour when one of the parties chose to act in ways that challenged the other's perceptions of and expectations for the bond. For masters, this occurred when servants were disobedient and disloyal. For servants, it happened when masters took grossly unfair advantage of their power.

A particularly critical time in master-servant relations occurred when boys and girls who had entered service at a very young age and were compliant to their masters' orders reached puberty or young adulthood and began to assert themselves.[81] Docile girls upon reaching puberty might suddenly find themselves the object of unwanted attention from their master and wish to escape, or they might find themselves the recipients of flattery from other men and chafe at the strictures of their master's household. Boys reaching their teens might suddenly balk at taking orders and the prospect of a life of service and go off in search of adventure. Fourteen-year-old Africo Negro, introduced in chapter 5, took leave of one master and was "going to ruin" [andava à ramengo] on Zante before he came under Giorgio da Brazzo's care. In his will, the oft-cited Procurator Marcantonio Morosini included a bequest to Zuan Piero da Brescia, who "was my boy" [fo mio ragazzo] but who left his service because "he wished to live in his own way" [habi voluto vivera suo modo]. According to Morosini, Zuan Piero also was going to ruin ("l'è andà ramengo").[82]

When masters and mistresses were actually confronted by acts of misbehavior or defiance, they responded in a variety of ways. Many, relying on their role as heads of household, admonished and cajoled. Paolino the Minorite and Glissenti both recommended the rod for servants, and there is plenty of evidence that servant keepers, both men and women, tried to beat their servants into submission. They justified this as part of their obligation to be stern but caring "parents."

At times, however, such beatings got out of hand and led to serious injury or even death. The signori di notte al criminal's register of those banished in contumacy for homicide between 1471 and 1507 includes one instance in which a master killed a servant. Both Niccolò Nicoloxo and his female servant, Margarita, were condemned in contumacy for the murder of Niccolò's Greek manservant, Eustachio.[83]

The second of the signori di notte's registers, covering the period 1523 to 1559, contains six cases in which masters or mistresses were condemned for murdering their servants. In 1533 Carolo, son of widow Elisabeta Theotonica, was convicted in contumacy for killing the family servant, Giacoma, with two wounds.[84] In 1539 Cristoforo Agata was banished for the murder of his male slave, Niccolò di Marimoiori, whom Agata had stabbed once in the stomach and once in the ribs.[85] The other four cases involved mistresses. Fineta, wife of Alvise a Curtino, and her sister, Elisabeta, were condemned for the murder of their massara, Urseta Feltrina; Agnesina, wife of Francesco a Tomaxiis, stabbed her maid, Antonia; Abadia, wife of the hatter Battista, beat to death her massara, Eva; and Caterinella Balbi beat her six-year-old slave Marcantonio so severely that he died.[86] The records do not provide clues to motivation, although it appears that in some cases mistresses committed these crimes in fits of uncontrolled rage, whereas in others there may have been some premeditation.

Tellingly, none of these cases involved members of the nobility, who proportionally employed the greatest number of servants in Venice. It may well be that nobles had little to fear from the Venetian justice system, did not flee the city, and so were not included in these records. Even Cristoforo Agata, who was sentenced for the murder of his servant, Niccolò di Marimoiori, in June 1539, was absolved by the Council of Ten in October of that same year.[87] It is also possible that some noble masters made their servants take the blame for certain crimes.[88]

In most cases of disobedience, it appears that masters relied on their personal power and authority to try to bring servants to heel. Another option, but one that was much less frequently exercised, was to take servants before the court of the censors. But going before them was, from the masters' point of view, a risky undertaking, since it publicized their inability to control their households and thus threatened their reputation. Perhaps it was for this reason that on average only eighteen cases were brought each year. On the other hand, by calling on the assistance of the authorities, masters could align themselves with the city fathers and, with the weight of the state behind them, try to discipline their servants. The censors' trial records provide our best evidence for the sources of tension in master-servant relations.

As noted in chapter 2, the most frequent charge masters made before the censors was that servants had broken their contracts. The breaking of contracts by servants annoyed and irritated masters because of the bother, inconvenience, and expense it caused. But the concern went much deeper, for when servants broke their contracts, they rejected their membership in the master's family, the affective ties associated with it, and, by implication, the master's position of dominance. The language masters used to describe these offenses illustrates these points.

In July 1570, for example, the censors heard the case the physician Tiberio Barbaro brought against his servant Galeatio, son of a ferryman. Barbaro claimed that when he took Galeatio into his service, he had outfitted him properly and "patiently" [patienter] cured him of trench. But Galeatio, whom he described as "unmindful and ungrateful for the benefits received" [immemor, et beneficiorque receptorum ingratus], had left his service, even though in April they had renewed the contract between them. Additionally, Barbaro claimed that the boy had taken the clothes he had furnished him, costing "a not insignificant sum."[89]

In another case, dated 30 October 1578, nobleman Francesco Bernardo recalled that he had taken Niccolò da Cattaro "from the pastures without any manners and raised him with good manners and taught him all that is required of a good servant." Bernardo probably emphasized this point in order to illustrate that he had assumed the role of a good father or patron. According to Bernardo, Niccolò had been "ungrateful" for the solicitude of his master and had begun "refusing orders" [sprezzando li comandamenti]. Eventually he had fled, but "not content with this," he had gone to a neighboring household, where he had gossiped to the servants of that house about his master's household, "with no respect for the house of his master and contrary to honest and peaceful living."[90]

Other masters expressed similar concerns. Niccolò da Venezia, who broke his contract with nobleman Marino Giustinian and engaged in sex with one of the household maids, was accused of being "unmindful of the benefits he had received from his master," as was Paolo, servant of nobleman Paolo Tron, when he broke his contract.[91] Nobleman Agostino Bembo strengthened the indictment against his servant Antonio da Venezia, whom he accused of breaking his contract, rendering bad service, and wounding another male servant, by claiming that he had left while his master was ill, despite entreaties to remain in service a few extra days.[92] Similarly, Paolo Drusi charged his ancilla, Zana Veronese, with breaking her contract at a time when her mistress, Drusi's wife, was sick.[93] When, in 1605, nobleman Antonio Diedo accused three persons of a number of crimes, including theft, one of the three, Diana, was considered especially culpable since she had been the recipient of favors from Diedo for thirty years. According to the censors' records, her action revealed that she feared "neither God nor Justice."[94]

What especially offended these masters (or what they imagined would offend the censors who were hearing the cases) was that servants appeared ungrateful for what the masters saw as the kindly, paternal treatment they had received. These masters had, in their own words, acted like good fathers to their servants; they had dressed them properly, cured them of illnesses, and taught them good manners. In return they were greeted with disobedience, indifference, and ingratitude. By fleeing, servants rejected the solicitude of their masters and suggested that the favors they had received required no long-term demonstrations of loyalty. When, for example, the censors tried two wet nurses for breaking their contracts and leaving their nurslings, they claimed that the women exhibited a "minimum of love."[95] What is more, individual acts of disobedience awakened fears about the loyalty of the subject classes in general.

Ironically, the patrician regime itself fostered and encouraged one form of disloyalty. Several writers of treatises on the household specifically warned that disgruntled or dismissed servants would go about revealing family secrets, as Niccolò da Cattaro had done. The privacy and honor of households could be held hostage by former employees. Despite this worry, the government recognized the potential of servants as informers. In 1484 the Senate passed a sumptuary law regulating the amount of money that could be spent on wedding feasts and festivals sponsored by the *compagnie della calza,* social clubs for elite young men, by trying to control what foods could be served. To enforce the law, the

Senate decided that part of any penalties levied against contraveners would go to informers. If the informers were slaves, they would be freed as a reward; if they were hired servants (either indentured or on salary), they were to be relieved of further contractual obligations.[96] By offering financial rewards, the government, perhaps without fully realizing the significance of its action, actually encouraged servants to betray their masters and to act in their own economic self-interest.

By breaking contracts, servants seemed to highlight the economically exploitative character of the master-servant tie, an aspect masters naturally tried to downplay in their everyday relations with servants. But when masters themselves charged servants with breaking contracts, they emphasized the financial loss they had suffered by listing the salary advances they had made and the clothes they had given to servants. In 1609, for example, the censors ruled that if Simeon, gondolier of nobleman Alvise Venier, were unfit for galley service, he was to be placed in the stocks at Rialto with a sign reading "for having left without permission of his master and for carrying off a salary advance."[97] And when the censors convicted Francesco da Romania for breaking his contract with nobleman Stefano Bollani, they noted that he had acted "in contempt of justice."[98] At the same time, masters reserved for themselves the right to dismiss servants with no prior warning. No law was enacted requiring masters to give servants notice of termination of contract.

Breaking contract was one of many deeds masters could interpret as acts of disloyalty and disobedience. Since masters were encouraged to think of the entire domestic complex, including family members, chattel, even the house itself, as a unit and a reflection of their own social position and moral probity, almost any violation of the household by servants could under the right circumstances be interpreted as a challenge to the master.

Theft in particular undermined the material welfare of the family and, like the breaking of contract, reminded masters and mistresses of the economic motives behind service. Closely associated with theft was the destruction of property. The gondola was an especially easy target. When Ioseph da Venezia, gondolier of nobleman Giovanni Battista Capello, was fired, he sank one of the Capello family gondolas at night by punching a hole in the bottom of the boat and filling it with rocks.[99] In 1587 nobleman Eustachio Duodo prosecuted his famulus, Melchiore da Oderzo, for verbally abusing and attempting to strike his son. The night after this incident, Melchiore destroyed Duodo's gondola.[100] Nobleman Vittore Malipiero claimed that his servant damaged and broke his gondola.[101] By stealing and destroying property, servants struck back at their masters and highlighted the underlying economic nature of their relationship.

While certain actions of servants exacerbated master-servant relations by underscoring the economic underpinnings of the bond, these were by no means the only sources of trouble and tension. The vast arena of sex and gender relations was another minefield threatening to complicate and disrupt ties. As Klapisch-Zuber has noted for Florence, a master's interest in his servants might aggravate and jeopardize cordial relations with his wife and throw the entire household into disarray.[102] The same was true in Venice. In 1423, for example, the avogadori di comun prosecuted a certain Margarita da Sibenico for attempting to poison her mistress. According to Margarita, her mistress was mistreating her because she was convinced that her husband, Stefano ab Oro, was in love with Margarita.[103]

Cases involving sexual relations between male servants and their mistresses or other family members seem to have been much rarer but were not unknown. Guido Ruggiero suggests that such liaisons were more widespread than the records indicate but that families refrained from prosecuting in order to avoid publicity.[104] Another possibility is that such offenses were considered so heinous that lower-class males were too fearful of the consequences to initiate such relations. In 1494 the signori di notte did prosecute Giorgio da Bovolenta, servant of ducal secretary Francesco Taiapietra, for "deflowering" and abducting Taiapietra's daughter. Described as a "servitor infidelis," he was captured at the Villa Bovolenta and sentenced to five years' exile.[105] Unfortunately, the records do not indicate whether the Taiapietra girl entered willingly into the relationship or her father presented it as a case of abduction in order to protect her reputation. However, the safest course for male servants was to appear neutered or asexual, like Buto in Alberti's dialogue.

As a rule servant keepers were much more concerned about sexual intrigues between servants than they were about illicit relations between masters and servants, at least those between masters and female servants. It was a preoccupation of legislators and a crime that was frequently prosecuted. Masters were worried for two reasons. First, sexual liaisons between servants undermined the order and morality of the entire household. Contemporaries believed that immorality was like a contagion, once introduced into a home, it would be difficult to eradicate; and treatises warned that daughters of the household were especially susceptible to the influence of immoral maids. Hence the entire household was threatened. Second, sexual activity on the part of servants signaled that they were not in fact docile and malleable children as masters liked to believe but rather independent-minded adults. It belied a one-dimensional understanding of servants and their personalities.

The prosecution of sex crimes reflects this concern. In 1587, for example, nobleman Francesco Barozzi prosecuted his ancilla, Margarita da Verona, and Andrea Furlan, a servant of the physician Octavio Zechio, for having sexual relations. Margarita had let Andrea into her master's house, and when Barozzi had caught them in flagrante delicto, Andrea had wounded Barozzi. The sexual intrigues of Margarita thus had led to an even greater evil, an attack on a nobleman in his own home. Andrea managed to flee and was banished for ten years. Margarita, who was captured, was to be placed in the stocks at Rialto with a sign around her neck reading "For having allowed her Pimp into the Home of her Master" [Per haver introdutto un suo Berton in Casa del suo Patron] and to spend two years in jail.[106] Nobleman Bernardo Navagero prosecuted his servants Marco Zon da Udine and Venturina Aethiops, nicknamed Moretta, for engaging in sex. According to the censors, they did this "against good customs and honesty, which especially are owed to noble houses."[107] Similar wording was used in a case in which nobleman Pietro Valier prosecuted his servant Pietro Ziozzeto for getting a housemaid pregnant and harassing the family.[108]

In a few special cases, cases involving wet nurses in charge of infants, masters believed that the unauthorized sexual activity of their servants literally threatened their kin. In 1579 Cristoforo Cithinio prosecuted his wet nurse, Maddalena Trentina, for talking to men from the balcony of her master's home, letting them in, and having sex with them. She had violated her master's home and tainted it with moral corruption, but the gravity of the offense was compounded by the fact that she was nursing Cithinio's infant son. According to the censors, she had committed these acts "with no little danger to the life of the boy that she is nursing and with much offence to the honor of her master and to all his household and with a most evil example to all respectable and honorable houses."[109] Nobleman Andrea Giustinian prosecuted his wet nurse, Caterina of Monselice, and his famulus, Giovanni, for having carnal relations and for robbing him. They had committed these acts "in the worst example to other male and female servants and especially to wet nurses, to whom is entrusted the care of nursing boys, endangering the life of the nursing boy, the son of the aforesaid nobleman Andrea, and with great dishonor to the aforesaid [noble] house."[110] Caterina's action cut to the very heart of the Venetian nobility, her promiscuity threatening Giustinian's male child, the lifeblood of a Venetian nobleman. It presented a double threat to the image of the family espoused by masters.[111]

Did noble and non-noble masters perceive the threat of servants differently? The aggregated data from the censors' trials allow us to answer that question partially. Table 6.2 presents the accusations leveled against servants according to the status of the plaintiffs during the period 1569–1600. Actually there are few surprises here. Nobles, who constituted 65 percent of known plaintiffs, leveled roughly that percentage of accusations in most categories. However, they seem to have been especially sensitive to harassment by servants; to their houses being left vulnerable; and to servants' refusal to take orders—all of which could be construed as challenges to their honor and authority. By contrast, noble plaintiffs were least concerned about the corruption of servants within households. Commoners appear to have been especially sensitive to verbal abuse and actual physical attack. This may indicate that servants were a bit less cowed by non-nobles and had the courage to challenge and even attack them. Generally speaking, however, plaintiffs of all status levels were concerned with the same issues, and under the right circumstances they could interpret almost any action as one of defiance. Ludovico Curelli, for example, charged his gondolier, Antonio, with "not rendering to him proper obsequiousness and despising his orders."[112] In 1609 Niccolò Tiepolo accused his gondolier, Sebastiano, of using words "contrary to the reverence which is owed to his master."[113] The censors condemned Lorenzo of Capodistria, gondolier of nobleman Alvise Soranzo, for, among other things, speaking to his master "in a derisory manner."[114]

Table 6.2
Accusations, by Plaintiff's Status, 1569–1600

| Accusation | Number of Accusations Made by | | | | | |
| | Nobles | | Commoners | | Others | |
| | No. | % | No. | % | No. | % |
| --- | --- | --- | --- | --- | --- | --- |
| Breaking contract | 173 | 67.1 | 48 | 18.6 | 37 | 14.3 |
| *Malam servitutem* | 14 | 58.3 | 6 | 25.0 | 4 | 16.7 |
| Theft of goods | 90 | 61.6 | 31 | 21.2 | 25 | 17.1 |
| Destruction of property | 13 | 68.4 | 3 | 15.8 | 3 | 15.8 |
| Leaving house vulnerable | 14 | 77.8 | 4 | 22.2 | 0 | 0.0 |
| Strangers in house | 8 | 72.7 | 2 | 18.2 | 1 | 9.1 |
| Refusing orders | 7 | 77.8 | 0 | 0.0 | 2 | 22.2 |
| Verbal abuse | 18 | 56.3 | 10 | 31.2 | 4 | 12.5 |
| Harassment | 13 | 86.7 | 2 | 13.3 | 0 | 0.0 |
| Physical attack or threat | 14 | 56.0 | 7 | 28.0 | 4 | 16.0 |
| Corruption of servants | 11 | 47.8 | 6 | 26.1 | 6 | 26.1 |
| Sex crimes | 85 | 63.0 | 31 | 23.0 | 19 | 14.0 |
| Miscellaneous | 34 | 54.0 | 13 | 20.6 | 16 | 25.4 |

*Source:* ASV, Censori, busta 3, registers 1–3.
*Note:* Data are for 412 plaintiffs, of whom 268 (65.1%) were nobles, 82 (19.9%), were commoners, and 62 (15.0%) were others. "Others" comprises foreigners, ecclesiastics, or plaintiffs whose status is unknown.

Masters considered public acts of disobedience especially grave. In July 1570 nobleman Benedetto Condulmer prosecuted his gondolier, Ioseph, before the censors. According to Condulmer, Ioseph had left his service without permission shortly after receiving a new set of clothes from him. Twice when he had met Ioseph on the street, he had demanded their return, but the gondolier had responded by drawing a weapon and threatening to toss his former master into a canal. According to the censors' records, this insolence had occurred on a public street, where it set a "most evil example that must not be tolerated."[115] When the censors tried Bartolomeo, servant of nobleman Andrea Gritti, for attacking his master, they noted that "what was worse" [quod peius est], he had yelled at him "in alta voce" in Campo Santa Maria Mater Domini.[116] Pietro da Cittadella screamed threats and obscenities at his former master, physician Fabricio Ancharanno, in public.[117] And after being fired, Bartolomeo da Pieve di Cadore verbally attacked his former master nobleman Luca Foscarini. This was a particularly serious affront since it occurred both in the Piazza San Marco and at Rialto, the centers of elite male culture and power in Venice. As the censors noted, by this behavior he had illustrated "no regard for [his master's] nobility.[118]

But what of servants? What did they see as the sources of tension in their relations with masters? It goes almost without saying that, given the extant sources, these questions are extremely difficult to answer. But two anonymous early printed texts, the *Dialogo del patron, et del Zane* and *L'ultima licenza della buona massara dalla cattiva patrona,* provide some evidence.[119]

The *Dialogo* revolves around the servant Zane's complaint that he is not given enough to eat. When he is asked by his master what he wants, Zane replies,

Every day a chicken, a lamb, and a veal
And a barrel of muscatel and thirty sausages
And a bushel of macaroni.

The patron replies that all the city's revenue would be insufficient to satisfy his appetite and accuses Zane of being "ungrateful" [sgratiato] and "unbridled" [sregolato] and threatens to give him a beating. In *L'ultima licenza,* the "good" housekeeper complains of the mistreatment she receives at the hands of her "bad" mistress, whose yelling "reaches to the stars." Every day the maid suffers a constant barrage of orders: "Wash these dishes . . . close that balcony . . . cook the sausage . . . set the table." The mistress is a harsh and demanding shrew.

Although these works were products of the elite that for comic effect intentionally exaggerated the complaints of servants, they do suggest that domestics were rankled when masters and mistresses failed to take seriously their obligation to care for them properly and to treat them with a minimum of respect.

Furthermore, the complaints by Zane and the housekeeper of inadequate food and mistreatment were echoed in the censors' records. For instance, Andriana, a nurse in the employ of Cristoforo Centoni, was hauled before the censors for taking some items, including bread and wine, hardly a serious offense.[120] When Raimondo Gritti accused his servants Pietro da Carrara and Santa of engaging in sex together, he also charged Santa with theft. Apparently she had given Pietro "more than his allotted ration" [ultra eius ordinanam (*sic*) portionem] of bread and wine.[121] And when nobleman Marino Gradenigo accused his famulus, Giovanni, of breaking his contract, he further accused him of stealing some wood.[122] These charges suggest that some masters were indeed miserly and that servants felt inadequately cared for.

Servants also resented and feared verbal, physical, and sexual abuse. When Francesco from Istria was accused by nobleman Antonio Bragadin of breaking his contract, he admitted his guilt but claimed that he had fled because his master beat him.[123] Pietro, servant of nobleman Timoteo Valier, likewise confessed that he had left service without permission but defended his action by claiming that one of Valier's children had beaten him.[124] And Daniele di Moretto claimed that he had left nobleman Francesco Querini's service "out of fear" [prae timore].[125]

Masters used their sexually dominant position to intimidate female (and more occasionally male) servants and especially to control male servants, to whom this kind of free sexual access to females was denied. There is no doubt that servants feared and resented their masters' unsolicited sexual advances. Cases of heterosexual misconduct have already been considered, but at least one of the cases heard by the censors hints at homosexual interest as well. In 1585 nobleman Pietro di Avocatis prosecuted his famulus, Geronimo da Narvesia, for breaking his contract. Geronimo confessed his guilt but claimed that he had left when his master "wished to offend him at a place called Fossalta, and out of fear, he threw himself into the river at Meolo."[126] By foisting themselves onto unwilling servants, masters betrayed their role as father figures whose job it was to protect their underlings.

Just as masters' reactions to servant disobedience ranged from tolerance to intimidation to actual murder, servants' reactions to their masters' treatment varied widely as well. Much of what servants thought and felt about their subordination, what James Scott calls "the hidden transcript" of the powerless, is irretrievably lost to us.[127] Some no doubt silently withstood abuse, while others muttered vague threats under their breath. Some probably found solace in religion. They may have found special meaning in depictions of the Last Judgment in which the proud are humbled or in the Carnival theme of the world turned upside down. Our one meager clue in this regard concerns Isabeta, wife of Zanmaria di Constantin, discussed in chapter 5, who compared her experience to that of the Israelites who fell into the hands of Pharaoh. Her words are reminiscent of those of Afro-American slaves who found solace, not, as masters hoped, in the New Testament messages of humility and perseverance, but in Old Testament themes of judgment and retribution.[128]

While some servants suffered in silence, others struck at their masters indirectly. We have noted the significance material objects had for servants, especially gondolas for male servants and linens and other household objects for female ones. Given the significance of these items as symbols of their masters' status, it is not surprising to find that some disgruntled servants struck at their masters through them. We have noted cases in which servants vandalized their masters' boats. By so doing, they not only relieved themselves of a few days work but also defied their masters. Masters clearly understood the symbolic significance of these acts. According to the censors who prosecuted Ioseph da Venezia for sinking his master's boat, he acted in contempt, or as they said, "in spretum," of his master.[129]

The desire to strike at masters without actually attacking their person may also explain at least some cases of theft by female servants. By stealing jewelry and linens, female servants were literally robbing the elite of the symbols of their status as well as trying to enrich themselves.[130] In 1398 the signori di notte tried Anna da Corone, former servant of Michele Abarcubus, for theft. Under threat of torture, Anna told her story. Soon after Anna had hired on with Abarcubus, her master had made unwelcome sexual advances toward her. When she refused him, he had beaten her and taken her tunic and silver-worked belt and locked them in a coffer. "Driven by anger" [furia ducta], she had found the keys to the coffer, stolen several items from it, fled the house, and gone to the home of a female friend in the parish of Sant'Aponal. According to her testimony, she had committed these acts "with the spirit and intention of avenging herself on her master and as a sign of disrespect for him."[131] In 1401 a certain Diada testified that she had stolen from her master because she was discontented.[132] In some unexpected ways, servants appropriated objects generally associated with the elite and instilled them with significance all their own. In so doing they found ways to defy their masters. Certain acts of sexual transgression may have been committed as acts of defiance as well.

Finally, under truly exceptional circumstances servants exploded, attacking or actually murdering their masters. The two registers of those condemned by the signori di notte in contumacy for homicide contain only three possible cases of servants' murdering their masters.[133] But those records provide only a partial view of the incidence of homicide, for scattered throughout the voluminous records of the avogadori di comun are other homicide cases.[134]

One involved the servants of a certain Francesco Bicharano. It seems that his gondolier, Giovanni da Savina, and his Russian slave, Uliana, were having an affair and that Uliana persuaded Giovanni to purchase some drugs. Her plan was to poison the master and mistress, steal their goods, and flee to Portogruaro. When Giovanni served the tainted food to his mistress, she became violently ill but did not die. Upon their discovery, Uliana drowned herself, and Giovanni was sentenced to a whipping, three years in jail, and then perpetual banishment from Venice.[135] This is but one of several cases of poisoning in the fifteenth century that involved female servants or slaves.[136] The desire for freedom and fear of further mistreatment were the forces that drove servants and slaves to commit or attempt murder.

In another case from 1459 the avogadori prosecuted ten-year-old Pietro da Cattaro, servant of Niccolò Pegoloto, for the murder of Pegoloto's wife, Peregrina. For reasons that remain unclear, Pietro had become furious with his mistress and begun hitting her with an andiron and threatening her infant son. According to the records of the avogadori, Peregrina had pleaded with Pietro, crying, "Oh Pietro, why do you wish to kill me?" [O petre quare me vis interficere?] Pietro's sentence was surprisingly light given the horror of the crime. He was sentenced to a year in jail, although on the first Sunday of each month he was to be taken to the piazza and whipped. After a year he was to be banished. In all likelihood, the Forty showed leniency in light of Pietro's youth.[137]

In October 1578 the avogadori prosecuted the ancilla Caterina, widow of Agostino Spatarii da Spilemburgo, for the murder of her master, Angelo Bisigati, a resident of Portogruaro. Bisigati, whom the records described as very rich, had been struck with sixteen wounds and his house had been robbed. The authorities believed that Caterina had had an accomplice, a certain Giacomo di Centiis da Gradisca, described as a "neighbor" [vicinius] of Bisigati. The case was transferred from Portogruaro to Venice for adjudication, but the two defendants escaped during a fire in the Ducal Palace, where they were incarcerated. Afterward, Giacomo voluntarily appeared before the court and was absolved of complicity. Caterina, by contrast, remained at large and was tried in contumacy; she was sentenced to perpetual banishment from Venice and its territories and, if caught, to beheading in the Piazza San Marco. The state attorneys described the case as a "most atrocious crime."[138]

And in yet another case, dated 1562, the avogadori tried Francesco da Piove di Sacco for the murder of his master, Giacomo Archerii. The two had gotten into an argument and drawn their weapons, at which point Francesco had mortally wounded his master. The avogadori tried him in contumacy and banished him in perpetuity. If caught, he was to be led up the Grand Canal and then tied to the tail of a horse and dragged to the parish of San Vitale, where the murder had taken place. There he was to have his right hand amputated. He was then to be led, with the amputated hand hung around his neck, to the Piazza San Marco, where between the twin columns of justice he was to be beheaded, drawn, and quartered. The attorneys noted that Francesco had committed the murder "with an evil spirit in the house of his master in terrible example to other servants and against the security and peaceful life of this city."[139]

The wording of the avogadori's condemnation suggests that the actual incidence of homicides by servants was less important than its perception by the elite. When they hired servants, masters allowed virtual strangers into their homes, giving them access to their person and property. They then projected onto servants their fears of murder and mayhem. For this reason, even the occasional homicide, which gained wide publicity, was sufficient to sustain and fuel masters' concerns.

Punishments like the one meted out to Francesco da Piove di Sacco were designed in part to shame them. The elite hoped that by humiliating servants, they might discourage others from acting in the same way. A widow who had received favors from the noble Diedo family and then helped the family servants rob their master was sentenced to spend an hour in the stocks with a sign identifying her "as a procuress and for having helped a housekeeper steal from her master" [come rufiana, et haver tenuto man à massare dar via la robba del patron].[140] When Maria dal Bo was convicted of theft, she was sentenced to wear a slogan with the words "For having robbed the home of her master" [Per haver robbado in casa del Patron].[141]

Yet such public punishments may have been less humiliating than members of the elite imagined and may not have had the desired affect, for it is uncertain that rich and poor shared the same standards of honor and shame.[142] In Glissenti's *Discorsi morali* the Philosopher claims that he would rather be subject to the whims of the sea or fortune than have his fate in the hands of servants, since they could destroy one's reputation by recounting "the sorrows, the insidious acts, the shameless deeds, the robberies they have perpetrated on their masters, *winning praise for themselves in these ribald deeds as if they were honorable and beautiful ones*" (emphasis mine).[143] Glissenti, for one, recognized that acts he considered reprehensible might not be universally so viewed.

A good example is the use of foul language by gondoliers. Laws forbade it, and members of the elite fulminated against it. Garzoni described gondoliers as having mouths "always full of filthy words, vain blasphemies of every sort and terrible curses."[144] Yet foul language was a mark of identification and even distinction among boatmen themselves. Glissenti's gondolier bragged that his lot were "accustomed to cursing, blaspheming, swearing, reproving, and vituperating from childhood on."[145] Such behavior defined gondoliers as a profession and created a sense of group identity. It is not inconceivable that within boatmen's circles those most adept at hurling curses gained a certain renown. In 1609 the censors ordered a ferryman to be placed in the stocks with the following slogan hung around his neck: "For nefarious words spoken at the traghetti" [Per parole nefande sopra i traghetti].[146] Whether or not his fellow boatmen saw this as a particularly shameful punishment is unknowable. It is possible that it made him a sort of hero within his own circle of acquaintances; at the very least it may have gained him some sympathy.

Such may also have been the case for the few servants who had the courage to bring charges before the court of the censors. As noted in chapter 2, between 1569 and 1600 there were only 4 such cases out of 416. One involved a servant who prosecuted another servant. In that case, dated 1590, a famulus de mezo in the employ of the Basadonna family charged Antonio, famulus of nobleman Silvano Capello, with throwing a rock at him. The censors found Antonio guilty and ordered him to spend a month in jail, although they subsequently pardoned him of the balance of his sentence.[147]

The other three cases involved servants taking their masters to court. In the first, Pasqua Trevisana, famula of Zaneta, charged her mistress and a certain Ludovico da cà Grado with beating and wounding her. The censors agreed and ordered Zaneta and Ludovico to pay Pasqua one hundred lire and to cover her medical expenses.[148] In 1599 Domenica, ancilla of Alvise Viggia, claimed that her master hit and abused her. Again the censors agreed, ordering Viggia to pay her twenty-five ducats plus her medical costs and to donate twenty-five ducats to charity.[149] And in the same year the widow Lucia brought suit against her master, the platter Marino. She charged him with beating and verbally abusing her. The censors found for Lucia and ordered Marino to pay her her salary plus interest as well as her medical expenses. Furthermore, he was not to be released from jail until she was paid.[150]

What is noteworthy about these suits is that all were pursued by female servants, all involved beatings, all concerned non-noble defendants, and all were successful. Of the six cases of servants prosecuting masters in the records of the censori between 1601 and 1609, five involved female plaintiffs, all involved beatings or verbal abuse by non-noble masters, and again all six plaintiffs won their cases.[151] The few servants who were courageous enough to prosecute their masters probably did so because they knew that the physical evidence of mistreat-

the authority of the state behind them, they could force obedience. But then a new option presented itself. Having brought the servant low, the master could forgive him or her and remit the punishment. In 15 of the 412 cases that masters brought before the censors, masters either decided at a certain point not to prosecute further or remitted the punishments after the servants were found guilty.

Vittore Malipiero, for example, who proceeded against his servant Natale for breaking his contract and for damaging his gondola and leaving it unattended, eventually decided to withdraw his complaint, and the censors released Natale from jail "pro nunc."[164] The censors were less forgiving of Andriana da Vicenza, ancilla of Giacomo à Sole, accused of allowing a man into her master's house. After the case was brought before the censors, the master dropped his complaint and "forgave" [pepercisset] Andriana. But the censors ordered her to ask forgiveness of her master—"petere debeat veniam supradicto eius patrono"—and then to suffer banishment for a year.[165] Battista Zancho was prosecuted by Alvise Balbi, the prior of the Cà di Dio, for rendering "malam servitutem" and for breaking his contract and leaving with his salary. When he confessed, Balbi withdrew the complaint, proclaiming himself satisfied for the expenses owed him, and Battista was released from jail.[166] And ducal secretary Marcantonio Novello dropped the case against his servant Bortolo da Mestre, who had stolen some wine and brought prostitutes into the house. But the censors were not as willing to dismiss the charges and ordered Bortolo to present their office with a two-pound candle embossed with an image of the Virgin Mary and to pay court costs.[167]

In 1566 nobleman Marco Antonio Pisani initiated proceedings against his servant Menego for unspecified crimes. The censors agreed to his release from jail when Pisani appeared before them and made the following statement: "I am content that as far as I am concerned, the aforesaid Menego presently jailed be prosecuted no further; and furthermore, I am willing that he be released from jail with this condition, that he return to my service and render me good service as is required. And rendering to me that which he ought to give me, as he used to do, and if he does otherwise, I reserve the right to appear again before these most Illustrious Lord Censors."[168]

By remitting penalties and forgiving servants after having brought the full force of the state to bear on them, masters publicly reestablished the proper relationship between superiors and inferiors. And there was no better moment than this for masters to demonstrate their superiority by displaying that most noble of qualities, mercy.

The best illustration of this process comes not, in fact, from the office of the censors but from the Holy Office, the Inquisition.[169] The case involved the lawyer

Giovanni Finetti and his servant Girolamo Badoer da Veglia. According to Finetti, he had taken Badoer into his household as his "servitore di barca," cared for him during his illnesses, and then given him largely unsupervised control of his household accounts.[170] In the brief he presented to the inquisitors he wrote, "[Girolamo] enjoyed every favor from me, he was *master of my household,* and I called him dear one, and he was called mister Girolamo by the others of the household, seeing that it was my intention that he enjoy precedence in the house" (emphasis mine).[171] When Finetti discovered that Badoer had been defrauding him, he threatened to charge him before the censors. But before he could do so, Badoer denounced his master to the Holy Office, accusing him of eating meat on prohibited days and denying a dying relative the services of a priest—sure signs of Protestant sympathies. The inquisitors, after calling a number of witnesses who refuted the charges, found for Finetti and then prosecuted Badoer and his brother, a priest, for making a false accusation. The case dragged on for a number of years but finally was resolved when Badoer appeared before the tribunal, confessing his guilt and asking for mercy. Finetti was also present, and according to the record, he was so moved by Christian charity that he chose to look beyond the injury done him and content himself "solely with the restitution of his honor, which is more dear than anything else."[172] Nevertheless, the inquisitors sentenced Badoer to banishment from Venice and its district for two years.[173]

By bringing the servant low, Finetti was able to restore his own damaged honor and reputation. As he himself admitted, he had made a terrible mistake: he had blurred social distinctions and allowed the servant to be the *patrone.* He paid dearly for this lapse, for when he tried to reassert his position, Badoer denounced him as a heretic. But in the end, with the disobedient servant humbled, the right order of things was restored and Finetti could assume the role of merciful master.

Finetti's action added new dimensions to his identity and created still further correspondences. In particular, by granting absolution, he mimicked the role of the priest as father, and by showing mercy, he created parallels to the image of God the Father. Religious associations were certainly not lacking in this case. Such allusions were present as well in the case involving ducal secretary Novello's servant Bortolo, for the censors ordered him to atone with a candle emblazoned with an image of the Madonna.[174] And when nobleman Girolamo Pisani prosecuted his gondolier Domenico da Udine for breaking his contract and for rendering bad service, Domenico confessed his "sin" and asked for "forgiveness and mercy."[175] The structure of the household found correspondence not only in the status systems of the polity but in universal hierarchies as well.

At the beginning of this chapter I noted that Lanteri wrote that a servant owed his master love, fear, and reverence and that those obligations appeared in some ways to be contradictory. Masters resolved the paradox by wanting servants to render them love as earthly fathers, fear as representatives of the city fathers, and reverence as symbols of the heavenly father.

~

In Renaissance Venice masters and servants were bound in constantly shifting symbiotic relationships, which meant that servants had to adopt various strategies for survival. By playing the role of good servants, they might gain financial security, satisfying affective ties, and a stream of favors. They could become literally indispensable members of elite families. On the other hand, disobedience might bring sympathy from friends or even honor and esteem among peers. One facet of servant subculture gained its meaning by opposing the prevailing elite culture.

Paradoxically, functional and dysfunctional master-servant relations played their role for masters as well. For masters, obsequious and obedient servants like Lucia Morosini through demonstrations of loyalty and reverence asserted the privileged place of the elite within both the household and the city. But disobedient servants did so as well. Through their acts of disobedience, servants confirmed in masters' minds the inherent inferiority of domestics and the rightness of their own elevated moral and social position and allowed opportunities for masters to demonstrate magnanimity and forgiveness. For masters, both obedient and disobedient servants affirmed the rectitude of their position at the apex of familial, civic, and sempiternal hierarchies.

# Chapter Seven

# The Significance of Service

After taking leave of the rascally servant who tricks and defrauds his master, the Philosopher and Courtier in Fabio Glissenti's *Discorsi morali* discuss the problems associated with servant keeping. The Courtier remarks to the Philosopher,

> In this city [Venice], more than in any other, servants are licentious, dissolute, vicious, and disrespectful, because the multitude of races and nationalities and the preoccupations of business overwhelm thoughts of correcting their evil ways. But in the [princely] courts, where I have passed my life, I have been served by good, loyal, sincere, and well-mannered servants.[1]

To Glissenti's fictional foreigner, Venice is a place where the proper order of society, the deferential humbling of inferiors before their superiors, falls victim to a heterogeneous population and the demands of capitalism. In Venice, where people of many nations and tongues mix freely and where moneymaking is king, the hierarchies and manners of courts are sacrificed. Unlike Jean Bodin and other observers who believed that positive qualities such as toleration and liberty emerged from Venice's mixed population and business community, Glissenti's Courtier saw only negative ones.[2]

Another foreigner, this time the real-life English traveler Thomas Coryat, also remarked on the unusual servant-keeping practices of the Venetians. Coryat traveled through Europe in 1608 recording his impressions. His description of the lagoon city was especially detailed and included, along with the obligatory description of buildings and discourse on government, vivid impressions of Venetian customs and habits. In his discussion of the lifestyle of the nobles he wrote,

> Howbeit these Gentlemen doe not maintaine and support the title of their Gentility with a quarter of that noble state and magnificence as our English Noblemen and Gentlemen of the better sort doe. For they keepe no honourable hospitality, nor gallant retinue of servants about them, but a very frugall table, though they inhabite most beautiful Palaces. . . . But I under-

stand that the reason why they so confine themselves within the bounds of frugality, and avoyde that superfluity of expenses in housekeeping that we Englishmen doe use, is, because they are restrained by a certaine kinde of edict made by the Senate, that they shall not keepe a retinue beyond their limitation.[3]

What struck Coryat about Venetian servant keeping was its meagerness and frugality. Michel de Montaigne had a similar reaction, noting that "a train of valets is of no use to us at all here, for everyone goes around by himself; and the expenses for clothes likewise; and then there is no need of a horse."[4] Compared with English and French nobles, Venetian patricians cut rather poor figures, having no "gallant retinue of servants." Coryat attributed this lack of display to governmental constraints, apparently referring to the Senate decrees enforced by the magistrato alle pompe limiting the number of servants nobles could employ at banquets.

These impressions of Venetian servant-keeping practices raise a number of questions that draw together the material of this study and serve as the focus of this chapter: Did the city's republican regime significantly modify or limit the elite's desire for display? Was Venetian servant keeping different in style or substance from that found in other societies, most notably in the absolutist regimes that increasingly dominated Italy and the rest of Europe? How did Venice's merchant economy influence service? Did servants act less deferentially in Venice than elsewhere? The answers to these questions illuminate the significance of service in Renaissance Venice.

## Domestic Service in Renaissance Venice

When the information presented in the preceding chapters is taken together, a pattern emerges, namely, that over the course of the fifteenth and sixteenth centuries a significant shift took place in the orientation of Venetian society and politics away from egalitarian republicanism and communal values and toward an ever more hierarchical and stratified society driven by notions of status and honor.[5] The outlines of that shift as reflected in an analysis of domestic service are worth reviewing.

The earliest writers of treatises on household management and wifely duties saw the household and all relations within households (between husbands and wives, fathers and sons, or masters and servants) as building blocks for larger political relationships, specifically of ruler and ruled. This view of the household as a microcosm of the polity was best expressed in the works of Fra Paolino the Minorite and Giovanni Caldiera. But during the course of the fifteenth and especially the sixteenth century a different understanding of the household and of master-servant relations came to predominate. Writers now saw in the hierarchy of the household and in the orderly marshaling of household resources an analogue to and justification for the stratification of society. Hierarchy was predicated not simply on a politicized vision of rights and responsibilities but also on a moralized vision of virtues and vices. Writers such as Tommaso Garzoni and Fabio Glissenti presented a highly ethical view of the world in which the virtuous were understood to have a responsibility to maintain order in the face of subversive tendencies by their vicious inferiors. The preservation of order took on an almost sacred significance—the elite had to sustain the divinely ordained system.

Venetian legislation concerning servants reflected a complementary transformation. The early-sixteenth-century capitulary of the capi di sestieri emphasized the contractual obligations of masters and servants and concentrated on female servants. The legislators were primarily concerned with maintaining dignified household establishments. But when the censors issued their first capitulary in 1541, worries over contracts yielded to increasing preoccupation with the moral failings of servants, especially males. Now unruly servants were perceived as threatening the honor and dignity of their master's person. Like sixteenth-century treatise writers, sixteenth-century legislators sought to impose moral order on society.

The changing gender concerns of masters are the most concrete indication that an important change had taken place not only in the elite's conception of service but also in the larger society. Specifically, male servants replaced females as the object of concern. In the introduction I noted that reliance upon male servants was the distinguishing characteristic of the aristocratic regimes of northern Europe, especially Old Regime France. In Venice the shift to male servants occurred in the very period (the early sixteenth century) when historians have noted a trend throughout Italy toward aristocratization—a movement characterized in the economy by a turn away from commerce toward safer investments in land and government bonds, in politics by the decline of republicanism and the emergence or strengthening of princely regimes, and socially in the growing emphasis on conspicuous consumption and personal honor. It was precisely in these same years that much of Italy came under the direct or indirect control of foreign monarchical states.

Accompanying these ideological transformations were perceptible changes in Venetian household structure and servant-keeping practices. Although conclusions must remain tentative until more definitive evidence is uncovered, it appears from the example of the Barbarigo family that the number of servants retained by members of the elite grew over the course of these two centuries. By the end of the period under study, it was almost obligatory for a major patrician to have at least two male servants to row his gondola and for every man with any pretensions to high status to have at least one male attendant.[6] Employing at least one female servant continued to separate moderately prosperous Venetians from those lower on the social ladder. The status animarum records indicate that some elite households grew fairly large, with eighteen or even twenty household members, including kinfolk and staff.

The increasing demand for male servants is one factor that may help explain the growing differential in male and female servants' wages. At the beginning of the fifteenth century wet nurses were the city's most highly paid servants; and throughout the century male servants made only a fraction more money than their female counterparts. But during the first half of the sixteenth century the gap between men's and women's wages widened considerably, so that by the second half of the century men were making almost three times as much money as women. The increase in men's wages was due to increased demand, a demand attested to by the new emphasis on livery and the inclusion of servants in portraits. Other explanations include the effect on the labor market of foreign invasions and the plague, which may have opened up opportunities in skilled trades for men traditionally excluded from them, thereby reducing the supply of male servants.

Evidence of judicial prosecution demonstrates the same preoccupation with male servants. Although there were always fewer male servants than female ones in Venice, masters prosecuted them at a much greater rate. Furthermore, the rhetoric of the censors' decisions shows that virtually all crimes committed by servants, including what at first appear to have been merely contractual concerns, such as breaking contracts, were perceived by masters as potential threats to their honor, status, and dignity.

Taken together, the evidence shows that among the wealthiest and most powerful members of the Venetian elite an aristocratic style of servant keeping gradually replaced the bourgeois style characteristic of the fourteenth and fifteenth centuries.[7] In the fourteenth century even the richest Venetian patricians were served by small staffs that were overwhelmingly female in composition and whose primary responsibility was maintenance of the household. By the sixteenth century, staffs had grown larger, more male in gender, and more public, in the sense that increasing emphasis was placed on the "display" function of retainers. In other words, in their servant-keeping practices, as in so much else, the Venetian elite had come to resemble more closely their northern European counterparts.

These conclusions are not altogether surprising, for historians have long noted a decline in the Venetian commitment to egalitarian republicanism and a trend toward aristocratization characteristic of the elites of sixteenth-century Italy generally. In politics Gaetano Cozzi and Felix Gilbert have detected the growing bifurcation of the ruling elite, especially as a consequence of the crisis of the League of Cambrai.[8] In the economic realm, Daniele Beltrami, S. J. Wolff, and others have noted a tendency toward more investments in land and away from commerce.[9] Brian Pullan has carefully documented the growing stratification of Venetian society as evidenced by the city's most important charitable organizations, the scuole grandi; and in the sphere of culture, scholars such as Manfredo Tafuri and Edward Muir have found in Doge Andrea Gritti's program of *renovatio* a new emphasis on decorum, dignity, and imperial pretensions.[10] This study provides further evidence for this shift in the Venetian elite's view of themselves, but it also suggests that the trend may have begun at the individual and household level and thence influenced the larger polity and society. Certainly that is how contemporaries would have understood such changes.[11] This work also illustrates a shift in the elite's relations with those who were in positions of subordination. Their new status consciousness transformed the elite's relations with their inferiors.

Overall, then, we have been able to document at the household level the increasingly hierarchical and stratified nature of Venetian society. But what of Glissenti's, Montaigne's, and Coryat's observations? According to them, Venetian servant-keeping practices pointed to differences rather than similarities between Venice and the aristocratic and absolutist regimes of other states of Italy and elsewhere. Their comments give us pause.[12]

If we compare Venetian servant-keeping practices with those of other European and Italian states, we do see some significant differences. This is most clearly evidenced by an examination of the size and composition of households. In England, for example, it is estimated that in 1507–8 the duke of Buckingham's household included anywhere between 100 and 200 people.[13] That was much larger than anything seen in Venice. More precise are figures for the household of William Cecil. In the mid-1550s his household of 35 included at least 22 salaried retainers. At the height of his career as Lord Treasurer to Elizabeth I he may have had as many as 120 servants.[14] It is estimated that in the period 1450–1500 the average "gentle" household in England numbered nearly 70 persons.[15] Of course many of the persons in these households were men of some status, such as secretaries and honored assistants, unlike the menials generally found in most Venetian households. Nevertheless, not without cause did Coryat comment on the modesty of Venetian patrician households.

Regardless of what was occurring in northern Europe, the model for Italian aristocratic households in the sixteenth century was the papal court and its satellite cardinalate households. Yet these establishments too dwarfed their Venetian counterparts. Peter Partner estimates that under Leo X the papal famiglia included 418 familiars and 265 servants.[16] According to David Chambers, in 1509 the average cardinal's household numbered 154 familiars; and Gigliola Fragnito has found that the number was 148 in 1526.[17] The maintenance of such large staffs was extremely costly, often averaging between four thousand and six thousand ducats or more per year.[18] The poorest cardinals struggled to maintain a minimum staff and were given subsidies allowing for "at least twenty servants."[19]

Size is one indication of elaboration, specialization of duties another. The primary distinction in cardinalate households was between familiars and servants. Familiars included relatives of the cardinal, prelates, gentlemen, resident scholars and artists, and those actually in charge of the household establishment. Servants were those who performed the more menial tasks and appeared as "salariati" in account books.[20] A number of treatises, including Paolo Cortese's *De cardinalatu* and Francesco Priscianese's *Del governo della corte d'un signore in Roma,* were written to help guide cardinals in the organization and management of these elaborate domestic establishments.[21]

Pierre Hurtubise studied one such household, that of Florentine cardinal Giovanni Salviati, and identified fifty-four distinct positions or offices on the staff. He grouped them into four categories: "intimate" offices, including the first secretary, confessor, pages, falconer, and others; the "management" staff, including treasurers, account keepers, gardeners, and launderers; the "offices of the mouth," comprising the wine steward, bakers, stewards, cook, and kitchen help; and the offices of the stable, including the master of the stable and stable hands. The cardinal's stable staff alone grew from about ten persons in 1520 to around thirty persons in 1550. In size and elaboration Salviati's household ranked among the more splendid of his time.[22]

The courts of the leading Italian secular princes were also huge complexes. As count of Pavia, that is, as heir to the Milanese throne, Galeazzo Maria Sforza had a household that numbered about forty persons, including five gentlemen, twelve camerieri, five *ragazzi,* a chaplain, a barber, four footmen, and thirteen other staff members, most of whom served in the kitchen. When he was duke, Galeazzo's court numbered in the hundreds; in 1476 the budget for all aspects of his court life, including household costs, clothing expenses, and patronage of musicians, was two hundred thousand ducats.[23] Sforza's mother, the dowager duchess Bianca Maria, maintained a court of two hundred, and Sforza's mistress was equipped with a household of at least thirty persons.[24]

In contrast to these large princely households with highly specialized staffs, the status animarum records for the end of the sixteenth century show that the most prominent Venetian nobles maintained far more modest establishments. Among the very largest was the fraternal household of three Priuli brothers (Antonio, Alvise, and Francesco) resident in the parish of San Felice. Seventeen Priuli kinsmen were served by twenty-four servants, including a factor, a provisioner, a steward, and a mistress of the house.[25] Another large household was that of Antonio Moro. According to the register for the parish of Santa Maria Formosa dated 1593, Moro's household included himself and his wife, his son and daughter-in-law, and five other Moro kin. These nine Moro family members were served by seven male "servitori" and eight female "serve."[26] By contrast, the household of Count Muzio Gambara, in the parish of Santa Maria Zobenigo, included as kinsmen only the count, his wife, and a niece; yet the three were served by twenty-nine retainers, including ladies-in-waiting, housekeepers, and bravi.[27] The priest of Santa Maria Formosa, who recorded the Moro family information, included virtually no classification of jobs in his description of their household, only the gender division of servants into males and females. Yet when the same priest surveyed the household of the patriarch of Aquileia, which included forty people, he noted their functions. The household included the patriarch, his niece and nephew, a vicar, four chaplains, fifteen camerieri, thirteen servitori, and four serve.[28] Similarly, the household of the ambassador from Savoy comprised the ambassador, his wife, his mother, and two sons, served by four ladies-in-waiting, two secretaries, a majordomo, two menservants, three pages, and a boatman.[29]

Florence provides the most instructive comparison with Venice since in the early Renaissance the bourgeois style of servant keeping was common to both. The patricians of fourteenth- and fifteenth-century Florence and Venice maintained modest staffs that were primarily female. In the mid-fifteenth century, for example, the wealthy patrician Giovanni Rucellai engaged only eight people to maintain both his town and country houses.[30] Unfortunately, the compilers of the catasto of 1427 did not list servants in the households they served, so it is difficult to gauge their presence in Florentine households at that time.[31] Yet several pieces of evidence suggest that Florence experienced a shift similar to the one in Venice. Klapisch-Zuber has noted the growing popularity of male servants in Florence by the beginning of the sixteenth century.[32] And she and David Herlihy have found evidence for "fantastic growth" in the overall number of servants by 1552. According to a census of that year, servants constituted 16.7 percent of the Florentine population.[33] This was a much greater percentage than in Venice, where in 1563 servants accounted for only 7.65 percent of the populace. Under the influence of the Medici grand dukes, the Florentine elite seem to have been much more willing than Venetian patricians to shed their old republican household modesty.[34]

The Medici household itself provides further evidence for the transformation in Florence. With the establishment of the duchy, the Medici domestic staff grew in size and elaboration. The court serving Cosimo I in 1550 included secretaries, stewards, physicians, artists (Cellini and Bronzino), and scores of humble servants, bringing the total household to about 280 persons. By the reign of Ferdinando I, who succeeded to the throne in 1587, the court had grown to 400. What is more, some of the higher positions in the household, such as those of majordomo, *maestro di casa,* and so on, were held by members of prominent families.[35] In Venice, by contrast, positions on the doge's personal staff were reserved for popolani and considered below the dignity of patricians. The differences between the Florentine ducal household and the Venetian one are instructive, for in both size and elaboration the Medici household far surpassed that of the doge.

Closer to home, valuable evidence exists for Verona, part of the Venetian terraferma dominion. Herlihy examined Veronese census data and found that the number of servants grew substantially between 1425 and 1502. In 1425 servants were 7.0 percent of the populace; by 1502 there were 1,311 servants, accounting for 12.3 percent of the populace. This was a greater percentage than ever reached in Venice. Not surprisingly, the growth in the number of servants was greatest in the richest households of the city, where by 1502 "staffs of fifteen or more servants, unknown in 1425, were not uncommon."[36]

Alison Smith has documented the servant-keeping practices of one Veronese aristocratic family, the Verità. Like Venetian and Florentine families, the Verità of the early fifteenth century maintained rather modest households. In 1433 no Verità establishment included more than three servants, most of whom were female. But by the beginning of the sixteenth century, Verità staffs had grown considerably and included more males. At the end of the century one of the most splendid Verità households, which included five kinsmen, was served by a tutor, two footmen, a provisioner, three coachmen, three stable hands, a steward, two grooms, and two cooks, as well as eleven other male and female servants.[37] At least some of the provincial elites of the Veneto were supporting more elaborate domestic establishments than their Venetian rulers.

In at least one respect, then, foreigners' perceptions of Venetian servant keeping were correct. Venetian households were smaller than those found in the aristocratic and absolutist regimes of northern Europe and other states in Italy. Their observations caution us not to overstate the transformation of the Venetian patriciate into an aristocracy like those found elsewhere. But they also beg the question what forces were at work that may have kept the Venetian move toward display in check.

As most historians who have studied the Venetian patriciate in the sixteenth century have noted, the elite were increasingly divided into two factions: a group of extremely rich and powerful patricians, who dominated the most important offices and concentrated their power in the Council of Ten and the Senate; and the majority of poorer patricians, whose sole claim to authority was their right to membership in the Great Council.[38] Tafuri has highlighted the ideological and cultural aspects of this factionalism by outlining a contest between the "Romanizing" tendencies of the upper elite and the traditional values of the lesser nobles, who favored a cultural style that emphasized modesty, gravity, and lack of display, what he terms *mediocritas*. Symbolic of the latter style was Doge Leonardo Donà's new palace on the Fondamenta Nuove, which in architectural terms was both "sober and laconic." As Tafuri notes, "The exhibition of 'modesty,' explicitly opposed to the wastefulness of Roman nobiliary building, was certainly a political message for Donà. Venetian *simplicitas* demonstrated its own vigor, upholding before Rome its own 'sanctity.'"[39]

Efforts by poorer and more traditionally minded nobles to limit the influence of their richer counterparts and subdue their power of display took a number of forms, including attempts to limit the power of the Council of Ten, support for the policies of a faction known as the *giovani*, and establishment of sumptuary rules, such as that cited by Coryat limiting servants. Political and cultural struggles within the patriciate thus functioned to check the further aristocratization of the class.[40]

The evidence of domestic servant keeping thus points both to the distance Venice had traveled in these centuries from its traditional values and the extent to which it remained attached to them. Some Venetian patricians came more and more to imitate their counterparts in the other European and Italian states, but those tendencies were held in check by an equally powerful Venetian republican tradition that emphasized a certain equality of members. Gasparo Contarini and others continued to highlight moderation as one of the essential keys to Venice's political and social success.[41] The ducal household was emblematic of the cultural and political style of Venice in this period. The sixteenth-century doges tried to increase the dignity and display of the office, but compared with rulers of other states, their households remained quite modest indeed. Service helped mark the anomalous position of republican Venice in sixteenth-century Europe.[42]

## Service, Honor, and Class Relations in Early Modern Venice

Foreign observers both real and fictional noted differences not only in the style of Venetian servant keeping but also in the behavior of Venetian servants and their relations with masters. According to Glissenti's courtier, Venetian servants were less deferential than servants elsewhere. He attributed this to the mix of peoples and the business of capitalism, which loosened discipline and order.

The Courtier's observations raise the issue of how master-servant relations in Venice were shaped and what that may say about interclass relations in early modern Europe more generally.

As we have seen, Glissenti's courtier based his opinion about servant behavior primarily on economics; in his view, the preoccupations of business made servants less deferential because masters were diverted from their job of commanding. In other words, he saw it as a failure on the part of masters. But that was only part of the problem, for Glissenti's portrait showed servants to be shrewd businessmen as well. They understood that the demand for servants in Venice far exceeded the supply, and this allowed them to manipulate their masters and change them frequently, in other words, to be less deferential. If Glissenti's servant is to be believed, Venetian masters' willingness to undercut one another by bidding away each others' employees destroyed the credibility of the servant-keeping class as a whole and gave servants some leverage. The marketplace environment undermined the mechanisms of deference.

Other evidence confirms this view. As we have seen, concern with regulating and controlling the labor market in favor of employers was a consistent feature of Venetian legislation from the thirteenth century on. The servant-keeping elite employed a variety of techniques in an effort to dominate the service market: they registered and enforced contracts, limited wages, and established minimum terms of service. Furthermore, masters prosecuted servants for breaking contracts more than for any other crime.

Yet while the Courtier's claim that the capitalist labor market rendered master-servant relations problematic is plausible, his claim that this situation was unique to Venice seems unlikely. Unfortunately, the particularity of Venice in this regard is difficult to ascertain given the paucity of studies of master-servant relations in other cities. Yet the few case studies that exist suggest that the demands of the capitalist labor market rendered relations difficult in some other cities as well.

In Florence, for example, servants understood the market and were able to manipulate it. Klapisch-Zuber found that female servants often remained with their masters for a very short time; according to her data, 19 percent left within a month of beginning service and 60 percent stayed a year or less. She believes that many terminated their employment as the only way to extract wages from their masters. Furthermore, servants quit because of the relative ease of finding new employment elsewhere. As early as 1415, Florentine servant keepers were trying to tip the balance in their own favor by establishing statutory limits on wages, something the Venetians did not do until the mid-sixteenth century.[43] While Klapisch-Zuber believes that sexual tension was the primary cause of conflict in master-servant relations in Florence, it seems clear that the issue of wages and contracts, what Glissenti might term the "preoccupations of business," played a role as well.

In contrast, Susan Mosher Stuard has found that medieval Ragusa did not have a particularly competitive labor market. In this Balkan city-state the low cost of slave labor relative to the cost of free labor in the thirteenth century led Ragusans to rely heavily on slaves. As a consequence, governmental intervention to control the labor market was unnecessary.[44] Even when Ragusans shifted to a system of contract labor in the fourteenth century, the tenor of master-servant relations having already been established, the overall result was a deferential society.[45] As Stuard observes, servants had few choices "but to serve and improve . . . [their] condition through striving for the incentives and rewards the noble household offered. Deference was the face of it, but the substance was a lack of viable choice."[46] The example of Ragusa thus supports the theory that where employment options for servants were limited, relations were, from the masters' point of view, more easily controlled. It may well be that in some of the smaller court centers, places like Ferrara and Urbino, a similar labor environment existed and servants were (or appeared to be) more deferential.

The issue raised here, namely, the relationship between the form of labor and its impact on political and social relations, leads to a broader consideration of the place of service in Venetian labor and class relations. That history has been written primarily with a view toward the guilds. The picture that has emerged is of an artisanal labor force that was politically disenfranchised and policed by the government and whose economic interests were subordinated to or made to work in tandem with those of the patrician merchant entrepreneurs. At the same time, subordination was mitigated by the religious and social benefits of guild membership, by a government that was at times sensitive to guild demands, and by the bestowal of honorific ritual functions on select sectors of the labor force, notably the Arsenalotti.[47] When guildsmen felt that their rights and privileges had been violated, they could express their discontent through petitions to the government, the lobbying of sympathetic patricians, and even, as the shearmen demonstrated in 1556, by staging a strike.[48] Guildsmen were able to mount opposition and do battle on statutory or contractual grounds precisely because the guild structure itself, as well as ancillary organizations such as the guild-sponsored confraternities, provided the associational means for artisans to act together.

Domestic servants were at a clear disadvantage in this regard; and elites worked hard to keep it that way by prohibiting them from undertaking any kind of collective action. As we have seen, in 1541 the censors issued a rule prohibit-

# Appendix A

## The *capi di sestieri*'s Capitulary of 1503

ASV, Signori di Notte al Civil, busta 1, capitulary A, 1270–1586,
Capitulary of the Signori di Notte, fols. 125v–126v

Die Ultimo Julii 1503

Sempre li precesori Et progenitori nostri In ciaschadun tempo hano cerchato con ogni sue forze remediar a chadauna mala intention et volunta de i cativi et molte leze hano statuide et ordinate per obviar ali Cativi et Cative sue male intention che adeffecto non sortischano: Et con cio sia che In lofficio di Capi de Sesstier sianno statuide molte leze et ordini sopra li fanti et fantesche che de zorno in zorno se scriveno, et scripte nel ditto officio sono che fu ben et sanctamente provisto et dove manchano le leze ge sono la bona et Antigua consuetudine In virida observantia ma per che non obstante le bone consuetudine, le bona et necesaria cosa proveder et ordenar le siano observate et non mutar le bone in cative. Imperho li magnifici et Clarissimi Signori Capi de Sesstier Infrascritti, Ordenando et statuendo hano termena In execution de le sancte leze prexe si ne lo Excellentissimo mazor conseglio Come ne li Altri consegli et colegii se Intenda statuidi et ordenadi Linfrascritti Capitoli et ordeni a bosoli et balote per la auctorita et liberta a loro concessa.

Primo, Sia statuido et firmiter ordinado che tuti li fanti over fantesche si da parte da mar come da terra non possi esser scripti in lofficio piui de Anni, diexe, Iusta la parte pressa In lo Excellentissimo Conseglio de pregadi del 1388, die .xi. maii.

Secundo, Sia ordinado che si Alcun acceptera, tignera, over torra alchun fante over fantescha in chasa che siano scripti in lofficio nostro siano chi esser se vogli nemine excepto Iqual siano partidi contra la volunta di sui patroni over patrone Incorri in remisibel pena statuida per la leze pressa nel mazor conseglio nel, 1284, die ultimo decembris, che sono de libre cento de pizoli.

Tercio, Sia statuito si alcun sia chi esser se voglia desviera over fara desviar Alcun fante over fantescha ne lofficio nostro scripta, per mali modi et razon che i ditti fanti over fantesche scampi da i suo patroni over patrone Cadi Ala pena de libre cento ["L. 100" is written above] ut supra et siano in liberta dei Capi de sextier ultra la pena soprascritta de farli star messe sex [?] in prigion serate. [125v/126r]

Quarto, Item se habia per statuido et ordinato Come sempre per consuetudine e sta observado se alcuni fante over fantescha scripti ne lofficio nostro scampera da li sui patroni over patrone Avanti el compir de quello sarano scripti et obligati a star per causa sua, et Anotado che sara el scampo, over crida del suo fuzir perder debiano tuto il suo salario Integraliter, et oltra di questo parendo cusi a I signori Capi de Sextier farli frustar per exempio de altri siano In sua liberta terminar segondo aloro parera pro qualitate delitti et persone Intendando perho chel non habi a perder il suo salario del tempo harano servito, se iterum el patron li acceptera in casa revertendo impristinum statum et hoc tociens quociens Acciderit.

Quinto, Siia statuido per obviar ogni mala fantasia over muodi excogitadi et nuove invention per I patroni over patrone vien tenuti et Aliquando adeffetto mandadi: Che sel sara Alcun che mandi via fanti over fantesche scripti nel officio imprincipio Al mezo over quasi Al fin inclusive del tempo li sono scripti, con volunta et Intention de non pagarli dagandoli de le botte over mal tratarli per farli scampar et perder el tempo servito senza legiptima causa siano obligati pagar li ditti fanti over fantesche pro rata del tempo hara servito, et siano depenati et In sua liberta posti et ulterius haver debino i drapi per suo vestir tuti fatti per suo patroni over patrone nel tempo sarano stati. Dechiarando che se iditti fanti over fantesche fusseno batudi per mal modo, over rotti in alcuna parte de la persona over havera batiture disoneste, siano In liberta di Signori Capi de Sextier farli pagar tuto il suo salario Integraliter et condennarli per qualitate delitti.

Sexto, Item sia statuido che se Alcun over Alcuna cometera et farano alcun latrocinio in casa o tora cosa alcuna de sustantia per robar oper mal modo darano fuora de casa a suo bertoni over altri se intendino esser ala condition del Capitolo quarto, et siano punite come a essi Signori Capi de Sextier parera meritar il delitto: et se Alcun de ditte fantesche scripte se farano conoscer [126r/126v] carnalmente in casa de li sui patroni over patrone siano et se intendano soto zaser al capitolo quarto ["terzo" is written underneath and corrected]. Et similiter li fanti che cognoscese carnalmente alcuna fantescha o altre in casa de i ditti sui patroni over patrone siano Ala condition del capitolo quarto sottoposti Et oltra siano puniti come parera ali signori Capi de Sextier meritar il manchamento et violation facta acio habiano causa de ben viver e siano Exempio de Altri.

Septimo, Item se alcun sia chi esser se vogli tora o fara tuor over consortera togli, alcuna cosa che fusse sta robata over per Altra via mal tolta over Acceptera

Alcuna cosa tolta per mala via ut supra per I ditti fanti over fantesche scripti le qual robe siano di suo patroni over patrone Cadi Ala pena de libre cinquanta ["L.50" is written above] et de star mesi do, in preson seradi et oltra cio siano obligati restituir tuto il mal tolto et sia In liberta de essi signor Capi de Sestier darli quella mazor over menor pena li parera.

Ottavo, Item, Ancor sia statuido che si Alcun patron deflorerano et violer-ano alcuna mamola scripta nel officio nostro over fioli de essi patroni sara Ale ditte sue fantesche tolta la verzenita siano obligati quelli tal patroni pagarli tuto il suo salario Integraliter Iusta il suo acordo et ultra cio debino pagar la dotta Iusta la qualita et condition segondo A essi signori Capi de sextier parera, et ca-schino ala pena ultra cio de lire cinquanta ["L.50" is written above] de pizoli et siano obligati ut supra.

Signor Capi de Sextier

Miser Zuan Donado.
Miser Zuan Batista
    Bondimier.
Miser Domenego Minio.
Miser Vidal Michiel.
Miser Lorenzo da Leze.
Miser Zuan Francesco
    Barbaro.

# Appendix B

## The Censors' Capitulary of 1541

ASV, Censori, busta 1, Capitulary 1541–1790, fols. 1v–3v

Li Clarissimi signori domino Alexandro Foscari, Federico Contarini Censori et Augustino Suriano Avogador de Comun, volendo per ben universal de tutti li nobeli, cittadini, et altri habitanti in questa citta Reffrenar la mandita rabbia, temerita Insolentia, et prosomptione Delle famegli, servitori, et Barcaruoli, de questa terra, per l'authorita a loro

Clarissimi signori data sotto di xvii del instante da lo Illustrissimo Conseglio di Diece di poter procieder contra li predetti famegli, servitori, et barcharoli, A tutte quelle severissime pene, che a loro parera, et ancho a pena di morte, A manifesta intelligentia de tutti fanno publicar l'infrascritti ordeni per loro pro nunc sanciti et determinati et prima

Primo. Che li famegli, servitori, et barcharoli i quali serveno si zentilhomeni come cittadini, over altri habitanti in questa citta de Venetia non possino da quatro in suso redursi in alcuna casa over altro loco per far alcuna unione o trattamento di sorte alcuna sotto pena a quelli [1v/2r] che se reduranno in simel lochi di esserli tagliata la man destra, et ulterius di esser perpetualmente banditi di Venetia, et destretto. Et se per alcun tempo contrafaranno al ditto bando, et serano presi siano condutti a Venetia, dove siano posti in prigione serrata et li star debbiano per un'anno, et poi siano rimessi al suo bando, et hoc totiens quotiens contrafecerint, et capti fuerint, et habbia chi quello o quelli prendera et dara nelle forze della Signoria nostra ogni volta lire dusento de sui beni se haver se ne potrano se non delli danari della cassa del Illustrissimo Conseglio di Diese. Et se in termine de giorni tre da poi che li preditti se haverano redutto alcuni de loro che saran stati in ditto redutto venirano a manifestar alli prefati Clarissimi signori censori et Avogador tal suo redur talmente che per la sua manifestation se habbia la verita sia libero da ogni pena soprascritta et habbia la taglia sopranominata. Se veramente alcun ch'havesse inditio scientia over notitia de questi simel redutti, et nel termine delli preditti giorni tre venira a manifestarlo alli prefati Clarissimi Signori Constando con verita de simel redutti habbino L.100 da esser pagate ut supra et se passati essi giorni tre non venirano cazino in pena de esser frustadi da San Marco a Rialto.

2. Item E se nelli anteditti reduti serano stati da quatro in suso al'hora a ciascaduno de loro, che se havera redutto da quatro in suso li sia tagliata la man destra et cavati tutti dui li occhi, talmente che siano privi del vedere, et da poi siano banditi perpetuo de Venetia et del destretto, come e ditto di sopra cum benefitio a quelli che accuserano come e superius dechiarito, et taglie anteditte.

3. Item se li preditti famegli, servitori o barcaruoli expetando in loco alcuno li loro patroni in barca se unirano da quatro in suso insieme cazino in pena di esser frustadi da San Marco fino a Rialto et da poi sia bolati di le quatro bole di foco consuete, et quello che li accusera habbia lire cento da esser pagate nel modo soprascritto, et se alcuno delli pridetti che si haverano redutto da quatro in suso venira ad accusar alli Clarissimi signori soprascritti li altri compagni in termine de giorni tre da poi fatta la unione sia assolto da le pene soprascritte et sia tenuto secreto.

4. Item se alcun de detti famegli, servitori, o barcaroli [2r/2v] persuaderano o exorterano alcun altro fameglio servitor o barcaruol a far piu a un modo cha a un altro in casa et contra li loro patroni vel desviandoli da li lor patroni, et si etiam alcun deli deli [sic] sopraditti impropererano alcun fameglio scritto chiamandolo fante scritto cadino ciascadun delli contrafacenti a quelle pene di esser frustati et bolati.

5. Item se ditti famegli, servitori, o barcaroli ne le case dove starano a salario farano violentia alcuna, Inducendo le massare a dar via la robba over tolendola loro aut userano alcuna deshonesta con le servitrice de ditte case, cazino a pena di esser frustati et bolati.

6. Item se alcun delli preditti famegli servitori o barcaroli havendo li loro patroni In barca, over non havendo faranno costion, o, rissa de sorte alcuna contra altri che havessero i loro patroni, o patrone in barca Cazino alla pena de esser frustati et bolati come e ditto di sopra et se in ditta costion o rissa intervenira sangue o morte contra di loro se intendi esser resservato de procieder come per giustitia a loro clarissimi signori parera.

7. Item se alcun de li preditti famegli servitori o barcaroli usera alcun modo de parole iniuriose contra alcun nobile cittadin o altro habitante in questa terra, cazi in pena di subito esser frustado da San Marco a Rialto et haver tre tratti de corda sopra la piazza de San Marco et di esser bolato de le quatro bole consuete, et se oltra le parole Iniuriose userano fatti sia reservato a loro signori punirli di quelle piu severe pene che a loro parerano per Giustitia.

8. Item se alcuno delli preditti famegli, servitori, o barcaruoli cosi in barca come altrove dira o usera parola alcuna dishonesta dove siano o possano aldir alcuna nobile, cittadina o altra habitante in questa citta cazino alle pene soprascritte di esser frustati bolati, et haver tre tratti de corda, et similmente cazino

a ditte pene, quelli che daranno stridor alle novize quando passarano per li canali et si de remi come con voce et altramente.

9. Item se alcuno delli predetti famegli, servitori, o barcaruoli da remo porteranno drapamenti de seda, over che habbino in seda de sorte alcuna berete, et scarpe di veluto, o, di seda over habito che non sia honesto cazino in pena di perder i drapi i quali siano de quelli capitanei, o, officiali che li prenderano: Li quali capitanei, et officiali tutti (nemine excepto) [2v/3r] senza alcuna licentia possino ritenirli, et ulterius siano frustati da San Marco a Rialto.

10. Item se alcuno delli detti famegli servitori o barcaruoli cercherano de desviar o desviarano alcuna massara o servitrice de alcuna de le case de i Nobili, cittadini o altri habitanti in questa terra cazino alla pena da esser frustadi et boladi ut supra.

11. Item se alcuno de predetti famegli, servitori, et Barcaroli porterano arme di sorte alcuna, over altra sorte de Instrumento da offender, et serano trovati, et si de notte come de giorno, et si in barca come per terra, cazino in pena di perder le arme, quale siano de quelli capitanei, o officiali che li prendera, et ulterius haver debbano sopra la piaza de San Marco tre tratti de corda, et siano poi frustati da San Marco a Rialto, exceptuando pero quelli che hanno licentia dal Illustrissimo conseglio di X di poter portar ditte arme.

12. Item che, quando li preditti famegli, servitori, et barcaruoli haverano vogati li loro patroni a palazzo a tempo et nelli giorni che si dovera redur il gran conseglio et desmontati ditti sui patroni in terra subito et immediate debbano uscir del rio de palazzo fora per il ponte dela paglia, et andar per il canal grande senza ritornar in rio fino che il gran conseglio non sera redutto: et altramente facendo quelli che contrafarano siano messi in berlina dove star debbano da terza fino a hore doi dapoi.

13. Item alcun barcaruol over altro con barca alcuna non possi star ne occupar la riva del palazzo per causa de far nolo, et guadagnar ma debbano quella lassar libera per comodita del montar et dismontar di barca, sotto pena a ciascadun de quelli che contrafaranno al presente ordine de star in berlina a hora di terza per due hore.

14. Item se alcun delli preditti famegli, servitori o barcaruoli stando in casa cum li loro patroni Andarano de di o de notte guadagnando et facendo noli, cazi in pena di esser frustado da San Marco a Rialto.

15. Item se alcuno delli preditti famegli, servitori, o, barcaruoli darano stridor, over farano violentia quando alcun capitaneo, over official vorano ritenir, over haveranno ritenuto alcuno si per causa civil come criminal cazino in pena de haver tre tratti de corda sopra la piazza de San Marco et di esser frustadi da San Marco a Rialto. [3r/3v]

16. Item se alcuno de li preditti famegli, servitori et barcaruoli daran recapito de di o de notte In casa de li loro patroni, ad homo alcuno, over donna, over in ditte case menerano putane cazi in pena di esser frustado da San Marco a Rialto si lui come quello, o quella che havera menato in casa, et se in termine de giorni tre dapoi che havera dato recapito o menato in casa quello, o quella, Alcuno de loro allozati in casa venirano a denunciar alli prefati Clarissimi Signori sia assolto dalla pena soprascritta.

17. Item se alcuno delli preditti famegli, servitori, o barcharuoli, haveranno havuto da li loro patroni a conto del suo salario danari avanti tratto, non possino da quelli partirse se prima non haveranno livrado i danari che haverano hauto et facendo altramente cazino in pena di esser frustadi da San Marco a Rialto et similiter sotto la soprascritta pena siano obligati per zorni xv Inanci il suo partir da li loro patroni fargelo intender a ditti loro patroni che se voleno partir accio possino haver custodia alla robba et provedersi di fameglio, servitor o barcaruol.

18. Item se li ditti famegli, servitori et barcaroli nel spender faranno per li loro patroni, cometteranno alcuno ingano si nel comprar la robba come da poi comprata darla ad altri o per se ritenirla cazino in pena di esser frustadi da San Marco a Rialto et di esser bolati delle quatro bolle consuete.

19. Se ditti famegli o servitori darano o porterano fora di casa cossa alcuna da manzar o da bever di quello li vien data per il loro viver, che li avanzasse cadino alla pena soprascritta.

20. Item se alcuno delli preditti fameglii servitori et barcaroli prometterano di tor o torano per moglie alcuna servitrice de quella casa dove i starano senza licentia delli loro patroni cazino l'un et l'altro in pena di esser frustadi da San Marco a Rialto.

21. Item de cetero Alcuno, et sia chi esser si voglia non possi in questa citta Traghetar ad alcun tragheto, si per si come per altri ne etiam andar guadagnando et si de di come di notte se prima non havera servito in questa citta in una over piu case per anni tre sotto pena a chi contrafara di esser frustado da San Marco a Rialto.

MDXLI Die XXV Augusti
Publicata fuit super scallis Rivoalti per Francescum a Vitualiis preconem.

# Notes

## Abbreviations

| | |
|---|---|
| AC | Avogaria di Comun |
| ACPV | Archivio Curia Patriarcale, Venezia |
| ASV | Archivio di Stato, Venezia |
| BNM | Biblioteca Nazionale Marciana, Venezia |
| CI | Cancelleria Inferiore |
| CP | Censimenti Parrocchiali |
| IRE | Archivio degli Istituzioni di Ricovero e di Educazione, Venezia |
| MC | Maggior Consiglio |
| MCC | Museo Civico Correr, Venezia |
| MV | More Veneto |
| NA | Notarile, Atti |
| NT | Notarile, Testamenti |
| PSM | Procuratori di San Marco |
| RPC, RBG | Registri Privati Contabili, Raccolta Barbarigo-Grimani |

Note that Latin names have been changed to their Italian equivalents. Some names have been maintained in the Venetian dialectical form.

## Introduction

1. Dennis Romano, *Patricians and Popolani: The Social Foundations of the Venetian Renaissance State* (Baltimore, 1987).

2. Theresa M. McBride, *The Domestic Revolution: The Modernisation of Household Service in England and France, 1820–1920* (New York, 1976), 9–10.

3. Charles Verlinden, *L'esclavage dans l'Europe médiévale*, 2 vols. (Bruges, 1955–77).

4. Domenico Gioffrè, *Il mercato degli schiavi a Genova nel secolo XV* (Genoa, 1971).

5. Susan Mosher Stuard, "Urban Domestic Slavery in Medieval Ragusa," *Journal of Medieval History* 9 (1983): 155–71; see also her "To Town to Serve: Urban Domestic Slavery in Medieval Ragusa," in *Women and Work in Preindustrial Europe*, ed. Barbara A. Hanawalt (Bloomington, 1986), 39–55.

6. McBride, 119.

7. Ibid., 14.

8. Cissie Fairchilds, *Domestic Enemies: Servants and Their Masters in Old Regime France*

(Baltimore, 1984); Sarah C. Maza, *Servants and Masters in Eighteenth-Century France: The Uses of Loyalty* (Princeton, 1983).

9. Maza, 276–98.

10. Fairchilds, 13–17.

11. Iris Origo, "The Domestic Enemy: The Eastern Slaves in Tuscany in the Fourteenth and Fifteenth Centuries," *Speculum* 30 (1955): 321–66.

12. Fairchilds takes her title from Origo's study; see Fairchilds, 245 n.1.

13. Piero Guarducci and Valeria Ottanelli, *I servitori domestici della casa borghese toscana nel basso medioevo* (Florence, 1982).

14. Jacques Heers, *Esclaves et domestiques au Moyen Age dans le monde méditerranéen* (Paris, 1981).

15. The documents for Venice were compiled for Heers by Elisabeth Crouzet-Pavan (see Heers, 289).

16. Bronislaw Geremek, *The Margins of Society in Late Medieval Paris*, trans. Jean Birrell (Cambridge, 1987), 251–52.

17. See also *Quaderni storici*, n.s., 68 (1988), entitled "I servi e le serve."

18. David Herlihy and Christiane Klapisch-Zuber, *Tuscans and Their Families: A Study of the Florentine Catasto of 1427* (New Haven, 1985); originally published as *Les Toscans et leurs familles: Une étude du catasto florentin de 1427* (Paris, 1978). The English edition is used throughout.

19. See Christiane Klapisch-Zuber, "Female Celibacy and Service in Florence in the Fifteenth Century" and "Blood Parents and Milk Parents: Wet Nursing in Florence, 1300–1530," in her *Women, Family, and Ritual in Renaissance Italy*, trans. Lydia G. Cochrane (Chicago, 1985); and idem, "Women Servants in Florence during the Fourteenth and Fifteenth Centuries," in *Women and Work in Preindustrial Europe*, ed. Barbara A. Hanawalt (Bloomington, 1986), 56–80.

20. Michael Goodich, "*Ancilla Dei*: The Servant as Saint in the Late Middle Ages," in *Women of the Medieval World: Essays in Honor of John H. Mundy*, ed. Julius Kirshner and Suzanne F. Wemple (Oxford, 1985), 119–36.

21. Frances E. Dolan, *Dangerous Familiars: Representations of Domestic Crime in England, 1550–1700* (Ithaca, 1994), 21–24, 86–88.

22. Kate Mertes, *The English Noble Household, 1250–1600: Good Governance and Politic Rule* (Oxford, 1988), 124–26.

23. As Mertes notes, "The household was very much a male institution" (ibid., 6 [quotation], 57).

24. Most of this information is taken from Mark Girouard, *Life in the English Country House: A Social and Architectural History* (New Haven, 1978), chs. 2–4.

25. See, Richard A. Goldthwaite, "The Florentine Palace as Domestic Architecture," *American Historical Review* 77 (1972): 1009. A recent study of domestic servants in late-seventeenth-century Rotterdam shows that households there conformed to the bourgeois model, that is, a small number of mainly female servants. See Marybeth Carlson, "A Trojan Horse of Worldliness? Maidservants in the Burgher Households of Rotterdam at the End of the Seventeenth Century," in *Women in the Golden Age: An International Debate on Women in Seventeenth-Century Holland, England, and Italy*, ed. Els Kloek, Nicole Teeuwen, and Marijke Huisman (Hilversum, Netherlands, 1994), 87–96. I wish to thank Wayne Franits for this reference.

26. Fairchilds, 12.

27. For the labels *bourgeois* or *mercantile* and *aristocratic,* see Daniel Roche, *The People of Paris: An Essay in Popular Culture in the Eighteenth Century,* trans. Marie Evans (Berkeley, 1987), 67–68.

28. See, for example, Klapisch-Zuber, *Women, Family, and Ritual,* 1–22; and Francis William Kent, *Household and Lineage in Renaissance Florence: The Family Life of the Capponi, Ginori, and Rucellai* (Princeton, 1977), 5.

29. Leon Battista Alberti, *I libri della famiglia,* ed. Ruggiero Romano and Alberto Tenenti (Turin, 1969), 226.

30. Donald R. Bender, "A Refinement of the Concept of Household: Families, Co-residence, and Domestic Functions," *American Anthropologist* 69 (1967): 493.

31. At least this is the hypothesis of Lucinda M. C. Byatt in her article "Aspetti giuridici e finanziari di una 'familia' cardinalizia del XVI secolo: Un progetto di ricerca," in *"Familia" del principe e famiglia aristocratica,* ed. Cesare Mozzarelli, 2 vols. (Rome, 1988), 2:612–14.

32. Klapisch-Zuber, "Women Servants in Florence," 56.

33. On this point, see also Susan Mosher Stuard, *A State of Deference: Ragusa/Dubrovnik in the Medieval Centuries* (Philadelphia, 1992), 123, 130, 132.

## Chapter One   Treatises on Household Management and Service

1. See *Le Ménagier de Paris,* ed. Georgine E. Brereton and Janet M. Ferrier (Oxford, 1981); and Goodman of Paris, *The Goodman of Paris (Le Ménagier de Paris): A Treatise on Moral and Domestic Economy by a Citizen of Paris (c. 1393),* trans. Eileen Power (New York, 1928).

2. See Gordon J. Schochet, *Patriarchalism in Political Thought: The Authoritarian Family and Political Speculation and Attitudes Especially in Seventeenth-Century England* (New York, 1975), 67.

3. Alberti, *I libri della famiglia.* For some recent considerations of the work, see Hans Baron, *In Search of Florentine Civic Humanism: Essays on the Transition from Medieval to Modern Thought,* 2 vols. (Princeton, 1988), 1:258–88; and Thomas Kuehn, *Law, Family, and Women: Toward a Legal Anthropology of Renaissance Italy* (Chicago, 1991), 157–75.

4. Aristotle, *Oeconomica and Magna Moralia,* trans. G. Cyril Armstrong (Cambridge, Mass., 1947). Scholars now ascribe the books of the *Oeconomica* to three different authors, although the first may well have been composed by a student of Aristotle (see Josef Soudek, "The Genesis and Tradition of Leonardo Bruni's Annotated Latin Version of the [Pseudo-] Aristotelian *Economics,*" *Scriptorium* 12 [1958]: 260–68).

5. Xenophon, *Memorabilia and Oeconomicus,* trans. E. C. Marchant (Cambridge, Mass., 1938).

6. See, among others, Alberto Tenenti, *Il senso della morte e l'amore della vita nel Rinascimento (Francia e Italia)* (Turin, 1957), esp. ch. 6.

7. Daniela Frigo, *Il padre di famiglia: Governo della casa e governo civile nella tradizione dell' "economica" tra Cinque e Seicento* (Rome, 1985), esp. 194–95.

8. Ibid., 26–31.

9. Ibid., 27.

10. Giorgio Politi, *Aristocrazia e potere politico nella Cremona di Filippo II* (Milan, 1976),

18: "La questione non avrebbe avuto senso poichè agli antipodi di espressioni quali appunto *bene pubblico* non si trova affatto il termine di *privato* ma quello di *particolare,* dal che si può dedurre come appunto il bene pubblico o generale non fosse concepito come alcunchè di *altro,* ma come la sommatoria o meglio la mediazione d'una pluralità d'interessi distinti." See also Frigo, 218 n.30.

11. See also some very sensible remarks in Richard A. Goldthwaite, *Wealth and the Demand for Art in Renaissance Italy, 1300–1600* (Baltimore, 1993), 210–12.

12. Fra Paolino Minorita, *Trattato de regimine rectoris,* ed. Adolfo Mussafia (Vienna, 1868).

13. Ibid., v–xxx.

14. Frigo, 20.

15. Minorita, 66–67.

16. The quotation reads, "ordene de li donzelli ben vestidhi, li qual servia zenza algun defecto" (ibid., 91–92).

17. "Se tu as servo fedel, siate caro co l'anema toa" (ibid., 92–93).

18. "A l'aseno se de' dar cibo, baston et encargo, et al servo pan e disciplina" (ibid., 93–94).

19. "Cosa serave che Mathan podesse viver zenza mi, et io no podesse viver zenza Mathan" (ibid., 94).

20. Frigo, 71–73.

21. Ibid., 78, 83.

22. For these changes, see Frederic C. Lane, "The Enlargement of the Great Council of Venice," in *Florilegium Historiale: Essays Presented to Wallace K. Ferguson,* ed. J. G. Rowe and W. H. Stockdale (Toronto, 1971), 241–42; and Roberto Cessi, *Storia della Repubblica di Venezia* (Florence, 1981), 365.

23. Francesco Barbaro, *De re uxoria liber,* ed. Attilio Gnesotto, *Atti e memorie della R. Accademia di SLA di Padova,* n.s., 32 (1916): 6–105. The translation of part 2, by Benjamin G. Kohl, is found in Benjamin Kohl and Ronald Witt, *The Earthly Republic: Italian Humanists on Government and Society* (Philadelphia, 1978), 179–228 (hereafter cited as Kohl).

24. Margaret Leah King, *Venetian Humanism in an Age of Patrician Dominance* (Princeton, 1986), 93.

25. For biographical information on Barbaro, see ibid., 92–93, 323–25; and Kohl, 180–81.

26. Kohl, 182.

27. My reading of Barbaro follows closely that of King; the translations are Kohl's.

28. King, 94.

29. Kohl, 192.

30. Ibid., 196; King, 96.

31. Kohl, 211. Kohl is my source for the information contained in the next several paragraphs.

32. Frigo, 17–64.

33. King, *Venetian Humanism,* 98. For Caldiera, see Juliana Hill Cotton, "Giovanni Caldiera," in *Dizionario biografico degli italiani,* vol. 16 (Rome, 1973), 626–28; King, *Venetian Humanism,* 344–45; idem, "Caldiera and the Barbaros on Marriage and the Family: Humanist Reflections on Venetian Realities," *Journal of Medieval and Renaissance Studies* 6 (1976): 19–50; and idem, "Venetian Ideology and the Reconstruction of Knowledge: Giovanni Caldiera (c. 1400–c. 1474)" (Ph.D. diss., Stanford University, 1972). Again, I follow closely King's reading of Caldiera, although I have also consulted the copy of

Caldiera's trilogy: Biblioteca Nazionale Marciana (hereafter BNM), Ms. La. cl. X, 356 (3261–62), Iohannes Caldierae, Physici, "De oeconomia veneta libri duo et de praestantia venetae politiae libri quinque" (hereafter cited as Caldierae).

34. King, *Venetian Humanism*, 98–112.

35. Caldierae, 50.

36. "Nam quidam honore potius quam utilitate domum reficiuntur" (ibid., 51).

37. The kinds of servants are discussed fully in King, "Venetian Ideology," 370–71; and idem, "Caldiera and the Barbaros," 24 n. 12.

38. King, "Venetian Ideology," 345–54.

39. "Et quia omnia Iconomia Policie assimilatur, et domus etiam civitatis similitudinem gerit" (King, *Venetian Humanism*, 105).

40. Ibid., 104 n. 36.

41. Ibid., 108, esp. n. 47.

42. Ibid., 102.

43. King, "Caldiera and the Barbaros," 28.

44. King, *Venetian Humanism*, 118–32. A critical edition of Quirini's *De republica* edited by Carlo Seno and Giorgio Ravegnani is found in *Lauro Quirini umanista*, ed. Vittore Branca (Florence, 1977), 123–61.

45. King, *Venetian Humanism*, 125.

46. Ibid., 125; Quirini, 128.

47. In his treatise *Della perfettione della vita politica*, Paolo Paruta wrote, "Gli huomini dunque nel formare una perfetta communanza, ogni parte di lei distinguendo, et altre al servire, et altre al comandare ordinando, imitarono questa loro madre, et maestra natura; dal cui instinto guidati, si posero ad habitare insieme, et à fabricarne le città" (Paolo Paruta, *Della perfettione della vita politica . . . libri tre* [Venice, 1579]).

48. For the modern edition, which reconstructs the fifteenth-century version, see Benedetto Cotrugli (Raguseo), *Il libro dell'arte di mercatura*, ed. Ugo Tucci (Venice, 1990). For the quotation, see Ugo Tucci, *Mercanti, navi, monete nel Cinquecento veneziano* (Bologna, 1981) 36–37. The tract was eventually edited and published by Elefanta of Venice in 1573.

49. Cotrugli, 229.

50. "[Il] pater familias della casa si possa chiamare rex domus sue, perchè come il re debbe reggiere il suo reame, così il padre della famiglia la sua casa" (ibid.).

51. "Una casa . . . non sia altro, che una picciola Città, et la Città una casa grande" (Alessandro Piccolomini, *Della institutione morale libri XII*, [Venice, 1560], 484). In his *De Iciarchia*, written about 1469, Alberti wrote that "the city . . . is almost like a very large family, and, conversely, the family is almost a small city" (cited in Baron, 1:282). For the friendship of Barbaro and Piccolomini, see Mary Rogers, "An Ideal Wife at the Villa Maser: Veronese, the Barbaros, and Renaissance Theorists of Marriage," *Renaissance Studies* 7 (1993): 382–86.

52. "Obedientia et servitù, non meno è loro utile, che à quegli altri sia il governo, e 'l principato" (Piccolomini, 486).

53. "In utile, et benefitio di tutte le parti della sua casa, secondo i gradi, che lor convengono" (ibid., 488).

54. "Una 'mappa' completa del vivere civile in tutte le sue sfumature e sottigliezze" (Frigo, 31).

55. Ibid., 26, 200.

56. Giacomo Lanteri, *Della economia . . . nel quale si dimostrano le qualità, che all'huomo et alla donna separatamente convengono pel governo della casa* (Venice, 1560). For a brief discussion of Lanteri, see Gino Barbieri, "Il trattatello 'Della economica' di Giacomo Lanteri, letterato e architetto bresciano del secolo XVI," in *Saggi di economia aziendale e sociale in memoria di Gino Zappa*, 3 vols. (Milan, 1961), 1:151–66.

57. Lanteri, 2.

58. "Credo certo, che i maggiori nimici, che habbiano le case, siano li servitori" (ibid., 18–19).

59. "In questa guisa premiando coloro che nel servirlo faranno il debito loro, et punendo chi facesse il contrario, gli spronerà ad essere ne gli uffici loro diligenti tutti, et fedeli" (ibid., 55).

60. Ibid., 169–70. For Deianira's advice about guarding the morals of female servants, see ibid., 139–40.

61. "Di bellissimo giudicio, virtuosa, et molto sofficiente" (ibid., 170).

62. Ibid., 13–14. See also Joanne M. Ferraro, *Family and Public Life in Brescia, 1580–1650: The Foundations of Power in the Venetian State* (Cambridge, 1993), 66.

63. Lanteri, 40: "A gli huomini di ciascuna conditione è lecito senza biasimo, di tenere servitù pel bisogno loro, onde quella commodità si cavi, che senza servi non si può havere."

64. On the connection of command with virtue, and service with vice, see Frigo, 83.

65. Stefano Guazzo, *La civil conversatione del sig. Stefano Guazzo gentilhuomo di Casale di Monferrato; divisa in quatro libri* (Venice, 1575).

66. For Guazzo's life and the work, see Maria Luisa Doglio, "Stefano Guazzo," in *Dizionario critico della letteratura italiana*, ed. Vittore Branca, 4 vols. (Turin, 1986), 2:460–62; and Amedeo Quondam, "La 'forma del vivere': Schede per l'analisi del discorso cortigiano," in *La corte e il 'Cortegiano,'* vol. 2, *Un modello europeo*, ed. Adriano Prosperi (Rome, 1980), 58–63. For his popularity in the Veneto, see Gino Benzoni, "Le accademie," in *Storia della cultura veneta*, vol. 4, *Il Seicento*, ed. Girolamo Arnaldi and Manlio Pastore Stocchi, pt. 1 (Vicenza, 1983), 131–32.

67. Guazzo, 436, 447–53.

68. "Che'l servitore è parte ad un certo modo del patrone, et che non vi è alcuna possessione migliore in questa vita, che'l buon servitore; onde è scritto, se hai un fedel servitore, sia a te quasi l'anima tua" (ibid., 454).

69. Lanteri, 161. According to Guazzo, a master needs three things from a servant: "amore, fede, et sofficienza" (Guazzo, 446).

70. Frigo, 85.

71. See ibid., 39–40. See also Elide Casali, "'Economica' e 'creanza' cristiana," *Quaderni storici* 41 (1979): 555–83.

72. For Valier's life, see, among other sources, G. Giuriato, "Memorie venete nei monumenti di Roma," *Archivio veneto*, n.s., 25 (1883): 133–34; Silvio Tramontin, "La visita apostolica del 1581 a Venezia," *Studi veneziani* 9 (1967): 453–533; and Lorenzo Tacchella and Mary Madeline Tacchella, *Il cardinale Agostino Valier e la riforma tridentina nella diocesi di Trieste* (Udine, 1974), 64–105.

73. Valier's *Della istruzione delle donne maritate* is printed in his *La istituzione d'ogni stato lodevole delle donne cristiane . . . novella impressione . . . illustrata da d. Gaetano Volpi* (Padua, 1744). An earlier edition was published in 1575 by Bolognino Zalieri in Venice.

For some brief remarks on the genre, see P. Renée Baernstein, "In Widow's Habit: Women between Convent and Family in Sixteenth-Century Milan," *Sixteenth Century Journal* 25 (1994): 789–90.

74. Valiero, *Della istruzione delle donne maritate*, 15: "Perchè le buone Madri di famiglia sono fermi fondamenti della disciplina delle città, onde poi nasce l'obbedienza, il buon reggimento, e la tranquillità de' popoli con onore, e gloria di Dio."

75. "Di far buone le Città, le Repubbliche, i Regni, educando buoni padri di famiglia, buoni cittadini, buoni gentiluomini, buoni principi, e finalmente . . . essendo . . . Madri del popolo di Dio" (ibid., 17).

76. Ibid., 29. The "Christian Institution" was probably a kind of catechism (see Tacchella and Tacchella, 77).

77. Valiero, *Della istruzione delle donne maritate*, 30.

78. Ibid., 39. The entire passage reads, "Questa benedizione dello Spirito Santo la quale ho con alcune parole dichiarata, desidero che caschi sopra tutte le Madri di famiglia di Verona, e sopra quelle della nostra patria, e finalmente sopra tutte le Donne Maritate del mondo: acciocchè colla buona lor disciplina si tengano lontani gli odi, e tutte le sorte di peccati: siano tutte le case veramente di Dio, alberghi di pace, e di concordia."

79. Edward Muir, "Images of Power: Art and Pageantry in Renaissance Venice," *American Historical Review* 84 (1979): 33.

80. This stands in contrast, for example, to the section on servants in the treatise *The Treasure of the City of Ladies*, by Christine de Pisan. Her description of corrupt behavior by servants seems to be drawn from experience rather than from ancient writers (see Christine de Pisan, *The Treasure of the City of Ladies or the Book of the Three Virtues*, trans. Sarah Lawson [New York, 1985], 168–71).

81. For biographical information, see Alessandro Gnavi, "Valori urbani e attività marginali nella *Piazza Universale* di Tommaso Garzoni," *Ricerche storiche* 20 (1990): 50–53.

82. I have used the 1595 edition: Tommaso Garzoni, *La piazza universale di tutte le professioni del mondo* (Venice, 1595).

83. It reads, "il bene, e il male, che posson fare tutti i professori [*sic*] del mondo" (ibid., dedication to Alfonso of Ferrara, unpaginated).

84. As Gnavi says, "Strumento ideologico, quindi, che, offerto da un ecclesiastico qual era il Garzoni, può essere letto come espressione del più generale sforzo di disciplinamento sociale perseguito dalla Controriforma" (Gnavi, 47).

85. Garzoni, 674–77.

86. "Ma quei vigliacchi Re de' furfanti, et schiuma de' poltroni, infedeli come i Mori, ladroni come i Cingari, assassini come gli Arabi, traditori come i Parthi, che furon creati dal niente . . . non meritano altro che stare alla servitù" (ibid., 676).

87. "Le rubbarie, le truffe, la fuga, l'arroganza, la dapocagine, l'ebrietà, l'ingordigia, il russar sempre, la tardità, e la poltroneria" (ibid., 677).

88. Gnavi, 60–61.

89. Garzoni, 554–58.

90. "In questi son congregati come in un mucchio tutti i vitii de gli altri, et nelle barche loro s'impara quanto di tristo sa un soldato, quanto di ghiotto sa un mercante, quanto di reo sa un ruffiano quanto di cattivo sa un'hebreo, quanto di furbo sa un scolare, quanto di maladetto sa una meretrice et tutta la somma si riversica addosso al barcaruolo" (ibid., 869).

91. "Costoro han sempre in bocca parole sporche, giuramenti vani d'ogni sorte, imprecationi terribili affatto. . . . in costoro non si trova una verità, non si scopre una creanza, non si vede una bontà, perche la più parte di loro è meza canaglia" (ibid., 869–70).

92. Ibid., 835–38. There is an error in the pagination of the text at this point.

93. "Coi cattivi costumi, co' vezzi, et coi diffetti che imprimono in loro" (ibid., 836).

94. "Circa le balie diceva il Barges, che tre cose mettono il foco in casa, un figliuol prodigo, una moglie adultera, et una Balia Ruffiana" (ibid., 837–38). Barges, who is otherwise unidentified, may well be the humanist Pietro Angeli (1517–96), who was also known by the name Bargaeus, after his hometown, Barga, near Lucca (see *Letteratura italiana: Gli autori: dizionario bio-bibliografico e indici*, 2 vols. [Turin, 1990–91], 1:83–84).

95. Garzoni, 869.

96. Cesare Vecellio, *De gli habiti antichi, et moderni di diverse parti del mondo libri due* (Venice, 1590). For biographical information on Vecellio, see *Dizionario enciclopedico Bolaffi dei pittori e degli incisori italiani dall'XI al XX secolo*, 11 vols. (Turin, 1972–76), 11:266–67.

97. Vecellio, 122v–123v.

98. For more on these points, see Dennis Romano, "The Gondola as a Marker of Station in Venetian Society," *Renaissance Studies* 8 (1994): 359–74.

99. See Rogers, 379–97.

100. See Paul H. D. Kaplan, "Sicily, Venice, and the East: Titian's Fabricius Salvaresius with a Black Page," in *Europa und die Kunst des Islam 15. bis 18. Jahrhundert* (Vienna, 1984), 127–36; see also Peter Burke, *The Historical Anthropology of Early Modern Italy* (Cambridge, 1987), 161–63.

101. Patricia Fortini Brown, *Venetian Narrative Painting in the Age of Carpaccio* (New Haven, 1988), 163. For illustrations of the works discussed in this paragraph see pp. 158–59.

102. Bartolomeo Spathaphòra di Moncata, *Quattro orationi di M. Bartolomeo Spathaphòra di Moncata gentil'huomo venetiano* (Venice, 1554). For the Accademia degli Uniti, see Antonio Pilot, "Gli 'ordini' dell'accademia veneziana degli uniti (1551)," *Ateneo veneto* 35, pt. 1 (1912): 193–207.

103. "Molto meglio è esser servo, che essere, come egli è, patrone" (Spathaphòra, 96–97).

104. "Non è adunque lodevole la libertà che voi havete diffinita, di potere liberamente fare quel che l'huom vuole; ma lodevole è ben la servitù del non poter far male; donde nasce, et procede la vera, et santa libertà di far bene" (ibid., 103–5). Here Spatafora is speaking of limitations on ducal power in Venice, contrasting the "servile" doges with tyrants, whose power is unlimited. For surprisingly similar comments about servants' lack of worries, but without Spatafora's ironic tone, see the remarks of the early-eighteenth-century bishop of Ely, William Fleetwood, cited in Schochet, 68.

105. Spathaphòra, 107–10.

106. For biographical information on Glissenti, see Leonardo Cozzando, *Libraria Bresciana prima, e seconda parte* (1694; reprint, Bologna, 1974), 78–79; and Vincenzo Peroni, *Biblioteca Bresciana*, 3 vols. (1818–23; reprint, Bologna, 1968), 2:127–29. I wish to thank Joanne Ferraro for these references. See also Giovanni Treccani degli Alfieri, ed., *Storia di Brescia*, vol. 3, *La dominazione veneta (1576–1797)* (Brescia, 1961), 230; and Ugo Vaglia, *Vicende storiche della Val Sabbia dal 1580 al 1915* (Brescia, 1955), 43–46. Glissenti's will dated 1615 is in Archivio di Stato, Venezia (hereafter ASV), Notarile, Testamenti (hereafter NT), busta 403, notary Giulio Figolino, unbound testament 392.

107. Fabio Glissenti, *Discorsi morali contra il dispiacer del morire. Detto Athanatophilia* (Venice, 1596). I have primarily used the edition published in Venice in 1609 by Bartolameo de gli Alberti. There are only minor differences between the editions.

108. "Hora considerate se questa non è una vita da Rè, da tenersela a cara, e di cercare di conservarsela più che si può" (ibid., 131v).

109. "Tu non sei il servo, come ben dicesti, ma il padrone" (ibid., 132r).

110. "Che non meritano il nome di servitori, ma piu'tosto di furfanti, di lecca taglieri, e di poltroni" (ibid., 132v–133r).

111. "Questi huomini, i quali si possono chiamar acquatici non sono così malitiosi come gli altri" (ibid., 139v).

112. Ibid., 142r.

113. For obedience as a political virtue, see Muir, "Images of Power," 42.

## Chapter Two   The Venetian Government and the Regulation of Domestic Service

1. For the Ten, see Giuseppe Maranini, *La costituzione di Venezia,* 2 vols. (1927–31; reprint, Florence, 1974), 2:385–472; Felix Gilbert, "Venice in the Crisis of the League of Cambrai," in *Renaissance Venice,* ed. J. R. Hale (London, 1974), 274–92; and Gaetano Cozzi, "Authority and the Law in Renaissance Venice," ibid., 293–345.

2. ASV, Censori, busta 1, capitulary dated 1541–1790, fols. 1r–1v: "Multiplicando di giorno in giorno tante querele alli capi di questo conseglio delle male conditione, Adunatione, et sette, che al continuo fanno li fameglì da barca et servitori di questa città, cum parole di male qualita, che publicamente usano, oltra diversi insolenti et dishonestissimi modi loro senza haver alcun rispetto alli Nobili, Nobile, cittadini, et cittadine nostre, et altre persone, cum malissimo exempio, et poco honore della citta: che non se li provedendo cresceranno tanto piu le Insolentie loro, quanto piu vederanno, quelle passar impunite. La qual materia per esser di quella importantia che cadauno, ben intende, si deve commetter a magistratto di Authorita, che summariamente habbia da expedirla, et metter quelli ordeni cerca cio, che li pareranno expedienti."

3. "Come se fusse fatto et deliberato per questo conseglio" (ibid., fol. 1r).

4. "Contra honorem domini ducis et eius consilio ac comunis Veneciarum" (see Giovanni Monticolo, ed., *I capitolari delle arti veneziane sottoposte alla giustizia vecchia dalle origini al MCCCXXX,* 3 vols. [Rome, 1896–1914], 2:23).

5. This phrase was deleted from the law (see ASV, Consiglio dei Dieci, Parti Comuni, filza 29, fol. 219).

6. Lia Sbriziolo, "Per la storia delle confraternite veneziane: Dalle deliberazioni miste (1310–1476) del Consiglio dei Dieci: *Scolae comunes,* artigiane e nazionali," *Atti dell'istituto veneto di scienze, lettere ed arti* 126 (1967–68): 405–42; idem, "Per la storia delle confraternite veneziane: Dalle deliberazioni miste (1310–1476) del Consiglio dei Dieci. Le scuole dei battuti," in *Miscellanea Gilles G. Meersseman,* 2 vols. (Padua, 1970), 2:715–63. See also Richard Mackenney, *Tradesmen and Traders: The World of the Guilds in Venice and Europe, c. 1250–c. 1650* (Totowa, N.J., 1987), 48.

7. Aldo Contento, "Il censimento della popolazione sotto la Repubblica Veneta," *Nuovo archivio veneto* 19 (1900): 231–32.

8. Ferruccio Zago, ed., *Consiglio dei Dieci: Deliberazioni miste,* vol. 1, *Registri I–II (1310–1324)* (Venice, 1962), 25–28; Marino Sanudo (il Giovane), *De origine, situ et magis-*

38. Ibid., fols. 204v–205r. Much of the fear centered on domestic slaves, who performed essentially the same tasks as other servants. For fear of slaves, see Origo, "Domestic Enemy."

39. For some evidence of the sexual exploitation of servants in Venice, see Ruggiero, *Boundaries of Eros,* 40–41, 107–8, and passim.

40. ASV, MC, Deliberazioni, register 22 (Ursa), fols. 47v–48r. The law, which was passed at a time when, after one hundred years of flux, the patriciate was becoming "a closed caste," contains some qualifications (see Lane, "Enlargement," 241–42; Stanley Chojnacki, "In Search of the Venetian Patriciate: Families and Factions in the Fourteenth Century," in Hale, *Renaissance Venice,* 47–90; and idem, "Marriage Legislation and Patrician Society in Fifteenth-Century Venice," in *Law, Custom, and the Social Fabric: Essays in Honor of Bryce Lyon,* ed. Bernard S. Bachrach and David Nicholas [Kalamazoo, 1990], 167).

41. For the sense of honor (and profit) among the merchant patricians of Renaissance Italy, see, among others, Benjamin Z. Kedar, *Merchants in Crisis: Genoese and Venetian Men of Affairs and the Fourteenth-Century Depression* (New Haven, 1976); Christian Bec, *Les marchands écrivains: Affaires et humanisme à Florence, 1375–1434* (Paris, 1967), esp. 20, 57, 63–64; and Ugo Tucci, "Il patrizio veneziano mercante e umanista," in *Venezia centro di mediazione tra oriente e occidente (secoli XV–XVI): Aspetti e problemi,* ed. Hans-Georg Beck, Manoussos Manoussacas, and Agostino Pertusi, 2 vols. (Florence, 1977), 1:335–57. For the household as the repository of honor, the best evidence comes from Leon Battista Alberti's treatise *I libri della famiglia.* There are few extant Venetian examples of such treatises; see, however, the fourteenth-century merchant's guide known as the *Zibaldone da Canal,* which includes, in addition to practical advice about trade, a number of aphorisms (see Alfredo Stussi, ed., *Zibaldone da Canal: Manoscritto mercantile del sec. XIV* [Venice, 1967]). The merchants' mentality is at least partially evoked in Frederic C. Lane, *Andrea Barbarigo: Merchant of Venice, 1418–1449* (Baltimore, 1944); Iris Origo, *The Merchant of Prato: Francesco di Marco Datini, 1335–1410* (New York, 1957); and Armando Sapori, *Le marchand italien au Moyen Age: Conferences et bibliographie* (Paris, 1952).

42. Ferro, vol. 2, tome 3, 130–37; Robert Finlay, *Politics in Renaissance Venice* (New Brunswick, 1980), 210–15.

43. Ferro, vol. 5, tome 10, 43–47.

44. The 1541 capitulary, printed as appendix B of this book, is in ASV, Censori, busta 1, capitulary dated 1541–1790, fols. 1v–3v. The chapters are cited either in the text or in the notes below.

45. For this wedding custom, see Francesco Sansovino, *Venetia città nobilissima et singolare, descritta in XIIII libri* (1663; reprint, Farnborough, England, 1968), 401.

46. The 1556 capitulary also warned "fanti, servitori, et barcharuoli" not to expose "le parte dis'honeste" (ASV, Censori, busta 1, capitulary dated 1541–1790, fol. 14r).

47. For crimes committed in boats, see Ruggiero, *Boundaries of Eros,* 101; and idem, *Violence,* 119.

48. ASV, Censori, busta 1, capitulary dated 1541–1790, fols. 1v–3v, chs. 6, 11, 15.

49. In 1514 two boatmen at the ferry station at the Ponte della Paglia apparently assisted some escapees from the prisons. The Council of Ten ordered the traghetto to move further down the riva (see ASV, Consiglio dei Dieci, Criminali, register 2, fols. 129v–130r).

50. ASV, Censori, busta 1, capitulary dated 1541–1790, fols. 1v–3v, chs. 17, 19, 18, 14, 21.

51. Ibid., ch. 9. For comparative purposes, see the discussion of municipal regulation

of domestic labor in German cities in Merry E. Wiesner, *Working Women in Renaissance Germany* (New Brunswick, 1986), 83–92.

52. ASV, MC, Deliberazioni, register 25 (Deda), fols. 184r–184v.

53. ASV, Compilazione delle Leggi, Serie Prima, busta 301, "Padroni e Servi," fols. 276r–276v. See also ASV, Signori di Notte al Civil, busta 1, capitulary A, fol. 128r.

54. See Raimondo Morozzo della Rocca and Maria Francesca Tiepolo, "Cronologia veneziana del Cinquecento," in *La civiltà veneziana del Rinascimento* (Florence, 1958), 221–22. For fistfights, see Robert C. Davis, *The War of the Fists: Popular Culture and Public Violence in Late Renaissance Venice* (New York, 1994).

55. These capitularies are found in ASV, Censori, busta 1, capitulary dated 1541–1790, fols. 11v–14r, 36v–38r, 58r–60v.

56. Ibid., fol. 52r.

57. See the essays in Manfredo Tafuri, ed., *"Renovatio urbis": Venezia nell'età di Andrea Gritti (1523–1538)* (Rome, 1984); and Edward Muir, *Civic Ritual in Renaissance Venice* (Princeton, 1981), 162–64.

58. Renzo Derosas, "Moralità e giustizia a Venezia nel '500–'600: Gli esecutori contro la bestemmia," in *Stato, società e giustizia nella Repubblica Veneta (sec. XV–XVIII)*, ed. Gaetano Cozzi (Rome, 1980), 431–528, esp. 444; Roberta Viaro, "La magistratura degli esecutori contro la bestemmia nel XVI secolo" (Tesi di laurea, Università degli Studi di Padova, 1969–70).

59. See John Martin, *Venice's Hidden Enemies: Italian Heretics in a Renaissance City* (Berkeley, 1993), 51–70.

60. See ASV, MC, Deliberazioni, register 26 (Diana), fols. 165v–166r.

61. The capitulary of 1541 was apparently also republished in 1558. The letters *mv* stand for *more veneto*. The Venetian year began on 1 March; hence, the date according to our calendar for a document dated 12 February 1555mv would be 12 February 1556.

62. ASV, Censori, busta 1, capitulary dated 1541–1790, fol. 11v.

63. "L'insolentia et tirannia de servitori, et massare, ch'usano nelle case et contra gli loro patroni" (ibid., fol. 58r).

64. The capitulary of 1556 only dealt with male servants, however, further evidence of the growing concern about their behavior.

65. Ibid., fols. 9r–9v. A printed version can be found in Museo Civico Correr (MCC), Ms. Donà dalle Rose 214, Leggi publiche, fol. 40.

66. ASV, Censori, busta 1, capitulary dated 1541–1790, fols. 9r–9v.

67. Ibid., esp. fol. 13r.

68. Ibid., fols. 58r–60v, chs. 5–6. References to specific chapters of the capitulary are given in the text. According to ch. 4, some servants were taking their rations and selling them. I wish to thank Giovanni Caniato for helping clarify some of these provisions for me.

69. Ibid., ch. 11. It should be noted that the capitulary of 1611 contained no wage controls, nor did other capitularies of the early seventeenth century. For the 1611 capitulary, see ibid., fols. 82r–86r; other early-seventeenth-century statutes can be found in ASV, Compilazione delle Leggi, Serie Prima, busta 301, fols. 174–78, 208–12, and passim.

70. "Non essendo conveniente, chegli patroni siano ridotti à tal miseria, che ogni giorno debbino esser occupati in cercar servitori, et massare" (ASV, Censori, busta 1, capitulary dated 1541–1790, fols. 58r–60v, ch. 4).

71. Again, Glissenti's servant confirms the view that demand for servants exceeded supply.

72. For the extensive literature on the aristocratization of Italian society in the sixteenth century, see chapter 1 above. See also Marvin B. Becker, *Civility and Society in Western Europe, 1300–1600* (Bloomington, 1988); and, for the Veneto, Angelo Ventura, *Nobiltà e popolo nella società veneta del '400 e '500* (Bari, 1964). For male servants as crucial to the aristocratic style of life, see Fairchilds; and Maza.

73. Burke, 140, 161–63.

74. I use the rather unconventional term *masculinization* to make an explicit contrast with the *feminization* of service that occurred in the nineteenth century. See Fairchilds; and Maza.

75. Burke, 150–67.

76. ASV, Censori, busta 1, capitulary dated 1541–1790, fol. 9r.

77. For court procedure and the competence of various courts and magistracies, see Ruggiero, *Violence*; idem, *Boundaries of Eros*; Stefano Piasentini, *"Alla luce della luna": I furti a Venezia, 1270–1403* (Venice, 1992); and Gaetano Cozzi, "La politica del diritto nella repubblica di Venezia," in Cozzi, *Stato, società e giustizia nella Repubblica Veneta (sec. XV–XVIII)*, 146–48.

78. ASV, Censori, busta 3, registers 1–3. The earliest extant register covers the years 1561 to 1569mv, although this cannot have been the first register actually maintained by the censors. Certainly records of their decisions were kept from the time of the office's inception in 1541 but have not survived. Only in 1569 did the notaries assigned to the censors begin to keep complete records of cases, including both summaries of the charges brought against defendants and verdicts; before 1569 they generally recorded only the sentences, seldom indicating the offenses. The second register covers cases heard between April 1570 and June 1591. The third and final extant register covers the period March 1598 to September 1609.

79. Ibid., register 2, fol. 142r.

80. For Scamozzi, see ibid., fol. 203v.

81. The cases involving female plaintiffs are recorded in ibid., fols. 116r–116v, 129v–130r, 153r, 187r.

82. Ibid., register 1, fols. 87v–88r.

83. Ibid., fols. 97r–97v.

84. Ibid., fols. 95v–96r.

85. Ibid., register 2, fols. 46r–46v.

86. Ibid., fols. 116r–116v.

87. Ibid., fols. 15r–15v.

88. Ibid., fols. 159r–160r.

89. Ibid., fols. 6v–7r.

90. Ibid., fols. 95r–96r.

91. Ibid., fols. 3r–3v.

92. Ibid., fols. 27v–28v. This obviously was not Doge Andrea Gritti.

93. An evaluation of accusations based upon the native or immigrant status of defendants is inconclusive largely because the status of 132 individuals cannot be identified. The following table presents the data. Questions of immigration are taken up more fully in chapter 3.

Table N1

Accusations by Immigrant/Native Status

| Type of Accusation | Immigrants No. | Immigrants % | Natives No. | Natives % | Unidentified No. | Unidentified % | Total |
|---|---|---|---|---|---|---|---|
| | Number of Accusations against | | | | | | |
| Breaking contract | 171 | 66.27 | 34 | 13.17 | 53 | 20.54 | 258 |
| *Malam servitutem* | 10 | 41.66 | 9 | 37.50 | 5 | 20.83 | 24 |
| Theft of goods | 105 | 71.91 | 13 | 8.90 | 28 | 19.17 | 146 |
| Destruction of property | 10 | 52.63 | 5 | 26.31 | 4 | 21.05 | 19 |
| Leaving house vulnerable | 16 | 88.88 | 1 | 5.55 | 1 | 5.55 | 18 |
| Strangers in house | 9 | 81.81 | 0 | 0.00 | 2 | 18.18 | 11 |
| Refusing orders | 7 | 77.77 | 0 | 0.00 | 2 | 22.22 | 9 |
| Verbal abuse | 23 | 71.87 | 2 | 6.25 | 7 | 21.87 | 32 |
| Harassment | 14 | 93.33 | 0 | 0.00 | 1 | 6.66 | 15 |
| Physical attack or threat | 16 | 64.00 | 2 | 8.00 | 7 | 28.00 | 25 |
| Corruption of servants | 17 | 73.91 | 2 | 8.69 | 4 | 17.39 | 23 |
| Sex crimes | 99 | 73.33 | 6 | 4.44 | 30 | 22.22 | 135 |
| Miscellaneous | 32 | 50.79 | 2 | 3.17 | 19 | 30.15 | 63 |

*Source:* ASV, Censori, busta 3, registers 1–3.
*Note:* Data are for 523 defendants, of whom 343 (65.58%) were immigrants, 49 (9.36%) were natives, and 132 (25.23%) are unidentified.

94. On the flexibility of Venetian justice, see Ruggiero, *Violence;* idem, *Boundaries of Eros;* Piasentini; and esp. Cozzi, "La politica del diritto," 29, 148–49.
95. ASV, Censori, busta 3, register 3, fols. 20v–21r.
96. Ibid., register 2, fol. 205r.
97. Ibid., fols. 89r–89v, 203v–204v.
98. Ibid., fols. 128v–129r.
99. Ibid., fols. 200v–201r.
100. Ibid., fol. 126r.
101. Ibid., fols. 67v–68r.
102. Ibid., fols. 159r–160r, 156r–156v.
103. Ibid., fols. 216r–216v.
104. Ibid., register 1, fols. 96r–96v.
105. Ibid., register 2, fols. 3v–4r.
106. Ibid., register 1, fols. 88v–89r.
107. Ibid., fols. 95v–96r.
108. Ibid., register 2, fol. 4v.
109. Ibid., fols. 215r–215v. For another decision in which the youth of the defendant affected the sentence, see ibid., fol. 159r.
110. Ibid., fol. 175r.
111. Ibid., fols. 213r–213v.

112. Ibid., fol. 155v.

113. Ibid., fols. 46r–46v.

114. Ibid., fol. 142r.

115. Ibid., register 3, fol. 6r.

116. Ibid., register 2, fols. 28v–29r.

117. Ibid., register 3, fols. 6v–7r. On the use of ritual punishments, see Ruggiero, *Violence*, 1–2.

118. After the whipping, Pietro was to be sent to the galleys for two years; Santa was banished for five. The whippings were carried out on 29 May (ASV, Censori, busta 3, register 2, fols. 99r–99v).

119. Ibid., register 3, fols. 55r–55v.

## Chapter Three   Servants in the Venetian Household

1. "Libera et spatiosa, et sia goduta come la si ritrova al presente" (ASV, NT, busta 1256, notary Cesare Ziliol, unbound testament 12, will dated 23 May 1562).

2. The Venetian family has been studied primarily in order to illustrate the operation of politics and commerce, subjects that traditionally have dominated Venetian historiography. See, among other sources, Stanley Chojnacki, "In Search of the Venetian Patriciate"; idem, "Kinship Ties and Young Patricians in Fifteenth-Century Venice," *Renaissance Quarterly* 38 (1985): 240–70; idem, "Dowries and Kinsmen in Early Renaissance Venice," *Journal of Interdisciplinary History* 4 (1975): 571–600; Bianca Betto, "Linee di politica matrimoniale nella nobiltà veneziana fino al XV secolo: Alcune note genealogiche e l'esempio della famiglia Mocenigo," *Archivio storico italiano* 139 (1981): 3–64; Lane, *Andrea Barbarigo;* Finlay, *Politics in Renaissance Venice;* and James C. Davis, *A Venetian Family and Its Fortune, 1500–1900* (Philadelphia, 1975).

3. For a definition of the household, see Bender.

4. For the dogeship, see Maranini, vol. 1; Cessi, *Storia della Repubblica;* Andrea da Mosto, *I dogi di Venezia nella vita pubblica e privata* (Florence, 1977); see also Edward Muir, "The Doge as *Primus Inter Pares:* Interregnum Rites in Early Sixteenth-Century Venice," in *Essays Presented to Myron P. Gilmore,* ed. Sergio Bertelli and Gloria Ramakus, 2 vols. (Florence, 1978), 1:145–60; and Asa Boholm, *The Doge of Venice: The Symbolism of State Power in the Renaissance* (Gothenburg, 1990).

5. Agostino Pertusi, "*Quedam regalia insignia:* Ricerche sulle insegne del potere ducale a Venezia durante il medioevo," *Studi veneziani* 7 (1965): 3–123; Muir, *Civic Ritual,* 251–89; Bernd Roeck, *Arte per l'anima, arte per lo stato: Un doge del tardo Quattrocento ed i segni delle immagini,* Centro Tedesco di Studi Veneziani, 40 (Venice, 1991), 20–21.

6. See Eugenio Musatti, *Storia della promissione ducale* (1888; reprint, Venice, 1983). For the texts of the earliest promissioni, see Gisella Graziato, ed., *Le promissioni del doge di Venezia dalle origini alla fine del Duecento* (Venice, 1986).

7. Graziato, viii–x, 1–4.

8. Ibid., 19.

9. Ibid., 37.

10. Ibid., 57–58.

11. Cessi, *Deliberazioni,* 2:216.

12. Ibid., 2:212.

13. Ibid., 2:232.

14. For the Querini-Tiepolo conspiracy, see Frederic C. Lane, *Venice: A Maritime Republic* (Baltimore, 1973), 114–17; and Dennis Romano, "The Aftermath of the Querini-Tiepolo Conspiracy in Venice," *Stanford Italian Review* 7 (1987): 147–59. For the threat of signorial rule, see Lane, "Enlargement," 236–74.

15. For Gradenigo's promissione, see Graziato, 132–63.

16. The *milites* first appear in the promissione of Giovanni Dandolo, dated 1280 (ibid., 123).

17. Ibid., 151.

18. Ibid., 151–52, 159.

19. In the fourteenth century the English royal household numbered in the hundreds. Of course these royal households had more functions than those of the doges (see Chris Given-Wilson, *The Royal Household and the King's Affinity: Service, Politics, and Finance in England, 1360–1413* [New Haven, 1986], 39–41, 278).

20. See the promissione of Foscari in MCC, Ms. Provinenze Diverse, 2362/II, Promissione ducale di Francesco Foscari, clauses 64–66; and of Barbarigo in ASV, CI, Doge, busta 157A, clauses 63, 64, 65, 94.

21. BNM, Ms. La. cl. X, 316 (3136), Promissione di Doge Pietro Lando, fols. 12r–13r. The oath refers to "Scudieri, over Donzelli." According to his promissione of 1486, Doge Agostino Barbarigo was still required to maintain twenty scudieri, referred to as "servitorum vel domicellorum" (see Roeck 43 n. 119). According to an eighteenth-century manuscript, the reduction to eighteen scudieri took place in 1522 (see MCC, Ms. Gradenigo 199, Doge, fol. 95r).

22. BNM, Ms. La. cl. X, 316 (3136), fols. 12r–13r.

23. Vecellio, 113v.

24. The treatise was edited and published by Nicolò da Rio as *Notizie d'antiche costumanze, diritti, e doveri de' dogi di Venezia* (Padua, 1840). See also the promissione of Doge Alvise Mocenigo, dated 1570, in BNM, Ms. La. cl. X, 192 (3557), fols. 18r–19v, 31r. For comparative purposes, in the fifteenth century the duke of Ferrara's court numbered around six hundred (see Werner L. Gundersheimer, *Ferrara: The Style of a Renaissance Despotism* [Princeton, 1973], 285–96).

25. "Serve bene spesso al Principe per appoggio, quando nell'andare à Consigli sale, et scende le scale di Palazzo" (Vecellio, 113r–114r. See also Giovanni Grevembroch, *Gli abiti de veneziani di quasi ogni età con diligenza raccolti e dipinti nel secolo XVIII*, 4 vols. [Venice, 1981], 3: no. 1).

26. For the patrician government as a gerontocracy, see Robert Finlay, "The Venetian Republic as a Gerontocracy: Age and Politics in the Renaissance," *Journal of Medieval and Renaissance Studies* 8 (1978): 157–78.

27. Pietro Casola was shown about the Ducal Palace, including the ducal apartments, by a "donzello del prefacto Duce" (see Roeck, 45 n. 127).

28. Vecellio, 114v–115r; see also Grevembroch, 3: nos. 3–6.

29. Grevembroch, 3: no. 2.

30. Da Rio, 31, 34, and passim.

31. His will, with the notice of his wife's dowry of 25 *lire di grossi*, is found in ASV,

PSM, de Citra, Commisssarie, busta 61, Commissaria of Andreas de Varnarussiis, parchment 22, 17 May 1381. For comparative information about dowries, see Romano, *Patricians and Popolani*, 34–36.

32. ASV, CI, Notai, busta 174, notary Giovanni Rizo, fol. 18v. Ventura's wife's will is in ASV, NT, busta 740, notary Alvise Nadal, unbound testament 134.

33. His will is in ASV, NT, busta 1261, notary Cesare Ziliol, unbound testament 868. Information about some other cavaliers and scudieri is found in MCC, Ms. Gradenigo 199, Doge, fols. 304r–307v. Several of the members of the ducal court seem to have been from the terraferma. These posts may have served as a way for the doge to bind some popolani in the subject cities to Venice. For brokers in the Ghetto, see Brian Pullan, *Rich and Poor in Renaissance Venice: The Social Institutions of a Catholic State, to 1620* (Cambridge, Mass., 1971), 549.

34. Archivio Curia Patriarcale, Venezia (hereafter ACPV), Censimenti Parrocchiali (hereafter CP), Sec. XVI–XVII, busta 3, Register of San Provolo, unpaginated (household of Ludovico Million [?], scudier).

35. See BNM, Ms. It. cl. VII, 134 (8035), Cronica Savina, fol. 371r.

36. The text reads, "che sarano al servitio nostro qua in casa al tempo della nostra morte . . . qualche pocho di beneficio da questo nostro Codicillo." Mocenigo's will and codicils are in ASV, NT, busta 1256, notary Cesare Ziliol, unbound testament 12.

37. Muir, *Civic Ritual*, 289–96.

38. ASV, Senato, Terra, register 42, fols. 48v–49r.

39. Ibid., fol. 138r.

40. Ibid., register 52, fols. 86r–86v. The act reads in part, "rappresentando ella massimamente la memoria felicissima d'un principe cotanto benemerito non solamente della nostra, ma di tutta la Republica Christiana."

41. Frederic C. Lane, *Venetian Ships and Shipbuilders of the Renaissance* (Baltimore, 1934), 176. Da Mosto says that the doges maintained, in addition to their personal servants, two camerieri, two staffieri, a chamberlain, and, on the terraferma, three "persone di stalla con 6 cavalli"; however, he gives no citation for these figures (Da Mosto, *I dogi*, xlvi).

42. Finlay, *Politics in Renaissance Venice*, 81–96.

43. Frederic C. Lane, "Family Partnerships and Joint Ventures," in *Venice and History: The Collected Papers of Frederic C. Lane* (Baltimore, 1966), 36–55; Davis, *A Venetian Family*, 85–86.

44. Davis, *A Venetian Family*, 7–8.

45. The ledger book is MCC, Ms. Provinenze Diverse, C 912/II.

46. For the Priuli family, see R. Fulin, "Girolamo Priuli e i suoi diarii," *Archivio veneto* 22 (1881): 137–54; and Lane, "Family Partnerships." See also MCC, Ms. Cicogna 2892 (with older number 3784), Arbore della nobilissima famiglia Priuli. Part of the diary of Girolamo Priuli has been published as *I diarii di Girolamo Priuli*, ed. Arturo Segre and Roberto Cessi, Rerum Italicarum Scriptores 24, pt. 3 (Bologna, 1912–38); see also Finlay, *Politics in Renaissance Venice*, 8–10.

47. MCC, Ms. Provinenze Diverse C 912/II, fols. 111, lxxi (the left-hand pages of the ledger have Arabic numeration; the facing right-hand pages have a corresponding Roman numeral). For the widespread practice of renting housing, see Laura Megna, "Comportamenti abitativi del patriziato veneziano (1582–1740)," *Studi veneziani*, n.s., 22 (1991): 272, 278.

48. On Girolamo's emancipation, see Fulin, 140.

49. Lane, "Family Partnerships," 39–40.

50. In one entry dated 1523, the sons refer to a "libreto tenuto de mano del quondam miser nostro padre per conto di salarii di servitori" (MCC, Ms. Provinenze Diverse, C 912/II, fol. 105).

51. Ibid., fol. 9.

52. According to Fulin, Girolamo was born on 26 January 1476 (Fulin, 137).

53. Only one child, Marina, is mentioned, but two wet nurses are listed. The other child was a son, Piero, also called Perin (MCC, Ms. Provinenze Diverse, C 912/II, fol. xviii).

54. Fulin, 139.

55. The fifty-eight ducats were for only ten months since on 4 January Lorenzo left for Cremona.

56. MCC, Ms. Provinenze Diverse, C 912/II, fols. 18, xviii, 27.

57. Ibid., fol. 58; the folio includes an entry "per fornir la Camera de Vincenzo." The other accounts appear on fol. lviii.

58. Catarina (also called Catarinela) first appears in the ledger in 1508, with the notation "s'pta," which I take to be short for "scripta," indicating indenture, after her name (ibid., fol. 37).

59. Ibid., fol. 105.

60. The children were sons Piero, Constantin, Andrea, and Bernardo and daughters Isabeta "granda," Isabeta "piccola," and Andriana. Perhaps one of the two Isabetas was an adoptee or even the Isabeta listed in 1511 as the daughter of the wet nurse.

61. Ibid., fol. lxxxvii.

62. Ibid., fol. lxviii.

63. On one level, of course, all servant keeping is culturally determined. It was in fact the cultural prejudice against upper-class women's nursing their own children that led to the hiring of nurses.

64. Although Lorenzo's masculine plural "mei famegli" may conceal women servants, none appear in entries for the years 1515–17, when he actually listed his servants by name. When Francesco Tiepolo drafted his second will, in 1611, he allowed that if any of his daughters did not wish to become a nun, but wished instead to live with her brothers as a spinster, she was to be given two hundred ducats a year "and a female servant" (see David Chambers and Brian Pullan, eds., *Venice: A Documentary History, 1450–1630* [Oxford, 1992], 249).

65. But when he drew up his will in 1546, Girolamo had at least two male servants and a massara named Maria. He also mentioned a certain "Suor Christina," a *conversa* (lay sister) at the convent of Ogni Santi, who "fù mia Massara." By this time Girolamo's brothers were dead, and he may have lived alone. This would have necessitated the maintenance of a female housekeeper. The will is in ASV, CI, Miscellanea Notai Diversi, busta 1, notary Avidio Branco; it is the only will in the fascicle.

66. For a survey of these books, see Lane, *Andrea Barbarigo,* 140–44. On the absence of family diaries in Venice, see James S. Grubb, "Memory and Identity: Why Venetians Didn't Keep *Ricordanze,*" *Renaissance Studies* 8 (1994): 375–87.

67. Barbarigo's career is summarized in Lane, *Andrea Barbarigo,* 15–33; on his renting a slave, see ibid., 21–22.

68. ASV, RPC, RBG, busta 42, register 4, ledger B; Lane calls the first unnumbered page a flyleaf. For Cristina's dowry, see Lane, *Andrea Barbarigo,* 28–29.

69. ASV, RPC, RBG, busta 42, register 4, ledger B, fol. 21 left. Facing pages bear the same Arabic numeral.

70. Ibid., fol. 29 right; see also Lane, *Andrea Barbarigo*, 191.

71. ASV, RPC, RBG, busta 42, register 4, ledger B, fols. 31 left, 31 right.

72. Ibid., fols. 66 left, 107 left.

73. By comparison, Marino Contarini, the builder of the magnificent Cà D'Oro, bequeathed five slaves to his wife, Lucia, in his will of March 1441 (see ASV, CI, Notai, busta 229, notary Leonardo de Valle, paginated parchment protocol, fols. 66r–66v). For further information about the servants in Contarini's household, see Richard J. Goy, *The House of Gold: Building a Palace in Medieval Venice* (Cambridge, 1992), 43–44.

74. On the slave trade at its height in Venice, see Vincenzo Lazari, *Del traffico e delle condizioni degli schiavi in Venezia nei tempi di mezzo* (Turin, 1862), 7, 34; and Alessandro Luzio and Rodolfo Renier, "Buffoni, nani e schiavi dei Gonzaga ai tempi d'Isabella D'Este," *Nuova antologia*, 3rd ser., 35 (1891): 137.

75. Lane, *Andrea Barbarigo*, 33–39, 43.

76. The servant contracts are found in ASV, RPC, RBG, busta 43, register 5 (the journal is unpaginated, but the servant contracts are recorded on what would be fol. 2r; the offices are recorded on the back flyleaf). The births and deaths of the children are in ibid., register 6, flyleaf (register 6 is paginated with Arabic numerals on the left and Roman numerals on the right).

77. Cristina's will is in ASV, NT, busta 1238, notary Tomaso Tomei, testament 158; in it she states that Lena "al prexentte sta con mi." See also the expenses for "Lena nostra bailla" in ASV, RPC, RBG, busta 43, register 6, fol. 92.

78. ASV, RPC, RBG, busta 43, register 5, fol. 2r.

79. Ibid., registers 5, fol. 2r, and 6, fol. 92.

80. Ibid., register 5, fol. 2r.

81. Ibid., register 6, fol. 92.

82. Ibid., register 5, entry dated 1 February 1478mv.

83. Ibid., register 5, entries dated 28 June 1473, 20 January 1473mv, 21 December 1474, 31 March 1475, 28 June 1476, 19 July 1476, 2 March 1477, 3 October 1478, 3 February 1480mv, 26 January 1481mv, and 1 March 1482; and register 6, fol. 161 and passim.

84. Ibid., busta 43, register 8, and busta 44, registers 9, 10. Frederic Lane (*Andrea Barbarigo*, 144) could not identify register 10, but an act dated 9 June 1525 on an unnumbered page at the front indicates that it must have belonged to Andrea. Andrea's book is examined in chapter 4 below as part of the analysis of servants' contracts and the geographic origins of servants.

85. Lane, *Andrea Barbarigo*, 39–40.

86. ASV, RPC, RBG, busta 43, register 8, entries dated 20 July 1501, 28 February 1508mv, 23 November 1518.

87. There is a cryptic reference in an entry that reads in part, "A chassa contadi per passar tragetto de ano uno mi [?] el fameio" (ibid., 29 February 1519mv).

88. The origins and salaries of these servants are analyzed more fully in chapter 4 below.

89. Lane, *Andrea Barbarigo*, 144.

90. Ibid., 40–43. For the dowry and the move back to San Barnaba, see ASV, RPC, RBG, busta 45, register 12, flysheet with entry dated 19 November 1565, and entry dated 23 July 1552 on unnumbered page.

91. ASV, RPC, RBG, busta 45, register 12, entry dated 26 February 1559mv.

92. Ibid., entry dated 28 February 1560mv.

93. Ibid., busta 47, unnumbered register with a "3" in pencil, section entitled "Spese de Casa," entries for 29 March, 18 and 24 May 1569.

94. Richard Goldthwaite, speaking of Italy generally, notes that in the sixteenth century more servants were needed to accommodate a new "style of social life within the home and to tend to the greater burden of household chores occasioned by more furnishings and new practices such as the use of carriages and the keeping of horses" (Goldthwaite, *Wealth and the Demand for Art*, 240).

95. Antonio Barbarigo stated that Zuane de Martin "servi fuor de Casa in pope" (ASV, RPC, RBG, busta 45, register 12, entry dated 26 February 1559mv. For another example, see ASV, AC, Raspe, register 3677, fols. 191v–192v).

96. Giorgio Gianighian and Paola Pavanini, *Dietro i palazzi: Tre secoli di architettura minore a Venezia, 1492–1803* (Venice, 1984), insert entitled "Ricostruzione . . . alla fine del Cinquecento," located between pp. 48 and 49.

97. ASV, Notarile, Atti (hereafter NA), busta 2549, fasc. 8, notary Girolamo Canal, parchment dated 4 February 1530mv.

98. Megna, 299–300 n. 237.

99. Ibid., 300–301.

100. See ACPV, CP, busta 3, San Benetto, fols. 3r, 4v, 5r.

101. ASV, CI, Notai, busta 231, notary Giovanni Vendramino, paginated parchment protocol, fols. 3r–3v.

102. ASV, NT, busta 870, notary Petrus de Rubeis, paginated parchment protocol, fols. 19r–19v.

103. Ibid., busta 190, notary Girolamo Canal, unbound testament 209. For another example, see the will of Ioannes Maria Giorgio in ibid., busta 889, notary Matteo Soliani, unbound testament 176.

104. See Juergen Schulz, "The Houses of Titian, Arentino, and Sansovino," in *Titian: His World and His Legacy*, ed. David Rosand (New York, 1982), 87.

105. Domenico Roberto Paolillo and Carlo Dalla Santa, *Il Palazzo Dolfin Manin a Rialto: Storia di un'antica dimora veneziana* (Venice, n.d.), 12 and pl. xv.

106. ASV, NA, busta 428, notary Rocco de Benedetto, protocol, fol. 164v. A block of apartments designed by Antonio Abbondi, known as Scarpagnino, for the scuola grande of San Rocco included "servant quarters in the attic" (see Manfredo Tafuri, *Venice and the Renaissance*, trans. Jessica Levine [Cambridge, Mass., 1989], 92).

107. ASV, NT, busta 411, notary Alessandro Falcon, protocol, fols. 70r–71v. Indeed, Dolfin left Iacomo use of a room for life.

108. Goy, 53.

109. ASV, NA, busta 436, notary Rocco de Benedetto, fols. 444v–448r. In the late fourteenth century, the male slave of Bishop Domenico Gaffaro of Eraclea slept in the same room as his master (see Giuseppe Tassini, *Alcune delle più clamorose condanne capitali eseguite in Venezia sotto la repubblica* [Venice, 1892], 25).

110. ASV, NT, busta 191, notary Girolamo Canal, testament 475. For another example, see, ASV, NA, busta 425, notary Rocco de Benedetto, pt. 2, fol. 153v.

111. Lanteri, 17–18.

112. For cittadini, see Pullan, *Rich and Poor*, 100–105; Mary Neff, "A Citizen in the Service of the Patrician State: The Career of Zaccaria de' Freschi," *Studi veneziani*, n.s., 5

(1981): 33–61; idem, "Chancellery Secretaries in Venetian Politics and Society, 1480–1533" (Ph.D. diss., University of California, Los Angeles, 1985); Andrea Zannini, *Burocrazia e burocrati a Venezia in età moderna: I cittadini originari (sec. XVI–XVIII)* (Venice, 1993); Stephen R. Ell, "Citizenship and Immigration in Venice, 1305 to 1500" (Ph.D. diss., University of Chicago, 1976); Matteo Casini, "Realtà e simboli del cancellier grande veneziano in età moderna (sec. XVI–XVII)," *Studi veneziani*, n.s., 22 (1991): 195–251; and Giuseppe Trebbi, "La società veneziana," in *Storia di Venezia*, vol. 6, *Dal Rinascimento al Barocco*, ed. Gaetano Cozzi and Paolo Prodi (Rome, 1994), 162–68.

113. "Quasi il Cancelliero rappresenti il doge del popolo" (quoted in Casini, 224).

114. Neff, "Chancellery Secretaries," 68–77; for the grand chancellor's salary, see ibid., 184.

115. ACPV, CP, busta 3, register 2, San Giovanni Novo. Surian became grand chancellor in 1586 (see Neff, "Chancellery Secretaries," 513).

116. Emmanuele Antonio Cicogna, *Delle inscrizioni veneziane*, 6 vols. (1824–53; reprint, Bologna, 1970–83), 4:19; Giuseppe Ellero, *L'archivio IRE: Inventari dei fondi antichi degli ospedali e luoghi pii di Venezia* (Venice, 1987), 169. See also Neff, "Chancellery Secretaries," 547–50.

117. Much of this information can be gleaned from Ellero, 169–72. For Angela's dowry, see Spinelli's will in Archivio degli Istituzioni di Ricovero e di Educazione, Venezia (hereafter IRE), Der E 195, fasc. 1, will dated 23 May 1588 with later codicils.

118. Ibid., fasc. 5, "Libro di debitori et creditori et cassa di contadi di Miser Agustin Spinelli." Facing folio pages bear the same Arabic numeral.

119. Ibid., fols. 3 left and right, 5 left and right, 18 left and right.

120. Ibid., fols. 17 left and right, 19 left and right, 24 left and right, 40 left and right, 43 left and right.

121. Ibid., fols. 63 left and right.

122. Ibid., fols. 68 left and right, 72 left and right, 82 left and right, 90 left and right.

123. Ibid., fols. 91 left and right.

124. Ibid., fols. 105 left and right; see also 97 left and right, 110 left and right, 123 left and right, 135 left and right, 144 left and right. For the promissory note and receipt, see ibid., fasc. 3, fol. 9r.

125. The dynamics of master-servant relations are treated more fully in chapter 6 below.

126. "Sapendo che offitio di Christiano è rendere bene per male" (IRE, Der E 195, fasc. 1, will dated 23 May 1588 with later codicils.

127. For much of my discussion of Lombardo I follow Cathy Santore, "Julia Lombardo, 'Somtuosa Meretrize': A Portrait by Property," *Renaissance Quarterly* 41 (1988): 44–83. Nowhere does Santore note the family's cittadino status. For the phrase "cittadina vinetiana," see IRE, Der E 131, fasc. 3, parchment dated 4 September 1559; on the reverse a notation reads, "N.o 74 Scrita del Mad.a Angelica con batista pellezaro." See also Neff, "Chancellery Secretaries," 462–63. The most famous Venetian courtesan, Veronica Franco, was also of cittadino background; see the excellent study by Margaret F. Rosenthal, *The Honest Courtesan: Veronica Franco, Citizen and Writer in Sixteenth-Century Venice* (Chicago, 1992).

128. Santore, 45–54.

129. Ibid., 79.

130. IRE, Der E 130, fasc. 1.

131. The contract is found in ibid., fasc. 3, act dated 9 August 1568. On the reverse a notation reads, "Scrito de Orsalina Sabato N.o 96."

132. Ibid., act dated 4 September 1559.

133. For Veronica Franco's servants, see Rosenthal, 81–82.

134. These acts are published in *Leggi e memorie venete sulla prostituzione fino alla caduta della republica* (Venice, 1870–72), 100–103. An earlier law of the Council of Ten dated 27 August 1500 forbade prostitutes or procuresses from housing any girls twelve years of age or under (ibid., 89; see also 276–77, 282–84).

135. Ibid., 102–3.

136. Pullan, *Rich and Poor,* 556–57.

137. Gino Fogolari, "Jacobello del Fiore e la sua famiglia (nuovi documenti)," *Archivio veneto,* 5th ser., 34–35 (1944): 33–50. Iacobello's second wife had had a dowry of five hundred ducats in her first marriage; it is unlikely that she brought less than that in her marriage to Iacobello. His will is printed in Michele Caffi, "Giacomello del Fiore: Pittore veneziano del sec. XV," *Archivio storico italiano,* 4th ser., 6 (1880): 402–13.

138. ASV, CI, Notai, busta 25, notary Marcus Basilio, protocol 1415–21, act dated 26 July 1418. See also Ruggiero, *Boundaries of Eros,* 150–51. Ivan Pederin notes that in fifteenth-century Spalato, "Talvolta non si notava la differenza tra figlia adottiva e serva" ("Appunti e notizie su Spalato nel Quattrocento," *Studi veneziani,* n.s., 21 [1991]: 395).

139. ASV, AC, Raspe, register 3652, fol. 78v.

140. ASV, CI, Notai, busta 24, notary Rolandinus de Bernardis, protocol 1406–32, fol. 62r.

141. Ibid., paginated protocol 1409–24, fols. 38v–39r. For another adoption agreement, see ibid., busta 174, notary Cristoforo Rizo, protocol 1414–19, act dated 18 July 1417.

142. See ibid., busta 174, notary Giovanni Rizo, protocol 1432–42, fol. 14r; and ASV, NA, busta 434, notary Rocco de Benedetto, protocol, fols. 313v–314r.

143. ASV, CI, Notai, busta 24, notary Rolandinus de Bernardis, protocol 1409–24, fol. 48r.

144. Ibid., fol. 26r. For another adoption agreement, see IRE, Der E 92, fasc. 2, parchment dated 15 May 1543.

145. Ferro, vol. 1, tome 1, 114. See also Ruggiero, *Boundaries of Eros,* 198 n. 7. For examples of the phrases used in conjunction, see ASV, NA, busta 445, notary Rocco de Benedetto, protocol, fols. 359v–360r; and ASV, NT, busta 360, notary Domenico Filosofi, unbound testament 13.

146. ASV, NT, busta 553, notary Rolandinus de Bernardis, unbound testament 317.

147. ASV, NA, busta 3345, notary Giovanni Maria Cavanis, protocol, fol. 321r.

148. In 1436 the government encouraged pious bequests to the hospital of Santa Maria della Pietà by requiring notaries to encourage testators to leave legacies to the hospital (see *Capitulare notariorum: Non tabellionibus solùm, verùm et iudicibus, Advocatis, causarum Procuratoribus, et aliis quislibet in Veneto foro versantibus* [Venice, 1591], 19–20).

149. ASV, NA, busta 435, notary Rocco de Benedetto, protocol, fols. 154r–155r; ASV, NT, busta 870, notary Petrus de Rubeis, protocol of wills, fol. 14r. Francesco Contarini bequeathed one hundred ducats to the dowry of "Diane quae educata fuit in domo mea," noting that that sum included her salary and some money she had lent him. He also left her six ducats as reward for her service during his illness.

150. The original reads, "quia fuit bona, fidelis, et honesta iuvenis in domo sua" (ASV, NA, busta 434, notary Rocco de Benedetto, protocol, fols. 313v–314r).

151. Ibid., busta 445, notary Rocco de Benedetto, protocol, fols. 359v–360r.

152. Caffi, 412. It is important to note that adoption did not necessarily imply legal obligation. Madile Gambier cites L. Manin's *Giurisprudenza veneta* as stating that the practice of taking in "figli d'anima" was a "vincolo di sola beneficenza ed affetto, che per sè non produceva conseguenze legali" (see Madile Gambier, "La donna e la giustizia penale veneziana nel XVIII secolo," in *Stato, società, e giustizia nella Repubblica Veneta [sec. XV–XVIII]*, ed. Gaetano Cozzi [Rome, 1980], 553 n. 76).

153. Lorenzo Lotto, *Il "Libro di spese diverse" con aggiunta di lettere e d'altri documenti*, ed. Pietro Zampetti (Venice, 1969). I wish to thank Professor Terisio Pignatti for bringing this important account book to my attention.

154. Ibid., 304–5.

155. Ibid., xxxvii, xxxix, xliii.

156. Ibid., 301.

157. Ibid., xxxiii, 93, 302.

158. Ibid., 126–27.

159. Ibid., 140–41.

160. "Quale me servite ne la mia infermità in casa del dito misser Bortolamio" (ibid., xxxviii–xxxix, 218–19).

161. Ibid., 154–56.

162. Ibid., 158–59, 198–99. Paolo's father agreed to pay Lotto thirty ducats and to pay for the boy's upkeep, as well as to supply him with a bed to sleep in alone.

163. Ibid., 110, 204–5.

164. "Tolto per servicij de casa, a parechiar e tenir netto et cocinar e spender et imparar l'arte mia" (ibid., 142–44).

165. Ibid., 49,52.

166. Ibid., 33–35. Rocha Contrada is the present-day Arcevia.

167. Ibid., 18–19, 166–67, 31. I have not included every apprentice or assistant in Lotto's service in this summary. Paolo was hired to "imparar l'arte et per servirme, sì ne li comuni servicij da fidele et acurato servitor, come ne le cose de l'arte."

168. For Zampetti's opinion, see ibid., xxviii.

169. See Benvenuto Cellini, *La vita di Benvenuto di M.o Giovanni Cellini fiorentino scritta (per lui medesimo) in Firenze*, in *Opere di Baldassare Castiglione, Giovanni della Casa, Benvenuto Cellini*, ed. Carlo Cordié (Milan, 1960) (hereafter cited as Cellini, *Vita*).

170. Maria Ciampi, "Notizie storiche riguardanti la vita e le opere di Palma il Giovane," *Archivio veneto*, 5th ser., 66 (1960): 1–19; Nicola Ivanoff and Pietro Zampetti, *Giacomo Negretti detto Palma il Giovane* (Bergamo, 1980); Stefania Mason Rinaldi, *Palma il Giovane: L'opera completa* (Milan, 1984).

171. ACPV, CP, busta 2, register 4, Santa Croce.

172. "Mi dole non aver molto per mostrar il moltto amor che li porto" (Ivanoff and Zampetti, 428). Francesco Sansovino referred to Cima da Conegliano as Giovanni Bellini's "allievo" (cited in Peter Humfrey, *Cima da Conegliano* [Cambridge, 1983], 180).

173. Ivanoff and Zampetti, 428.

174. The rather humble artist Cima da Conegliano, who was active at the end of the fifteenth century and in the early sixteenth century, had, according to a tax declaration

of 1516, a household made up of himself, his wife, six children, and a fantesca (see Humfrey, 207. See also V. Botteon and A. Aliprandi, *Ricerche intorno alla vita e alle opere di Giambattista Cima* [1893; reprint, Bologna, 1977], 34, 47).

175. See, among others, John Larner, *Culture and Society in Italy, 1290–1420* (New York, 1971), 264–348; Anthony Blunt, *Artistic Theory in Italy, 1450–1600* (Oxford, 1956), 48–57.

176. On workshops, see Humfrey, 61–69; Felton Gibbons, "Practices in Giovanni Bellini's Workshop," *Pantheon* 23 (1965): 146–55; M. Roy Fisher, *Titian's Assistants during the Later Years* (New York, 1977), esp. i–xxii; and Bruce Cole, *The Renaissance Artist at Work: From Pisano to Titian* (New York, 1983), 13–30. One of the crucial criteria for establishing one's right to cittadino originario status was that one had not engaged in the mechanical arts (see Pullan, *Rich and Poor*, 103). For the similarity between artists and other craftsmen, see Cole, 13.

177. ASV, NA, busta 428, notary Rocco de Benedetto, protocol, fols. 59r–59v.

178. "Per conto di mercede che ella potesse dimandarli di servitù ch'havesse fatto in casa sua il tempo che vi è stata." Valentin in turn agreed not to seek repayment for the expenses he had incurred for her upkeep (ibid., busta 431, notary Rocco de Benedetto, protocol, fols. 286r–286v).

179. Ibid., busta 433, notary Rocco de Benedetto, protocol, fols. 492v–493r.

180. "Non può essere maestro chi non è prima discepolo: e però non avere a sdegno servire a l'arte che vuoli imparare, ché servendo s'impara" (Paolo Da Certaldo, *Libro di buoni costumi,* ed. Alfredo Schiaffini [Florence, 1945], 140).

In his *Libro dell'arte,* Cennino Cennini wrote to apprentices, "Adunque, voi che con animo gentile sete amadori di questa virtù, principalmente all'arte venite, adornatevi prima di questo vestimento: cioè amore, timore, ubbidienza, e perseveranza." He also advised, "E quanto più tosto puoi, incomincia a metterti sotto la guida del maestro a imparare; e quanto più tardi puoi, dal maestro ti parti" (see Cennino D'Andrea Cennini, *Il libro dell'arte o trattato della pittura,* ed. Fernando Tempesti [Milan, 1984], 31).

181. For the terms *famulus* and *discipulus* used in conjunction, see Keith Christiansen, *Gentile da Fabriano* (Ithaca, 1982), 164.

182. "Item dimitto illi qui serviet mihi in mea egritudine" (ASV, NT, busta 552, notary Rolandinus de Bernardis, unbound testament 119).

183. Ibid., busta 86, notary Vettore Solimano, unbound testament 32.

184. Ibid., busta 832, notary Alberto Pertempo, unbound testament dated 8 May 1408. For other examples of the poor receiving service, see ibid., busta 889, notary Matteo Soliani, testament 91, and busta 411, notary Alessandro Falcon, testament 271.

185. Ibid., busta 595, notary Angelo Locatello, protocol, fol. 2r.

186. Daniele Beltrami, *Storia della popolazione di Venezia dalla fine del secolo XVI alla caduta della repubblica* (Padua, 1954), 9–27; Contento.

187. Paolo Preto, "Peste e demografia," 97–98.

188. Andrea Zannini, "Un censimento inedito del primo Seicento e la crisi demografica ed economica di Venezia," *Studi veneziani,* n.s. 26 (1993): 87–116.

189. MCC, Ms. Donà dalle Rose 53, Istoria veneta, fols. 156r–159v.

190. Contento, 19:180–81.

191. The instruction reads, "Avertendo nelle case delli ARTEFICI, che alla casella de Servitori và il .o." The census organizers did recognize that female servants (massere) could be found in artisan households (see MCC, Ms. Donà dalle Rose 351, Anagrafi, quaderno en-

titled "S. Polo 1607"; also printed in Contento, 20:222–23. For census forms as indicators of the social system, see Burke, 27–39).

192. MCC, Mss. Donà dalle Rose 351, fascicle for the parish of San Polo. For example, a male servant was listed in the house of Dominico calegher. But the priest then changed the "1" to a "0" and added a "1" under the box for men aged eighteen to fifty. The same thing occurred for the households of Dominico tentor and others. See other examples in the fascicles for the parishes of San Ubaldo (households of Salvador galliner, Zuan Maria botter) and Sant'Aponal (households of Constantin capeler, Iacomo bombaser).

193. See Brian Pullan, "Wage-Earners and the Venetian Economy 1550–1630," in Crisis and Change in the Venetian Economy in the Sixteenth and Seventeenth Centuries, ed. Brian Pullan (London, 1968), 159–60. Pullan is not sure, however, whether wages improved for less skilled workers. See also Richard Tilden Rapp, Industry and Economic Decline in Seventeenth-Century Venice (Cambridge, Mass., 1976), 98; and Zannini, "Censimento," 103.

194. Rapp, 96–106; Lane, Venice, 400–402.

195. In the aftermath of the plague, the government generally tried to limit wage increases (see Pullan, "Wage-Earners," 164–66).

196. Zannini, "Censimento," 99–100. Again, Glissenti, writing in this period, noted that the demand for servants exceeded the supply.

197. Beltrami, 23–24; John Bossy, "The Counter-Reformation and the People of Catholic Europe," Past and Present, no. 47 (1970): 51–70.

198. ACPV, CP, buste 1–3 (the registers are not paginated; in all cases I refer to my own informal pagination). For an excellent thesis utilizing these records, see Michela Dal Borgo, "Venezia alla fine del 1500: La zona di San Zaccaria" (Tesi di laurea, Università degli Studi di Venezia, 1977–78); see also Sylvie Favalier, "Le attività lavorative in una parrocchia del centro di Venezia (San Polo—secolo XVI)," Studi veneziani, n.s., 9 (1985): 187–97; Monica Elena Chojnacka, "City of Women: Gender, Family, and Community in Venice, 1540–1630" (Ph.D. diss., Stanford University, 1994); and Paolo Ulvioni, Il gran castigo di Dio: Carestia ed epidemie a Venezia e nella terraferma, 1628–1632 (Milan, 1989), 16–17.

199. The difficulties of working in the Archivio Curia Patriarcale in 1988–89 made a more systematic and thorough analysis of the status animarum records impossible. I selected parishes in different parts of the city and parishes with smaller populations.

200. A few servants lived on their own. Ulvioni (17) reaches slightly different totals: San Benetto, 504; San Basilio, 1,643; San Provolo, 875; San Zan Degolà, 625.

201. Dal Borgo found for the same period that servants made up 9.79 percent of the population of San Giovanni Novo and 17.24 percent of the population of San Severo (see Dal Borgo, "Venezia alla fine del 1500," 230–31). The same phenomenon is observed in the 1642 census. Few servants were employed in households in the area around the Arsenal, a poor part of the city. According to Richard Rapp, 730 Arsenal worker families employed just 32 servants (Rapp, 81). According to Robert Davis, the 4 Arsenal parishes employed about 80 live-in maids, compared with 6,500 for the entire city (Robert C. Davis, Shipbuilders of the Venetian Arsenal: Workers and Workplace in the Preindustrial City [Baltimore, 1991], 233 n. 73).

202. ACPV, CP, busta 3, San Basilio, fols. 4v, 6r, 6v, 8v, 9v, 16v.

203. Ibid., busta 2, San Zan Degolà, fols. 1r, 3v, 4v, 5r.

204. Ibid., busta 3, San Basilio, fol. 23r.

205. Ibid., San Provolo, fol. 4v.

206. Ibid., San Benetto, fols. 5r–5v.

207. For other examples, see chapter 7 below.

208. And one of the noble households was headed, not by a Venetian noble, but by a terraferma noble(ACPV, CP, busta 2, San Zan Degolà, fol. 6r [household of the cavalier Signor Pietro Mont'Albano]).

209. According to Megna, in the period she studied (1582–1740) there were no "residenza patrizia di proprietà nella . . . contrada di San Provolo." That means that all the patricians resident in the parish rented their housing (see Megna, 306).

210. Chojnacka's figures indicate that 9 percent of patrician households were without servants (Chojnacka, 235).

211. These forms of address include *magnifico, eccellente, signor, miser, ser,* and *maistro,* as well as titles for priests and widows. As Dal Borgo notes for the parishes she examined, the title *messer,* "si trovano a capo di una azienda artigianale a condizione familiare abbastanza vasta, con più di due-tre persone come lavoranti e/o garzoni, e con la possibilità anche di avere personale domestico, come massere e servi" (Dal Borgo, "Venezia alla fine del 1500," 153).

212. Another guide is the tallies the priest of San Zan Degolà included at the end of his register. According to his calculations, there were 626 souls in the parish, of whom 50 were noble and 113 were cittadini. According to the priest, the nobles employed 35 servants and the cittadini, 45. Like the census takers of 1563, the priest listed no servants among the homes of "artesani," although he did list "garzoni" and "homeni à mese."

213. As Dal Borgo notes, "Si può avanzare dunque l'ipotesi che l'avere al proprio servizio una persona di sesso maschile . . . rappresenti un elemento distintivo dell'appartenenza ad una classe sociale elevata" (Dal Borgo, "Venezia alla fine del 1500," 219).

214. For other examples, see the first page of the register for the parish of San Severo (ACPV, CP, busta 3, San Severo).

215. Ibid., busta 2, San Zan Degolà fol. 6v.

216. Ibid., busta 3, San Basilio fols. 8r, 11v, 14r, 15v.

217. For example, entry number 20 reads, "Antonia Spagnuola, alli Servi, pieza una so massera"; and number 43, "Cornelia Guantera, a Santo Apostolo, dona maridà, pieza Lucia so massera." The catalogue is printed in Rita Casagrande di Villaviera, *Le cortigiane veneziane nel Cinquecento* (Milan, 1968), 275–93; see also Rosenthal, 39–40.

218. ACPV, CP, busta 3, San Benetto, fols. 3r, 4v, 5r. According to Richard Rapp, the 1642 census likewise showed many servant-headed households in the sestiere of Dorsoduro (Rapp, 79).

219. The instructions for the 1607 census takers indicate that gondoliers in personal service were to be listed in the household of their masters, but their families were to be listed separately. The instructions read, "Se sarà Barcaruol che servi, doppo il suo nome si farà un S. non mettendo lui in altre caselle, dovendo esser descritto nella fameglia del Patrone, ma si metterà la sua fameglia nelle proprie caselle" (MCC, Ms. Donà dalle Rose 351, quaderno entitled "S. Polo 1607").

Chapter Four    Recruitment, Contracts, and Wages: The Mechanics of Labor

1. ASV, RPC, RBG, busta 44, register 10, unnumbered penultimate page. I wish to thank Linda Carroll and Michela Dal Borgo for their help with the translation.

2. The tradition runs from Paolo da Certaldo and others in the fourteenth century to Francesco Guicciardini in the sixteenth (see Bec).

3. ASV, RPC, RBG, busta 44, register 10, fols. 24 left ("stette sempre amalado"); 31 right ("schanpo da nui e porte con lei tutti li soi drappi"); 68 right ("ando via con suo marido zenza dir niente"); 97 right ("schanpa via da nui et nerobe . . . una soa chamixa nuova e mase 10 di fil e do tovagnoli nuove").

4. For the Piazza del Campo as the place to locate domestic servants, see Oscar Di Simplicio, "Le perpetue (Stato senese, 1600–1800)," *Quaderni storici,* n.s., 68 (1988): 388.

5. "Ho cerchato cum ogni diligentia per aver una moretta che fusse al proposito suo, et erami stato proposto una de etade de circa quatro anni molto negra et ben facta, non gia' da vendere ma figliola de uno barcharolo" (Luzio and Renier, 140).

6. "Io ho posto sottosopra tutta questa terra per ritrovare una moretta per la Ex. V., et tandem ne ho trovato una a l'hospitale de la Pietà de etade de dui anni o pocho più, la quale è molto negra . . . bastarà fare qualche elemosina ad esso hospitale" (ibid., 141).

7. Marino Sanuto, *I diarii di Marin Sanuto,* ed. Rinaldo Fulin et al., 58 vols. (Venice: 1879–1903), 16:579; see also ASV, AC, Raspe, register 3662, fols. 85r–85v.

8. Glissenti, 130r.

9. ASV, RPC, RBG, busta 43, register 5, entries dated 1 August 1474 and 13 March 1475.

10. "Per mezzo de donna Lucia da Cadore lavandaia de drapi in corte da chà Barozi a san Moysé" (Lotto, 140).

11. ASV, Archivio Privato Donà in Archivio Privato Marcello/Grimani/Giustinian (hereafter Archivio Donà), busta 169, leatherbound notebook with "117" on cover, accounts of Francesco de Priuli, 1518–24, fol. 30 left.

12. "Conciosia che altre volte donna Pasqua relicta q. ser Francisco de Corte de Padoa acordasse donna Laura fiola de ser Andrea portador da vino a star per massara in casa di miser Zacaria Fondra" (ASV, NA, busta 8094, notary Vettor Maffei, protocol, fols. 244r–244v). For female brokers in Siena, see Di Simplicio, 388.

13. "Io son stado favorevele ai homeni dela dita villa de Roncha" (ASV, NT, busta 360, notary Natale Colonna, parchment protocol, fols. 29v–34v, testament 42).

14. Barbaro's will is in Charles Yriarte, *La vie d'un patricien de Venise au XVIe siècle* (Paris, 1884), 361–66.

15. ASV, Ospedali e Luoghi Pii Diversi, busta 921, fasc. 5, "Osp. Derelitti, Atti Diversi," dated 9 December 1554.

16. Jacopo Bernardi, *Antichi testamenti tratti dagli archivii della Congregazione di Carità di Venezia,* 12 fascicles (Venice, 1882–93), 10 (1891): 25, 32–33.

17. ASV, RPC, RBG, busta 43, register 9, fol. 142 left.

18. Lotto, 33.

19. Ibid., 127.

20. ASV, RPC, RBG, busta 44, register 10, fol. 52 right. For examples of servants from the same town serving in the same household, see ASV, Censori, busta 3, register 2, fols. 100v–101r, 111v.

21. "Come a Antonio suo chuxin a cha Lion" (ASV, RPC, RBG, busta 44, register 10, fol. 46 right).

22. ASV, NA, busta 433, notary Rocco de Benedetto, protocol, fols. 151r–151v.

23. Ibid., fol. 153v.

24. ASV, Censori, busta 3, register 2, fols. 26v–27v.

25. I do not believe that this is the case with the Barbarigo books. Andrea Barbarigo had a very difficult time retaining employees. They came and went with such frequency

(some stayed only a few days) that it is difficult to imagine that servant networks were in operation here.

26. ASV, RPC, RBG, busta 42, register 4, ledger B, fol. 21 left.

27. Ibid., busta 44, register 10, fol. 82 right.

28. IRE, Der E 195, fasc. 5, "Libro," fols. 43 left, 63 left.

29. ASV, RPC, RBG, busta 44, register 10, fol. 82 right.

30. Ibid., fol. 89 right.

31. Lotto, 126–127.

32. See Alain Ducellier, "Les Albanais a Venise aux XIVe et XVe siècles," in *L'Albanie entre Byzance et Venise, Xe–XVe siècles* (London, 1987), 407–9. Another indication that the flow of immigrants to Venice from Dalmatia and Albania was great is that the scuola of Santa Maria degli Albanesi was founded in 1442 and the scuola of San Giorgio degli Schiavoni was founded in 1451 (see ibid.; and Guido Perocco, *Carpaccio nella scuola di S. Giorgio degli Schiavoni* [Venice, 1964], 18). Even in the early sixteenth century, many of Venice's sailors came from Dalmatia (see Frederic C. Lane, "Wages and Recruitment of Venetian Galeotti, 1470–1580," *Studi veneziani*, n.s., 6 [1982]: 31–32).

33. The woman from Crete was called Benedetta da Chaneia (ASV, RPC, RBG, busta 43, register 8, entry dated 28 February 1520mv). The Barbarigo family had holdings at Canea (see Lane, *Andrea Barbarigo*, 23, 40).

34. The German monk and pilgrim Felix Faber, who visited Venice in 1483 on his way to the Holy Land, wrote that he stayed at an inn where everyone—the owner, his wife, and the servants—spoke German (Philippe Braunstein, "Remarques sur la population allemande de Venise à la fin du moyen age," in *Venezia centro di mediazione tra oriente e occidente (secoli XV–XVI): Aspetti e problemi,* ed. Hans-Georg Beck, Manoussos Manoussacas, and Agostino Pertusi, 2 vols. [Florence, 1977], 1:238). On the other hand, Jacopo Foscari, son of Doge Francesco, employed at least two German male servants (see Samuele Romanin, *Storia documentata di Venezia*, 10 vols., 3rd ed. [Venice, 1973], 4:195–97).

35. ASV, PSM, de Citra, Commissarie, busta 115, fasc. 8, "Sopra affari, e Bene possessia da q. Zaccaria Zustinian," fols. 43 right, 84 left.

36. MCC, Ms. Provinenze Diverse, C 912/II, fols. lxxvii, 82, lxxxvii.

37. See chapter 3 above.

38. Of course we must keep in mind possible prejudices of the source. Perhaps native-born Venetians were more likely to get involved in civil disputes with their masters.

39. See Verlinden, 2:550–666; and Lane, *Venice*, 332.

40. Very few notarial contracts for service are extant, and they may indeed have been illegal (see Lazzarini, 69–71; and the discussion in chapter 2 above). However, the notary Rocco de Benedetto and a few others did redact several service agreements.

41. Bernardi, 10:33. A 1490 Great Council deliberation spoke of "quelibet manicipia, servi, serve, famule, et ancille servientes, scripte vel ad salarium" (see ASV, MC, Deliberazioni, register 24 [Stella], fols. 108r–108v, 25 July 1490).

42. The text reads: "In nomine dei eterni amen. Anno ab incarnation domini nostri Yhesu Christi millesimo quadringentesimo septimo mensis marcii die septimo, Indictione quintadecima Rivoalti. Manifestum facio ego Iacobus de Clemona nunc habitator Venetiarum in confinio Sancti Paterniani cum meis heredibus et successoribus, Quia do et affirmo vobis domine Clare relicte ser Petri de Avanzo de confinio Sancti Laurentii

tra per vos mihi commissa die ac nocte licita semper et honesta, et vobis semper esse obediens per totum dictum tempus. Et vos debeatis mihi facere expensas victus et vestitus, et me tenere in domu vostra per totum tempus suprascriptum. Et in fine temporis mihi dare debetis pro meo sallario ducatos Decem auri. De quibus ex nunc fateor habuisse et recepisse pro parte ducatos quatuor auri, quos meo nomine exbursastis et soluistis suprascripto domino Nicolao de Committibus, cui eram obligatus in dictis pecuniis. Declarando inter nos quod se recederem a vobis domino Michaele ante tempus suprascriptum ex mea propria causa vel defectu, quod perdere debeam totum meum salarium suprascriptum. Et vobis tenear restituere ducatos quatuor suprascriptos quos pro me exbursastis. Si vero ex causa vestra recederem a vobis, habere debeo totum meum suprascriptum sallarium tamquam si dicti anni quatuor tunc fuissent completi. Testes: d. Franciscus Trivisanus ser Nasinue (?), Franciscus Cremondinus preco, et Iohannes Zilla" (ibid., busta 14821, notary Giovanni Battista Renier, protocol 1457–76, fol. 46r, act 215; I wish to thank Sergio Perini for this reference).

56. Ibid., busta 426, notary Rocco de Benedetto, protocol, fol. 247r.

57. See n. 49 above.

58. ASV, RPC, RBG, busta 44, register 10, fols. 56 right, 64 right.

59. ASV, CI, Notai, busta 81, notary Domenico de Philosophis, large protocol, fol. 3r.

60. Ibid., busta 24, notary Rolandinus de Bernardis, protocol 1406–32, fol. 61r.

61. See Monticolo, 1:124–25; 2:85, 294; 3:78–79, 104, 167, 189, 226, 241, 338.

62. Rapp, 44–45.

63. ASV, RPC, RBG, busta 43, register 5, unpaginated second page with list of servant contracts, and entry for Manoli dated 26 November 1465.

64. Ibid., busta 44, register 10, fol. 10 right, entry for Ieronima Schiavona.

65. Ibid., fols. 52 right, 72 right.

66. The cancellation reads, "Il detto ser Rado debbi et possi andar liberamente à far li fatti suoi." See n. 54 above.

67. ASV, NA, busta 8094, notary Vettor Maffei, protocol of 1548, fols. 93r–93v.

68. ASV, NT, busta 89, notary Rocco de Benedetto, unbound testament 140, 12 May 1559.

69. BNM, Ms. It. cl. VII, 2022 (8558), Matricola della Scuola del Corpo di Cristo o del SS.mo Sacramento, a S. Gregorio, 1523, fols. 29r–30r.

70. See chapter 2 above.

71. ASV, PSM, de Citra, Commissarie, busta 269bis, Account book "IV," fol. 67v.

72. "De ducatis decem auri qui sunt pro salario octo annorum in quibus ego tenebar stare vobiscum ad vestras expensas oris et vestitis. Item de ducatis duodecim auri qui sunt pro salario duorum annorum in quibus ego steti vobiscum ultra predictos octo annos" (ASV, CI, Notai, busta 24, notary Rolandinus de Bernardis, protocol 1409–24, fol. 70r).

73. ASV, RPC, RBG, busta 43, register 5, entry dated 15 February 1478mv.

74. See Herlihy and Klapisch-Zuber, 136–37; and Klapisch-Zuber, *Women, Family, and Ritual*, 107–8.

75. Pullan, "Wage-Earners," 161.

76. See chapter 2 above.

77. Klapisch-Zuber has found that between 1400 and 1480 wet nurses earned between eighteen and twenty florins a year, "more than any other category of paid domestics" (see Klapisch-Zuber, *Women, Family, and Ritual*, 136).

78. ASV, NT, 1260, notary Cesare Ziliol, unbound testament 794.

79. See Pullan, "Wage-Earners," 159–61; Zannini, "Censimento," 103.

80. Glissenti, 130r.

81. Pullan, "Wage-Earners," 164–66.

82. For the factor's agreement, see IRE, Der E 131, fasc. 3, act dated 4 September 1559, on the reverse of which is written, "N.o 74 Scrita del Mada. Angelica con batista pellezaro."

83. Cited in Gino Luzzatto, *Storia economica di Venezia dal'XI al XVI secolo* (Venice, 1961), 234. According to Pierre Sardella, domestics in the years 1496–1510 were making on average about 7 ducats per year (*Nouvelles et spéculations à Venise au début du XVIe siècle* [Paris, 1948], 52).

84. See Lane, *Venetian Ships*, 161.

85. Ibid., 162.

86. MCC, Ms. Provinenze Diverse, C 912/II, fols. 9, 37, 44, and passim.

87. Goldthwaite, *Wealth and the Demand for Art*, 210.

88. Gino Luzzatto, *Studi di storia economica veneziana* (Padua, 1954), 170–71, 188.

89. Lane, *Andrea Barbarigo*, 33.

90. Ibid., 29. For other examples of renting slaves, see ASV, CI, Notai, busta 230, notary Nicolò Venier, protocol, fols. 35r–35v; and ibid., busta 23, notary Giovanni Borghi, protocol, act dated 15 April 1407.

91. ASV, RPC, RBG, busta 45, register 12, entry dated 28 February 1557mv.

92. Ibid., entries dated 26 February 1559mv and 1 August 1560.

93. Ibid., entry dated 28 February 1560mv.

94. Lotto, 93.

95. Ibid., 127, 140–41.

96. Ibid., 74.

97. Ibid., xxxii.

98. Lane, *Andrea Barbarigo*, 29.

99. MCC, Ms. Provinenze Diverse, c 912/II, fol. lxxvii.

100. Ibid., fol. 82.

101. Ibid., fol. lxxxvii.

102. Ibid., fols. 105, cviiii.

103. ASV, NA, busta 8094, notary Vettor Maffei, protocol of 1548, fols. 93r–93v.

104. IRE, Der E, 189, fasc. 3 (and within fasc. 3, fasc. 32), act dated 11 September 1604.

105. See chapter 6 below.

106. BNM, Ms. It. cl. VII, 2022 (8558), fols. 23r–23v, 29r–30r.

107. "Et parte per sua mercede della servitù fattali gia molto tempo" (ASV, NA, busta 434, notary Rocco de Benedetto, fols. 70v–71r).

108. ASV, NT, busta 1208, notary Antonio Marsilio, unbound testament 448.

109. ASV, NA, busta 8094, notary Vettor Maffei, protocol, fols. 206v–207r. For another example, see ASV, CI, Miscellanea Notai Diversi, busta 66, testament 64. In this will Nicolosa Paleologa stated that her massara Susana had loaned her some money.

110. See ASV, Archivio Donà, busta 170, quaderno 2, "Memorial de mi Hieronimo Donado, Die 13 Setembre 1553 . . . ," unpaginated, entry for Agnola, massara, dated 28 February 1542. For other examples of holding money "in salvo," see ASV, NT, busta 553, notary Rolandinus de Bernardis, unbound testaments 250, 325; and IRE, Der E 195, fasc. 5, fol. 63 right.

111. In a collection of legislation found in the Querini-Stampalia is the following act:

28. ASV, NA, busta 433, notary Rocco de Benedetto, protocol, fols. 459r–459v. The act is dated 1566, but the marriage contract was made about ten years earlier.

29. The meaning of *buttarius* is not entirely clear. He may have been a wine seller of some sort or even a butler (see Charles Du Cange, *Glossarium mediae et infimae latinitatis*, 10 vols. [Niort, 1883–87], 2:795–97).

30. ASV, CI, Notai, busta 195, notary Antonio de Sereni, protocol 1448mv–1481, act dated 13 January 1450mv.

31. For Ioseph Basello, see ASV, NA, busta 428, notary Rocco de Benedetto, protocol, fols. 110r–110v; for Colona, see ASV, CI, Notai, busta 84, notary Canciano de Florinis, fragmentary protocol, act dated 13 April 1494.

32. However, for purposes of comparison, one might note that Andrea Barbarigo received a dowry of 4,000 ducats when he married Cristina Capello in 1439; his son Niccolò received a dowry of 2,437 ducats in the 1460s; and Niccolò's grandson got 4,000 ducats in 1552 (see Lane, *Andrea Barbarigo,* 28–29, 36; and ASV, RPC, RBG, busta 45, register 12, entry dated 23 July 1552). In the previous year (1551) the Senate had set an upper limit of 5,000 ducats for dowries (see Giulio Bistort, *Il magistrato alle pompe nella republica di Venezia* [1912; reprint, Bologna, 1969], 112).

33. ASV, NA, busta 441, notary Rocco de Benedetto, protocol, fols. 3r–4v.

34. Ibid., busta 8092, notary Vettor Maffei, protocol, fols. 168r–168v.

35. Ibid., busta 428, notary Rocco de Benedetto, protocol, fols. 199r–199v.

36. See, generally, Romano, *Patricians and Popolani,* 131–39; and idem, "Aspects of Patronage in Fifteenth- and Sixteenth-Century Venice," *Renaissance Quarterly* 46 (1993): 712–33.

37. ASV, NT, busta 86, notary Vettore Solimano, unbound document 35, dated 7 July 1476.
The goods portion of the dowry included the following items:

Una vesta de sarza nuova ducati cinque
una vesta de rasa do ducati
una gonela de rasa do ducati
una investura de pano tre ducati e mezo
una vesta de pano nuovo diese ducati
un fostagno fornido ducati cinque
sie cai sete ducati
cinque cape tre ducati
do pelixe quatro ducati
sete braza de sarza sete lire
camise e traverse sie ducati
fazoleti e fazuoli e binde e altre cosse menude ducati sie
quatro case un ducato.

Boerio defines *caia* as pieces of cloth (Giuseppe Boerio, *Dizionario del dialetto veneziano* [1856; reprint, Venice, 1973], 116). According to the *Grande dizionario della lingua italiana,* 6:508, *fustagno* could mean "vestito con abiti di questo tissuto, caratteristico della gente umile, povera."

38. ASV, NA, busta 442, notary Rocco de Benedetto, protocol, fols. 393r–394v.

39. Ibid., busta 430, notary Rocco de Benedetto, protocol, fols 235v–236r.

40. Ibid., fols. 187v–188r.

41. ASV, NT, busta 889, notary Matteo Solani, unbound testament 48.

42. Ibid., busta 411, notary Alessandro Falcon, unbound testament 215.

43. "Tra Orsa, et Pasqua massere di miser Lorenzo Bernardo, tra d. Pasqua, et sua fiola dalle Gambarare massere domina Marieta Venier, et tra Lucia, et la cuoga che hora sono in casa domina Isabeta da cha Valaresso mia commissaria, et tra d. Catarina sta in corte da cha Capello, la qual dieba andar a tuor i perdoni per mi, et tra la gastalda dalle Trinita, qual dieba andar a tuor i perdon dalla Trinita per mi" (ibid., busta 296, notary Girolamo de Capi [seniore], unbound testament 60).

44. Ibid., busta 1195, notary Vettor de Rosatis, protocol, fols. 53v–54r.

45. Ibid., busta 360, notary Natale Colonna, protocol, fols. 30v–34v, testament 42.

46. Pullan, *Rich and Poor,* 163.

47. "Spontaneamente mosso da christian pietà" (ASV, NA, busta 431, notary Rocco de Benedetto, protocol, fol. 73v). For another example, see Guido Ruggiero, *Binding Passions: Tales of Magic, Marriage, and Power at the End of the Renaissance* (New York, 1993), 177.

48. "Nel tempo di diti ani zinque fazi bon portamento, et servire mie fioli, et quando fazese [i]l cativo portamento non sia benefiziati ni liberi" (ASV, NT, busta 1195, notary Vettor de Rosatis, protocol, fols. 67v–68v).

49. For the importance of honor and its relationship to dowries, see Donald E. Queller and Thomas F. Madden, "Father of the Bride: Fathers, Daughters, and Dowries in Late Medieval and Early Renaissance Venice," *Renaissance Quarterly* 46 (1993): 685–711.

50. ASV, NA, busta 453, notary Antonio Brinis, protocol, fols. 24v–25r.

51. Ibid., busta 425, notary Rocco de Benedetto, protocol, pt. 2, fols. 9r–9v.

52. ASV, CI, Notai, busta 27, notary Francesco de Benzon, protocol, act dated 9 November 1462.

53. ASV, NA, busta 514, notary Giacomo de Beni, protocol, pt. 1, fols. 11r–12r.

54. MCC, Ms. Donà dalle Rose 174, Procuratia de Citra, Tomo Primo, sec. 4, entitled "Memoria della distributione . . . ," fols. 3 left and right, and passim.

55. See, for example, the rules for the distribution of dowries to girls in the parish of San Pantalon dated 1560, which stated that most girls who fell into "mala vita" did so "per non haver habudo li sui modo [sic] de maritarle" (IRE, Patr 1S, fasc. 46, unnumbered pages at front).

56. The receipt reads, " . . . quos ego habere debebam a predicto ser Antonio Albergno ut apparet in quaternus dominorum capitum sexteriorum pro tempore quo ego servire tenebar predicto ser Antonio Albergno" (ASV, CI, Notai, busta 24, notary Rolandinus de Bernardis, protocol 1409–24, fol. 74v, two acts dated 24 October 1422 and one act dated 7 November 1422). Perhaps Constantia used two of the ducats from her salary for purposes other than her dowry, which would account for the dowry of only thirty ducats.

57. ASV, NA, busta 431, notary Rocco de Benedetto, protocol, fols. 272v–274r. For Brombilla's identification as a "sanser da biave," see ibid., busta 435, fol. 98v.

58. ASV, NA, busta 436, notary Rocco de Benedetto, protocol, fols. 51v–52v.

59. With some modifications, I have used the professional categories used in Pullan, *Rich and Poor,* 96.

60. ASV, CI, Notai, busta 231, notary Nicolò de Varsi, protocol, fol. 11r, act dated 14 June 1449.

101. Vecellio, 150r.

102. For female space in Venice, see Romano, "Gender and Urban Geography." For an example of female escorts, see ASV, AC, Raspe, register 3651, fol. 104v.

103. Ibid., register 3648, fols. 10r–10v.

104. Ibid., register 3647, fols. 28r–28v.

105. See Marisa Milani, "Il caso di Emilia Catena 'Meretrice, striga et herbara,'" *Museum patavinum* 3 (1985): 75–97. For transcriptions of various cases, see idem, ed., *Streghe e diavoli nei processi del S. Uffizio, Venezia, 1554–1592* (Padua, 1989), esp. 102, 195–97. See also Ruggiero, *Binding Passions*, 37, 71, 91, 112, 124.

106. ASV, NT, busta 870, notary Petrus de Rubeis, protocol, fols. 11v–12r.

107. "Novem caritatis sive novem helymosinas novem pauperibus personis mee contrate" (ibid., unbound testament 254).

108. The will is a bit confusing on one point. Margarita refers to the monastery as San Cipriano on the island of "Burano maris" and endows the caritade on that island, yet the monastery was actually located on Murano. It is difficult to explain this problem, although it is clear that she intended a caritade to be given either on Murano or on Burano (ASV, NT, busta 746, notary Marcilianus de Naresis, protocol, testament 53). By the mid-fifteenth century the practice of endowing love feasts was quite rare (see Dennis Romano, "Charity and Community in Early Renaissance Venice," *Journal of Urban History* 11 [1984]: 63–81).

109. I have garnered from a wide variety of notaries 115 wills of present or former female servants (representing 113 women—I have 2 wills for 2 of the women) and 15 wills of present or former male servants or slaves. The disproportion between men's and women's wills was common in Venice. It should also be noted that many persons, both male and female, who at some time in their life served as domestics were not identified as such in their wills. I have used only those of persons who either were specifically identified as servants or refer to their masters, thereby indicating servant status. For purposes of comparison, I have also gathered 45 wills of boatmen's wives and widows and 31 wills of boatmen themselves.

110. ASV, NT, busta 1230, notary Federigo de Steffani, unbound testament 181.

111. Two of forty-five boatwomen remembered the scuola of Sant'Ursula, compared with no male servants or boatmen. For the scuola, see Brown, *Venetian Narrative Painting*, 56–60.

112. The parishes were: Santa Maria Nuova, Santa Marina (2), San Giacomo dall'Orio, Santa Maria Formosa, San Giovanni Degolà, San Marcuola, and Santa Luca.

113. ASV, NT, busta 746, notary Marcilianus de Naresis, unbound testament 49.

114. For the scuole, see Maurice E. Cope, *The Venetian Chapel of the Sacrament in the Sixteenth Century* (New York, 1979).

115. ASV, NT, busta 66, notary Priamo Busenello, unbound testament 269.

116. Pullan, *Rich and Poor*, 98. One male servant, Zuane, a former traghetto operator and servant of cà Grimani, asked that the scuola grande of the Misericordia be represented at his funeral (see ASV, NT, busta 1208, notary Antonio Marsilio, unbound testament 448).

117. For indulgences generally and that granted by Nicholas III, see Giovanni Diclich, *Indulgenze plenarie e parziali perpetue che si trovano nelle chiese della diocesi di Venezia* (Venice, 1827), esp. 14; see also Sansovino, 559.

118. Flaminio Corner, *Notizie storiche delle chiese e monasteri di Venezia, e di Torcello*, reprint of 1758 edition (Bologna, 1990), 135–36; Sansovino, 201.

119. Seeking indulgences as a form of patronage and clientage is considered more fully in chapter 6.

120. ASV, Censori, busta 3, register 2, fols. 25r–25v.

121. Sansovino, 201.

122. Thirteen of forty-five boatwomen (28.88%) made such a bequest, compared with only three of thirty-one boatmen (9.67%).

123. ASV, NT, busta 86, notary Vettore Solimano, unbound testament 32.

124. "Item dimitto cui vogabit dictum meum commissarium ad dispensandum legata mea suprascripta ducato uno pro suo labore" (ibid.).

125. ASV, CI, Notai, busta 28, notary Pietro Bogotichi, protocol, fol. 17v.

126. In the wills I examined, 20.86 percent of female servants' wills contain bequests to other servants (of their own or other households), compared with 26.66 percent of the male servants' wills.

127. For example, Pietro da Cittadella, famulus of physician Fabrizio Ancharanno, beat Lucrezia, a maid in the household (ASV, Censori, busta 3, register 2, fols. 188r–188v).

128. For some examples, see ASV, Signori di Notte al Criminal, register 12, fol. 76v; ASV, Censori, busta 3, register 1, fols. 99v–100r. In their capitulary of 1541 the censori specifically warned male servants not to insult or lead female servants into theft (see chapter 2 above).

129. Male servants as well could be sexually intimidated. Martini cites a case from 1628 in which the Council of Ten prosecuted for sodomy an adult cameriere and a fourteen-year-old servant. The cameriere was identified as the "active" partner, but Martini does not indicate whether the two worked in the same household or whether the fourteen-year-old was coerced (Martini, 119).

130. ASV, AC, Raspe, register 3646, fols. 116v–117r.

131. Gene A. Brucker, ed., *The Society of Renaissance Florence: A Documentary Study* (New York, 1971), 224–28; see also Piasentini, 90.

132. ASV, AC, Raspe, register 3677, fols. 191v–192v.

133. Ibid., register 3690, fols. 62v–63v. For another example, see ibid., fols. 70r–70v.

134. ASV, Signori di Notte al Criminal, registers 15, "Banditi in contumacia per omicidio distinti per sestiere," and 22, "Banditi in contumacia per omicidio."

135. Ibid., register 22, fols. 24r, 103r.

136. Ibid., register 15, fols. 41r, 74r.

137. Apparently, some gondoliers wrote into their contracts that they would get Sundays off in order to participate in the gang fistfights, but I found no such clause in any of the sixteenth-century contracts I examined. See Davis, *War of the Fists*, 83.

138. "A di primo zenar contadi a Madonna per pagar bona man alla famegia" (ASV, RPC, RBG, busta 47, register 16, fol. 1r). See also ibid., register with a "3" in pencil, section entitled "Diverse," entry for 1 January 1580mv ("per piu bone man in casa").

139. ASV, NT, busta 1261, notary Cesare Ziliol, testament 810.

140. See Gino Luzzatto, *Studi di storia economica veneziana*, 202–4. For the Sensa more generally, see Lina Padoan Urban, "La festa della Sensa nelle arti e nell'iconografia," *Studi veneziani* 10 (1968): 291–353.

141. According to Girolamo Bardi [Francesco Sansovino], on Maundy Thursday, "è

vietato alle donne di poter entrar in San Marco, si come è vietato a gli huomini l'entrarvi la vigilia della Sensa, entrandovi solamente le donne per veder il medesimo sangue, alle quali si mostra" (*Delle cose notabili della città di Venezia, libri II* [Venice, 1587], 76).

142. For Spinelli, see IRE, Der E 195, fasc. 5, fol. 123 left; for Barbarigo, ASV, RPC, RBG, busta 47, register with "3" in pencil, section entitled "Salariati," entry for Lutia da Este, left. For other examples, see ASV, Archivio Donà, busta 170, quaderno 5, fol. 12 left, entry dated 10 June 1546, and busta 171, quaderno 9, fol. 38 right.

143. "Unam vestem panni quam emi in hac assensiam" (ASV, NT, busta 66, notary Priamo Busenello, unbound testament 99).

144. For the Sensa as a fertility festival, see Muir, *Civic Ritual*, 131–32.

145. Lotto, 223.

146. Boerio, 821.

147. ASV, RPC, RBG, busta 43, register 5, entry dated 10 February 1466mv.

148. "Dui famegli, cioè quelli che vuogaranno le novizze" (Bistort, 392). For evidence of clothing being given to servants at the time of marriages, see ASV, Censori, busta 3, register 2, fols. 26r–26v.

149. For soccer, see ASV, AC, Raspe, register 3651, fol. 109r; for the lyre, ibid., register 3677, fols. 37r–37v; for a mattinata involving twelve youths, including a boatman, ibid., register 3648, fols. 151v–152r; and for the fistfights, Davis, *War of the Fists.*

150. Sanuto, *Diarii,* 37:578, cited in Trebbi, 146.

151. For lullabies, see Giovanni Musolino, "I santi nel folklore," in *Santità a Venezia*, ed. A. Niero, G. Musolino, and S. Tramontin (Venice, 1972), 193–94."

152. The aged were also especially susceptible to violence. See the case of the aged freed slave Margherita as reported in Piasentini, 93 n. 31.

153. Lotto, 126–27.

154. Milani, "Il caso di Emilia Catena," 78.

155. ASV, NT, busta 189, notary Girolamo Canal, unbound testament 67.

156. The parish registers housed in the Archivio Curia Patriarcale contain many instances of women living together. For an old woman, a former servant, gathering herbs, see ASV, AC, Raspe, register 3646, fols. 194v–195r.

157. For candle-selling by former slaves, see ASV, MC, Deliberazioni, register 22 (Ursa), fol. 36v.

158. ASV, CI, Miscellanea Notai Diversi, busta 1, notary Avidio Branco, testament dated 27 March 1546.

159. Polisena, former wet nurse of Bianca Dolfin, asked to be buried at Santa Maria dei Miracoli in the habit of the nuns and that her body be escorted by the converse of the site (see ASV, NT, busta 889, notary Matteo Soliani, unbound testament 278).

160. Franca Semi, *Gli "Ospizi" di Venezia* (Venice, 1983), 54–61.

161. The doge enjoyed patronage rights over the Cà di Dio and the hospital of San Marco (see Filippo Nani-Mocenigo, "Testamento del Doge Agostino Barbarigo," *Nuovo archivio veneto,* n.s., 17 [1909]: 249).

162. ASV, NT, busta 360, notary Antonius de Rovellis, protocol, fols. 1r–2r, testament 2.

163. Ibid., busta 870, notary Petrus de Rubeis, protocol, fols. 5v–6r. For another example of a former servant in a hospital, see ibid., busta 889, notary Matteo Soliani, unbound testament 276 (bequest to Antonia Granda).

164. See the will of Lorenza printed in Bernardi, 12 (1893): 39; see also Semi, 235.

165. ASV, CI, Miscellanea Notai Diversi, busta 66, testament 64.

166. MCC, Ms. Donà dalle Rose 174, Procuratia de Citra, Tomo Primo, sec. 4, entitled "Memoria della distributione . . .," fols. 14 right and 14 left.

167. ASV, NA, busta 425, notary Rocco de Benedetto, protocol, pt. 1, fol. 133v. On 22 April 1558 Caterina acknowledged receipt of the first two bushels.

168. ASV, NT, busta 1208, notary Antonio Marsilio, unbound testament 365. For another example, see ibid., busta 372, notary Lorenzo Cagnolino, protocol, fols. 6v–7v, testament 7.

169. Ibid., busta 889, notary Matteo Soliani, unbound testament 132.

170. ASV, NA, busta 426, notary Rocco de Benedetto, protocol, fol. 247r.

171. "Per carita e per amor prima del Signor Dio et poi anche per amor mio" (ASV, NT, busta 372, notary Donati Viti, protocol, fols. 11v–14r, testament 14).

172. ASV, CI, Miscellanea Notai Diversi, busta 66, testament 38.

173. "Mai la voglino arbandonar ne in vechieza ne in malatia ne mai mandarla via de casa" (ASV, NT, busta 265, notary Ioseph Cigrignis, protocol, testament 6). For another example, but with conditions, see ibid., busta 740, notary Alvise Nadal, unbound testament 15 (bequest to Menega Veronese).

174. See Romano, *Patricians and Popolani*, 112–18.

175. "E messe e altre elemoxine" (ASV, RPC, RBG, busta 43, register 6, fol. 92).

176. IRE, Der E 195, fasc. 5, fol. 63 left.

177. ASV, NT, busta 889, notary Matteo Soliani, unbound testament 57.

178. See ibid., busta 86, notary Vettore Solimano, unbound testament 32.

179. For some examples, see ibid., busta 889, notary Matteo Soliani, unbound testaments 81, 191, 219.

180. Ibid., busta 89, notary Rocco de Benedetto, unbound testament 105.

181. Ibid., busta 553, notary Rolandinus de Bernardis, unbound testament 415.

182. Ibid., busta 66, notary Priamo Busenello, unbound testament 17.

183. Ibid., busta 89, notary Rocco de Benedetto, unbound testament 34.

184. Ibid., busta 672, notary Bernardo Morosini, protocol, fols. 37v–38r, testament 31. For some other examples, see ibid., busta 66, notary Priamo Busenello, unbound testament 269, and busta 86, notary Vettore Solimano, protocol, testament 17.

185. Ibid., busta 754, notary Antonio de Vataciis, unbound testament dated 4 July 1435.

186. Ibid., busta 296, notary Girolamo de Capi (seniore), unbound testament 184.

187. Ibid., busta 66, notary Priamo Busenello, unbound testament 99; busta 189, notary Girolamo Canal, unbound testament 91; and busta 746, notary Marcilianus de Naresis, unbound testament 49.

188. Ibid., busta 889, notary Matteo Soliani, unbound testament 132. For a request for burial in a scuola associated with the Madonna, see ibid., testament 57.

189. Ibid., busta 86, notary Vettore Solimano, unbound testament 32.

190. For Niccolò, see ASV, NA, busta 376, notary Domenico Bonamor, protocol, fols. 19v–20r. For Martha, see ASV, NT, busta 191, notary Girolamo Canal, unbound testament 492, which reads, "in caemiterio Sancti Hieremie in archis schole traiectus macelli.

191. Cicogna, 4:202; see also 6:699.

192. This is not to deny, of course, that social distinctions found their way even into the scuole piccole.

193. This seems especially so since one boatman wished to be buried next to his first

wife, and the son of a boatman wished to be interred next to his father (see ASV, NT, busta 553, notary Rolandinus de Bernardis, unbound testament 440, and busta 889, notary Matteo Soliani, unbound testament 161).

194. Ibid., busta 754, notary Antonio de Vataciis, protocol, testament 231.

195. Ibid., busta 191, notary Girolamo Canal, unbound testament 475.

196. "Monasterio de madona S. Anna dove ancora riposano le osse de la quondam magnifica madonna Maria Morexini mia amoreudissima patrone et madre" (ibid., busta 410, notary Alessandro Falcon, unbound testament 160).

197. "Il mio corpo voglio sia sepulto in l'arca del mio patron à S. Lorenzo da ca Malipiero" (ibid., busta 89, notary Rocco de Benedetto, unbound testament 140).

198. Ibid., busta 889, notary Matteo Soliani, unbound testament 189.

199. Ibid., busta 86, notary Vettore Solimano, unbound testament 32).

200. "Pro anima mea et meorum defunctorum" (ibid., busta 740, notary Alvise Nadal, unbound testament 87).

201. "Meza casa de muro coverta de paia et campo uno di terra vinga [*sic*]" (ibid., busta 190, notary Girolamo Canal, unbound testament 417).

202. Maza, 115–33, 138–50.

203. McBride, 17, 83–88.

204. See the historiographical discussion in the Introduction.

205. See Romano, *Patricians and Popolani,* 65–90; and John Martin, "A Journeymen's Feast of Fools," *Journal of Medieval and Renaissance Studies* 17 (1987): 149–74.

206. On patriarchy in Venice, see John Martin, "Out of the Shadow: Heretical and Catholic Women in Renaissance Venice," *Journal of Family History* 10 (1985): 21–33.

## Chapter Six   The Dynamics of Master-Servant Relations

1. Lanteri, 161.

2. Alberti cites the same three qualities when Giannozzo says, "Vuolsi sapere da' servi essere riverito e amato non meno che ubidito" (Alberti, *I libri della famiglia,* 280).

3. My analysis in this chapter has been influenced by James Scott's *Domination and the Arts of Resistance: Hidden Transcripts* (New Haven, 1990).

4. For the notion of strategies rather than rules for explaining behavior, see Pierre Bourdieu, *Outline of a Theory of Practice,* trans. Richard Nice (Cambridge, 1977), 9. I wish to thank Edward Muir for this and the preceding reference.

5. ASV, NA, busta 8090, notary Vettor Maffei, protocol 1542–54, fols. 4r–4v.

6. "Quella compagnia in ditta casa non come massara ma come fiola propria" (ASV, CI, Miscellanea Notai Diversi, busta 29, doc. 3046, dated October 1554). The contract was mistakenly collated with this collection of wills and numbered as such.

7. In an entry in his account book in which he recorded that he had taken "per garzone" a certain Piero da Venezia, Lorenzo Lotto wrote that he promised to maintain the boy "et insegnarli fidelmente e governato et amaestrato de fiol" (Lotto, 154). In his will Andrea Badoer stated that he had maintained his servant Felice "non da servitor, ma da fiol" (ACPV, Testamenti, Archivio Antico, fols. 65r–65v).

8. ASV, NT, busta 192, notary Girolamo Canal, protocol, fols. 135v–137v, testament 156.

9. Ibid., busta 191, notary Girolamo Canal, unbound testament 589, dated 4 March 1524. For another example, see ASV, CI, Miscellanea Notai Diversi, busta 27, testament 2594.

10. This was to be done after Marco had served the sons for four years following Giova's death (ASV, NT, busta 192, notary Girolamo Canal, protocol, fols. 67v–69v, testament 80).

11. ACPV, Testamenti, Archivio Antico, fol. 44r.

12. ASV, NT, busta 1256, notary Cesare Ziliol, unbound testament with codicils dated 10 November 1574 and 15 September 1576.

13. Ivanoff and Zampetti, 428.

14. ASV, NT, busta 1260, notary Cesare Ziliol, unbound testament 759 (second codicil), and busta 727, notary Ioseph de Moysis, testament 135.

15. ASV, Archivio Donà, busta 171, quaderno 9, Account book of Francesco de Priuli, 1535–37, fols. 31 right, 32 left, 114 left and right, 127 right, 146 left and right, 163 left and right, 166 left and right, 199 left and right.

16. Ibid., fols. 56 right, 59 left, 127 right, 146 right, 166 left.

17. The will is published in Bernardi, 10 (1891): 23–47.

18. "L'è ben rasonevole me ricordi de i miei servidori et massime de queli i quali longamente con fede e amore me hanno servito" (ibid., 30).

19. "Ultra le qual i lasso tutti i lavori damaschini cum el caramal de hebano tegno per uso et ornamento del mio studio. Ancora i lasso tutti i geti de bronzo è in dicto studio, el mapamundo, el quadro pizolo de sancto Hieronymo, et el quadro de musaico, e tute le mie medaie si doro, arzento, laton e rame" (ibid.).

20. "A viver virtuosamente e da homo da ben" (ibid., 32).

21. "El mio messale e breviario in bona carta scriti a pena et el mio breviario stampato azio el se ricordi pregar Dio per mi" (ibid., 33).

22. "I quali legati e lassi fati ai dicti tre, zoè Zuane, Antonello, e Gasparo se intendi e habbi executione stando in casa e continuando a servirme, ma partendosse alcuno de loro, se intendi et sia privo dei legati e lassi fatoli, e queli ritorni in la mia comessaria" (ibid., 33).

23. ASV, NA, busta 435, notary Rocco de Benedetto, protocol, fols. 154r–155r.

24. Ibid., busta 436, protocol, fols. 112v–113r.

25. ASV, NT, busta 740, notary Alvise Nadal, unbound testament 17.

26. For this Iacoba would receive the "elemosina consueta" (ASV, CI, Miscellanea Notai Diversi, busta 29, testament 2945).

27. "A fidel servitude et exemplar vita di dita loro cameriera" (ASV, NT, busta 8092, notary Vettor Maffei, protocol, fols. 103r–103v).

28. "Per esser sempre statto fedelissimo in tute le chosse nostre" (Nani-Mocenigo, 249–50).

29. On the public rather than private nature of making a will, see Lorenzo Polizzotto, "Dell'arte del ben morire: The Piagnone Way of Death, 1494–1545," I Tatti Studies: Essays in the Renaissance 3 (1989): 61–63.

30. ASV, NT, busta 1195, notary Vettor de Rosatis, protocol, fols. 67v–68v.

31. Ibid., busta 870, notary Petrus de Rubeis, unbound testament 105.

32. Nani-Mocenigo, 249–50.

33. ASV, NT, busta 1190, notary Galeazzo Secco, testament 50.

34. Alberti, I libri della famiglia, 321. I follow idem, The Family in Renaissance Florence, trans. Renée Neu Watkins (Columbia, S.C., 1969), 247 (hereafter cited as Watkins).

35. Alberti, I libri della famiglia, 319–20; Watkins, 246.

36. "Che alla presenza del padrone me ne stò avvertito, e quanto giovami assai: perche

egli non mi viene à conoscere, e mostro d'esser in presenza sua quel, ch'io non sono" (Glissenti, 130v).

37. This may be explained by the fact that Caterina was from Venice (ASV, NT, busta 1230, notary Federigo de Steffani, unbound testament 98).

38. Bernardi, 10:34.

39. For the notion of plurivocality, see Carlo Poni, "Norms and Disputes: The Shoemakers' Guild in Eighteenth-Century Bologna," *Past and Present*, no. 123 (1989): 108.

40. For the transmission of character via milk, see James Bruce Ross, "The Middle-Class Child in Urban Italy, Fourteenth to Early Sixteenth Century," in *The History of Childhood*, ed. Lloyd deMause (New York, 1974), 184–96; and Klapisch-Zuber, *Women, Family, and Ritual*, 132–64.

41. ASV, NT, busta 189, notary Girolamo Canal, unbound testament 39, will dated November 1519.

42. Ibid., busta 411, notary Alessandro Falcon, unbound testament 211.

43. Ibid., testament 257.

44. MCC, Ms. Donà dalle Rose 174, Procuratia de Citra, Tomo Primo, sec. 4, entitled "Memoria della distributione...," fols. 14 left and 14 right. Richard Trexler suggests that one reason why masters cared for aged servants was to protect their own family honor (see his "Charity and the Defense of Urban Elites in the Italian Communes," in *The Rich, the Well Born, and the Powerful: Elites and Upper Classes in History*, ed. Frederic Cople Jaher [Urbana, 1973], 82).

45. Throughout this chapter, *family* has the meaning ascribed to it by Klapisch-Zuber: a "cluster of values" (see Klapisch-Zuber, "Women Servants in Florence," 56).

46. On family strategies to preserve wealth, see Davis, *A Venetian Family*. For bachelors, see Stanley Chojnacki, "Subaltern Patriarchs: Patrician Bachelors in Renaissance Venice," in *Medieval Masculinities: Regarding Men in the Middle Ages*, ed. Clare A. Lees et al. (Minneapolis, 1994), 73–90.

47. "Mia dilectissima consorte, la qual non me e stata mogier, ma schiava che lhastendato sempre con mi che ha latado tutti suoi fioli" (ASV, NT, busta 372, notary Donati Viti, protocol, fols. 24v–26r, testament 25).

48. Ibid., busta 191, notary Girolamo Canal, unbound testament 588.

49. Ibid., busta 89, notary Rocco de Benedetto, protocol, fols. 17r–19r, testament 21. For an example of an unmarried man who had a child with his slave, see ibid., busta 832, notary Alberto Pertempo, unbound and unnumbered will dated 25 April 1398. See also, Ruggiero, *Binding Passions*, 190–91.

50. ASV, NT, busta 191, notary Girolamo Canal, unbound testament 589. In actuality, two of Soranzo's three wills are included as number 589—the wills of 4 March 1524 and 12 May 1526; Soranzo's third will, dated 21 January 1525mv, is number 594 in the same busta.

51. See Maureen Flynn, *Sacred Charity: Confraternities and Social Welfare in Spain, 1400–1700* (Ithaca, 1989), 76–77.

52. Nani-Mocenigo, 249.

53. ASV, CI, Miscellanea Notai Diversi, busta 29, testament 2945.

54. Bernardi, 10:30.

55. "Duas capsellas pictas et unam anchonam in qua picta est ymago beate virginis Marie" (ASV, CI, Notai, busta 24, notary Rolandino de Bernardis, protocol 1406–32, fols. 46v–47r, testament 119).

56. "Per lanima mia et per i sui meriti et fadige" (ASV, NT, busta 189, notary Girolamo Canal, unbound testament 98).

57. "Lasso à D. Stana sta in casa con mi, et mi governa per sua mercede" (ibid., busta 372, notary Lorenzo Cagnolino, unbound testament 27).

58. For the *madonneri*, see Sergio Bettini, *La pittura di icone cretese-veneziana e i madonneri* (Padua, 1933); and Rodolfo Pallucchini, *La pittura veneziana del Trecento* (Venice, 1964), 215–16.

59. See Roger Chartier, "Culture as Appropriation: Popular Cultural Uses in Early Modern France," in *Understanding Popular Culture: Europe from the Middle Ages to the Nineteenth Century*, ed. Steven L. Kaplan (Berlin, 1984), 229–53.

60. ASV, NT, busta 750, notary Nicolaus de Varsis, protocol, testament 39. For possible meanings of the term *agnus dei*, see Boerio, 25; Pietro Sella, *Glossario latino italiano: Stato della Chiesa—Veneto—Abruzzi* (1944; reprint, Modena, 1979), 9; J. F. Niermeyer, *Mediae Latinitatis Lexicon Minus* (Leiden, 1976), 31; and Klapisch-Zuber, *Women, Family, and Ritual*, 149–50. It may even have been some kind of painted object attached to the bed (see Laudedeo Testi, *La storia della pittura veneziana* 2 vols. [Bergamo, 1909–15], 1:107).

61. ASV, NT, busta 1208, notary Antonio Marsilio, unbound testament 448. The bequest of cash was made in part to fulfill a legacy that Zuane's wife had left to Paola Grimani, whom he described as "mia carissima patrona."

62. Ibid., busta 1230, notary Federigo de Stefano, unbound testament 30.

63. "Et questo per la bona compagnia ho halauto da lui, et per havermi tratado come fiola" (ibid., busta 296, notary Girolamo de Capi [seniore], unbound testament 257).

64. For a much fuller consideration of the circulation of paintings and other luxury items between servants and masters, see Romano, "Aspects of Patronage."

65. For a good summary of the issue, see Michela Dal Borgo, "L'abbigliamento come storia. Note sulla società veneziana attraverso i costumi dei barcaruoli dal XV secolo ai nostri giorni," in *Le marinerie adriatiche tra '800 e '900*, ed. Pasqua Izzo (Rome, 1989), 17–24.

66. Bistort, 392.

67. ASV, Censori, busta 3, register 2, fols. 155r–155v.

68. Fairchilds, 102–3.

69. Domenico Malipiero, *Annali veneti dall'anno 1457 al 1500*, in *Archivio storico italiano* 7, pts. 1 and 2 (1843–44), 2:718. For another example, see ASV, AC, Raspe, register 3679, fols. 193v–194v. Sarah Maza notes the same phenomenon among servants in Old Regime France (see Maza, 213–14).

70. Romanin, 4:195–97, 200–204.

71. ASV, Signori di Notte al Criminal, register 22, fol. 25r.

72. "Cum offensione etiam dicti nob. de familia Cornelii" (ASV, Censori, busta 3, register 3, fol. 87r). Some writers of treatises on the duel noted that an affront to a servant constituted contempt for the master (see Frederick Robertson Bryson, *The Point of Honor in Sixteenth-Century Italy: An Aspect of the Life of the Gentleman* [New York, 1935], 53).

73. ASV, AC, Raspe, register 3647, fols. 143r–143v.

74. ASV, CI, Notai, busta 28, notary Biagio Bogotichi, paper protocol, fol. 17v.

75. ASV, NT, busta 889, notary Matteo Soliani, unbound testament 298. It reads, in part, "me ha indotta mia fia de parte de la sua dotta per conto del mio salario, et me ha governato nelle mie mallatie, et me ha satisfatto in piu volte de tutto quello dovea haver per conto del mio salario et per la bona conpagnia ho hautto da esso."

76. Ibid., busta 410, notary Alessandro Falcon, unbound testament 160.

77. Ibid., busta 740, notary Alvise Nadal, unbound testament 6, with codicils. The last part reads, "Et hoc facio quia ipse Lucia et Helesabet se male gesserunt erga me, et quod peius est aufugerunt e domo mea cum maximo dedecore et summa anema mee desplecemia."

78. "Li servidori che saranno beneficiadi servir debino continuamente li sui patroni stando in casa sua" (ibid., busta 741, notary Alvise Nadal, unbound testament 283).

79. Ibid., busta 1256, notary Cesare Ziliol, unbound testament with codicils dated 10 November 1574 and 15 September 1576. In her will dated 1478 Lena Morosini left several items and ten ducats to her "mamola," Tunina. But the bequests were to be voided if Tunina married before Morosini died or if she committed any "shameful act" [cossa de vergonza] (see ASV, CI, Miscellanea Notai Diversi, busta 27, testament 2594).

80. ASV, NT, busta 1261, notary Cesare Ziliol, unbound testament 810 with codicil dated 16 May 1572.

81. On this point, see Mertes, 180.

82. Bernardi, 10:34.

83. ASV, Signori di Notte al Criminal, register 15, fols. 49r–49v. The case is very confusing. Apparently Niccolò was suspected but fell out of suspicion when he appeared in court. Suspicion then fell on Margarita, who did not appear.

84. Ibid., register 22, fol. 42v.

85. Ibid., fol. 65v.

86. Ibid., fols. 29r, 41v, 45v, 76v.

87. Ibid., fol. 65v.

88. For example, the signori di notte charged Niccolò Saraceno, slave of nobleman Marino de Garzoni, with the death of a twelve-year-old boy named Giovanni, who in all likelihood was another of Garzoni's servants. The judges accepted the testimony of Garzoni's son Alvise (ibid., register 15, fol. 59v).

89. ASV, Censori, busta 3, register 2, fol. 4v.

90. Ibid., fols. 109r–109v. It reads in part, "Che essendo da detto suo patron stato tolto dalle pasture senza alcuna creanza, et alevato con boni costumi, et ammaestrato di tutto quello conviene à buon servitor esso sii stato cosi ingrato." And the final phrase reads, "non havendo rispetto alla casa di detto suo patron, et contra l'honesto et pacifico viver."

91. Ibid., fols. 49r–49v, 123r–123v. For another example, see ibid., fols. 125r–125v.

92. Ibid., fols. 154v–155r.

93. Ibid., fols. 157r–157v.

94. "Non timens Deum, nec Iustitiam" (ibid., register 3, fols. 97v–98v). Diana's relationship with Diedo is unclear.

95. Ibid., fols. 91v, 129v.

96. Bistort, 367.

97. "Per haversi partito senza licentia dal patron et portato via dannari havuti à conto di salario anticipato" (ASV, Censori, busta 3, register 3, fols. 138v–139r).

98. "In spretum iustitiae" (ibid., fols. 12r–12v).

99. Ibid., register 2, fols. 3r–3v.

100. Ibid., fols. 183v–184r.

101. Ibid., fols. 30v–31r.

102. Klapisch-Zuber, "Women Servants in Florence," 71–72.

103. ASV, AC, Raspe, register 3647, fol. 177r. For an example of a master who had sexual relations with a servant, see ibid., register 3652, fol. 96v. For a twist on this dynamic, see Ruggiero, *Binding Passions,* 126–29.

104. Ruggiero, *Boundaries of Eros,* 63.

105. ASV, Signori di Notte al Criminal, register 14, "Registro assente per omicidio e laddri," fol. 29v. There is certainly ample evidence of harassment of women, especially when they were in boats.

106. ASV, Censori, busta 3, register 2, fols. 187r–187v.

107. "Contra bonos mores, et honestatem, quae praecipue domibus nobilium debetur" (ibid., fols. 217v–218r).

108. Ibid., fols. 182v–183r.

109. "Con non picciol pericolo della vita del figliolo che lata, con molta offesa nell'honore de ditto suo patron, et di tutta casa sua, et con mallissimo essempio di tutte le case da bene et de honore" (ibid., fols. 121v–122r).

110. "In pessimum exemplum aliorum famulorum et ancilarum, et precipue bailarum, quibus comissa est cura puerorum infantium, cum periculo vitae pueri lactantis filii supracripti viri nobili ser Andreae et cum maximo dedecore supradictae domus" (ibid., fols. 92r–92v).

111. For other examples of servants accused of abandoning or otherwise threatening the lives of nursing children, see ibid., registers 2, fols. 140r, 157v, 166r, and 3, fols. 91v, 129v.

112. "Non prestando ei debitum obsequium despiciendoque eius mandata ac male tratando alias et alios servientes" (ibid., register 3, fols. 88v–89r).

113. "Ausus fuerit proferre verba contra riverentiam que debetur domino suo" (ibid., fol. 142r).

114. "Quasi in modum derisionis" (ibid., register 2, fol. 107r).

115. "In pessimum exemplum nullatenus tolerandum" (ibid., fol. 5r).

116. Ibid., fols. 46v–47r.

117. Ibid., fols. 188r–188v.

118. "Nulla habita ratione nobilitatis" (ibid., fols. 61r–61v).

119. The *Dialogo del patron, et del Zane* is found in *Nuova scielta di vilanele et altre canzoni ingeniose, et belli.* I consulted the copy BNM Misc. 2223.5. The *L'ultima licenza* is found in *Capricii et nuove fantasie alla Venetiana di Pantalon de' Bisognosi* (Brescia, 1601). I consulted the copy BNM Misc. 2402.5.

120. ASV, Censori, busta 3, register 2, fol. 175r.

121. Ibid., fols. 99r–99v.

122. Ibid., fol. 99v.

123. The censors released him from further contractual obligations (ibid., fols. 158v–159r).

124. Ibid., fol. 160v.

125. Ibid., fol. 217r.

126. "Voluit ipsum offendere in loco dicto la fossetta, et metu se proiecit in flumine Meoli" (ibid., fol. 159r). For other cases, see Ruggiero, *Boundaries of Eros,* 115–16. Ruggiero also notes that diarist Marino Sanuto may have used one of his male servants sexually (ibid., 189 n. 15).

127. Scott.

128. Albert J. Raboteau, *Slave Religion: The "Invisible Institution" in the Antebellum*

*South* (New York, 1978), 250–51, 311–13. In this regard, it is interesting to speculate why Venetian masters bequeathed images of the Virgin to their servants. Masters may have hoped that servants would thereby emulate the patience and humility associated with Mary.

129. ASV, Censori, busta 3, register 2, fols. 3r–3v.

130. In 1585 Domenica, ancilla of Lucretia Argentina, was accused of stealing "ornamenta muliebria" (ibid., fol. 153r).

131. "Ad animum et intentionem vindicandi se de dicto domino suo et ob despectum suum" (ASV, Signori di Notte al Criminal, register 12, fol. 52v). The case is also discussed in Piasentini, 33–34, 40.

132. Cited in Piasentini, 94–95.

133. ASV, Signori di Notte al Criminal, registers 15, fols. 28r, 46v, and 22, fol. 78v.

134. I have examined the registers of the raspe of the avogadori di comun for the years 1410–19, 1460–69, 1510–19, and 1560–69.

135. ASV, AC, Raspe, register 3646, fol. 247r.

136. See ibid., registers 3647, fol. 177r, and 3648, fols. 10r–10v.

137. Ibid., register 3651, fol. 57v. He was also to be branded.

138. Ibid., register 3683, fols. 205r–206r.

139. "Committendo predicta malo animo in domo eius patroni in peximum exemplum aliorum servitorum et contra securitatem et pacificum vivere huius civitatis" (ibid., register 3676, fols. 177v–178r).

140. ASV, Censori, busta 3, register 3, fols. 97v–98v.

141. Ibid., fol. 145r.

142. For the notion of varying ideas of honor and shame, see Ida Fazio and Gabriella Gribaudi, "Onore e storia nelle società mediterranee," *Quaderni storici*, n.s., 73 (1990): 277–84, esp. 283.

143. The text reads, "Et è stato cosi pericoloso, che meglio sarebbe lui il ritrovarsi alla discrettione delle onde del mare, e della fortuna, che nelle man di questi tali; perche oltre ogni danno, che maggior far gli possono, gli vanno questi tristi servitori di poi togliendo anco la fama; raccontando in altre case per diletto à suoi pari le tristitie, le insidie, li svergognamenti, li rubamenti fatti à lor padroni, lodandosi in queste ribalderie, come di cose honorate, e belle" (Glissenti, 133v).

144. "Costoro han sempre in bocca parole sporche, giuramenti vani d'ogni sorte, imprecationi terribili" (Garzoni, 869–70).

145. "Impercioche avezzi siamo a maledire, bestemmiare, giurare, rimproverare, e vituperare fin da fanciulli" (Glissenti, 142r).

146. ASV, Censori, busta 3, register 3, fol. 143v. It should be noted, however, that it was the gastaldus of the traghetto and his associates who brought the case to the censors.

147. Ibid., register 2, fols. 210r–210v.

148. Ibid., register 3, fol. 14r.

149. Ibid., fol. 18r.

150. Ibid., fol. 19v.

151. Ibid., fols. 37v, 47r, 94r, 117r, 124v, 126v–127r.

152. Ibid., register 2, fols. 141v–142r; Burke, 97.

153. "In spretum legum, et ordinum, in materia famulorum disponentium, nec non in spretum Nobilitatis huius civitatis" (ASV, Censori, busta 3, register 2, fols. 43v–44r).

154. See chapter 2 above.

155. "Un dannoso imperio, una misera soggettione, et ignominiosa conditione" (Glissenti, 134r).

156. A law of 1582 concerning the Council of Ten referred to its "paterna carità." It is cited in Gaetano Cozzi, "Considerazioni sull'amministrazione della giustizia nella repubblica di Venezia (secc. XV–XVI)," in *Florence and Venice: Comparisons and Relations*, ed. Sergio Bertelli et al., 2 vols. (Florence, 1979–80), 2:126.

157. "Sia certo ch'è servi son quanto è signori li sanno volere obedienti" (Alberti, 280; Watkins, 218). See also Guazzo, 439–41.

158. Minorita, 94.

159. The original reads, "E per questo erra il servidore, che proferisce il suo servigio al padrone, perciocché egli se lo reca ad onta e pargli che il servidore voglia metter dubbio nella sua signoria, quasi a lui non istia l'imporre e il comandare" (see Giovanni della Casa, *Prose di Giovanni della Casa e altri trattatisti cinquecenteschi del comportamento*, ed. Arnaldo di Benedetto [Turin, 1970], 224. I follow the translation of Konrad Eisenbichler and Kenneth R. Bartlett, *Galateo* [Toronto, 1986], 28).

160. "Non vedi tu che sarà non servidore, ma signore nostro?" (Alberti, 282; Watkins, 219).

161. Cited in Iris Origo, *The World of San Bernardino* (London, 1963), 70.

162. Glissenti, 129v–132r.

163. Lotto, 52. In a letter to her exiled son, Florentine patrician Alessandra Macinghi degli Strozzi complained that her slave Caterucia "pays no more heed to me than if I were the slave and she the lady" [che fa quel conto di me, che s'io fussi la schiava e ella la donna] (see Alessandra Macinghi negli Strozzi, *Lettere di una gentildonna fiorentina del secolo XV ai figliuoli esuli*, ed. Cesare Guasti [Florence, 1877], 104. I follow the translation in Origo, "Domestic Enemy," 343).

164. ASV, Censori, busta 3, register 2, fols. 30v–31r. For another example of a master withdrawing a complaint, see ibid., fol. 191r.

165. Ibid., fol. 80r. For other cases in which the master "pepercisset" the servant, see ibid., fols. 87v, 106v–107r, 132v, 142r–142v, 167v, 184v.

166. Ibid., fol. 212v.

167. Ibid., fols. 25r–25v. For another example in which the defendant was required to pay for illumination of an image of the Virgin, see ibid., register 3, fol. 87r.

168. "Io me contento, che quanto aspetta à me non sii piu processo contra il sopradetto Menego al presente carcerato, et di piu Io son contento, chel sia cavato di pregione con questo, chel vegni a servirmi facendomi quella bona servitù, che se convien, et scontando quel tanto el me die' dar, come faceva esso in prima, et facendo lui altrimente, me risservo comparer dinanci a questi Illustrissimi Signori Censori." (ibid., register 1, fol. 68r).

169. ASV, Sant'Uffizio, Processi, busta 21 (it includes three filze). I wish to thank John Martin for bringing this important case to my attention. For Finetti, see also Gino Benzoni, "Un Ulpiano mancato: Giovanni Finetti," *Studi veneziani*, n.s., 25 (1993): 35–71; and Marion Leathers Kuntz, "Voices from a Venetian Prison in the Cinquecento: Francesco Spinola and Dionisio Gallo," *Studi veneziani*, n.s. 27 (1994): 79–126.

170. ASV, Sant'Uffizio, Processi, busta 21, filza entitled "Scripturae productae in dies in causa ex.tis D. Iois Fineti," fol. 7v.

171. "Che costui havendo ogni gratia appresso di me, era patrone di casa mia, et Io lo

chiamava il mio diletto, et dagli altri di casa era chiamato miser Hieronimo, vedendo che era mia intentione, che havesse maggioranza in casa." (ibid., fol. 9r).

172. Ibid., filza entitled "Processus in causa Ex.tis D. Iois Fineti contra Hier.m Baduarium, et Pbrum Aloysium eius frem," fols 69v–70v. It reads, "mosso da charità debita, et conveniente ad huomo civile Catholico, et Christiano, contendandose solamente della restitutione dell'honor suo, che hà più d'ogni altra preciosa cosa caro."

173. Ibid., fols. 70v–71r.

174. ASV, Censori, busta 3, register 2, fols. 25r–25v.

175. "Petendo veniam, et misericordiam" (ibid., fol. 211v).

## Chapter Seven   The Significance of Service

1. The text reads, "Stimo ben, replicò il Cortigiano, che in questa città, più che in ogn'altra, vi siano i servitori licentiosi, dissoluti, vitiosi, e poco rispettanti: perche la moltitudine delle genti, delle nationi, e la confusione degli affari, toglie il pensiero del corregimento de tristi lor andamenti. Ma nelle Corti, dove io praticai per certo, che v'hò scorto di buoni, leali, schietti, et accostumati servitori" (Glissenti, 132v–133r).

2. In his *Colloquium ~~~~~~~~~~~res de Rerum Sublimium Arcanis Abditis,* Jean Bodin wrote that people went to Venice ~~to spend~~~~~~~~~~~~~~~~~~~~ quility of spirit, whether they are interested in commerce or crafts or leisure pursuits as befit free men" (see Jean Bodin, *Colloquium of the Seven about Secrets of the Sublime: Colloquium Heptaplomeres de Rerum Sublimium Arcanis Abditis,* trans. Marion Leathers Daniels Kuntz [Princeton, 1975], 3). For the reputation of Venice as tolerant and free, see also William J. Bouwsma, "Venice and the Political Education of Europe," in *Renaissance Venice,* ed. J. R. Hale (London, 1974), 73; and Martin, *Venice's Hidden Enemies,* 28–29.

3. Thomas Coryat, *Coryat's Crudities,* 2 vols. (Glasgow, 1905), 1:415. Elsewhere Coryat is amazed that Venetian nobles do their own shopping for "flesh, fish, fruites," stating, "but me thinkes it is not an argument of true generosity, that a noble spirit should deject it selfe to these petty and base matters, that are fitter to be done by servants than men of a generose parentage" (1:396–97).

While not referring specifically to servants, Machiavelli also noted differences between the Venetian patriciate and the aristocrats of the rest of Europe (see William J. Bouwsma, *Venice and the Defense of Republican Liberty: Renaissance Values in the Age of the Counter Reformation* [Berkeley, 1968], 58).

4. Michel de Montaigne, *The Complete Works of Montaigne: Essays, Travel Journal, Letters,* trans. Donald M. Frame (Stanford, 1957), 921.

5. The notion of egalitarian republicanism of course refers to equality within the patriciate. See Cozzi, "Authority and Law," 308. For communal values, see Romano, *Patricians and Popolani.*

6. A definitive statement is impossible given the lack of census data before 1563. As table 3.3 suggests, for the later sixteenth century the census data are equivocal since servants declined as a percentage of the total population between 1563 and 1586. But that decline probably reflects the effects of the plague of the 1570s. By 1642 the percentage of servants had rebounded and reached a new high. For further evidence of a rebound even earlier, see Zannini; and Chojnacka, 217–19.

7. For the bourgeois and aristocratic styles, see Roche, 67–68.

8. Cozzi, "Authority and Law"; Gilbert.

9. S. J. Wolff, "Venice and the Terraferma: Problems of the Change from Commercial to Landed Activities," in *Crisis and Change in the Venetian Economy in the Sixteenth and Seventeenth Centuries,* ed. Brian S. Pullan (London, 1968), 175–203.

10. Pullan, *Rich and Poor,* ch. 2; Tafuri, *Venice and the Renaissance,* 108–12; Muir, *Civic Ritual,* 163.

11. Susan Mosher Stuard notes that in the sixteenth century, theorists "saw the private or personal as the first line of attack for solving the larger problems of the commonwealth" (Stuard, *State of Deference,* 220).

12. In fairness we should note that foreigners often made similar claims about the paucity of servants in other Italian cities as well (see Goldthwaite, *Wealth and the Demand for Art,* 174).

13. Girouard, 15.

14. Richard C. Barnett, *Place, Profit, and Power: A Study of the Servants of William Cecil, Elizabethan Statesman* (Chapel Hill, 1969), 9–10.

15. Mertes, 218.

16. Peter Partner, *Renaissance Rome, 1500–1559* (Berkeley, 1976), 118.

17. David S. Chambers, "The Economic Predicament of Renaissance Cardinals," *Studies in Medieval and Renaissance History* 3 (1966): 293; Gigliola Fragnito, "Cardinals' Courts in Sixteenth-Century Rome," *Journal of Modern History* 65 (1993): 26 n. 1.

18. Partner, 134.

19. Fragnito, 45.

20. For the distinction between familiars and servants, see Pierre Hurtubise, "La 'familia' del Cardinale Giovanni Salviati (1517–1553)," in *"Familia" del principe e famiglia aristocratica,* ed. Cesare Mozzarelli, 2 vols. (Rome, 1988), 2:593–96.

21. These works are discussed in Chambers and in Hurtubise, among others.

22. Hurtubise, esp. 590, 601–4.

23. Gregory Lubkin, *A Renaissance Court: Milan under Galeazzo Maria Sforza* (Berkeley, 1994), 29, 249.

24. Ibid., 31–32, 197.

25. ACPV, CP, busta 1, San Felice, unpaginated.

26. Ibid., busta 3, Santa Maria Formosa, unpaginated.

27. Ibid., Santa Maria Zobenigo, unpaginated.

28. Ibid, Santa Maria Formosa, unpaginated.

29. Ibid., busta 2, San Cassano, unpaginated. The priest who recorded the household of Thomà Contarini "Kavalier" in the parish of Sant'Agnese did list a "mistro de Casa," a spenditor, and a cook, as well as three camerieri, two barcaroli, and four massere (ibid., busta 3, Sant'Agnese, unpaginated). But in Sant'Antonin the household of the bishop of Vicenza included a secretary, a physician, a maestro di casa, a spenditor, a despenser, a cook, a scullery boy *(squataro),* a porter, a butler *(credencier),* and a factor, as well as two chaplains, four camerieri, six servitori, and two barcaroli (ibid., Sant'Antonin, unpaginated).

30. Goldthwaite, *Wealth and the Demand for Art,* 239.

31. Herlihy and Klapisch-Zuber, 12–13.

32. Klapisch-Zuber, *Women, Family, and Ritual,* 176–77.

33. Herlihy and Klapisch-Zuber, 332. According to Merry Wiesner, servants made up 15–20 percent of the population of German towns in the Renaissance (Wiesner, 92).

34. Gene Brucker noted the lessening of that modesty even under Cosimo il Vecchio

(see Gene A. Brucker, *Renaissance Florence* [Berkeley, 1983], 120–27).

35. R. Burr Litchfield, *Emergence of a Bureaucracy: The Florentine Patricians, 1530–1790* (Princeton, 1986), 27–35.

36. David Herlihy, "The Population of Verona in the First Century of Venetian Rule," in *Renaissance Venice*, ed. J. R. Hale (London, 1974), 109, 112.

37. Alison Andrews Smith, "The Establishment of an Aristocratic Family in Renaissance Verona: The Verità from the Fifteenth to the Early Seventeenth Century,," (Ph.D. Diss., Johns Hopkins University, 1990), 266–70.

38. Cozzi, "Considerazioni," esp. 125–27. See also M. J. C. Lowry, "The Reform of the Council of Ten, 1582–1583: An Unsettled Problem?" *Studi veneziani* 13 (1971): 275–310.

39. Tafuri, *Venice and the Renaissance*, generally chs. 1 and 7, particularly 112–14; quotation on 188. For some perceptive remarks on stratification within the patriciate, see Trebbi, 130–52.

40. As early as 1509, Girolamo Priuli was lamenting the nobility's turn away from commerce and toward frivolous expenditures (see Ventura, 304–5). For the continuing struggle in the seventeenth century, see Gaetano Cozzi, "Venezia, una repubblica di principi?" *Studi veneziani*, n.s., 11 (1986): 139–57.

41. Elizabeth Gleason argues that Contarini belonged to the circle around Andrea Gritti; nevertheless, he upheld the notion of moderation (see Elizabeth G. Gleason, *Gasparo Contarini: Venice, Rome, and Reform* [Berkeley, 1993], 116. See also Bouwsma, *Venice and the Defense*, 148).

42. Later-sixteenth-century doges tried to increase the dignity of the office by increasing the ceremonial role of the dogaressa (see Muir, *Civic Ritual*, 292–96).

43. Klapisch-Zuber, *Women, Family, and Ritual*, 174–77.

44. Stuard, "Urban Domestic Slavery," 169. For an extremely useful survey, see Steven A. Epstein, *Wage Labor and Guilds in Medieval Europe* (Chapel Hill, 1991).

45. Stuard, *State of Deference*, 132–34.

46. Stuard, "To Town to Serve," 51.

47. See, in particular, the works of Robert Davis, Mackenney, and Rapp, as well as Romano, *Patricians and Popolani*.

48. The strike is discussed in Lane, *Venice*, 314.

49. The Ragusan Great Council also passed a law forbidding servants to assemble (see Stuard, *State of Deference*, 125).

50. Frigo, 202.

51. On England E. P. Thompson notes, "It is exactly in servant-master relations of dependency, in which personal contacts are frequent and personal injustices are suffered against which protest is futile, that feelings of resentment and of hatred can be most violent and most personal" (E. P. Thompson, "The Crime of Anonymity," in *Albion's Fatal Tree: Crime and Society in Eighteenth-Century England*, ed. Douglas Hay et al. [New York, 1975], 307 n. 1).

52. For the decline of popular protest in the face of new state action in Florence and the rise of isolated personal acts of protest, see Victor Rutenburg, *Popolo e movimenti popolari nell'Italia del '300 e '400* (Bologna, 1971), 331–68, esp. 361; and Samuel Kline Cohn Jr., *The Laboring Classes in Renaissance Florence* (New York, 1980), 165–67, 193–94.

53. Bryson.

54. Bryson, 15–26. For further consideration of the concept of honor in this period, see

Claudio Donati, *L'idea di nobiltà in Italia, secoli XIV–XVIII* (Bari, 1988); Francesco Erspamer, *La biblioteca di Don Ferrante: Duello e onore nella cultura del Cinquecento* (Rome, 1982) 25–54; Edward Muir, *Mad Blood Stirring: Vendetta and Factions in Friuli during the Renaissance* (Baltimore, 1993), 252–72; and Ruggiero, *Binding Passions*, 57–87.

55. The Spaniard Jerónimo Jiménez de Urrea, whose *Dialogo della verdadera honrra militar* was published in an Italian translation in Venice in 1569, wrote that since insults often resulted in duels, only persons practiced in arms could give or receive them. This automatically excluded the vast majority of men and all women (see Bryson, 33; and Erspamer, 40–42).

56. For these Aristotelian categories, see Bryson, 27–28.

57. The seventeenth-century Bolognese writer Berlinguero Gessi argued that when the social distance between individuals was great, the terms *insult* and *injury* did not apply, only simple *disgrace*. Such lesser offenses were not properly resolved through dueling, but rather through the courts (for Gessi, see Lucia Ferrante, "Differenza sociale e differenza sessuale nelle questioni d'onore [Bologna, sec. XVII]," in *Onore e storia nelle società mediterranee*, ed. Giovanna Fiume [Palermo, 1989], 108).

58. For an example of conflict between a master and journeymen being played out as a contest over honor, see Robert Darnton, *The Great Cat Massacre and Other Episodes in French Cultural History* (New York, 1984), 74–104, esp. 99. And in his autobiography, Benvenuto Cellini provides an excellent example of how he manipulated social codes to extract concessions from his patron, Madonna Porzia. They even sparred over the theme of the world turned upside down when Porzia spoke of the poor giving to the rich (see Cellini, *Vita*, 532–37. See also the translation by George Bull in Benvenuto Cellini, *The Autobiography of Benvenuto Cellini*, trans. George Bull [London, 1956], 40–44).

Susan Amussen notes a similar shift in seventeenth-century England. She believes that after the Restoration, with the elite more securely in power, "insults challenged the character, not the authority of the elite" (see Susan Dwyer Amussen, *An Ordered Society: Gender and Class in Early Modern England* [New York, 1988], esp. 186–88).

59. McBride, 9.

60. The topic of relations between social classes was of such import in the sixteenth century that Giovanni Della Casa was prompted to write a treatise entitled *De officiis inter potentiores et tenuiores amicos* (also known as the *Trattato degli uffici communi tra gli amici superiori e inferiori*). It can be found in Della Casa, *Prose*, 135–89.

# Bibliography

Primary Sources

**Archival Sources**

*Archivio Curia Patriarcale, Venezia*

Censimenti Parrocchiali, Sec. XVI–XVII, buste 1–3.
Testamenti, Archivio Antico.

*Archivio degli Istituzioni di Ricovero e di Educazione, Venezia*

Der E 92, 130, 131, 189, 195.
Patr 1S.

*Archivio di Stato, Venezia*

Archivio Privato Contarini in Archivio Privato Marcello/Grimani/ Giustinian, busta 3.
Archivio Privato Donà in Archivio Privato Marcello/Grimani/Giustinian, buste 165, 167, 169–71, 173.
Avogaria di Comun, Raspe, registers 3646–48, 3651–53, 3661–63, 3672, 3676–79, 3683, 3687, 3690–91.
Cancelleria Inferiore
Doge, busta 157A.
Miscellanea Notai Diversi, buste 1, 27–30, 66–67.
Notai, buste 23–25, 27–28, 81, 84, 121, 123, 150, 174, 176, 195, 229–31.
Censori, buste 1–3.
Compilazione delle Leggi
Serie Prima, busta 301.
Serie Seconda, busta 24.
Consiglio dei Dieci
Criminali, register 2.
Parti Comuni, filza 29.
Giustizia Vecchia, buste 112–16.
Maggior Consiglio, Deliberazioni, registers 19, 21–28, 30–32.
Miscellanea Gregolin, buste 14–15.
Notarile, Atti, buste 5–6, 24–25, 356–57, 376–79, 425–54, 479–81, 514–17, 2549, 3345–46, 6615, 7821, 8090, 8092–94, 14534, 14630, 14821.
Notarile, Testamenti, buste 10, 41–42, 66, 86, 89, 131, 189–92, 265, 296, 360, 372, 378, 403, 410–11, 416, 449, 552–53, 570, 595, 598, 656, 672, 727, 740–41, 746, 750, 754, 810, 824, 832, 858, 870, 889, 915, 927, 985, 1060, 1070, 1149, 1183–84, 1186, 1190, 1192, 1195, 1207–9, 1211, 1230, 1238, 1256, 1258, 1260–61.

*Domestic Economy by a Citizen of Paris (c. 1393)*. Translated by Eileen Power. New York: Harcourt, Brace & Company, 1928.

Graziato, Gisella, ed. *Le promissioni del doge di Venezia dalle origini alla fine del Duecento.* Venice: Il Comitato Editore, 1986.

Grevembroch, Giovanni. *Gli abiti de veneziani di quasi ogni età con diligenza raccolti e dipinti nel secolo XVIII.* 4 vols. Venice: Filippi, 1981.

Guazzo, Stefano. *La civil conversatione del sig. Stefano Guazzo gentilhuomo di Casale di Monferrato; divisa in quatro libri.* Venice: Bartolomeo Robino, 1575.

Kohl, Benjamin G., and Ronald G. Witt. *The Earthly Republic: Italian Humanists on Government and Society.* Philadelphia: University of Pennsylvania Press, 1978.

Lanteri, Giacomo. *Della economia . . . nel quale si dimostrano le qualità, che all'huomo et alla donna separatamente convengono pel governo della casa.* Venice: Vincenzo Valgrisi, 1560.

*Leggi e memorie venete sulla prostituzione fino alla caduta della republica.* Venice: Marco Visentini, 1870–72.

Le Ménagier de Paris. *Le Ménagier de Paris.* Edited by Georgine E. Brereton and Janet M. Ferrier. Oxford: Clarendon Press, 1981.

Lotto, Lorenzo. *Il "Libro di spese diverse" con aggiunta di lettere e d'altri documenti.* Edited by Pietro Zampetti. Venice: Istituto per la Collaborazione Culturale, 1969.

*L'ultima licenza della buona massara dalla cattiva patrona.* In *Capricii et nuove fantasie alla Venetiana di Pantalon de' Bisognosi.* Brescia: n.p., 1601.

Malipiero, Domenico. *Annali veneti dall'anno 1457 al 1500. Archivio storico italiano* 7, pts. 1 and 2 (1843–44).

Milani, Marisa, ed. *Streghe e diavoli nei processi del S. Uffizio, Venezia, 1554–1592.* Padua: Centrostampa, 1989.

Minorita, Fra Paolino. *Trattato de regimine rectoris.* Edited by Adolfo Mussafia. Vienna: Tendler & Vieusseux, 1868.

Montaigne, Michel de. *The Complete Works of Montaigne: Essays, Travel Journal, Letters.* Translated by Donald M. Frame. Stanford: Stanford University Press, 1957.

Monticolo, Giovanni, ed. *I capitolari delle arti veneziane sottoposte alla giustizia vecchia dalle origini al MCCCXXX.* 3 vols. Rome: Istituto Storico Italiano, 1896–1914.

Paruta, Paolo. *Della perfettione della vita politica . . . libri tre.* Venice: Domenico Nicolini, 1579.

Piccolomini, Alessandro. *Della institutione morale libri XII.* Venice: Giordano Ziletti, 1560.

Priuli, Girolamo. *I diarii di Girolamo Priuli.* Edited by Arturo Segre and Roberto Cessi. Rerum Italicarum Scriptores 24, pt. 3. Bologna: Zanichelli, 1912–38.

Quirini, Lauro. *De republica.* Edited by Carlo Seno and Giorgio Ravegnani. In *Lauro Quirini umanista,* edited by Vittore Branca, 121–61. Florence: Olschki, 1977.

Sansovino, Francesco. *Venetia città nobilissima et singolare, descritta in XIIII libri.* 1663. Reprint. Farnborough, England: Gregg International Publishers, 1968.

Sanudo, Marino (il Giovane). *De origine, situ et magistratibus urbis Venetae ovvero la città di Venezia (1493–1530).* Edited by Angela Caracciolo Aricò. Milan: Cisalpino-Goliardica, 1980.

———. *I diarii di Marin Sanuto.* Edited by Rinaldo Fulin et al. 58 vols. Venice: Visentini, 1879–1903.

Sebellico, Andreina Bondi, ed. *Felice de Merlis: Prete e notaio in Venezia ed Ayas (1315–1348).* 2 vols. Venice: Il Comitato Editore, 1973–78.

Spathaphòra di Moncata, Bartolomeo. *Quattro orationi di M. Bartolomo Spathaphòra di Moncata gentil'huomo venetiano*. Venice: Plinio Pietrasanta, 1554.

Strozzi, Alessandra Macinghi negli. *Lettere di una gentildonna fiorentina del secolo XV ai figliuoli esuli*. Edited by Cesare Guasti. Florence: Sansoni, 1877.

Stussi, Alfredo, ed. *Zibaldone da Canal: Manoscritto mercantile del sec. XIV*. Venice: Il Comitato Editore, 1967.

Valiero, Agostino. *La istituzione d'ogni stato lodevole delle donne cristiane . . . novella impressione . . . illustrata da d. Gaetano Volpi*. Padua: Giuseppe Comino, 1744.

Vecellio, Cesare. *De gli habiti antichi, et moderni di diverse parti del mondo libri due*. Venice: Damian Zeparo, 1590.

Xenophon. *Memorabilia and Oeconomicus*. Translated by E. C. Marchant. Loeb Classical Library. Cambridge: Harvard University Press, 1938.

Zago, Ferruccio, ed. *Consiglio dei Dieci: Deliberazioni miste*. Vol. 1. *Registri I–II (1310–1324)*. Venice: Il Comitato Editore, 1962.

## Secondary Sources

Amussen, Susan Dwyer. *An Ordered Society: Gender and Class in Early Modern England*. New York: Columbia University Press, 1988.

Barbieri, Gino. "Il trattatello 'Della economica' di Giacomo Lantieri, letterato e architetto bresciano del secolo XVI." In *Saggi di economia aziendale e sociale in memoria di Gino Zappa*, 3 vols., 1:151–66. Milan: Gioffrè, 1961.

Barnett, Richard C. *Place, Profit, and Power: A Study of the Servants of William Cecil, Elizabethan Statesman*. Chapel Hill: University of North Carolina Press, 1969.

Baron, Hans. *In Search of Florentine Civic Humanism: Essays on the Transition from Medieval to Modern Thought*. 2 vols. Princeton: Princeton University Press, 1988.

Baernstein, P. Renée. "In Widow's Habit: Women between Convent and Family in Sixteenth-Century Milan." *Sixteenth Century Journal* 25 (1994): 787–807.

Bec, Christian. *Les marchands écrivains: Affaires et humanisme à Florence, 1375–1434*. Paris: Mouton, 1967.

Becker, Marvin B. *Civility and Society in Western Europe, 1300–1600*. Bloomington: Indiana University Press, 1988.

Beltrami, Daniele. *Storia della popolazione di Venezia dalla fine del secolo XVI alla caduta della republica*. Padua: CEDAM, 1954.

Bender, Donald R. "A Refinement of the Concept of Household: Families, Co-residence, and Domestic Functions." *American Anthropologist* 69 (1967): 493–504.

Benzoni, Gino. "Le accademie." In *Storia della cultura veneta*, vol. 4, *Il Seicento*, edited by Girolamo Arnaldi and Manlio Pastore Stocchi, pt. 1:131–62. Vicenza: Neri Pozza, 1976–86.

———. "Un Ulpiano mancato: Giovanni Finetti." *Studi veneziani*, n.s., 25 (1993): 35–71.

Bettini, Sergio. *La pittura di icone cretese-veneziana e i madonneri*. Padua: CEDAM, 1933.

Betto, Bianca. "Linee di politica matrimoniale nella nobiltà veneziana fino al XV secolo: Alcune note genealogiche e l'esempio della famiglia Mocenigo." *Archivio storico italiano* 139 (1981): 3–64.

Bistort, Giulio. *Il magistrato alle pompe nella republica di Venezia*. 1912. Reprint. Bologna: Forni, 1969.

Blunt, Anthony. *Artistic Theory in Italy, 1450–1600.* Oxford: Clarendon Press, 1956.

Boerio, Giuseppe. *Dizionario del dialetto veneziano.* 1856. Reprint. Venice: Filippi, 1973.

Boholm, Asa. *The Doge of Venice: The Symbolism of State Power in the Renaissance.* Gothenburg, Sweden: Institute for Advanced Studies in Social Anthropology, 1990.

Bossy, John. "The Counter-Reformation and the People of Catholic Europe." *Past and Present,* no. 47 (1970): 51–70.

Botteon, V., and A. Aliprandi. *Ricerche intorno alla vita e alle opere di Giambattista Cima.* 1893. Reprint. Bologna: Forni, 1977.

Bourdieu, Pierre. *Outline of a Theory of Practice.* Translated by Richard Nice. Cambridge: Cambridge University Press, 1977.

Bouwsma, William J. *Venice and the Defense of Republican Liberty: Renaissance Values in the Age of the Counter Reformation.* Berkeley: University of California Press, 1968.

———. "Venice and the Political Education of Europe." In *Renaissance Venice,* edited by J. R. Hale, 445–66. London: Faber & Faber, 1974.

Braunstein, Philippe. "Remarques sur la population allemande de Venise à la fin du moyen age." In *Venezia centro di mediazione tra oriente e occidente (secoli XV–XVI): Aspetti e problemi,* edited by Hans-Georg Beck, Manoussos Manoussacas, and Agostino Pertusi, 2 vols., 1:233–43. Florence: Olschki, 1977.

Brown, Judith C. "A Woman's Place Was in the Home: Women's Work in Renaissance Tuscany." In *Rewriting the Renaissance: The Discourses of Sexual Difference in Early Modern Europe,* edited by Margaret W. Ferguson, Maureen Quilligan, and Nancy J. Vickers, 206–24, 363–70. Chicago: University of Chicago Press, 1986.

Brown, Patricia Fortini. *Venetian Narrative Painting in the Age of Carpaccio.* New Haven: Yale University Press, 1988.

Brucker, Gene A. *Giovanni and Lusanna: Love and Marriage in Renaissance Florence.* Berkeley: University of California Press, 1986.

———. *Renaissance Florence.* Berkeley: University of California Press, 1983.

———, ed. *The Society of Renaissance Florence: A Documentary Study.* New York: Harper & Row, 1971.

Burke, Peter. *The Historical Anthropology of Early Modern Italy.* Cambridge: Cambridge University Press, 1987.

Bryson, Frederick Robertson. *The Point of Honor in Sixteenth-Century Italy: An Aspect of the Life of the Gentleman.* New York: Columbia University Press, 1935.

Byatt, Lucinda M. C. "Aspetti giuridici e finanziari di una 'familia' cardinalizia del XVI secolo: Un progetto di ricerca." In *"Familia" del principe e famiglia aristocratica,* edited by Cesare Mozzarelli, 2 vols., 2:611–30. Rome: Bulzoni, 1988.

Caffi, Michele. "Giacomello del Fiore: Pittore veneziano del sec. XV." *Archivio storico italiano,* 4th ser., 6 (1880): 402–13.

Caniato, Giovanni. "Traghetti e barcaroli a Venezia." In *La civiltà delle acque,* edited by Manlio Cortelazzo, 149–67. Milan: A. Pizzi, 1993.

Carlson, Marybeth. "A Trojan Horse of Worldliness? Maidservants in the Burgher Households of Rotterdam at the End of the Seventeenth Century." In *Women in the Golden Age: An International Debate on Women in Seventeenth-Century Holland, England, and Italy,* edited by Els Kloek, Nicole Teeuwen, and Marijke Huisman, 87–96. Hilversum, Netherlands: Verloren, 1994.

Casagrande di Villaviera, Rita. *Le cortigiane veneziane nel Cinquecento.* Milan: Longanesi, 1968.

Casali, Elide. "'Economica' e 'creanza' cristiana." *Quaderni storici* 41 (1979): 555–83.

Casini, Matteo. "Realtà e simboli del cancellier grande veneziano in età moderna (sec. XVI–XVII)." *Studi veneziani*, n.s., 22 (1991): 195–251.

Cessi, Roberto. *Storia della Repubblica di Venezia*. Florence: Giunti Martello, 1981.

Chambers, David S. "The Economic Predicament of Renaissance Cardinals." *Studies in Medieval and Renaissance History* 3 (1966): 287–313.

Chartier, Roger. "Culture as Appropriation: Popular Cultural Uses in Early Modern France." In *Understanding Popular Culture: Europe from the Middle Ages to the Nineteenth Century*, edited by Steven L. Kaplan, 229–53. Berlin: Mouton, 1984.

Chojnacka, Monica Elena. "City of Women: Gender, Family, and Community in Venice, 1540–1630." Ph.D. diss., Stanford University, 1994.

Chojnacki, Stanley. "Dowries and Kinsmen in Early Renaissance Venice." *Journal of Interdisciplinary History* 4 (1975): 571–600.

———. "In Search of the Venetian Patriciate: Families and Factions in the Fourteenth Century." In *Renaissance Venice*, edited by J. R. Hale, 47–90. London: Faber & Faber, 1974.

———. "Kinship Ties and Young Patricians in Fifteenth-Century Venice." *Renaissance Quarterly* 38 (1985): 240–70.

———. "Marriage Legislation and Patrician Society in Fifteenth-Century Venice." In *Law, Custom, and the Social Fabric: Essays in Honor of Bryce Lyon*, edited by Bernard S. Bachrach and David Nicholas, 163–84. Kalamazoo: Medieval Institute Publications, 1990.

———. "Subaltern Patriarchs: Patrician Bachelors in Renaissance Venice." In *Medieval Masculinities: Regarding Men in the Middle Ages*, edited by Clare A. Lees et al., 73–90. Minneapolis: University of Minnesota Press, 1994.

Christiansen, Keith. *Gentile da Fabriano*. Ithaca: Cornell University Press, 1982.

Ciampi, Maria. "Notizie storiche riguardanti la vita e le opere di Palma il Giovane." *Archivio veneto*, 5th ser., 66 (1960): 1–19.

Cicogna, Emmanuele Antonio. *Delle inscrizioni veneziane*. 6 vols. 1824–53. Reprint. Bologna: Forni, 1970–83.

Cohn, Samuel Kline, Jr. *The Laboring Classes in Renaissance Florence*. New York: Free Press, 1980.

Cole, Bruce. *The Renaissance Artist at Work: From Pisano to Titian*. New York: Harper & Row, 1983.

Contento, Aldo. "Il censimento della popolazione sotto la Repubblica Veneta." *Nuovo archivio veneto* 19 (1900): 5–42, 179–240; 20 (1900): 5–96, 171–235.

Cope, Maurice E. *The Venetian Chapel of the Sacrament in the Sixteenth Century*. New York: Garland, 1979.

Corner, Flaminio. *Notizie storiche delle chiese e monasteri di Venezia e di Torcello*. 1758. Reprint. Bologna: Forni, 1990.

Cotton, Juliana Hill. "Giovanni Caldiera." *Dizionario biografico degli italiani* 16:626–28. Rome: Istituto della Enciclopedia Italiana, 1973.

Cozzando, Leonardo. *Libraria Bresciana prima, e seconda parte*. 1694. Reprint. Bologna: Forni, 1974.

Cozzi, Gaetano. "Authority and Law in Renaissance Venice." In *Renaissance Venice*, edited by J. R. Hale, 293–345. London: Faber & Faber, 1974.

———. "Considerazioni sull'amministrazione della giustizia nella repubblica di Venezia (secc. XV–XVI)." In *Florence and Venice: Comparisons and Relations,* edited by Sergio Bertelli et al., 2 vols., 2:101–33. Florence: La Nuova, 1979–80.

———. "La politica del diritto nella repubblica di Venezia." In *Stato, società e giustizia nella Repubblica Veneta (sec. XV–XVIII),* edited by Gaetano Cozzi, 15–152. Rome: Jouvence, 1980.

———. "Venezia, una repubblica di principi?" *Studi veneziani,* n.s., 11 (1986): 139–57.

Dal Borgo, Michela. "L'abbigliamento come storia. Note sulla società veneziana attraverso i costumi dei barcaruoli dal XV secolo ai nostri giorni." In *Le marinerie adriatiche tra '800 e '900,* edited by Pasqua Izzo, 17–24. Rome: De Luca Edizioni d'Arte, 1989.

———. "Venezia alla fine del 1500: La zona di San Zaccaria." Tesi di laurea, Università degli Studi di Venezia, 1977–78.

Da Mosto, Andrea. *L'Archivio di Stato di Venezia: Indice generale, storico, descrittivo ed analitico.* 2 vols. Rome: Biblioteca d'Arte, 1937–40.

———. *I bravi di Venezia.* Milan: Ciarrocca, 1950.

———. *I dogi di Venezia nella vita pubblica e privata.* Florence: Giunti Martello, 1977.

Darnton, Robert. *The Great Cat Massacre and Other Episodes in French Cultural History.* New York: Vintage Books, 1985.

Davis, James C. *A Venetian Family and Its Fortune: 1500–1900.* Philadelphia: American Philosophical Society, 1975.

Davis, Robert C. *Shipbuilders of the Venetian Arsenal: Workers and Workplace in the Preindustrial City.* Baltimore: Johns Hopkins University Press, 1991.

———. *The War of the Fists: Popular Culture and Public Violence in Late Renaissance Venice.* New York: Oxford University Press, 1994.

Derosas, Renzo. "Moralità e giustizia a Venezia nel '500–'600: Gli esecutori contro la bestemmia." In *Stato, società e giustizia nella Repubblica Veneta (sec. XV–XVIII),* edited by Gaetano Cozzi, 431–528. Rome: Jouvence, 1980.

Diclich, Giovanni. *Indulgenze plenarie e parziali perpetue che si trovano nelle chiese della diocesi di Venezia.* Venice: Tipografia Rizzi, 1827.

Di Simplicio, Oscar. "Le perpetue (Stato senese, 1600–1800)." *Quaderni storici,* n.s., 68 (1988): 381–412.

*Dizionario enciclopedico Bolaffi dei pittori e degli incisori italiani dall'XI al XX secolo.* 11 vols. Turin: Giulio Bolaffi, 1972–76.

Doglio, Maria Luisa. "Stefano Guazzo." In *Dizionario critico della letteratura italiana,* edited by Vittore Branca, 4 vols., 2:460–62. Turin: UTET, 1986.

Dolan, Frances E. *Dangerous Familiars: Representations of Domestic Crime in England, 1550–1700.* Ithaca: Cornell University Press, 1994.

Donati, Claudio. *L'idea di nobiltà in Italia, secoli XIV–XVIII.* Bari: Laterza, 1988.

Du Cange, Charles. *Glossarium mediae et infimae latinitatis.* 10 vols. Niort: L. Favre, 1883–87.

Ducellier, Alain. "Les Albanais a Venise aux XIVe et XVe siècles." In *L'Albanie entre Byzance et Venise, Xe–XVe siècles,* 405–20. London: Variorum Reprints, 1987.

Ell, Stephen R. "Citizenship and Immigration in Venice, 1305 to 1500." Ph.D. diss., University of Chicago, 1976.

Ellero, Giuseppe. *L'archivio IRE: Inventari dei fondi antichi degli ospedali e luoghi pii di Venezia.* Venice: Istituzioni di Ricovero e di Educazione, 1987.

Epstein, Steven A. *Wage Labor and Guilds in Medieval Europe.* Chapel Hill: University of North Carolina Press, 1991.

Erspamer, Francesco. *La biblioteca di Don Ferrante: Duello e onore nella cultura del Cinquecento.* Rome: Bulzoni, 1982.

Fairchilds, Cissie. *Domestic Enemies: Servants and Their Masters in Old Regime France.* Baltimore: Johns Hopkins University Press, 1984.

Favalier, Sylvie. "Le attività lavorative in una parrocchia del centro di Venezia (San Polo—secolo XVI)." *Studi veneziani,* n.s., 9 (1985): 187–97.

Fazio, Ida, and Gabriella Gribaudi. "Onore e storia nelle società mediterranee." *Quaderni storici,* n.s., 73 (1990): 277–84.

Ferrante, Lucia. "Differenza sociale e differenza sessuale nelle questioni d'onore (Bologna, sec. XVII)." In *Onore e storia nelle società mediterranee,* edited by Giovanna Fiume, 105–27. Palermo: La Luna, 1989.

Ferraro, Joanne M. *Family and Public Life in Brescia, 1580–1650: The Foundations of Power in the Venetian State.* Cambridge: Cambridge University Press, 1993.

———. "The Power to Decide: Battered Wives in Early Modern Venice." *Renaissance Quarterly* 48 (1995): 492–512.

Ferro, Marco. *Dizionario del dritto comune, e veneto.* 10 tomes in 5 vols. Venice: Modesto Fenzo, 1778–81.

Finlay, Robert. *Politics in Renaissance Venice.* New Brunswick: Rutgers University Press, 1980.

———. "The Venetian Republic as a Gerontocracy: Age and Politics in the Renaissance." *Journal of Medieval and Renaissance Studies* 8 (1978): 157–78.

Fisher, M. Roy. *Titian's Assistants during the Later Years.* New York: Garland, 1977.

Flynn, Maureen. *Sacred Charity: Confraternities and Social Welfare in Spain, 1400–1700.* Ithaca: Cornell University Press, 1989.

Fogolari, Gino. "Jacobello del Fiore e la sua famiglia (nuovi documenti)." *Archivio veneto,* 5th ser., 34–45 (1944): 33–50.

Fragnito, Gigliola. "Cardinals' Courts in Sixteenth-Century Rome." *Journal of Modern History* 65 (1993): 26–56.

Frigo, Daniela. *Il padre di famiglia: Governo della casa e governo civile nella tradizione dell' "economica" tra Cinque e Seicento.* Rome: Bulzoni, 1985.

Fulin, R. "Girolamo Priuli e i suoi diarii." *Archivio veneto* 22 (1881): 137–54.

Gambier, Madile. "La donna e la giustizia penale veneziana nel XVIII secolo." In *Stato, società, e giustizia nella Repubblica Veneta (sec. XV–XVIII),* edited by Gaetano Cozzi, 529–75. Rome: Jouvence, 1980.

Geremek, Bronislaw. *The Margins of Society in Late Medieval Paris.* Translated by Jean Birrell. Cambridge: Cambridge University Press, 1987.

Gianighian, Giorgio, and Paola Pavanini. *Dietro i palazzi: Tre secoli di architettura minore a Venezia, 1492–1803.* Venice: Arsenale, 1984.

Gibbons, Felton. "Practices in Giovanni Bellini's Workshop." *Pantheon* 23 (1965): 146–55.

Gilbert, Felix. "Venice in the Crisis of the League of Cambrai." In *Renaissance Venice,* edited by J. R. Hale, 274–92. London: Faber & Faber, 1974.

Gioffrè, Domenico. *Il mercato degli schiavi a Genova nel secolo XV.* Genoa: Fratelli Bozzi, 1971.

Girouard, Mark. *Life in the English Country House: A Social and Architectural History.* New Haven: Yale University Press, 1978.

Giuriato, G. "Memorie venete nei monumenti di Roma." *Archivio veneto,* n.s., 25 (1883): 119–43.

Given-Wilson, Chris. *The Royal Household and the King's Affinity: Service, Politics, and Finance in England, 1360–1413.* New Haven: Yale University Press, 1986.

Gleason, Elizabeth G. *Gasparo Contarini: Venice, Rome, and Reform.* Berkeley: University of California Press, 1993.

Gnavi, Alessandro. "Valori urbani e attività marginali nella *Piazza Universale* di Tommaso Garzoni." *Ricerche storiche* 20 (1990): 45–73.

Goldthwaite, Richard A. "The Florentine Palace as Domestic Architecture." *American Historical Review* 77 (1972): 977–1012.

———. *Private Wealth in Renaissance Florence.* Princeton: Princeton University Press, 1968.

———. *Wealth and the Demand for Art in Renaissance Italy, 1300–1600.* Baltimore: Johns Hopkins University Press, 1993.

Goodich, Michael. "*Ancilla Dei:* The Servant as Saint in the Late Middle Ages." In *Women of the Medieval World: Essays in Honor of John H. Mundy,* edited by Julius Kirshner and Suzanne F. Wemple, 119–36. Oxford: Basil Blackwell, 1985.

Goy, Richard J. *The House of Gold: Building a Palace in Medieval Venice.* Cambridge: Cambridge University Press, 1992.

*Grande dizionario della lingua italiana.* Edited by Salvatore Battaglia. Turin: UTET, 1961–.

Grendler, Paul F. *Schooling in Renaissance Italy: Literacy and Learning, 1300–1600.* Baltimore: Johns Hopkins University Press, 1989.

Grubb, James S. "Memory and Identity: Why Venetians Didn't Keep *Ricordanze.*" *Renaissance Studies* 8 (1994): 375–87.

Guarducci, Piero. "La servitù domestica nella Toscana bassomedievale: Una precisazione sulle modalità di assunzione." *Erbe d'Arno* 35 (1985): 42–50.

Guarducci, Piero, and Valeria Ottanelli. *I servitori domestici della casa borghese toscana nel basso medioevo.* Florence: Salimbeni, 1982.

Gundersheimer, Werner L. *Ferrara: The Style of a Renaissance Despotism.* Princeton: Princeton University Press, 1973.

Heers, Jacques. *Esclaves et domestiques au Moyen Age dans le monde méditerranéen.* Paris: Arthème Fayard, 1981.

Herlihy, David. "Family Solidarity in Medieval Italian History." In *Economy, Society, and Government in Medieval Italy,* edited by David Herlihy, Robert S. Lopez, and Vsevolod Slessarev, 173–84. Kent, Ohio: Kent State University Press, 1969.

———. "The Population of Verona in the First Century of Venetian Rule." In *Renaissance Venice,* edited by J. R. Hale, 91–120. London: Faber & Faber, 1974.

Herlihy, David, and Christiane Klapisch-Zuber. *Tuscans and Their Families: A Study of the Florentine Catasto of 1427.* New Haven: Yale University Press, 1985. Originally published as *Les Toscans et leurs familles: Une étude du catasto florentin de 1427* (Paris: École des Hautes Études en Science Sociales, 1978).

Hughes, Diane Owen. "From Brideprice to Dowry in Mediterranean Europe." *Journal of Family History* 3 (1978): 262–96.

Humfrey, Peter. *Cima da Conegliano.* Cambridge: Cambridge University Press, 1983.

Hurtubise, Pierre. "La 'familia' del Cardinale Giovanni Salviati (1517–1553)." In *"Familia" del principe e famiglia aristocratica,* edited by Cesare Mozzarelli, 2 vols., 2:589–609. Rome: Bulzoni, 1988.

Ivanoff, Nicola, and Pietro Zampetti. *Giacomo Negretti detto Palma il Giovane.* Bergamo: Poligrafiche Bolis, 1980.

Kaplan, Paul H. D. "Sicily, Venice, and the East: Titian's Fabricius Salvaresius with a Black Page." In *Europa und die Kunst des Islam 15. bis 18. Jahrhundert*, 127–36. Vienna: Böhlau, 1984.

Kedar, Benjamin Z. *Merchants in Crisis: Genoese and Venetian Men of Affairs and the Four-teenth-Century Depression.* New Haven: Yale University Press, 1976.

Kent, Francis William. *Household and Lineage in Renaissance Florence: The Family Life of the Capponi, Ginori, and Rucellai.* Princeton: Princeton University Press, 1977.

King, Margaret Leah. "Caldiera and the Barbaros on Marriage and the Family: Human-ist Reflections on Venetian Realities." *Journal of Medieval and Renaissance Studies* 6 (1976): 19–50.

———. *Venetian Humanism in an Age of Patrician Dominance.* Princeton: Princeton Uni-versity Press, 1986.

———. "Venetian Ideology and the Reconstruction of Knowledge: Giovanni Caldiera (c. 1400–c. 1474)." Ph.D. diss., Stanford University, 1972.

Klapisch-Zuber, Christiane. *Women, Family, and Ritual in Renaissance Italy.* Translated by Lydia G. Cochrane. Chicago: University of Chicago Press, 1985.

———. "Women Servants in Florence during the Fourteenth and Fifteenth Centuries." In *Women and Work in Preindustrial Europe,* edited by Barbara A. Hanawalt, 56–80. Bloomington: Indiana University Press, 1986.

Kuehn, Thomas. *Law, Family, and Women: Toward a Legal Anthropology of Renaissance Italy.* Chicago: University of Chicago Press, 1991.

Kuntz, Marion Leathers. "Voices from a Venetian Prison in the Cinquecento: Francesco Spinola and Dionisio Gallo." *Studi veneziani,* n.s. 27 (1994): 79–126.

Lane, Frederic C. *Andrea Barbarigo: Merchant of Venice, 1418–1449.* Baltimore: Johns Hop-kins Press, 1944.

———. "The Enlargement of the Great Council of Venice." In *Florilegium Historiale: Es-says Presented to Wallace K. Ferguson,* edited by J. G. Rowe and W. H. Stockdale, 236–74. Toronto: University of Toronto Press, 1971.

———. "Family Partnerships and Joint Ventures." In *Venice and History: The Collected Pa-pers of Frederic C. Lane.* Baltimore: Johns Hopkins Press, 1966.

———. *Venetian Ships and Shipbuilders of the Renaissance.* Baltimore: Johns Hopkins Press, 1934.

———. *Venice: A Maritime Republic.* Baltimore: Johns Hopkins University Press, 1973.

———. "Wages and Recruitment of Venetian Galeotti, 1470–1580." *Studi veneziani,* n.s., 6 (1982): 15–43.

Larner, John. *Culture and Society in Italy, 1290–1420.* New York: Charles Scribner's Sons, 1971.

Lazari, Vincenzo. *Del traffico e delle condizioni degli schiavi in Venezia nei tempi di mezzo.* Turin: n.p., 1862.

Lazzarini, Vittorio. *Proprietà e feudi, offizi, garzoni, carcerati in antiche leggi veneziane.* Rome: Edizioni di storia e letteratura, 1960.

*Letteratura italiana: Gli autori: Dizionario bio-bibliografico e indici.* 2 vols. Turin: Einaudi, 1990–91.

Litchfield, R. Burr. *Emergence of a Bureaucracy: The Florentine Patricians, 1530–1790.* Princeton: Princeton University Press, 1986.

Lowry, M. J. C. "The Reform of the Council of Ten, 1582–1583: An Unsettled Problem?" *Studi veneziani* 13 (1971): 275–310.

Lubkin, Gregory. *A Renaissance Court: Milan under Galeazzo Maria Sforza.* Berkeley: University of California Press, 1994.

Luzio, Alessandro, and Rodolfo Renier. "Buffoni, nani e schiavi dei Gonzaga ai tempi d'Isabella D'Este." *Nuovo antologia,* 3rd ser., 34 (1891): 618–50; 35 (1891): 112–46.

Luzzatto, Gino. *Storia economica di Venezia dal'XI al XVI secolo.* Venice: Centro Internazionale delle Arti e del Costume, 1961.

———. *Studi di storia economica veneziana.* Padua: CEDAM, 1954.

Mackenney, Richard. *Tradesmen and Traders: The World of the Guilds in Venice and Europe, c. 1250–c. 1650.* Totowa, N.J.: Barnes & Noble, 1987.

Maranini, Giuseppe. *La costituzione di Venezia.* 2 vols. 1927–31. Reprint. Florence: La Nuova Italia, 1974.

Martini, Gabriele. *Il "vitio nefando" nella Venezia del Seicento: Aspetti sociali e repressione di giustizia.* Rome: Jouvence, 1988.

Martin, John. "A Journeymen's Feast of Fools." *Journal of Medieval and Renaissance Studies* 17 (1987): 149–74.

———. "Out of the Shadow: Heretical and Catholic Women in Renaissance Venice." *Journal of Family History* 10 (1985): 21–33.

———. *Venice's Hidden Enemies: Italian Heretics in a Renaissance City.* Berkeley: University of California Press, 1993.

Mason Rinaldi, Stefania. *Palma il Giovane: L'opera completa.* Milan: Electa, 1984.

Maza, Sarah C. *Servants and Masters in Eighteenth-Century France: The Uses of Loyalty.* Princeton: Princeton University Press, 1983.

McBride, Theresa M. *The Domestic Revolution: The Modernisation of Household Service in England and France, 1820–1920.* New York: Holmes & Meier, 1976.

Mertes, Kate. *The English Noble Household, 1250–1600: Good Governance and Politic Rule.* Oxford: Basil Blackwell, 1988.

Megna, Laura. "Comportamenti abitativi del patriziato veneziano (1582–1740)." *Studi veneziani,* n.s., 22 (1991): 253–323.

Milani, Marisa. "Il caso di Emilia Catena 'Meretrice, striga et herbara.'" *Museum patavinum* 3 (1985): 75–97.

Morozzo della Rocca, Raimondo, and Maria Francesca Tiepolo. "Cronologia veneziana del Cinquecento." In *La civiltà veneziana del Rinascimento,* 197–249. Florence: Sansoni, 1958.

Muir, Edward. *Civic Ritual in Renaissance Venice.* Princeton: Princeton University Press, 1981.

———. "The Doge as *Primus Inter Pares:* Interregnum Rites in Early Sixteenth-Century Venice." In *Essays Presented to Myron P. Gilmore,* edited by Sergio Bertelli and Gloria Ramakus, 2 vols., 1:145–60. Florence: La Nuova Italia, 1978.

———. "Images of Power: Art and Pageantry in Renaissance Venice." *American Historical Review* 84 (1979): 16–52.

———. *Mad Blood Stirring: Vendetta and Factions in Friuli during the Renaissance.* Baltimore: Johns Hopkins University Press, 1993.

Musatti, Eugenio. *Storia della promissione ducale.* 1888. Reprint. Venice: Filippi, 1983.

Musolino, Giovanni. "I santi nel folklore." In *Santità a Venezia,* edited by A. Niero, G. Musolino, and S. Tramontin, 167–227. Venice: Edizioni dello Studium Cattolico Veneziano, 1972.

Nani-Mocenigo, Filippo. "Testamento del Doge Agostino Barbarigo." *Nuovo archivio veneto*, n.s., 17 (1909): 234–61.

Neff, Mary Frances. "Chancellery Secretaries in Venetian Politics and Society, 1480–1533." Ph.D. diss., University of California, Los Angeles, 1985.

———. "A Citizen in the Service of the Patrician State: The Career of Zaccaria de' Freschi." *Studi veneziani*, n.s., 5 (1981): 33–61.

Niermayer, J. F. *Mediae Latinitatis Lexicon Minus*. Leiden: E. J. Brill, 1976.

Origo, Iris. "The Domestic Enemy: The Eastern Slaves in Tuscany in the Fourteenth and Fifteenth Centuries." *Speculum* 30 (1955): 321–66.

———. *The Merchant of Prato: Francesco di Marco Datini, 1335–1410*. New York: Knopf, 1957.

———. *The World of San Bernardino*. London: Jonathan Cape, 1963.

Pallucchini, Rodolfo. *La pittura veneziana del Trecento*. Venice: Istituto per la Collaborazione Culturale, 1964.

Paolillo, Domenico Roberto, and Carlo Dalla Santa. *Il Palazzo Dolfin Manin a Rialto: Storia di un'antica dimora veneziana*. Venice: Alfieri, n.d.

Partner, Peter. *Renaissance Rome, 1500–1559*. Berkeley: University of California Press, 1976.

Pederin, Ivan. "Appunti e notizie su Spalato nel Quattrocento." *Studi veneziani*, n.s., 21 (1991): 323–409.

Perocco, Guido. *Carpaccio nella scuola di S. Giorgio degli Schiavoni*. Venice: Ferdinando Ongania, 1964.

Peroni, Vincenzo. *Biblioteca Bresciana*. 3 vols. 1818–23. Reprint. Bologna: Forni, 1968.

Pertusi, Agostino. "*Quedam regalia insignia:* Ricerche sulle insegne del potere ducale a Venezia durante il medioevo." *Studi veneziani* 7 (1965): 3–123.

Piasentini, Stefano. *"Alla luce della luna": I furti a Venezia, 1270–1403*. Venice: Il Cardo, 1992.

Pilot, Antonio. "Gli 'ordini' dell'accademia veneziana degli uniti (1551)." *Ateneo veneto* 35, pt. 1 (1912): 193–207.

Politi, Giorgio. *Aristocrazia e potere politico nella Cremona di Filippo II*. Milan: SugarCo, 1976.

Polizzotto, Lorenzo. "*Dell'arte del ben morire:* The Piagnone Way of Death, 1494–1545." *I Tatti Studies: Essays in the Renaissance* 3 (1989): 27–87.

Poni, Carlo. "Norms and Disputes: The Shoemakers' Guild in Eighteenth-Century Bologna." *Past and Present*, no. 123 (1989): 80–108.

Preto, Paolo. "Peste e demografia: L'età moderna: Le due pesti del 1575–77 e 1630–31." In *Venezia e la peste 1348/1797*, 97–98. Venice: Marsilio, 1979.

Pullan, Brian. *Rich and Poor in Renaissance Venice: The Social Institutions of a Catholic State, to 1620*. Cambridge: Harvard University Press, 1971.

———. "Wage-Earners and the Venetian Economy, 1550–1630." In *Crisis and Change in the Venetian Economy in the Sixteenth and Seventeenth Centuries*, edited by Brian Pullan, 146–74. London: Methuen, 1968.

Queller, Donald E., and Thomas F. Madden. "Father of the Bride: Fathers, Daughters, and Dowries in Late Medieval and Early Renaissance Venice." *Renaissance Quarterly* 46 (1993): 685–711.

Quondam, Amedeo. "La 'forma del vivere': Schede per l'analisi del discorso cortigiano." In *La corte e il "Cortegiano,"* vol. 2, *Un modello europeo*, edited by Adriano Prosperi, 15–68. Rome: Bulzoni, 1980.

Thompson, E. P. "The Crime of Anonymity." In *Albion's Fatal Tree: Crime and Society in Eighteenth-Century England,* edited by Douglas Hay et al., 255–308. New York: Pantheon Books, 1975.

Tramontin, Silvio. "La visita apostolica del 1581 a Venezia." *Studi veneziani* 9 (1967): 453–533.

Trebbi, Giuseppe, "La società veneziana." In *Storia di Venezia,* vol. 6, *Dal Rinascimento al Barocco,* edited by Gaetano Cozzi and Paolo Prodi, 129–213. Rome: Enciclopedia Italiana, 1994.

Trecanni degli Alfieri, Giovanni, ed. *Storia di Brescia.* 4 vols. Brescia: Morcelliana, 1961–64.

Trexler, Richard C. "Charity and the Defense of Urban Elites in the Italian Communes." In *The Rich, the Well Born, and the Powerful: Elites and Upper Classes in History,* edited by Frederic Cople Jaher, 64–109. Urbana: University of Illinois Press, 1973.

Tucci, Ugo. "Il patrizio veneziano mercante e umanista." In *Venezia centro di mediazione tra oriente e occidente (secoli XV–XVI): Aspetti e problemi,* edited by Hans-Georg Beck, Manoussos Manoussacas, and Agostino Pertusi, 2 vols., 1:335–57. Florence: Olschki, 1977.

———. *Mercanti, navi, monete nel Cinquecento veneziano.* Bologna: Il Mulino, 1981.

———. "The Psychology of the Venetian Merchant in the Sixteenth Century." In *Renaissance Venice,* edited by J. R. Hale, 346–78. London: Faber & Faber, 1974.

Ulvioni, Paolo. *Il gran castigo di Dio: Carestia ed epidemie a Venezia e nella terraferma, 1628–1632.* Milan: Franco Angeli, 1989.

Urban, Lina Padoan. "La festa della Sensa nelle arti e nell'iconografia." *Studi veneziani* 10 (1968): 291–353.

Vaglia, Ugo. *Vicende storiche della Val Sabbia dal 1580 al 1915.* Brescia: Fratelli Geroldi, 1955.

Ventura, Angelo. *Nobiltà e popolo nella società veneta del '400 e '500.* Bari: Laterza, 1964.

Viaro, Roberta. "La magistratura degli esecutori contro la bestemmia nel XVI secolo." Tesi di laurea, Università degli Studi di Padova, 1969–70.

Verlinden, Charles. *L'esclavage dans l'Europe médiévale.* 2 vols. Bruges: De Tempel, 1955–77.

Wiesner, Merry E. *Working Women in Renaissance Germany.* New Brunswick: Rutgers University Press, 1986.

Wolff, S. J. "Venice and the Terraferma: Problems of the Change from Commercial to Landed Activities." In *Crisis and Change in the Venetian Economy in the Sixteenth and Seventeenth Centuries,* edited by Brian S. Pullan, 175–203. London: Methuen, 1968.

Yriarte, Charles. *La vie d'un patricien de Venise au XVIe siècle.* Paris: J. Rothschild, 1884.

Zannini, Andrea. *Burocrazia e burocrati a Venezia in età moderna: I cittadini originari (sec. XVI–XVIII).* Venice: Istituto Veneto di Scienze, Lettere ed Arti, 1993.

———. "Un censimento inedito del primo Seicento e la crisi demografica ed economica di Venezia." *Studi veneziani,* n.s., 26 (1993): 87–116.

Zordan, Giorgio. *L'ordinamento giuridico veneziano: Lezioni di storia del diritto veneziano con una nota bibliografica.* Padua: CLEUP, 1980.

# Index

Abarcubus, Michele, 218
adoption, 99–101, 156
Adriatico, Girolamo, 195
Aethiops, Venturina, 214
Afeita, Ludovico del, 185
Agata, Cristoforo, 209, 210
Albanese, Lena, 153
Albanese, Maria, 153
Albanese da Montagnana, Tognetto, 153
Alberegno, Antonio, 162
Alberti, Giannozzo, 223
Alberti, Leon Battista, xxiii, 3, 198, 223
Albinoni, Giovanni Battista, 113
Albona, Marin d', 166
Alborante, Santo Giovanni, 161
Alborello, Giacomo, 104
Alcherio, Francesco, 185
Alcherio, Marco, 185
Aldioni, Niccolò, 183
Alemanea, Philipo da, 162
Alesio, Andrea, 179
anime, 47–48
Aperlis, Clara, 184
apprentices: contracts of, 131–32, 136; func-
    tions of, 104–5; of Lorenzo Lotto, 102–3,
    121; registration of, 46–47
Archerii, Giacomo, 219–20
Arengo, 9
Argusani, Francesco, 183
Arimondo, Catarina, 130, 136, 152
Aristotle, 4, 8, 23
Armelino, Matteo, 105
Arquà, Gasparo d', 120
art, servants depicted in, 27–35
artisans: children of, 154; marriage of, 155;
    servant keeping by, 99–106

Athanatophilia. See Discorsi morali contra
    il dispiacer del morire
Avanzo, Clara di, 129–30
Avanzo, Pietro di, 129
Avocatis, Pietro di, 217

**B**
Badoer, Marino, 5
Badoer da Veglia, Girolamo, 225
Balanzan, Augustin, 200
Balbi, Alvise, 224
Balbi, Caterinella, 209
Baldagara, Domenico, 180
Ballota, Francesco, 160
Ballota, Lucia, 160
Barbarigo, Agostino, 80, 86, 179, 197, 203
Barbarigo, Alvise, 46, 90, 91, 120, 125, 137,
    140, 178, 182
Barbarigo, Andrea, 90–91, 122–23, 144, 145,
    149
Barbarigo, Andrea (son of Niccolò), 92,
    121–22, 123, 137; aphorisms of, 118–19
Barbarigo, Antonio, 92–93, 144, 177
Barbarigo, Giovanni Alvise, 92, 121, 177
Barbarigo, Marco, 86
Barbarigo, Niccolò, 46, 90, 91–92, 120, 123,
    125, 137, 140, 178, 182
Barbarigo, Paola, 86, 88
Barbarigo family, account books of,
    90–93, 122–26
Barbaro, Daniele, 16
Barbaro, Francesco, 10–13, 20, 23, 32
Barbaro, Giovanni Francesco, 49
Barbaro, Giustiniana, 32
Barbaro, Leonardo, 72
Barbaro, Marcantonio, 121

Barbaro, Marina, 94
Barbaro, Tiberio, 71, 210
Barbaro, Zaccaria, 10, 94
Barbo, Benedetto, 201
Barbo, Giovanni, 52
Barbo, Niccolò, 52, 58
Barbo, Pietro, 201
Bardolino, Piero da, 137
Barges, 27
Bari, Battista di, 131
Barozzi, Francesco, 214
Bartolani, Biagio, 160
Bartolani, Marieta, 160
Basadonna, Girolamo, 166
Basadonna, Pietro, 35
Basalu, Piero, 95
Basello, Ioseph, 158
Basello, Regina, 158
Basilischis, Giovanni di, 156
Battochio, Zuan Piero, 152
Belino, Giovanni Vittore, 100
Bellini, Gentile, 32
Bello, Antonio di, 163
Beltrami, Daniele, 231
Bembo, Giovanni Maria, 159
Bembo, Pietro, 94
Benedetto, Rocco di, 151
Bentio, Bernardino, 161
Bereti, Francesco di, 121
Bergamasco, Alessandro, 166
Bergamo, Zaneto da, 88, 146, 147
Bernardo, Andrea, 175
Bernardo, Francesco, 94, 210
Bernardo, Lorenzo, 160
Bernardo, Niccolò, 72–73
Bertoldi, Niccolò di, 162
Bertoldi, Vittoria di, 162
Bethinis, Giacoma di, 222
Bianchinin, Zuan Antonio, 201
Bicharano, Francesco, 219
Bo, Maria dal, 220
boatmen, 170–71; dowries of, 158; Garzoni's view of, 26; prevented from organizing, 55; as servants, 166; Vecellio's view of, 28, 31. *See also* gondoliers

boats, 26, 34, 55–56, 152; bequests of, 194, 203; described, 28, 31, 168; purchase of, 166; significance of, to servants, 170–71; on tombs, 184; vandalism of, 212, 224
Bodin, Jean, 227
Boerio, Giuseppe, 178
Bollani, Stefano, 212
Bonacorsi, Giovanni, 140
Bonzanina, Angela, 180
Borromeo, Carlo, 21
Borromeo, Isabella, 17
Bortholuzzi, Francesco, 66
Bortholuzzi, Paolo Gasparini, 66
Bovolenta, Giorgio da, 213
Bracciolini, Poggio, 15
Bragadin, Antonio, 217
Bragadin, Cecilia, 204
Bragadin, Francesco, 160, 161
Bragadin, Giovanni Francesco, 120–21
Brazzo di Maina, Giorgio da, 151, 209
Brazzo di Maina, Michele Cosmo da, 151
Brescia, Julio da, 207
Brescia, Zuan Piero da, 209
Bressano, Paolo, 102
brokers, for servants, 120
Brombilla, Ventura, 162
Brown, Patricia Fortini, 34
Broylo, Giovanni di, 176
Brucker, Gene, 176
Budua, Ruosa da, 156, 157, 159, 197
Bugatto, Giovanni Pietro, 167
Buranello, Agostino, 100–101
Buranello, Hippolita, 100–101
burial. *See* funerals
Buzzuola, Francesco, 65, 71

C

Cà di Dio, 84, 179, 208, 224
Cadore, Lucia da, 120, 121
Cadore, Marina da, 146
Caffa, Margarita da, 172
Cagneto, Francesco, 157
Calbo, Pietro, 177, 208
Caldiera, Giovanni, 13–16, 19, 23, 228
Calegari, Francesco di, 137

Calegari, Menega, 137
Capello, Coronea, 90
Capello, Cristina, 90
Capello, Giovanni Battista, 66, 212
Capello, Silvano, 170
Capello family, 170
Capi, Gironimo di, 183, 185
*capi di contrade*, 44
*capi di sestieri*: and Capitulary of 1503,
    49–54, 229, 241–43; and registration of
    servants, 44–48; and transfer of author-
    ity to *censori*, 43–44, 54–59
Capitulary of 1503, 49–54, 229, 241–43
Capitulary of 1544, 54–59, 244–48
Caravaggio, Domenichina da, 185
Carchassa, Uliana, 171
cardinals, households of, 231–32
Carnival, 178, 217
Carpaccio, Vittore, 34, 223
Carpan, Antonio, 101
Carpan, Bartolomeo, 102
Carrara, Giovanni da, 206
Carrara, Pietro da, 73, 217
Casa, Giovanni della, 62, 223
Castellane, Simone di, 170
Castrignano, Giovanni di Tomasi da, 69
Catalenich, Zorzi, 102
Catena, Emilia, 179
Cattaro, Alegreto, 170
Cattaro, Anna da, 153
Cattaro, Maddalena da, 137, 140
Cattaro, Niccolò da, 210–11
Cattaro, Petrussa da, 137, 182
Cattaro, Pietro da, 219
Cattaro, Zuane da, 147, 204
Cavalcanti, Ginevra, 10
cavaliers, 80, 81
Cecil, William, 231
Cefalonia, Dorothea dalla, 184
*censori*: as judges, 63–73, 212, 216–17, 224;
    legislation enacted by, 55–62; punish-
    ment determined by, 68–69; transfer of
    authority to, 54–59
census data, 106–17; recorded by clergy,
    110–17

Centiis da Gradisca, Giacomo di, 219
Centoni, Cristoforo, 72, 217
Certaldo, Paolo da, 105
Cesarea, Madonna, 151
chambermaids, 171
Chambers, David, 232
children: education of, 11–12; father's duty
    to, 6; as servants, 152–55
Christian economy, 21–23, 41
Cimador, Paolo, 97
Cinganetto, Marco di Vivian, 148
*cinque alla pace*, 63
Circulis da Verona, Ventura di, 81–84
Cithinio, Cristoforo, 214
Cittadella, Pietro da, 216
*cittadini*, 13; categories of, 95; servants of,
    95–99, 105–6
Civran, Luca, 175, 206
Civran, Pietro, 156
Cleaver, Robert, 3
Cleopatra, 25
Climento da Alemania, Stefano di, 164
Colalto, Margarita da, 120
Colbigot, Antonio, 185
Colbigot, Maria, 185
Colona, Giovanni Domenico, 158
Comin, Zuane di, 96
Comnena, Deianira, 17, 18–19
*compagnie della calza*, 211
Condulmer, Aurelio, 164
Condulmer, Benedetto, 216
Condulmer, Domenica, 162
Condulmer, Giovanni Battista, 49
Conegliano, Philipo da, 70
confraternities. See *scuole*
Constantin, Isabeta di, 151–52, 218
Constantin, Zanmaria di, 151–52, 218
Constantin da Cadore, Battista di Zuanne
    di, 122, 153
Contarini, Cecilia, 85
Contarini, Federico, 54
Contarini, Gasparo, 95, 235
Contarini, Girolamo, 151
Contarini, Marino, 94, 138

Cividale, Pietro da, 71

Contarini, Paolo, 142, 163
Contarini, Piero, 138
Conte, Niccolò di, 134
Contento, Aldo, 106, 107
contracts: of apprentices, 131–32; regard-
  ing children, 132; inscription, 129–31,
  135–36; length of, 135–38; between mas-
  ters and servants, 122, 129–35, 210–11,
  212, 224; of salaried servants, 132–35
Corner, Giovanni, 160
Corner, Nadal, 90
Corner, Pietro, 71, 205
Corone, Anna da, 218
Correr, Francesco, 122
Corte, Francesco di, 120
Cortese, Paolo, 232
Coryat, Thomas, 227–28, 231, 235
Cotrugli, Benedetto, 16
Council of Ten, 43–44, 63
courtesans, 39, 97–98
Cozzi, Gaetano, 67, 231
Cristoforo da Monzambano, Leonardo
  Bettino, 162
Cristoforo da Monzambano, Mattea, 162
Curelli, Ludovico, 215
Curtino, Alvise, 209
Curtino, Fineta, 209

**D**
Da Canal family, 204
Damiani da Montagnana, Francesca di, 153
Damiani da Montagnana, Zuanalvise di,
  153
damigelle, 19
Dandolo, Enrico, 78
Dandolo, Fantino, 63–64
Dandolo, Vittore, 65, 72
Dandolo, Zilia, 85
Davis, James C., 86
De cardinalatu (Cortese), 232
De gli habiti antichi, et moderni di diverse
  parti del mondo libri due (Vecellio),
  27–32
Del governo della corte d'un signore in
  Roma (Priscianese), 232

Della economica (Lanteri), 17–21
Della instituzione morale (Piccolomini), 16
De oeconomica veneta (Caldiera), 14
De origine, situ et magistratibus urbis
  Venetae (Sanuto), 44
De praestantia venetae politicae (Caldiera),
  14
De regimine principum (Giles of Rome), 5
De regimine rectoris (Paolino), 5–9, 13
De republica (Querini), 15
De re uxoria (Barbaro), 10–13
De virtutibus moralibus et theologicis
  (Caldiera), 14
Dialogo del patron, et del Zane, 216
Diedo, Antonio, 211
Diogenes, 7, 9, 223
Discorsi morali contra il dispiacer del
  morire (Athanatophilia) (Glissenti),
  37–40, 220, 227
Dod, John, 3
dogaressa, position of, 84–85
doges: bodyguards of, 79; court of, 80–81;
  households of, 77–85
Dolan, Frances, xix
Dolfin, Girolamo, 94
Dolzego, Zorzi da, 120
Donà, Antonio, 163
Donà, Cristina, 65
Donà, Giovanni, 49, 167
Donà, Girolamo, 147
Donà, Leonardo, 161, 180, 200, 235
Donà, Michele, 163
Donà, Zuan Simon, 94
Donà da Sclavonia, Marco, 163
dowries: of servants, 155–63; sources of,
  159–62
Drisgna, Lucia da, 156
Drisgna, Michele da, 156
Drusi, Paolo, 211
Duodo, Eustachio, 212

**E**
Ecclesiasticus, 7, 20
Emo, Antonio, 69
esecutori contro la bestemmia, 58

Este, Isabella d', 119–20
Este, Lucia da, 177
Este, Maddalena da, 73

**F**
*Fabricius Salvaresius with a Black Page* (Titian), 32
Fairchilds, Cissie, xvii, 205
Falla, Alem, 153
Falla, Lotho, 153
family: defined, xxiii–xxiv; governance of, 5–6; as metaphor for the state, 13–16. *See also* households
fantesche, 19, 31
fathers, role of, in household, 6, 8–9, 222
Fauro, Stefano, 180
Feltrin, Francesco, 130, 153
Feltrin, Maria, 130–31, 153
Feltrina, Franceschina, 119
Feltrina, Isabeta, 119
Feltrina, Maddalena, 96, 97, 123, 148–49, 182
Feltrina, Urseta, 209
Ferrante, Antonio, 172
Ferro, Federico, 137, 147
Ferro, Marco, 172
Finetti, Giovanni, 225
Fiore, Ercole del, 99
Fiore, Francesco del, 99
Fiore, Iacobello del, 99, 101, 104
Fiore, Matteo del, 99
Fiorito, Giovanni Battista, 64
Fiume, Marco da, 102
Flambro, Constantin da, 122
Florence, Italy, servant keeping in, xviii–xix, 233–34, 236
Fondra, Andriana, 103
Fondra, Zaccaria, 120
Fontana, Andrea de la, 197
Fontana, Barbarela de la, 197
Formento, Franceschina, 172
Fornasier, Bastian, 153
Fornasier, Battista, 132, 153
Foscari, Alessandro, 54
Foscari, Francesco, 80, 81, 204

Foscari, Jacopo, 204, 205
Foscari, Niccolò, 105, 159, 175, 183, 204
Foscarini, Alvise, 73
Foscarini, Luca, 216
Fragnito, Gigliola, 232
Francesco da Montello, Baldisera di, 201, 202
Francesco da Montello, Benetto di, 202
Francesco da Montello, Lucia di, 201
Francia, Giovanni da, 100
Franco, Giacomo, 172
*fraterna*, 86, 146–47
Frigo, Daniela, 4, 8, 17, 21, 238
funerals, of servants, 182–85
Furlan, Andrea, 214
Furlan, Battista, 176
Furlana, Agatha, 96
Furlana, Isabetta, 117

**G**
Gabia, Giacomo di Francesco, 163
Galasso, Michiel, 196
*Galateo* (della Casa), 62, 223
Garabaldo, Zaneto, 166
Garzoni, Tommaso, 23–27, 31, 35, 40, 41, 170, 220–21, 229
Garzoni, Vincenzo di, 70
Gentili, Pierantonio, 94
Geremek, Bronislaw, xviii
Gibelino, Ciprian di, 183
Gilbert, Felix, 231
Giles of Rome, 5
Gioffrè, Domenico, xvi
Giova, Bernardino, 194
Giovanni da Ferrara, Vito di, 199
Giustinian, Andrea, 214
Giustinian, Leonardo, 122
Giustinian, Lorenzo, 160
Giustinian, Marco, 170
Giustinian, Marino, 211
Giustinian, Zaccaria, 126
giustizieri vecchi, 44–47
Glissenti, Fabio, 24, 37–40, 120, 142, 198, 209, 220, 221, 222, 223, 229, 231, 235–36
Gnavi, Alessandro, 24

*Godly Form of Household Government, for the Ordering of Private Families, A* (Dod and Cleaver), 3
Goldthwaite, Richard, 144
gondolas. *See* boats
gondoliers: foul language used by, 220–21; Garzoni's view of, 26; Glissenti's depiction of, 37, 39–40, 221; penalties imposed upon, 55–56; responsibilities of, 168; Vecellio's view of, 28; wages of, 60, 141–42
Gonzaga, Laura, 17
Gonzaga, Lodovica, 117
Goodrich, Michael, xix
Gorizia, Gironima da, 97, 177, 197
governesses, role of, 27, 171, 200
Gradenigo, Laura, 22
Gradenigo, Marino, 217
Gradenigo, Pietro, 79–80
Grado, Ludovico da cà, 221
grand chancellor, 95
Grando, Antonio, 170
Great Council: legislation affecting servants, 49–54, 57; Serrata of, 9, 80
Greca, Zanina, 171
Greco, Giorgio, 183
Gregorio, Marco di, 147
Grimani, Isabeta, 156–57, 197
Grisson, Pietro, 46
Gritti, Andrea, 66, 216
Gritti, Andrea (doge), 58–59, 84, 180, 231
Gritti, Franceschina, 84
Gritti, Giovanni, 66
Gritti, Laura, 100, 156
Gritti, Marcantonio, 70
Gritti, Pietro, 70
Gritti, Raimondo, 73, 217
Guarducci, Piero, xviii
Guazzo, Stefano, 20–21, 223
guest quarters, 17
guilds, 237

**H**
*Healing of the Possessed Man, The* (Carpaccio), 34
Heers, Jacques, xviii

Herlihy, David, xviii, 233, 234
Hesiod, 11
household management, treatises on, 228–29; and Christian economy, 21–23; hierarchy as subject of, 40–42; political metaphor used in, 13–16; popularity of, 3–5; and social utility of servants, 16–21; Venetian tradition of, 5–13; and wifely duties, 21–23
households, Venetian: artisan, 99–106; cardinals' households as model for, 231–32; *cittadino,* 95–99; compared with European households, 231; compared with Florence, 233–34; ducal, 77–85; as hierarchy, 8–9, 14–16, 19, 40–42, 191, 229; ideal, 14; largest, 232–33; as microcosm of state, 14–16, 228; patrician, 85–95, 222–23; as symbol of social system, 17–21
Hurtubise, Pierre, 232

**I**
*I libri della famiglia* (Alberti), xxiii, 3, 198
*Il libro dell'arte de mercatura* (Cotrugli), 16
*Il Savio Industrioso* (Zambelli), 150
indulgences, 160, 173, 203
Istria, Bona da, 99

**J**
Jerome, Saint, 7

**K**
King, Margaret, 10
Klapisch-Zuber, Christiane, xviii, xxi, xxiv, 132, 213, 233, 235–36
knights. *See* cavaliers

**L**
labor and class relations, 149–50, 237–39
*La civil conversatione* (Guazzo), 20
Lando, Pietro, 80
Lane, Frederic, 9, 86, 87, 144
Lanteri, Giacomo, 17–21, 31, 36, 41, 95, 192, 226
Lanteri, Lucretia Bona de, 18

legal disputes, between masters and servants, 63–73
Lemesanis, Battista da, 64
Lena, Donna, 179–80
Leon, Caterina, 148
Leon, Leonardo Giovanni, 148
Leoncini, Angelica, 97–98
Leoncini, Zuane, 97
Leono, Luca, 193
Leono, Lucretia, 193
Lepanto, Marro da, 137, 146
Lesina, Caterina da, 140
Lezze, Lorenzo da, 49
Lezze, Marin da, 194
Lion, Antonio, 153
Lion, Tommaso, 64
Lion, Vincenzo, 153
Lippomano, Bartolomeo, 113
Lippomano, Elena, 91
Lippomano, Francesco, 113
Lippomano, Geronimo, 205
Lippomano family, 87
Locadello, Zuan Giacomo, 180
Locadello family, 135
Lombardo, Julia, 97–98, 99, 117
Lombardo, Lorenzo, 71
Longo, Francesco, 70
Loredan, Francesco, 132–33
Loredan, Giorgio, 157
Lotto, Lorenzo, 101–3, 104, 120, 121, 145, 178, 179, 223
Lovatina, Simon da, 135, 180
Lovatina, Tonina da, 135, 180
*L'ultima licenza della buona massara dalla cattiva patrona,* 216
Lupatino, Gioanbattista, 17–18, 19
Lupatino, Pietro Antonio, 17
Lupini, Angela, 96
Luzzatto, Gino, 144, 177

**M**

McBride, Theresa, xvii, 186, 239
Macipo, Alvise, 180
Madiotis, Francesco di, 72
Maffei, Vettor, 148

Malipiera, Laura, 117
Malipiera, Lucietta, 117
Malipiero, Beta, 203
Malipiero, Domenico, 205
Malipiero, Marco, 203
Malipiero, Marino, 172
Malipiero, Paolo, 94
Malipiero, Priamo, 137, 185
Malipiero, Vittore, 212, 224
Malumbra, Mattea, 200
Malumbra, Michele, 200
Mansueti, 34
Mantoana, Margarita, 184
Marcello, Elena, 92, 178
Marcello, Giovanni, 183
Maria, Giovanni, 122
Marimoiori, Niccolò, 209, 210
Marino, Gaspare, 69
marriage: as political alliance, 85; purpose of, 10; Renaissance theories of, 32; of servants, 155–67
Martinengo, Brunori da, 167
Massimi, Paolo di, 147–48
masters: as executors of servants' wills, 198–99; murdered by servants, 218–20; responsibilities of, 223; risks to, 52; sexual advances of, 52–53, 57
master-servant relationships, 146–47; contractual nature of, 53–54, 61, 73–74, 122, 192, 210–11, 212, 224; dynamics of, 191–93; importance of loyalty, 20–21, 192, 193–94, 197–98; judicial decisions affecting, 63–73; sexual liaisons, 213–14, 217, 236–37; variety of, 200–203, 226; views of, 238. *See also* masters; servants
Mathan (servant), 7, 9, 223
Maximus, Valerius, 16
Maza, Sarah, xvii, 185–86
Medici, Cosimo I de, 234
Medici, Cosimo il Vecchio de, 10
Medici, Ferdinando I de, 234
Medici, Giovanni di Bicci de, 10
Medici, Lorenzo de, 10, 12
Medici household, 233–34
Memo, Zuan Maria, 133–34, 137

Mercatello, Antonio di, 99
Mercatello, Caterina di, 99
Mestre, Bartolomeo da, 173
Mestre, Bortolo da, 224
Mestre, Pietro da, 171
Michiel, Alvise, 122
Michiel, Diana, 94
Michiel, Francesco, 153
Michiel, Giulio, 66
Michiel, Niccolò, 71, 180
Michiel, Tomà, 166
Michiel, Vitale, 44, 49
Minio, Domenico, 49
Miona, Maria, 194
*Miracle at the Bridge of San Lio* (Mansueti), 34
*Miracle at the Bridge of San Lorenzo* (Bellini), 32
Mocenigo, Alvise, 77; will of, 84, 194, 208
Mocenigo, Marina, 94
Mocenigo, Pietro, 94
Modena, Flaminio da, 132
Modon, Manoli da, 137
Molin, Bernardo da, 94
Molin, Francesco da, 70
Molin, Marco da, 166
Montagnana, Maria da, 120, 121, 145
Montagnana, Sebastiano da, 65
Montagnana, Zuanalvise di Damiani da, 121
Montaigne, Michel de, 228, 231
Montenegro, Rado da, 137
Moretto, Daniele di, 217
Moro, Antonio, 233
Morosini, Alvise, 72
Morosini, Angelo, 161
Morosini, Antonia, 196
Morosini, Bartolomeo, 177
Morosini, Donata, 196, 203
Morosini, Gaudenzi, 171
Morosini, Giacomo, 122, 177
Morosini, Helena, 100
Morosini, Lucia, 184–85, 206, 207
Morosini, Marcantonio, 206

Morosini, Marcantonio (procurator), 121, 129, 165; will of, 195–97, 209
Morosini, Marco, 100
Morosini, Maria, 185, 207
Morosini, Marino, 79
Morosini, Michele, 184, 206
Morosini, Morosina, 171
Morosini, Paolo, 160
Morosini, Piero, 206
Morosini, Pietro, 171, 172
Morosini, Zorzi, 121
Morosini, Zuane, 206
Mosto, Pietro da, 35
Mugla, Andrea da, 134, 135
Muir, Edward, 231

**N**
Nani, Caterina, 153
Nani, Francesco, 153
Nani, Lorenzo, 153
Nani, Niccolò, 153
Narvesia, Geronimo da, 217
Navagero, Bernardo, 214
Negretti, Giacomo. *See* Palma il Giovane
Negro, Africo, 151, 152, 209
Negro, Alvise, 94, 184
Negroponte, Niccolò da, 184
Niccolò, Francesco di, 208
Nicholas III, Pope, 173
Nicoloxo, Niccolò, 209
Nigro, Theodoro, 156
Novello, Marcantonio, 173, 224

**O**
Obici, Andriana, 117
Oderzo, Melchiore da, 212
*Oeconomicus* (Xenophon), 3
*On the Instruction of Married Women* (Valier), 22–23
Origo, Iris, xvii–xviii
Orio, Girolamo, 64
Oro, Agnesina dal, 203
Oro, Francesco dal, 203
orphans, 100–101

Ottanelli, Valeria, xviii
Ottobon, Gian Francesco, 176

**P**
Pace, Sebastiano di, 148
Padoan, Lunardo, 119
Padova, Bartolomeo di Gobbati da, 70
Padova, Maria da, 177
Paduana, Benedetta, 159
painters. *See* artisans
paintings, 32–35, 203–4
Palazzo, Gioanandrea, 17
Paleologa, Francesca, 19
Palma il Giovane, 103–4, 194
Palma il Vecchio, 103, 104
Paolino the Minorite, Fra, 5–9, 14, 19, 41,
    209, 223, 228
Paparoto, Vittore, 72
Partner, Peter, 232
Pasqualigo, Giovanni, 183
Patento, Bartolomeo di, 105
Patras, Caterina da, 183
Patras, Niccolò da, 132–33
patricians, households of, 85–95
Paxeto, Piero, 90
Pegoloto, Niccolò, 219
Pegoloto, Peregrina, 219
Peraga, Guglielmo da, 81
Pericles, 11
Permuta, Natalino, 69
Peschiera, Anzolo da, 207
Petrarch, xviii
*Piazza universale di tutte le professioni del
    mondo* (Garzoni), 24–27
Piccolomini, Alessandro, 16
Pieve di Cadore, Bartolomeo da, 216
Piove di Sacco, Francesco da, 219–20
Pisani, Marco Antonio, 224
Pisani, Vittore, 183
Pizzuol, Zuan Battista, 130–31
plagues, impact on population, 108–9
Plutarch, 10, 12
Polangelo, Quintiliano, 70
Politi, Giorgio, 4

Polonia, Philippo da, 99, 100
Pordenone, Sebastiano da, 122
Pozzo, Giovanni Matteo, 102
Priscianese, Francesco, 232
Priuli, Alvise, 232–33
Priuli, Antonio, 232–33
Priuli, Chiara, 89
Priuli, Domenego, 194, 195
Priuli, Francesco, 70, 86, 87, 88, 89, 120,
    194, 207, 232–33
Priuli, Giacomo, 120
Priuli, Giovanni da cà, 170
Priuli, Girolamo, 81, 86, 87, 88, 89, 179
Priuli, Laura, 88–89, 207
Priuli, Lorenzo, 85, 147; family ledger of,
    86–89, 143, 145–46
Priuli, Lucretia, 161
Priuli, Marina, 87
Priuli, Niccolò, 153
Priuli, Priula, 161
Priuli, Vincenzo, 86, 87–89
professions: encyclopedia of, 24–27; of
    servants' fathers, 154–55
*promissioni*, 78–79, 80
prostitutes, 56, 66, 98, 117
Pullan, Brian, 173, 231
Purliliis, Leonardo di, 69

**Q**
Querini, Carlo, 200
Querini, Francesco, 166, 217
Querini, Guglielmo, 144
Querini, Lauro, 15
Querini-Tiepolo conspiracy of 1310, 79

**R**
Ragusa, xvi–xvii, 237
Ragusa, Giovanni da, 156
Ragusa, Rado da, 156
Ragusa, Zanetto da, 121, 137
Raimondo, Leonardo, 137, 146
Raphanellis, Cristina di, 136
Raphanellis, Marco di, 136
Rapp, Richard, 136

registration: of apprentices, 46–47; of in-
dentured servants, 47–48; of servants,
44–48
Renée of France, duchess of Ferrara, 17
Ricio, Francesco, 72
Rimondo, Marcantonio, 147
Rini, Scipione, 146
Rizzo, Andrea, 180
Rizzo, Maria, 180
Rocha Contrada, Caterina della, 102, 121
Rocha Contrada, Ercole della, 102, 121, 223
Romania, Francesco da, 212
Rossi, Pascha di, 200
Rucellai, Giovanni, 233
Ruggiero, Guido, 213

**S**

Salamon, Michele, 134
Salò, Innocente da, 170
Sàlo, Zuane da, 121–22
Salviati, Giovanni, 232
Sansovino, Francesco, 55, 173
Sansovino, Jacopo, 94
Santa Sofia, Battista di, 197
Sant'Ursula, scuola of, 172, 184
Sanuto, Clara, 105
Sanuto, Marino, 44, 120, 142, 178
San Vito da Salvacono, Angelica di, 207
San Vito da Salvacono, Blanchino di, 207
Saon, Giovanni dal, 101, 178
Saraxina, Lucia, 123
Savina, Giovanni da, 219
Scamozzi, Vincenzo, 64
Scandori, Michelin, 151
Schiavona, Ruosa, 179
Schiavona da Sibenico, Lena, 123
Schio, Orsa da, 160, 161
Scodra, Girolamo, 193
Scorzoni, Gerolamo, 72
Scott, James, 217
*scudieri*, 80, 81
*scuole*, importance of, to servants, 172–75
Scutari, Agnese da, 137, 204
Scutari, Catarina da, 177
Scutari, Giorgio da, 100

Scutari, Giovanni da, 156
Scutari, Pantaleone da, 204
Segna, Giovanni da, 167
Sensa fair, 177–78
Serena, Virgilio, 122
Serravalle, Gaspare da, 166
servants: as accouterments of nobility,
61–62; adolescence of, 208–9; as depicted in art, 27–35; in artisan households, 99–106; of Barbarigo family,
90–93, 122–26; beatings of, 209, 221–22;
bequests from, 204–5; bequests to,
195–97, 203–4; as bodyguards, 79; census data on, 106–17; charges brought
against, 64–66; children as, 152–55; of
*cittadini*, 95–99, 105–6; clothes worn by,
56, 205; contracts of, 122, 129–38; cost of
maintaining, 143–45; death and burial
of, 182–85; as defendants, 63–73, 215–17;
disloyalty and disobedience of, 207–26;
distribution of, by gender, 116–17; distribution of, by social class, 113–16;
dowries of, 155–63; in ducal households, 78–85; employed by Jews, 98;
employed by prostitutes, 98, 117; female, 18–19, 26–27, 28, 31, 61, 66, 66, 109,
140, 165, 171–72; Garzoni's view of,
25–27; geographic origins of, 123–25,
127–29; Glissenti's view of, 37–40; governance of, 6–7, 20; holidays celebrated
by, 177–78; household position of, 8–9;
housing of, 93–95; ideal, 206–7; indentured, 47–48, 135–37; as informers,
211–12; inscribed, 129–31, 139–40; and
labor and class relations, 237–39; legislation affecting, 49–54, 59–62, 229;
leisure activities of, 177–78; loyalty as
virtue of, 20–21, 192, 193–94, 197–98;
male, 31, 56, 61, 109–10, 140, 167–69, 230;
marriage of, 155–67; masters murdered
by, 218–20; masters' view of, 36–37;
murder of, 209–10; necessity of, 10–11;
neighborhood-based friendships,
171–72; in non-noble households,
95–99; in old age, 178–82; in patrician

households, 87–95; payment schedules, 145–49; of Priuli family, 87–89; punishment for crimes, 69–71, 219–20, 222–26; recruitment of, 119–29, 149; registration of, 44–48, 73; regulations affecting, 43–44; relationships among, 56, 175–77; responsibilities of, 167–69, 171–72; rewarding and punishing of, by masters, 7, 11, 16, 18; role of, in society, 185–87; salaried, 132–35, 137; *scuole* as important to, 172–75; selection of, 18; sexual conduct of, 51, 52–53, 57, 66, 213; social backgrounds of, 154; social life of, 171–75; social utility of, 16–21; Spatafora's view of, 35–37; surnames of, 123, 206; terminology for, xxiii–xxv; theft by, 51–52, 66, 212, 218; tips for, 138, 177; turnover among, 138, 149; Vecellio's view of, 28–32; violence among, 176–77, 205–6; wages of, 59–60, 121–22, 138–45, 149, 230; wills of, 175–76; wives' treatment of, 22
servitude, Spatafora's defense of, 35–37
Sforza, Bianca Maria, 232
Sforza, Galeazzo Maria, 232
Sheba, Queen of 6, 9
Sibenico, Caterina da, 137
Sibenico, Francesco da, 69
Sibenico, Margarita da, 213
Sibenico, Zuan da, 120
Siena, Italy, 119
*signori di notte*, 48, 54, 176–77, 205, 209–10, 218
Simbaldi, Giovanni, 95
slaves, 84, 170, 180, 194, 206–7, 209; in art, 32; of Barbarigo family, 90–91; burial of, 183–85; intimidation of, 176; manumission of, 161, 197, 212; marriage of, 164; networks of, 171–72; origins of, 122–23, 128–29; poisonings by, 52, 58, 219; religion of, 218; renting of, 90, 92, 93, 144; terminology for, xxv; trade in, 90–91
Smith, Alison, 234
society, hierarchical nature of, 62

Sole, Giacomo à, 224
Soranzo, Alvise, 215
Soranzo, Chiara, 201
Soranzo, Isabeta, 201
Soranzo, Pietro, 194, 201–2
Soranzo, Zuane, 201, 202
Spada, Zuan Giacomo, 131
Spalato, Bona da, 136, 152
Spalato, Matteo da, 130, 136, 152
Spalato, Michele da, 177
Spatafora, Bartolomeo, 24, 25, 35–37
Spatarii da Spilemburgo, Agostino, 219
Spatarii da Spilemburgo, Caterina, 219
Spinelli, Agostino, 96, 98–99, 123, 127, 148–49, 177, 182, 197
Spinelli, Polissena, 96, 97
state, household as microcosm of, 14–16
*status animarum records*, 110–17
Stauri, Tomà Zane, 151
stewards, 81
Stuard, Susan Mosher, xvi–xvii, 237
sumptuary laws, 56–57, 205, 211–12
Surian, Agostino, 54
Surian, Andrea, 95, 98, 113

**T**
Tafuri, Manfredo, 231, 235
Taia, Domenego, 104–5
Taiapietra, Francesco, 213
Terzo, Gasparo, 195, 196, 202
Terzo, Zuan, 121, 195, 196, 199
Theotonica, Carolo, 209
Theotonica, Elisabeta, 209
Tiepolo, Girolamo, 66
Tiepolo, Jacopo, 78–79
Tiepolo, Niccolò, 215
Titian, 27, 32, 158
Todesco, Roberto, 207
Tomasini, Cesare, 47
Tomaxiis, Agnesina a, 209
Tomaxiis, Francesco a, 209
Toniolis, Andrea di, 161
Toniolis, Francesca di, 161
traghetti, 168–70, 184, 186
Trau, Constantia da, 162

Trau, Lucia da, 137, 147
Trau, Matheo da, 165
Trentina, Maddalena, 214
*tre savi all'eresia*, 58
Trevisan, Agatha, 96
Trevisan, Domenego, 96
Trevisan, Francesco, 72, 100, 132, 153
Trevisan, Giovanni, 167
Trevisan, Marco Antonio, 35
Trevisan, Pasquale, 170
Trevisan, Zaccaria, 10
Trevisana, Lucieta, 96
Trevisana, Pasqua, 221
Treviso, Lucia da, 119
Tron, Alvise, 120
Tron, Francesco, 120
Tron, Lucieta, 156, 159
Tron, Paolo, 211
Tron, Piero, 207–8
Tucci, Ugo, 16
Turcho, Zorzi, 92, 93

**U**
Udine, Domenico da, 225
Udine, Marco Zon da, 214

**V**
Valaresso, Isabeta, 160
Valentin, Marin, 105
Valier, Agostino, 21–23, 41
Valier, Andrea, 66
Valier, Giulio, 222
Valier, Pietro, 214
Valier, Timoteo, 217
Varnarussiis, Andrea di, 81, 164
Vecellio, Cesare, 24, 27–32, 80, 81, 84, 168, 171, 223
Vedregnano, Jacopo, 207
Vendramin, Luca, 161, 197
*Venetia città nobilissima et singolare* (Sansovino), 55
Venezia, Catarina da, 199
Venezia, Galeatio da, 147
Venezia, Gaspar da, 73
Venezia, Ioseph da, 212

Venezia, Niccolò da, 211
Venezia, Piero da, 102
Venice, Italy, servant keeping in, 229–35; census data, 106–17; compared with other European states, 231. *See also* households, Venetian
Venier, Alvise, 212
Venier, Antonio, 172
Venier, Francesco, 35, 206
Venier, Lucrezia, 180
Venier, Marieta, 160
Venier, Santo, 113
Venier, Sebastiano, 84, 85, 180
Vercia, Margarita, 171–72
Verità family, 234
Verlinden, Charles, xvi
Verona, Andrea da, 65
Verona, Guarino da, 10
Verona, Italy, servant keeping in, 234
Verona, Margarita da, 214
Veronese, Paolo, 32
Veronese, Zana, 211
Vesentina, Isabella, 117
Vetor, Zuan, 193
Vexentina, Lucia, 123
Vicenza, Andriana da, 224
Vicenza, Francesca da, 180, 184
Vicenza, Giacoma da, 179, 203
Vidali, Silvestro di, 8
Vidali, Zuanne, 84
Viggia, Alvise, 221
Virilis, Iacobello, 100
Virilis, Lucia, 100
Visentin, Agnolo, 194
Visentin, Lucia, 194
Vitale, Francesco di, 156
Volta, Giovanni dalla, 101, 121

**W**
wet nurses, 26–27, 28, 42, 60, 89, 165, 171, 200, 211; salaries of, 141; sexual behavior of, 214, 222
wives: desirable qualities of, 5–6, 10; duties of, 10–11, 12, 21–23; servants as, 155, 165
Wolff, S. J., 231

**X**

Xanthippus the Elder, 11

Xenophon, 3, 10, 23

**Z**

Zambato, Francesco, 222

Zambelli, Leone, 150

Zamboni, Domenego di, 121

Zamengo, Salvatore, 176

Zancarolo, Antonio, 206

Zancho, Battista, 224

Zane, Andrea, 166, 176

Zane, Giovanni, 170

Zannini, Andrea, 106

Zara, Caterina da, 180

Zara, Lucia da, 203

Zara, Zorzi da, 203

Zechio, Octavio, 214

Zeno, Andrea, 130

Zeno, Georgina, 130

Zeno, Ranieri, 79

Ziozzeto, Pietro, 214

Zorzi, Antonio, 201

Zorzi, Fantino, 167

Zorzi, Paolo, 201

Zuane da Bergamo, Bortolo di, 204

Library of Congress Cataloging-in-Publication Data

Romano, Dennis, 1951–
    Housecraft and statecraft : domestic service in Renaissance Venice, 1400–1600 /
Dennis Romano.
        p.      cm.
Includes bibliographical references and index.
ISBN 0-8018-5288-9 (alk. paper)
1. Domestics—Italy—Venice—History.  2. Domestics—Legal status, laws, etc.—Italy—
Venice—History.  3. Venice (Italy)—History.  I. Title.
HD8039.D52I865    1996
305.5'62—dc20        95-53743